Control Characters in C

Action	Cont
Break Menu Line	+
Cancel active command	^C
Change Viewport	^V
Display active screen submenu	=* (e.g.: $i=*)
Echo Text to Printer	^Q
Invoke Macro Expression	$M= (e.g.: $M=$(getvar,clayer))
Override Redefined Command	. (e.g.: .LINE)
Pause for User Input	\
Press Backspace	^H
Press Enter	; (also ^M)
Press TAB	^I
Reference Menu Subsection	$ (e.g.: $S=)
Repeat Command Indefinitely	*^C^C (e.g.: *^C^CLINE)
Set Isometric angle	^E
Toggle Coordinate Display	^D
Toggle Grid Display	^G
Toggle Menu Echo	^P
Toggle Ortho	^O
Toggle Snap	^B
Toggle Tablet	^T
Translate International Command	_ (e.g.: _LINE)

Computer users are not all alike.
Neither are SYBEX books.

We know our customers have a variety of needs. They've told us so. And because we've listened, we've developed several distinct types of books to meet the needs of each of our customers. What are you looking for in computer help?

If you're looking for the basics, try the **ABC's** series. You'll find short, unintimidating tutorials and helpful illustrations. For a more visual approach, select **Teach Yourself,** featuring screen-by-screen illustrations of how to use your latest software purchase.

Running Start books are really two books in one—a tutorial to get you off to a fast start and a reference to answer your questions when you're ready to tackle advanced tasks.

Mastering and **Understanding** titles offer you a step-by-step introduction, plus an in-depth examination of intermediate-level features, to use as you progress.

Our **Up & Running** series is designed for computer-literate consumers who want a no-nonsense overview of new programs. Just 20 basic lessons, and you're on your way.

We also publish two types of reference books. Our **Instant References** provide quick access to each of a program's commands and functions. SYBEX **Encyclopedias** and **Desktop References** provide a *comprehensive reference* and explanation of all of the commands, features, and functions of the subject software.

Our **Programming** books are specifically written for a technically sophisticated audience and provide a no-nonsense value-added approach to each topic covered, with plenty of tips, tricks, and time-saving hints.

Sometimes a subject requires a special treatment that our standard series don't provide. So you'll find we have titles like **Advanced Techniques, Handbooks, Tips & Tricks,** and others that are specifically tailored to satisfy a unique need.

We carefully select our authors for their in-depth understanding of the software they're writing about, as well as their ability to write clearly and communicate effectively. Each manuscript is thoroughly reviewed by our technical staff to ensure its complete accuracy. Our production department makes sure it's easy to use. All of this adds up to the highest quality books available, consistently appearing on best-seller charts worldwide.

You'll find SYBEX publishes a variety of books on every popular software package. Looking for computer help? Help Yourself to SYBEX.

For a brochure of our best-selling publications:
SYBEX Inc. 2021 Challenger Drive, Alameda, CA 94501
Tel: (510) 523-8823/(800) 227-2346 Telex: 336311
Fax: (510) 523-2373

SYBEX is committed to using natural resources wisely to preserve and improve our environment. As a leader in the computer book publishing industry, we are aware that over 40% of America's solid waste is paper. This is why we have been printing the text of books like this one on recycled paper since 1982.

This year our use of recycled paper will result in the saving of more than 15,300 trees. We will lower air pollution effluents by 54,000 pounds, save 6,300,000 gallons of water, and reduce landfill by 2,700 cubic yards.

In choosing a SYBEX book you are not only making a choice for the best in skills and information, you are also choosing to enhance the quality of life for all of us.

ADVANCED
AutoCAD
Release 12

ADVANCED AutoCAD® Release 12
3rd Edition

Robert M. Thomas

San Francisco ■ Paris ■ Düsseldorf ■ Soest

Acquisitions Editor: Dianne King
Developmental Editor: Christian Crumlish
Editor: James A. Compton
Technical Editor: Kurt Hampe
Book Series Designer: Suzanne Albertson
Production Artist: Charlotte Carter
Screen Graphics: Aldo Bermudez, Cuong Le
Page Layout and Typesetting: Len Gilbert
Series Program Font Created by: Len Gilbert
Proofreader/Production Coordinator: Arno Harris
Indexer: Ted Laux
Cover Designer: Ingalls + Associates
Cover Photographer: David Bishop
Screen reproductions produced with Collage Plus.

Collage Plus is a trademark of Inner Media Inc.

SYBEX is a registered trademark of SYBEX Inc.

TRADEMARKS: SYBEX has attempted throughout this book to distinguish proprietary trademarks from descriptive terms by following the capitalization style used by the manufacturer.

SYBEX is not affiliated with any manufacturer.

Every effort has been made to supply complete and accurate information. However, SYBEX assumes no responsibility for its use, nor for any infringement of the intellectual property rights of third parties which would result from such use.

First edition copyright ©1988 SYBEX Inc.; second edition copyright ©1989 SYBEX Inc..

Copyright ©1993 SYBEX Inc., 2021 Challenger Drive, Alameda, CA 94501. World rights reserved. No part of this publication may be stored in a retrieval system, transmitted, or reproduced in any way, including but not limited to photocopy, photograph, magnetic or other record, without the prior agreement and written permission of the publisher.

Library of Congress Card Number: 92-63117
ISBN: 0-7821-1187-4

Manufactured in the United States of America
10 9 8 7 6 5 4 3 2 1

To Krista, with Love

ACKNOWLEDGMENTS

Many thanks to all the people who worked so hard on this book. Special thanks to Jim Compton, Savitha Varadan, and Doug Robert, Copy Editors, for making it readable and consistent with itself; and to Kurt Hampe, Technical Editor, who provided many helpful comments and suggestions for the example programs. Also thanks to Christian Crumlish, Developmental Editor, for his support; Charlotte Carter, design; Len Gilbert, typesetting; and Arno Harris, Proofreading.

The WALLS.LSP routine that appears in these pages is an extensive update of a routine of mine that first appeared in *CADalyst* magazine in July, 1990. Likewise, UND.LSP is a slightly modified version of a "hot tip" that appeared in *CADalyst* in July, 1989. My thanks to David Cohn at *CADalyst* for his kind permissions.

Closer to home, thanks to Francia Friendlich and Rich Teich of the Aquarian Age Computer Center in San Francisco. Finally, thanks as always to Roscoe and Elaine, for their undying faith in the fundamental goodness of all things.

CONTENTS AT A GLANCE

	Introduction	xix
1	Overview	1
2	Using Custom Line Types and Hatch Patterns	19
3	Using Shapes and Fonts	37
4	Creating Custom Menus	79
5	Custom Menu Macros	123
6	Introduction to AutoLISP	151
7	Creating AutoLISP Routines	175
8	Entity Association Lists	223
9	Introduction to ADS	267
Appendix A	AutoLISP/ADS Quick Function Reference	319
Appendix B	Short AutoLISP Routines and Useful Functions for Study	433
	Index	465

TABLE OF CONTENTS

Introduction	xix
1 Overview	**1**
What Does Customization Involve?	2
Why Bother Customizing?	3
Introduction to ASCII Files	4
AutoCAD's Modifiable Source-Code Files	5
*.DCL	5
*.EXE and *.EXP	5
*.LIN	5
*.LSP	6
*.MNL	6
*.MNU	6
*.SHP	7
ACAD.PAT	8
ACAD.PGP	8
Customizing the DOS Environment	8
Accessing Multiple Drawing Directories	8
The ACAD Variable	9
Using AUTOEXEC.BAT	10
Setting Up Multiple AutoCAD Configurations (Release 11 and Earlier)	10
Creating Batch Files	12
Using a Text Editor inside AutoCAD	12
Modifying ACAD.PGP	14
Spaces in Response to Prompts	16
A Last-Resort Batch File	17
A Word about Experimenting	18
2 Using Custom Line Types and Hatch Patterns	**19**
Custom Line Types	20
Using the Drawing Editor	22
Using the Word Processor	23
Custom Hatch Patterns	25

The Structure of a Hatch-Pattern Definition	26
Creating New Hatch Patterns	31

3 Using Shapes and Fonts — 37

Shape Files	38
Editing Shape Files	39
Shape-Description Elements	40
Creating a Shape Description	44
Complex Shape Descriptions	47
Shapes Using Nonstandard Lines and Arcs	59
Text-Font Files	69
Comparing Text-Font Files to Shape Files	70
Special Shape Descriptions in a Text-Font File	71
Designing Text-Character Shapes	73
Dual-Orientation Text-Font Files	74
Reading a PostScript Font in Release 12	75
Turning Text into Line Entities	76
Editing Compiled Shape and Font Files	78

4 Creating Custom Menus — 79

Creating the Custom Menu	80
Knowing What You Want	81
Making a Copy of the AutoCAD Standard Menu	82
Loading the Custom Menu	82
The Screen Menu Structure	83
Major Sections	84
Subsections	85
Syntax	85
Examining the AutoCAD Standard Menu	91
First Changes to the Custom Menu	96
Customization Using the Digitizer	101
Designing the Template	102
Configuring the Tablet	103
Placing Commands on the Digitizing Tablet	104
Creating a New Menu Subsection	106
Creating New Pull-Down Menus	107

Table of Contents

The Structure of Pull-Down Menus	108
Controlling the Pull-Down Menu Display	109
Other Pull-Down Menu Features	114
Creating Icon Menus	114
Creating the AutoCAD Slide Files	116
Creating a Slide Library File	116
Creating the Icon Menu in ACAD.MNU	118
Displaying the Icon Menu on the Screen	120

5 Custom Menu Macros — 123

Utility Macros	124
Layer Macros	124
Menu Subsections to Save Keystrokes	126
Quick Undo	128
Quick Zoom In and Out	128
Quickly Clear the Screen	129
Rotating the Crosshairs	129
Word Processor Macros	130
Macros That Aid the Editing Process	131
Quick Selection Macros	131
Macros That Combine Drawing and Editing Commands	133
Macros That Combine Editing and Display Commands	134
Macros for Block Operations	141
Inserting Blocks	141
Inserting Blocks with Attributes	144
Editing around the Inserted Block	146
Other Editing and Display Macros	147

6 Introduction to AutoLISP — 151

Planning an AutoLISP Routine	153
Syntax Conventions	154
Functions	154
Memory Variables	157
Nesting	159
System Variables	160
Radians	161
Fundamental AutoLISP Data Types	161

xiii

Entity Names	161
File Descriptors	162
Integers and Real Numbers	162
Lists	163
Strings	163
Symbols	164
Selection Sets	164
Managing AutoLISP Routines in AutoCAD	165
Loading AutoLISP Routines	165
Memory Management	165
Making a LISP File More Readable	169
Comments	170
Indentation	170
Getting Out of Trouble	171
Console Break with Ctrl-C	172
The Unbalanced Function Prompt	172

7 Creating AutoLISP Routines   175

Defun	177
Global and Local Variables	178
Parametric Programming	179
A Basic LISP Routine	181
Stating the Problem	181
Writing the Pseudocode	182
Pseudocode for GEAR.LSP	182
The GEAR.LSP Routine	185
Remembering Default Values	190
Global Functions	190
G:DTR	191
G:STR	191
G:INT	192
G:DIST	193
G:PT	194
GETP	194
CALCP	196
DRAW	197
NOTCH	197

C:GEAR	197
Enhancements to GEAR.LSP	198
Error Trapping in GEAR.LSP	199
Entering Parameters Using Dialog Boxes (Release 12 Only)	200
Designing a Dialog Box	202
Controlling Data Input via a Dialog Box	208
Placing LISP Routines on a Custom Menu	220
Sharing Functions—ACAD.LSP	221

8 Entity Association Lists — 223

Entity Names and Association Lists	224
Entity Handles	226
Entity Access Functions	227
Creating Entities with Entmake	227
Retrieving Entities from the Database	233
WALLS.LSP	237
Drawing the Faces	254
Managing Variable Names	254
Global Functions	257
Entity-Access Functions in WALLS.LSP	257
Makeline	257
Makeface	258
Modify	259
Accum	260
Addset	261
Rdwset	261
Other Functions in WALLS.LSP	262
C:WALLS	262
Wdraw	263
Wedit	263
Wallpt	263
Getll	263
Getwindow	264
D_pwall and D_wwall	264
Getoffset	264
Closeup	264

Direct Entity Access versus the Command Function	264
Using WALLS.LSP	265

9 Introduction to ADS — 267

Who This Chapter Is For	268
ADS Features	269
Programming for Productivity, Profit, and Fun	270
Requirements for ADS Development	271
Books on C Programming	272
Supported Compilers for ADS	272
Compiling AutoCAD's Sample ADS Programs	273
The ADS Development Process—Basic Steps	275
Creating an ADS Function from Scratch—FPROMPT.C	275
Executing Functions in ADS	280
TEMPLATE.C	281
Testing the Function	285
CUTOUT.C	285
Pseudocode for CUTOUT.C	288
Function Tables	303
Macros and Constants	304
Functions in CUTOUT.C	305
External Variables in CUTOUT.C	306
Using Ads_ssfree() and Ads_relrb()	307
Managing Program Behavior	307
Handling Points	307
Setting Up and Resetting the AutoCAD Environment	309
Using UNDO	309
Creating Entities in ADS Programs	310
Working with Entities	312
Working with Selection Sets	314
Searching the Block Table	316
Moving On	317

Appendices

A AutoLISP/ADS Quick Function Reference — 319

B Short AutoLISP Routines and Useful Functions for Study — 433

Index — 465

INTRODUCTION

If you have mastered the basics of AutoCAD and are looking for ways to increase your drawing productivity and make the CAD process faster and easier, this book was written for you. It will show you how to use your own drawing style to create a unique, customized version of AutoCAD built around your needs.

Who Should Read This Book

You can use this book even if you are not an AutoCAD expert; the only requirements are that you understand the basic command structure and have some practice in using the program. This book refers to many AutoCAD commands, but it does not explain their fundamental use. If you are completely new to the program, you should come back to this book a little later.

AutoCAD's Advanced Development System (ADS), discussed in Chapter 9, requires that you understand the C programming language in addition to AutoCAD; but otherwise you do not need to be a computer expert or programmer to use this book. Except for the material on ADS, computer programming concepts are touched upon in these pages only when they are necessary for teaching you AutoCAD customization skills.

This book assumes that you are a drawing professional, more interested in maximizing your use of AutoCAD than in becoming a professional computer programmer. Thus, you should not think of this book as a programming tutorial. If it inspires you to learn more about computer programming, so much the better. Many good books that deal with this subject in depth are available to you in your local library or computer bookstore.

Customization is worthwhile. To use AutoCAD only in its off-the-shelf version is to waste this product, because AutoCAD is expressly written to be customized. The off-the-shelf product is only a foundation for the elegant drawing product you can create.

Learning to customize an AutoCAD program is no more difficult than learning basic AutoCAD. You must learn some new terminology, study the examples, and above all, practice and experiment. Customization is really an investment in time and patience. The investment is well worth it, because customization can offer you significant profit. You will make AutoCAD easier for yourself and for those who use the systems you develop. If you persist, you might even develop a third-party AutoCAD application you can market to other users.

How to Use This Book

The best way to use this book is to read it while you have AutoCAD up and running. You can then run through the examples for yourself and assimilate the underlying ideas as fully and quickly as possible.

This book should be read from front to back. The chapters build upon each other, moving from simpler material to the more complex. Everyone should read Chapter 1, "Overview." After that, you may skim ahead to material that is of particular interest to you. However, be prepared to back up to previous chapters if you suddenly find yourself too far ahead.

Although the examples in this book will stand alone and you may be able to put several of them to use right away, that is not all they are intended to do. Their primary purpose is to spark your imagination and get you thinking about your needs and the steps necessary to create completely original features, commands, and routines. You may get your money's worth just typing in the examples, but taking the time to read and understand the commentary and explanations will pay the biggest dividends.

What This Book Is About

This book serves as a bridge between the customization concepts presented in AutoCAD's documentation and the user who is apt to skim over those ideas because of limited background in what the documentation is presenting. You cannot successfully use this book as a replacement for AutoCAD's documentation. After completing this book you will want to return to the documentation, which you will then find much easier to understand. The contents of the book include the following:

- Chapter 1 presents an overview of AutoCAD customization features.
- Chapters 2 and 3 show you how to expand and modify some standard AutoCAD features: line types, hatch patterns, and shapes.
- Chapters 4 and 5 present techniques for reconfiguring the AutoCAD screen and digitizer menus, for creating new menus from scratch, and for automating frequently used AutoCAD command sequences by creating macros.
- Chapter 6 introduces fundamental techniques for developing AutoLISP and ADS source code files. You should read this chapter if you are new to programming.
- Chapter 7 introduces you to AutoCAD's internal instruction language, AutoLISP. This chapter shows you how to create new commands, features, and utilities that can improve performance and increase AutoCAD's power to serve you.
- Chapter 8 expands your understanding of AutoLISP by demonstrating how you can directly access AutoCAD's underlying database and link your own special information to AutoCAD drawing entities.
- Chapter 9 introduces you to the Advanced Development System. This chapter describes in detail the process of creating, compiling, and executing a custom AutoCAD application using the C programming language.

The book has two appendices. Appendix A summarizes and compares AutoCAD's predefined functions in AutoLISP and ADS. Appendix B presents sample functions you may use to increase your productivity, or for further study.

Which Version of AutoCAD Should You Use?

If you have not done so already, I recommend that you upgrade to the latest version of AutoCAD (Release 12 at the time of this writing). Each new release of AutoCAD has offered significant new improvements and features, plus important enhancements to existing commands. Among the many new and improved features of

Release 12 are increased overall speed, improved plotting, easier entity selection, programmable dialog boxes, easier links to external databases, and significant enhancements to ADS and AutoLISP.

Among the features described in this book, hatch patterns, shape files, line type files, most of the menu macros, and many predefined AutoLISP functions will work with versions as early as 2.5. Each AutoLISP routine listed in this book includes a comment indicating the earliest version of AutoCAD with which it is compatible. Some routines have been written to demonstrate unique Release 12 features, and will only work under Release 12.

All AutoLISP code in this book is upwardly compatible, meaning that code written for an earlier release also will work in later releases, at least through Release 12.

Obtaining the Examples on Disk

If you do not wish to type the examples and AutoLISP programs yourself, you can obtain them on disk. Use the order form at the end of this book. You must be using version 2.5 or later. For the benefit of users of versions prior to Release 12, the disk contains a bold outline font in a style similar to Helvetica (both SHP and SHX). The disk also includes a special public-domain utility that converts SHX files to their ASCII equivalent, allowing you to make custom modifications.

CHAPTER ONE

Overview

OVERVIEW

CH. 1

AutoCAD's adaptability is a major reason for its position as the standard for PC-based CAD. AutoCAD can be modified to meet the needs of drafters and designers of virtually any discipline. Learning to modify the program is, of course, up to AutoCAD users. Most users are drawing professionals under strict deadlines with little time to master the skills needed to customize and reconfigure computer programs. However, the basic ideas related to the customization of AutoCAD are simpler to learn than they may first appear, and the results easily justify the investment of time taken to learn them.

This book shows what parts of the program can be customized. It demonstrates the techniques necessary to design and develop a version of AutoCAD containing specialized features to make your drawing process as efficient as possible.

To benefit from this book, you must have at least a working knowledge of the fundamentals of AutoCAD. If you can create and make changes to drawing entities in AutoCAD, you should be able to understand the material presented here. To learn about developing custom applications using the Advanced Development System, you should also have a good working knowledge of the C programming language.

What Does Customization Involve?

Customizing AutoCAD can take a variety of forms, from creating simple custom drawing entities, through creating custom screen menus and command macros, to developing unique AutoCAD commands based on AutoCAD's internal programming languages, AutoLISP and ADS.

Chapter 2 shows how to develop libraries of your own custom line types and hatch patterns. Chapter 3 shows how to create and compile shape files that contain your basic drawing entities and symbols. These resources save you from having to recreate the same patterns and symbols repeatedly and from maintaining large numbers of external block-drawing files.

Chapters 4 and 5 demonstrate how the AutoCAD screen menu works and how it can be changed to suit your drawing preferences. You also will learn how to incorporate AutoCAD commands into macros that accomplish a series of tasks with a single screen-menu selection.

Chapters 6, 7, and 8 examine AutoLISP. You can use AutoCAD's internal programming language to create your own AutoCAD commands for performing calculations and analysis, and for producing drawing entities. You can also use it to develop special utility commands to simplify and speed up the drawing process.

Chapter 9 guides you through the process of writing, compiling, and executing a custom AutoCAD application using ADS.

Why Bother Customizing?

AutoCAD users spend most of their time selecting and/or typing commands in a precise order, and then selecting the correct options within those commands. For the experienced AutoCAD user, customization can make the process of drawing more efficient by allowing you to combine long series of keystrokes into just a few. In addition, if the process of creating a drawing involves calculations, customization can build these calculations right into the drawing commands.

Some part of the AutoCAD drawing process undoubtedly will be spent managing the program—changing layers, turning them on and off, adjusting the grid, setting drawing parameters, and so on. A customized version of AutoCAD will reduce the amount of time spent on these management tasks and allow the user to focus on drawing and design.

A customized AutoCAD installation, once developed, also benefits the inexperienced user by presenting a more compact, familiar interface that reduces learning time and offers the opportunity to produce usable drawings as soon as possible.

Why didn't AutoCAD provide these things in the first place? In a way, it did provide them. AutoCAD is not just a drawing program. It is also a large, comprehensive toolbox containing many drawing tools. These tools are the basis for a program that can be used by many different kinds of drafters. Undoubtedly some tools will be more useful to you than others. The process of customizing AutoCAD, therefore, is the process of arranging the tools in a way that is most efficient for you, bringing the more frequently used tools together, and using the existing tools to create new drawing tools of your own.

OVERVIEW

CH. 1

Introduction to ASCII Files

Most word processors and some text editors add special codes to your document as you produce it. These embedded codes handle printing and formatting tasks such as underlining, boldfacing, word wrapping, and paragraph reforming. An *ASCII file* is simply a file that does not contain any of these special codes. ASCII files contain only letters of the alphabet, numerals, and standard punctuation marks.

Customizing AutoCAD involves creating and editing ASCII files, which AutoCAD reads and uses at various times during its processing. The DOS text editor, EDIT or EDLIN, can be used to produce and edit an ASCII file, but the most efficient way to do this is to use a word processor or text editor.

Computer instructions are called *source code;* thus, ASCII files that contain computer instructions are called *source-code files*. AutoCAD handles source-code files in one of two ways: either it reads the source code directly, interpreting each line in the file in sequence, or it compiles the source code into a different, machine-readable format. Each treatment has its advantages, but in either case the result is the same: AutoCAD carries out the instructions that it finds in the source-code file.

When you give AutoCAD a command that causes it to read one of its source-code files, it may do one of two things:

- Locate the appropriate file and copy the entire contents of that file into an area of memory reserved for that purpose. This process of placing the contents of the file into memory is called *loading* the file. Once the file is loaded, AutoCAD can respond to its contents more efficiently. AutoLISP files and AutoCAD shape files, for instance, are loaded in this fashion.

- Locate the appropriate file and copy into memory only the part of the file that it has been instructed to find. In the case of long ASCII files, such as the file containing the standard AutoCAD hatch patterns or a file containing line-type definitions, this approach is more efficient.

AutoCAD's Modifiable Source-Code Files

AutoCAD recognizes a source-code file by its file-name extension, a group of three letters placed after the file's unique name and separated from the name by a period. The file-name extensions recognized by AutoCAD are DCL, EXE, EXP, LIN, LSP, MNL, MNU, PAT, PGP, and SHP. The following are brief descriptions of each of these types of files. In cases where a file type may have several different names, an asterisk represents the file name.

*.DCL

An ASCII file with this extension contains instructions for the design and layout of custom dialog boxes in Release 12. You can create new dialog boxes using Autodesk's Dialog Control Language (DCL), a special language used exclusively for managing dialog boxes. Refer to Chapter 7 for more details on DCL.

*.EXE and *.EXP

Previously compiled ADS files have these extensions. They must be compiled according to ADS parameters that are specific to the compiling software that created them. AutoCAD does not include compiling software; it must be purchased separately. An example of such a product is MetaWare's High C software compiler, which was used to compile the ADS programs in this book. Many files have these extensions; only those files that have been specifically compiled for use with AutoCAD's ADS may be loaded within the drawing editor. Source-code files for these ADS programs normally have the extension C; for example, MYAPP.C would be compiled into MYAPP.EXP (for extended-mode ADS) or MYAPP.EXE (for real-mode ADS). Refer to Chapter 9 and your compiler's documentation for more details on creating these files.

*.LIN

An ASCII file with this extension contains information required by AutoCAD to draw different line types. ACAD.LIN contains AutoCAD's standard line types. You can add line types of your own to this file or build up a library of line types in different files, provided that each file has a unique name and the extension LIN.

Individual line types are also given unique names to identify them within the LIN file. When you wish to use a new line type in a drawing session, its information must be retrieved from the LIN file and stored within the drawing database. The AutoCAD command for loading a new line type is LINETYPE. When you issue this command, AutoCAD prompts first for the name of the line type, and then for the name of the file to search for the line-type information. When AutoCAD locates the information, it displays a message to that effect.

New line-type definitions can be added to LIN files from within AutoCAD's Drawing Editor, giving you the capability of creating new line types "on the fly" as drawing progresses.

*.LSP

An ASCII file with this extension contains source code written in AutoLISP, AutoCAD's internal programming language. Customized AutoCAD installations commonly use many different AutoLISP files. Files containing AutoLISP source code can have any valid name, but they usually have the default extension LSP. The default extension makes it easier for AutoCAD to recognize them and interpret their contents. AutoCAD does not compile these files. Instead, it loads them into memory and interprets their instructions in sequence.

*.MNL

An ASCII file with this extension contains AutoLISP code that is associated with a Release 12 menu file. Whenever you load a menu file in Release 12, AutoCAD looks for a file with the MNL extension and the same name as the menu file. If AutoCAD finds such a file, it loads the file after loading the new menu.

*.MNU

This file extension identifies an AutoCAD menu file, which contains screen-menu prompts and commands executed when you choose a displayed prompt with your pointing device. You can create any number of AutoCAD menus; each must have its own unique name and the extension MNU.

AutoCAD's Modifiable Source-Code Files

Earlier versions of AutoCAD treat this file differently than later versions. Versions 2.18 and earlier read the file directly and display it on the screen. Versions 2.5 and later compile the menu file and display the compiled version. This process of compiling the menu takes place automatically the first time AutoCAD loads the MNU file into the drawing editor and whenever the file is edited. By compiling the menu file (which is often quite large), AutoCAD saves time both in the loading process and the menu display during drawing sessions.

Once compiled, the machine-readable version of the menu file is contained in a separate file that has the same name but a new extension, MNX. Thereafter, only this compiled version of the menu is loaded and displayed. The source-code version remains available, in case you want to make additional changes to it.

The compiled version of AutoCAD's standard menu is contained in the file ACAD.MNX. The source code for the standard menu is contained in the file ACAD.MNU. ACAD.MNU is normally installed on your hard disk in a separate subdirectory, \ACAD\SUPPORT. If you modify this file, you must instruct AutoCAD to look in this subdirectory for its menu files to recompile it into the MNX version.

It is wise to make a copy of ACAD.MNU using a different name, then modify and load the copy using AutoCAD's MENU command. This prevents AutoCAD from overwriting its standard menu with any unwanted changes you happen to make. For more details, refer to Chapter 4.

*.SHP

An ASCII file with this extension contains definitions of drawing symbols, shapes, or objects that can be inserted into a drawing in ways similar to a block. AutoCAD compiles this file into another file, with the file extension SHX. These files are called *shape files*. You load shape files into the drawing database using the AutoCAD LOAD command. After loading the shape file, you can insert the shapes into the drawing using the AutoCAD SHAPE command. Shape insertion is faster than block insertion, but it is intended to be used with relatively simple drawing symbols. For complex symbols or one-time insertions, block insertion is the preferred method.

A *text font file* is a special type of SHP file, which contains shapes that correspond to text fonts, along with special shape definitions that indicate the overall scale and orientation of those characters. For example, the source code for AutoCAD's standard text fonts is stored in files such as the following: TXT.SHP, SIMPLEX.SHP, COMPLEX.SHP, ITALIC.SHP, MONOTXT.SHP, and VERTICAL.SHP. These files are normally installed on the \ACAD\SOURCE subdirectory of your hard disk.

ACAD.PAT

This file contains AutoCAD hatch patterns. Unlike the previous extensions, PAT cannot be used with other files—AutoCAD recognizes only ACAD.PAT. You can add hatch pattern definitions of your own to the list of standard patterns contained in this file, using your text editor.

ACAD.PGP

ACAD.PGP contains special AutoCAD commands that can be accessed from within the drawing editor. This file is the only one that can use the extension PGP. This file is normally installed on the \ACAD\SUPPORT subdirectory. You will begin customizing AutoCAD by making a modification to this file. Once it is modified, you will be able to move back and forth quickly between AutoCAD and your text editor.

Customizing the DOS Environment

By executing certain DOS commands before running AutoCAD, you can do a lot to customize the program without major alterations to its accompanying ASCII files. While these commands do not directly modify the performance of AutoCAD, they have a significant effect on the DOS environment in which AutoCAD works and can thereby make your CAD work much easier and faster.

Accessing Multiple Drawing Directories

For many users, maintaining different drawings in separate hard disk subdirectories is a necessity of drawing life. By organizing related drawings in their own subdirectories, users can simplify the process of locating them or backing them up.

Once you have organized your drawing files this way, you can further simplify the process of locating them using one of the following techniques.

It is a good practice to add the AutoCAD system subdirectory to the operating system's search path. In many systems, this subdirectory is \ACAD. For example, the following command, issued at the DOS prompt, adds the subdirectory C:\ACAD to the existing search path, C:\DOS:

```
PATH=C:\DOS;C:\ACAD
```

This command alters the operating system configuration. To make this change permanent, use your text editor to add or modify the PATH statement in the AUTOEXEC.BAT file on your system's root directory. Once the AutoCAD system subdirectory is added to the DOS search path, AutoCAD may be invoked from other currently logged directories. For example, imagine that you have drawing files located in two subdirectories called DRAWING1 and DRAWING2. To use AutoCAD with the drawings on DRAWING1, enter the following at the DOS prompt before starting AutoCAD:

```
CD\DRAWING1
```

Next, invoke AutoCAD from this subdirectory. AutoCAD will execute normally, because you have issued the DOS PATH command and told DOS where to search for command files that aren't on the currently logged drive. With AutoCAD now up and running, drawing files will be accessed from the DRAWING1 subdirectory. You can still access drawing files on other drives and subdirectories by typing out the full path name of the desired drawing.

The ACAD Variable

If you wish, you can set up a special search path for AutoCAD to use when it searches for files from the drawing editor. You can accomplish this in DOS prior to entering AutoCAD, by setting the ACAD variable to indicate a list of subdirectories.

When you install AutoCAD Release 11 and later, it attempts to create this variable with the name of at least two directories containing AutoCAD files.

After you install AutoCAD, you may find this command in your ACADR12.BAT file. The DOS command for your system is similar to the following:

```
SET ACAD=C:\ACAD;C:\ACAD\SUPPORT
```

This instructs AutoCAD to look for files on the subdirectories \ACAD and \ACAD\SUPPORT, besides looking for them on whatever subdirectory happens to be logged at the time. Notice that the two subdirectories in the above list are separated by a semicolon, and include a drive letter. You can add additional subdirectories to this list. For example:

`SET ACAD=C:\DRAWING1;C:\DRAWING2;C:\ACAD;C:\ACAD\SUPPORT`

Once you have set the ACAD variable to include these new subdirectories, AutoCAD will look there for existing drawing files when you enter the drawing file name.

Be wary of adding many subdirectory names to the search path. There are some pitfalls. A long search path will slow the search for drawing files. If files with the same name reside in two different directories, AutoCAD will load only the first one found on the path.

Also, long search paths use up the operating system's environment space. You can enlarge the DOS environment space by making changes in the CONFIG.SYS file. Consult your DOS documentation if you receive the message *Out of environment space* when rebooting your computer or invoking the SET ACAD command with a long search path.

Using AUTOEXEC.BAT

As you settle on the appropriate DOS environment for AutoCAD, you may find that some DOS commands (for example, PATH) remain consistent regardless of any specific configuration. You can, if you wish, add such commands to the AUTOEXEC.BAT file instead of your system batch files. DOS looks for AUTOEXEC.BAT when booting, and if found, AUTOEXEC.BAT will then execute automatically. This can save time and disk space.

Setting Up Multiple AutoCAD Configurations (Release 11 and Earlier)

Some AutoCAD users have more than one set of peripheral hardware devices that they use with AutoCAD. For example, you may have more than one plotter.

Setting Up Multiple AutoCAD Configurations (Release 11 and Earlier)

Release 12 allows you to configure AutoCAD for multiple plotting devices, and select one of the configured devices at plot time. Previous versions of the program, however, require you to use a special DOS variable, ACADCFG, which points to a subdirectory containing the configuration file ACAD.CFG. When AutoCAD starts up, it finds the information in this file and thus sets itself up for use with your hardware. By setting up different configuration files in different subdirectories, you can switch from one configuration to the other, by changing the value of the ACADCFG variable before running AutoCAD.

The following example assumes that the AutoCAD system files are located in the subdirectory ACAD. The example configures AutoCAD for use with two different display configurations: one that includes a screen menu, and one that does not. Two special subdirectories are used to keep the configurations separate, named MENU and NOMENU.

To begin the process, create the two subdirectories on the hard disk. These subdirectories will exist for the sole purpose of holding our two versions of ACAD.CFG, and will contain no other files. At the DOS prompt, enter:

```
MD C:\MENU
MD C:\NOMENU
```

With the two subdirectories created, the next step is to use the DOS command SET, which will cause AutoCAD to place the ACAD.CFG file in the appropriate subdirectory:

```
SET ACADCFG=C:\MENU
```

Next, invoke AutoCAD and configure it according to your hardware, indicating that your screen display includes a screen menu. Once you have configured AutoCAD and it is running properly, exit the program and return to the DOS prompt. Enter:

```
SET ACADCFG=C:\NOMENU
```

Start AutoCAD as you did before. Again, you will be called upon to configure ACAD. Again, answer the configuration prompts, this time indicating that the display will not include a screen menu. When AutoCAD is configured and running, exit, and you are finished.

From here on, if you wish to use the screen display with a menu, enter the following at the DOS prompt before you begin AutoCAD:

```
SET ACADCFG=C:\MENU
```

OVERVIEW
CH. 1

If you wish to use the display without a screen menu, enter:

`SET ACADCFG=C:\NOMENU`

before running AutoCAD.

You can use any subdirectory names you choose, and you can have as many different configurations as you need, but each ACAD.CFG file must be on its own subdirectory.

Creating Batch Files

All this typing of DOS commands prior to entering AutoCAD does not have to be done at the keyboard each time. You can create another type of ASCII file, called a *batch file*, which contains DOS commands in sequence, one to a line. Once you've created a batch file, you can type its name and the DOS commands in the file will be issued automatically. This is a convenient alternative to remembering which set of DOS commands goes with which version of AutoCAD.

If you are not familiar with the process of creating batch files, refer to your DOS documentation. You can have as many batch files as you need to handle your various combinations of drawing file subdirectories and hardware configurations. Be sure to make backup copies of all the files you create, to save time in the event you inadvertently lose your originals.

Using a Text Editor inside AutoCAD

Customizing AutoCAD involves switching back and forth between your text editor and AutoCAD, first to modify the ASCII files, then testing the results in AutoCAD. Since you probably will want to switch back and forth fairly frequently, it would be most useful to access your text editor without leaving AutoCAD's drawing editor. By doing this, you will save a lot of time, because you will not have to wait for AutoCAD to reload each time you make a change to an ASCII file.

You can access most text editors from inside the drawing editor by making a modification to the file ACAD.PGP, usually found on the \ACAD\SUPPORT subdirectory.

Using a Text Editor inside AutoCAD

Before you begin modifying this file, you will want to be sure how AutoCAD and your chosen text editor work together. To begin, you will need to decide the best means to activate your text editor when you are logged in the AutoCAD system subdirectory.

The simplest approach is this: If your text editor is small and can reside comfortably on the same subdirectory as AutoCAD, you may simply place a copy of it there. This approach is acceptable and efficient, and by doing so, you've ensured that all your text editor commands will work just fine. However, if your text editor is large, or if for any reason you don't want it on the same subdirectory as AutoCAD, you may be able to place it on its own subdirectory. Some text editors will allow you to start from a subdirectory other than their own, but others have trouble with this.

If you choose to place your text editor on a different subdirectory than AutoCAD, it is worthwhile to test your ability to access it from AutoCAD's subdirectory. Following is an example of how to do this.

For this example, suppose that the text editor is on a subdirectory named TEXT; AutoCAD is installed on the subdirectory ACAD. Add the text editor's subdirectory to the DOS search path, using a command like the following:

```
PATH=C:\DOS;C:\ACAD;C:\TEXT
```

This DOS command will ensure that both AutoCAD and your text editor files can be accessed from anywhere on your hard disk. Now log onto AutoCAD's subdirectory. Try calling your text editor. Check for the following:

- Did your text editor appear on the screen, perhaps after only a few seconds longer than usual?
- If you can access a list of files on the default subdirectory, are they the ACAD files? If not, can you change the subdirectory to the AutoCAD subdirectory while inside your text editor?
- While inside your text editor, open a test file, type some characters and save the file. Leave the text editor program, enter it again and edit the same test file. Did everything work?
- Exit the text editor. Are you in the ACAD subdirectory? If not, can you set up your text editor so that it will exit to the ACAD subdirectory?

OVERVIEW
CH. 1

If you can configure your text editor to function fully while logged onto the AutoCAD subdirectory, and if it will place you in the AutoCAD subdirectory when you exit, then you will be able to use it while inside the drawing editor.

There is one other thing you will need to know: the amount of computer memory (RAM) required by your text editor. This information can be found in your text editor's documentation. Text editors usually require between 64Kb and 256Kb. Look it up to be sure, and make a note of it. The maximum amount of memory you will be able to use is 512K. If your text editor needs more than this (which is unusual), you must use a different one, or use it outside AutoCAD.

Check your text editor's documentation to learn if it requires increasing amounts of memory for editing files as they become larger. Some text editors will expand their memory requirements to accommodate whatever size file you are working on. If this is the case with your text editor, plan on using the maximum amount of memory.

Modifying ACAD.PGP

You are now ready to modify ACAD.PGP, using your text editor. Remember to edit the file as an ASCII file (or non-document file, or whatever name your text editor uses for ASCII files). When your text editor locates the file, something like this should appear on the screen:

```
; acad.pgp - External Command and Command Alias definitions
; Examples of External Commands for DOS
CATALOG, DIR /W, 0, File specification: ,0
DEL,DEL,        0, File to delete: ,4
DIR,DIR,        0, File specification: ,0
EDIT,EDLIN,     0, File to edit: ,4
SH,,            0, *OS Command: ,4
SHELL,,         0, *OS Command: ,4
TYPE,TYPE,      0, File to list: ,0
```

If the file is not found, be sure you are accessing files from the appropriate subdirectory. Check the \ACAD\SUPPORT subdirectory for the existence of the file.

ACAD.PGP contains a list of DOS commands. Each command occupies its own line in the file. Each line contains five separate elements of information, separated by commas. These items are:

1. the command to be issued while within the drawing editor;
2. the actual command AutoCAD passes to DOS when the drawing-editor command is issued;
3. the amount of memory required to execute the command;
4. a prompt offered to the user for any additional information needed;
5. a special number code used by AutoCAD when it returns to the drawing editor.

Move the cursor just below the line that begins "TYPE,TYPE" and type the new AutoCAD command you wish to use to access your text editor when inside the drawing editor. This command can be the same as your text editor command, or it can be an abbreviation. Any brief combination of letters will work, but do not use an existing AutoCAD command. Type the command in capital letters. The example just ahead uses the command TE. Type a comma after the command.

Next, type the command that will access your text editor, followed by another comma. In this example, the command is the same, TE.

Next, add the memory requirement of your text editor. If you are using Release 12, you may simply add a zero. Otherwise, enter the memory requirement as specified in your text editor's documentation. In this example, the memory requirement is 128Kb. As you will see, the memory requirement is typed out fully, as 128000. An abbreviation like "128Kb" will not work. If your text editor has the expandable memory feature mentioned earlier, you may wish to type in the maximum allowable amount, which is 512000. Type another comma after the number.

Next comes an optional prompt that will be displayed whenever you type the command TE at the AutoCAD command prompt. If you don't intend to supply additional information (such as the name of the file you intend to edit) you can leave this field empty. Simply type another comma.

However, some text editors allow you to type a file name at the DOS level, before you enter the text editor. This can save a little time. If your text editor has this feature and you wish to take advantage of it, you may do so here by entering a prompt for AutoCAD to display. For example, you might want to include the prompt "File to Edit? ", so that you can type a file name before entering your text editor. Type your chosen prompt, plus a space for the sake of screen appearance, followed by a comma.

Lastly, add a single-digit *response code* that AutoCAD will use when it returns from the text editor to the drawing editor. If this code is zero, AutoCAD will remain in text mode when it returns to the drawing editor. If this code is 4, AutoCAD will "flip" back to graphics mode upon its return. (Other numbers execute specific technical functions beyond the scope of this book. See the AutoCAD documentation for details.) In this example, the return code used is 4, so that AutoCAD will "flip" back to graphics mode automatically. Press ↵ instead of typing a comma.

If you have followed these instructions exactly, this how the new line looks in ACAD.PGP:

```
TE,TE,128000,File to Edit? ,4
```

Of course, you may have substituted specific parameters of your own. The cursor should be just below the first character in the line. This completes the necessary modifications.

Take a moment to study the other lines in the file. Notice that they all use the same basic structure. Using the technique described here, you can make additional modifications to ACAD.PGP, calling other programs like a spreadsheet or database, all from within the drawing editor.

Double-check your work and save the file onto the AutoCAD system subdirectory. You can test the results of your work by starting AutoCAD, beginning a new drawing, and typing the text editor command from inside the drawing editor.

Spaces in Response to Prompts

AutoCAD normally responds in the same way whether you press the space bar or the ↵ key. This feature applies to responses to any optional prompts in ACAD.PGP. If you choose to make further edits to ACAD.PGP and a response to the optional prompt may require spaces, you can precede your optional prompt with an asterisk (*). With this notation, only ↵ will work as a finish to the user's response. Refer back to the printed example of ACAD.PGP to see examples of this feature.

A Last-Resort Batch File

If you find that your text editor simply will not work from within the drawing editor, there is a batch file named SWING.BAT that will allow you to "swing" back and forth between AutoCAD and a text editor, provided that both programs are accessible using the DOS search path. It will save you keystrokes, but you must wait for AutoCAD to load each time you wish to test a change you have made.

You also may want to create a variation on this file to handle editing and compiling ADS files. Most C compilers require too much memory to run inside the drawing editor. In this case, you have no choice but to exit AutoCAD to make changes.

This batch file should be located on the same subdirectory as the AutoCAD system files. The file is invoked by typing the command SWING followed by the name of the ASCII file you wish to edit. For example:

```
SWING ACAD.PGP
```

In the lines that follow, substitute your text editor's startup command for TE. SWING.BAT contains the following lines:

```
IF "%1"=="" GOTO END
TE
PAUSE
REM Add ADS compiler commands here before returning to AutoCAD,
REM if required. Also, consider adding another PAUSE after
REM exiting the compiler, to provide additional opportunity
REM to break out of the loop.
ACAD
PAUSE
SWING %1
:END
```

The first line of the file tests to be certain that a file name was used when SWING.BAT was invoked. If not, the line instructs DOS to skip to the last line of the file, which causes the batch process to end. The next line invokes the text editor. The PAUSE command will cause DOS to pause execution of the batch file and issue the prompt *Press any key to continue...* When you no longer wish to swing back and forth between AutoCAD and your text editor, simply issue a CONTROL-C in response to this prompt. You will then see the message,

```
Terminate Batch Job (Y/N)?
```

Answer Y and you will return to the DOS prompt. If you press any other key, the batch file will continue.

The lines beginning REM do not execute. They contain comments. If you want to include compiler commands, replace these lines with them.

The next line invokes AutoCAD, and the following line again pauses execution. If you choose to continue, the next line of the batch file calls itself and the whole process is repeated.

The last line marks the end of the file. The batch file skips to this line if no file was named when the batch file was invoked.

This batch file is an example of an *endless loop*, a series of commands that will repeat indefinitely until interrupted by the user.

A Word about Experimenting

You may have to experiment a bit with AutoCAD and your text editor to learn the best possible configuration and subdirectory organization. For example, you may decide to create a single subdirectory for use as your development subdirectory, placing your text editor files on that directory and logging there before calling AutoCAD for customizing and development work. This experimentation is not harmful to your hardware. At worst, your system may "lock," offering you no response and forcing you to reboot. Once you have completed the process and set up an effective development environment, the investment will pay off in time saved during development.

CHAPTER TWO

Using Custom Line Types and Hatch Patterns

USING CUSTOM LINE TYPES AND HATCH PATTERNS
CH. 2

AutoCAD comes equipped with eight standard line types (plus two variations on each) in the file ACAD.LIN and as many as 53 standard hatch patterns in the file ACAD.PAT. This is a generous number, but you are not limited to these. If your drawing requires a unique line type or hatch pattern, AutoCAD is equipped with the tools to create line types and hatch patterns that are distinctly your own. This chapter introduces you to these tools and provides some examples of their use.

Custom Line Types

Besides a standard continuous line type, AutoCAD can construct many other line types composed of various combinations of dashes and dots. AutoCAD creates these dashes and dots from a *line-type definition*, a series of numbers that represent up and down movements of an imaginary "pen" as it creates a line between points. The numbers representing the various dashes and dots, plus the amount of space between them, are the *elements* of the line type.

In addition to the numbers in the line-type definition, AutoCAD requires some additional information: a unique name for each line type, plus an approximation of the line type's appearance in the ASCII file, using underline characters and periods to represent dashes and dots.

By supplying AutoCAD with various line-type definitions, you can create a variety of custom line types. You can store these definitions in an ASCII file, giving the file a name of your own choosing and the extension .LIN. AutoCAD stores definitions for standard line types in ACAD.LIN. It is a short file and can easily accommodate additional definitions of your own. This section shows how to add new line-type definitions to this file, emphasizing the principles involved so that you can then create whatever line types suit your fancy.

There are two ways to add line-type definitions to the file ACAD.LIN. You can define new line types "on the fly" while within AutoCAD's drawing editor, or you can edit the file ACAD.LIN directly with your word processor.

Before attempting to create a new line type, it is useful to sketch it out on a piece of paper or draw it using AutoCAD. The goal is to have a clear idea of the relationships between the lengths of the dots, dashes, and spaces that make up the new line type.

Custom Line Types

As an example, Figure 2.1 illustrates a new line type consisting of dashes separated by a group of three dots. It looks a bit like the boundary lines used on highway maps, so you will call this line type BOUNDRY.

While analyzing this line type, you can make some reasonable assumptions about the relationships between its elements. Begin by arbitrarily assuming that the line's shortest dash element has a length of one AutoCAD drawing unit. Having assigned this value to the dash, you can surmise that the spaces in the line type are about one-quarter of a drawing unit long. When writing line-type definitions, you must express fractions as their decimal equivalents.

AutoCAD reads spaces as negative numbers, to differentiate them from dashes. A space that is one-quarter of a drawing unit long, therefore, is expressed as –.25.

Dots have no significant length. They are always assigned a length of zero.

A list of these numbers in a line-type definition will create the BOUNDRY line type in AutoCAD.

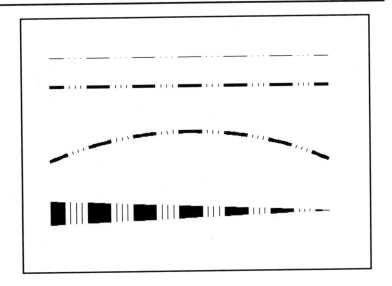

FIGURE 2.1:
The BOUNDRY line type, drawn as various AutoCAD polylines.

USING CUSTOM LINE TYPES AND HATCH PATTERNS
CH. 2

Using the Drawing Editor

To add this line-type definition to AutoCAD, enter AutoCAD, start a new drawing, and enter the Linetype command. AutoCAD responds with this prompt:

`?/Load/Create:`

Select the Create option by typing C. AutoCAD prompts:

`Name of linetype to create:`

Respond by typing the name of the new line type, in this example, **BOUNDRY**. AutoCAD then asks for the name of the line-type file, offering ACAD as the default.

If you respond to this prompt by pressing ↵, AutoCAD will store the line-type definition in ACAD.LIN. If you want to create or use a new file of line-type definitions, type the name of the file you wish to create or use at this point. The extension .LIN is assumed.

AutoCAD checks to see if a line type with the name BOUNDRY already exists in the named file. Since it does not, AutoCAD prompts:

`Descriptive text:`

In response to this prompt, type a rough approximation of the line by entering periods and underline characters in the same pattern as the dots and dashes of the new line, until the pattern repeats enough to represent the line type to your eye. The periods and underline characters used in this rough approximation need not line up with each other as precisely as the actual dots and dashes in the line type that AutoCAD draws. When you enter the command **Linetype ?**, AutoCAD displays a list of these approximations.

For the BOUNDRY line type, type three underlines, a space, three periods, and a space. Repeat this pattern two or three times, until it represents the line type to your eye. Press ↵.

Next, AutoCAD supplies an "**A,**". These two characters are required in all line-type definitions. Therefore, leave them in place and begin entering numbers to represent the BOUNDRY line type. Separate each number with a comma. The definition will appear as follows:

`A,1,-.25,0,-.25,0,-.25,0,-.25`

Custom Line Types

The first number, 1, represents a dash, one drawing unit long. The next number, –.25, represents a space, one-quarter of a drawing unit long. The next number, 0, represents a dot, followed by –.25, another quarter-unit space. The dot-and-space combination repeats twice more, completing the definition.

Press ↵, and AutoCAD will store the definition in the file and return to the drawing editor.

At this point, you may wish to load the BOUNDRY line type, create a layer for it, and draw some lines to see how it looks. The first thing you may notice is that the scaling of the line type needs to be changed, using the AutoCAD command Ltscale. You can establish whatever scale is necessary to achieve a pleasing line in the drawing editor.

If you decide to change the line-type definition, you can reissue the Linetype command, select the Create option, and use the name BOUNDRY again. AutoCAD will ask whether to overwrite the previous line definition. When you respond with a Y, AutoCAD will allow you to re-create the definition from scratch, including the descriptive text.

The major advantage of creating line-type definitions in the drawing editor is the ability to create such definitions and test their appearance while editing a drawing. You can use any combination of dashes, dots, and spaces in your custom definitions, but a few inflexible rules apply:

- Do not begin a line type with a space. Begin it with either a dash or dot.
- You must have at least two line elements, and you must have no more than 12. Otherwise, the definition won't work.
- The line-type text definition, including the name, should be no more than 47 characters long.
- The numerical line-type definition should fit on a single 80-character line.

Using the Word Processor

Once you have created line types, you may want to edit them using your word processor. Using your word processor to edit line types is often faster, especially if the intended change is small—for example, if you intend to change only a single element, update the descriptive text, or change the line type's name.

USING CUSTOM LINE TYPES AND HATCH PATTERNS
CH. 2

To see how this is done, enter your word processor and call up the file ACAD.LIN. When it appears on the screen, you will see something similar to Listing 2.1.

Listing 2.1: The contents of the file ACAD.LIN.

```
*BORDER,__ __ . __ __ . __ __ . __ __ . __ __ .
A,.5,-.25,.5,-.25,0,-.25
*BORDER2,_ . _ . _ . _ . _ . _ . _ . _ . _ . _ . _
A,.25,-.125,.25,-.125,0,-.125
*BORDERX2,____ ____ . ____ ____ . ____ ____ .
A,1.0,-.5,1.0,-.5,0,-.5
*CENTER,____ _ ____ _ ____ _ ____ _ ____ _ ____
A,1.25,-.25,.25,-.25
*CENTER2,___ _ ___ _ ___ _ ___ _ ___ _ ___
A,.75,-.125,.125,-.125
*CENTERX2,_____ __ _____ __ _____ __ _____
A,2.5,-.5,.5,-.5
*DASHDOT,__ . __ . __ . __ . __ . __ . __ . __ .
A,.5,-.25,0,-.25
*DASHDOT2,_._._._._._._._._._._._._._._._.
A,.25,-.125,0,-.125
*DASHDOTX2,____ . ____ . ____ . ____ . ____ .
A,1.0,-.5,0,-.5
;; These two line types are custom, added for this book:
*BOUNDRY,____ . . . ____ . . . ____ . . . ____
A,1,-.25,0,-.25,0,-.25,0,-.25
*BOUNDRY2,_____ _____ _____ _____ _____ _____
A,1,-.125
```

Notice how the BOUNDRY line type has been added to the list. AutoCAD has stored the information you supplied in response to the prompts as a two-line definition. This first line is called the *header line*. It begins with an asterisk, followed immediately by the name of the line type, followed by a comma, followed by the approximation of the line type using periods and underlines. This structure is required. Because you supplied the information in response to prompts in the drawing editor, AutoCAD created the proper header line structure for you. Now that you are working within the word processor, however, it is up to you to supply the correct structure. On the next line, first comes an uppercase A followed by a comma, followed by the numbers that represent the dashes, dots, and spaces. Notice that there is no comma at the end of the line of numbers, but there always is a carriage return.

Custom Hatch Patterns

Since you are here, try typing in another line type. Figure 2.2 illustrates another example, called BOUNDRY2. This line type consists of two long dashes separated by varying spaces.

FIGURE 2.2:
BOUNDRY2 line type, drawn as various polylines, plus its line-type definition.

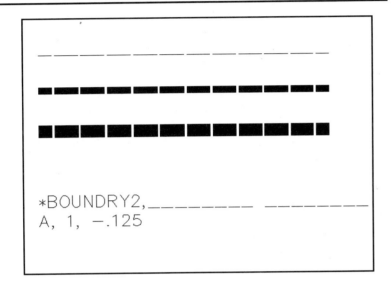

Custom Hatch Patterns

There are some similarities between the ASCII file definitions AutoCAD uses to construct its line types and the ASCII file definitions it uses to construct hatch patterns.

When a hatch pattern is constructed, AutoCAD first draws a line type, then copies the line parallel to itself at a distance you specify. It continues to copy parallel lines until a specified area is filled. In addition, a hatch-pattern definition may include definitions of more than one line type. Each line type in a hatch pattern is individually drawn and then copied parallel to itself, until all line types defined in the pattern are drawn. This feature allows you to draw patterns of considerable complexity.

USING CUSTOM LINE TYPES AND HATCH PATTERNS
CH. 2

As was the case with custom line types, you tell AutoCAD how to move its "pen" by means of a series of numbers that are separated by commas. However, with hatch patterns, you have to supply some extra information.

Hatch patterns that contain more than one line type usually draw these various line types at different angles. The combination of the angles at which the line types are drawn, their starting position, their direction and distance from each other, and their pattern of dashes, dots, and spaces can all combine into many possible patterns. Interestingly enough, a simple set of definitions can yield a surprisingly complex hatch pattern, as you will see.

This discussion begins with a look at AutoCAD's ASCII file of standard hatch patterns. You will examine the elements of a standard hatch-pattern definition and make changes to create a different pattern. You will see an example of how AutoCAD can be used as a tool for designing and developing custom hatch patterns from scratch.

The Structure of a Hatch-Pattern Definition

AutoCAD's standard hatch patterns are contained in the file ACAD.PAT. It can be found on the AutoCAD support files subdirectory (and should remain there). It contains about 53 definitions of various hatch patterns.

To look at the file, enter your word processor and call up the file ACAD.PAT. The first few lines in the file should look something like Listing 2.2.

Listing 2.2: The first lines in File ACAD.PAT.

```
;;
;;   Ver. 12.0 - AutoCAD Hatch Pattern File
;;
*ANGLE, Angle steel
0, 0,0, 0,.275, .2,-.075
90, 0,0, 0,.275, .2,-.075
*ANSI31, ANSI Iron, Brick, Stone masonry
45, 0,0, 0,.125
*ANSI32, ANSI Steel
45, 0,0, 0,.375
45, .176776695,0, 0,.375
*ANSI33, ANSI Bronze, Brass, Copper
45, 0,0, 0,.25
45, .176776695,0, 0,.25, .125,-.0625
```

Custom Hatch Patterns

```
*ANSI34, ANSI Plastic, Rubber
45, 0,0, 0,.75
45, .176776695,0, 0,.75
45, .353553391,0, 0,.75
45, .530330086,0, 0,.75
*ANSI35, ANSI Fire brick, Refractory material
45, 0,0, 0,.25
45, .176776695,0, 0,.25, .3125,-.0625,0,-.0625
*ANSI36, ANSI Marble, Slate, Glass
45, 0,0, .21875,.125, .3125,-.0625,0,-.0625
```

Each hatch-pattern definition begins with a header line, which has a structure similar to the header line in line-type definitions. That is, it begins with an asterisk (*) followed by the name of the pattern. The pattern name is followed by a comma and then a short text description of the hatch pattern. (Unlike the description of a line type, it is not a visual representation, just a description.) This name and description will appear in the listing of hatch patterns invoked by AutoCAD's **Hatch ?** command. The description is optional, but I recommend that you supply one. If you don't supply a description, do not supply the comma after the pattern name, either.

The line(s) following the header line contain the numbers that describe the various line types used to construct the hatch pattern. Each numerical line definition occupies its own text line in the file. These definitions adhere to a rigid structure. The first five numbers are required. As many as six additional numbers follow. The additional numbers describe noncontinuous line types and are optional. All numbers are separated by commas. Each numerical line definition ends with a carriage return.

No line in a hatch-pattern definition can extend past column 80 (the rightmost column on most computer screens). If any line in your pattern is longer than this, AutoCAD will display an error message when you attempt to use the pattern.

For example, following is the first hatch pattern in ACAD.PAT:

```
*ANGLE, Angle steel
0, 0,0, 0,.275, .2,-.075
90, 0,0, 0,.275, .2,-.075
```

The name of the line type is "angle" and the description is "Angle steel." Because there are two numerical line definitions below the hatch pattern name, this hatch pattern is composed of two line types.

USING CUSTOM LINE TYPES AND HATCH PATTERNS
CH. 2

The first number in the numerical line definition refers to the angle at which the line type is to be drawn. Subsequent parallel lines will be drawn at the same angle. In the angle hatch pattern, the two lines are drawn at angles of zero and 90 degrees.

The second and third numbers are the X- and Y-coordinates of the initial line's starting point. The starting point of the first line in a hatch pattern may be arbitrarily assigned, and is frequently given a starting point of 0,0. The starting point is a reference point for determining the starting points of other lines in the pattern. In the angle hatch pattern, both lines begin at point 0,0.

The fourth number, also a zero in this example, is the *offset number*. It will always be zero when the line type is continuous. It can be given a nonzero value when the line type is composed of dashes and/or dots. Figures 2.3–2.5 illustrate the meaning of the offset number.

Figure 2.3 shows a set of parallel dashed lines. The length of all dashes and spaces is one drawing unit. Because the offset value is zero, the dashes and spaces appear to line up "on top" of one another. In Figure 2.4, the lines have been given an offset value of one drawing unit. This causes the dashes and spaces to line up differently. In Figure 2.5, the lines have been given a fractional offset, .5. This causes the dashes and spaces to overlap each other.

FIGURE 2.3:
Dashed lines at offset value of zero.

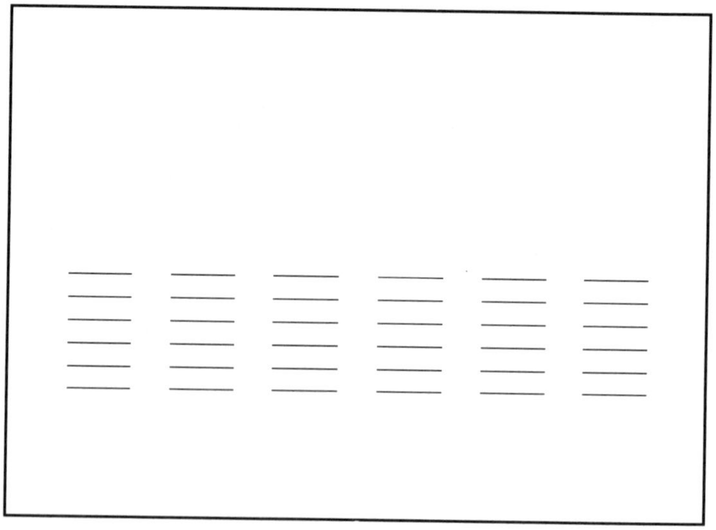

Custom Hatch Patterns

FIGURE 2.4:
Dashed lines at offset value of 1.

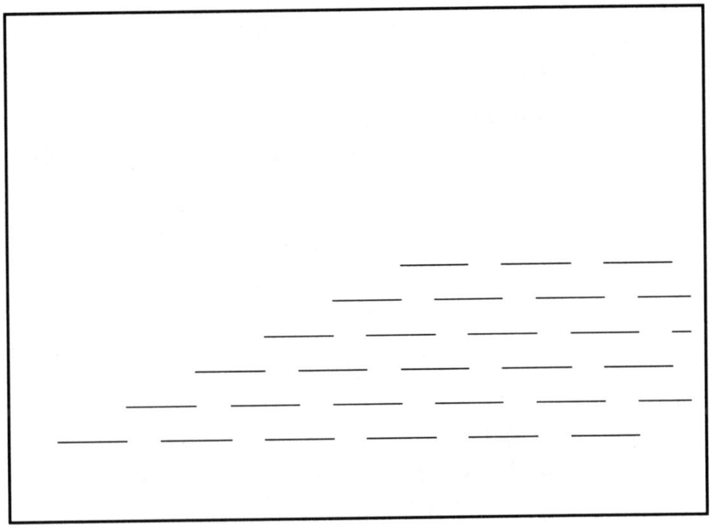

FIGURE 2.5:
Dashed lines at offset value of .5.

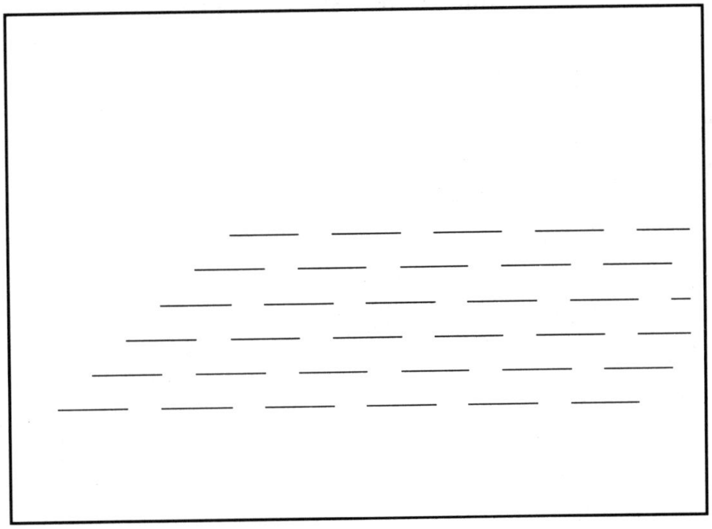

In the angle hatch pattern, the offset is set to zero. Therefore, the dashes and spaces in the parallel lines will line up "on top" of one another, similar to Figure 2.5.

The fifth number in each numerical line definition expresses the distance in drawing units between the parallel lines. By definition, parallel lines must have some distance between them, so zero is not possible as a value for this line.

The numbers that follow the fifth number move AutoCAD's "pen" up and down, exactly as in definitions of custom line types. If there are no numbers after the fifth number, the line type is assumed to be continuous. In the angle hatch pattern, the line type for both sets is composed of a dash .2 drawing units long and a space .075 drawing units long.

Hatch patterns allow a maximum of only six pen motions per line type. The Angle Steel hatch pattern uses two pen motions per line type. Following is a repeat of the first numerical line definition of the angle hatch pattern:

```
0, 0,0, 0,.275, .2,-.075
```

In English, you can read this pattern as follows: "At an angle of zero degrees, starting at point 0,0, at an offset of zero, a dashed line type, pen down .2 units, pen up .075 units." The resulting parallel lines look like Figure 2.6.

FIGURE 2.6:
The first set of lines in the angle hatch pattern.

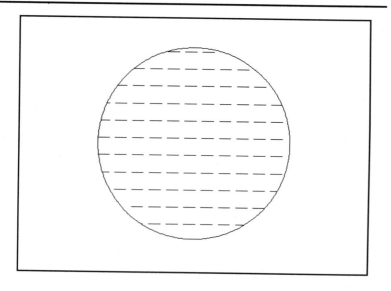

Custom Hatch Patterns

When you hatch using this pattern, AutoCAD will read this first line and fill the entities to be hatched with parallel lines according to this definition. Then, it will move onto the next line in the hatch pattern and fill the entities again:

`90, 0,0, 0,.275, .2,-.075`

The parallel lines that result from this numerical line definition look like Figure 2.7. When these two sets of lines are combined, they form the complete hatch pattern shown in Figure 2.8.

Creating New Hatch Patterns

Now that you understand how hatch patterns are constructed, you are ready to create your own. One of the most important things you can do when creating new hatch patterns is to sketch the pattern out before attempting to write the numerical line definitions. You don't need to sketch the entire thing, just enough so that you can compute the necessary angles and offsets, plus any necessary dashes and dots.

Hatch patterns can require complex geometrical math. AutoCAD is useful for developing the hatch pattern and calculating all the necessary dots, dashes, spaces, angles, and offsets.

FIGURE 2.7:
The second set of lines in the angle hatch pattern.

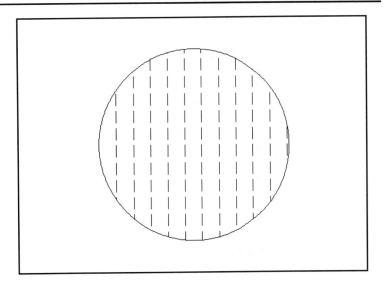

FIGURE 2.8:
The complete angle steel hatch pattern.

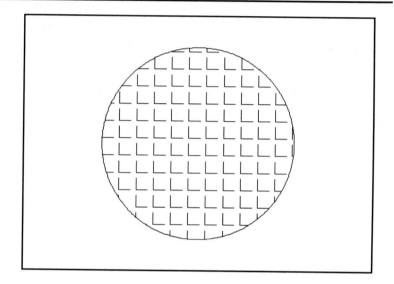

In this example you will use AutoCAD to sketch the hatch pattern and measure the distances and offsets necessary to create it. The hatch pattern you intend to create is a common brick paving effect, and the finished pattern is illustrated in Figure 2.9. Listing 2.3 shows the complete brick paving pattern definition.

Listing 2.3: The brick paving pattern definition.

```
*PAVING, Brick Paving Pattern
0,   0,   0,    4.5, 4.5, 1,-.5,1,-.5,1,-5
0,   4.5, 0,    4.5, 4.5, 4,-5
0,   4.5, 1,    4.5, 4.5, 4,-5
0,   4.5, 1.5,  4.5, 4.5, 4,-5
0,   4.5, 2.5,  4.5, 4.5, 4,-5
0,   4.5, 3,    4.5, 4.5, 4,-5
0,   4.5, 4,    4.5, 4.5, 4,-5
0,   0,   4,    4.5, 4.5, 1,-.5,1,-.5,1,-5
90,  0,   0,    4.5, 4.5, 4,-5
90,  0,   4.5,  4.5, 4.5, 1,-.5,1,-.5,1,-5
90,  1,   0,    4.5, 4.5, 4,-5
90,  1.5, 0,    4.5, 4.5, 4,-5
90,  2.5, 0,    4.5, 4.5, 4,-5
```

Custom Hatch Patterns

```
90, 3,   0,    4.5, 4.5, 4,-5
90, 4,   0,    4.5, 4.5, 4,-5
90, 4,   4.5,  4.5, 4.5, 1,-.5,1,-.5,1,-5
```

To prepare AutoCAD as a tool for helping create hatch patterns, begin a new AutoCAD drawing named HATCHES. Because hatch patterns are defined using decimal drawing units, you may need to use the Units command to select default decimal drawing units. Set the snap spacing to one-half drawing unit. Draw the pattern using the Line and Copy commands. Start the pattern at point 0,0. Each brick in the pattern is four units long and one unit wide; the bricks are spaced one-half unit apart.

The paving pattern is composed entirely of horizontal and vertical lines. After you have drawn the complete pattern, you can use AutoCAD to see this for yourself. Use the CHPROP command to move the horizontal line to a separate layer, then turn layers on and off to isolate the horizontal and vertical lines.

You will notice that there are two basic line patterns. One consists of three one-unit segments followed by a four-unit segment, and these segments are separated by half-unit spaces. The other line pattern consists of a four-unit segment, followed by a five-unit space. Use the AutoCAD DIST and DIM commands to confirm this. Use the ID command to confirm the starting coordinate locations of the initial segments

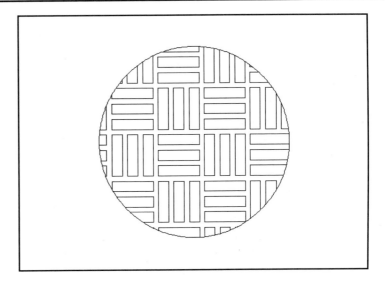

FIGURE 2.9:
The brick paving hatch pattern.

in each line. In addition, you will observe that each line pattern repeats at an offset of 4.5 units, and the spacing between each copy of a line pattern is also 4.5 units.

Notice that there are six horizontal lines and six vertical line types in the basic pattern. Each line within the basic pattern begins at a unique starting location. This would seem to indicate that you will need six horizontal and six vertical line definitions in the hatch pattern, to account for each starting location.

However, there are some additional complications. As mentioned earlier, you can include only six pen movements when defining hatch line segments. The line pattern with both short and long segments requires eight pen movements, two more than the limit. Therefore, this pattern must be split between two definition lines in the hatch file. Look at the paving pattern's first two definition lines:

```
0,   0,   0,    4.5, 4.5, 1,-.5,1,-.5,1,-5
0,   4.5, 0,    4.5, 4.5, 4,-5
```

The first line accounts for the three short line segments. It indicates an angle of zero, a 0,0 starting point, a distance of 4.5 drawing units between copies of the line, and an offset that is also 4.5 units. The line-type pattern is a one-unit segment, a half-unit space, another one-unit segment, another half-unit space, a final one-unit segment, and lastly a five-unit space.

The next definition line covers the rest of the pattern. Again the angle is zero, but the starting point is now 4.5,0. This causes the pen to skip over the short segments. The distance and offset are the same, and the line type includes a four-unit segment followed by a five-unit space.

The next five lines in the hatch definition have the same angle, distance, offset, and line type. However, the starting position is changed for each. Since these hatch lines are horizontal, the Y-coordinate is incremented, and the effect is that of "stacking" these hatch lines above one another.

The final horizontal hatch line in the definition is also composed of three short segments. It has the effect of finishing the bricks' opposite side. Compare this line to the first line in the file, and notice the difference in the starting location.

You can demonstrate the effect of each of these definition lines by adding them to the pattern one at a time, then hatching a large rectangle in your drawing to see the effect as each new definition is added to the overall pattern. This also will help you to understand how angle, starting point, distance, offset, and line type work together and build into a complex pattern.

Custom Hatch Patterns

The vertical lines work similarly to the horizontal lines. Notice that the angle is now 90, and pay close attention to the changes in the starting locations. Notice the similarities in the pen movement numbers.

When developing your own hatch patterns, be sure to draw them out first, and use AutoCAD extensively to analyze the relationships between the lines. The time you spend analyzing the original drawing will pay off in time saved writing the pattern definition, and it will reduce the number of times you must switch between AutoCAD and your word processor as you fine-tune your custom hatch definitions.

CHAPTER THREE

Using Shapes and Fonts

USING SHAPES AND FONTS
CH. 3

AutoCAD shape and text-font files are ASCII files with the extension SHP. You can name these files with any valid DOS file name. The files are edited using your text editor, and must be compiled before they can be used in a drawing. When a shape or text-font file is compiled, a new file is created. This new file is given the original file name plus the extension SHX. The SHX file is the file used by AutoCAD during a drawing session.

Shape Files

Shape files contain basic drawing entities and symbols. By learning to create and compile these files, you can avoid having to create your shapes repeatedly. Instead, you can call up the appropriate file with a few simple steps.

Shape files are similar to blocks, in that their purpose is to simplify the process of repeating fundamental elements of a drawing throughout drawing files, or between several drawing files. However, shapes have certain advantages over blocks:

1. They are faster to insert and regenerate on screen.
2. They are more memory-efficient.
3. They conserve disk space. Shapes take less space in a drawing file, several shape definitions can be stored in a single shape file, and several drawings can share the same shape file.
4. Many commercially prepared shape files are available as third-party products, containing standard symbol libraries for a variety of drafting disciplines.

Shapes also have certain disadvantages when compared to blocks:

1. Custom shapes must be defined in a separate file, and the file must be compiled into machine-readable form before the shapes can be used.
2. When transferring drawings from one machine to another, the shape file must accompany the drawing.
3. They cannot contain complex entities such as solids, polylines, and 3D faces, so you must reserve them for simpler symbols that only contain line entities.

Editing Shape Files

If you decide that blocks are too unwieldy for simple drawing symbols, and you cannot find or prefer not to purchase a commercially prepared shape file, you will want to define your own custom shapes. Shape files are ASCII files; prepare them using your text editor.

Since your custom shape files may not work the first time, it may be necessary to make a few trips back and forth between the text editor and AutoCAD to reedit and refine them. If you can access your text editor from inside AutoCAD's drawing editor, the following procedure is an efficient one:

1. Enter the drawing editor.
2. Call your text editor to create or edit the shape file.
3. Return to the drawing editor.
4. If you are using a version earlier than Release 12, issue an END command to return to AutoCAD's main menu.
5. At the main menu, select Task #7 (Compile a shape/text font description file). In Release 12, issue the COMPILE command inside the drawing editor.
6. AutoCAD prompts you for the name of the shape file and proceeds with compilation.
7. Save and reload the drawing.
8. If necessary, use the LOAD command to load the newly compiled shape file.
9. Use the SHAPE command to place shapes into the drawing.
10. If necessary, repeat steps 2–9.

By editing and compiling your shape files while inside AutoCAD, you save the time that it would take to reload AutoCAD from DOS. Also, if you have inserted a shape in a drawing, saved the drawing, changed the shape's description, and recompiled the shape file, AutoCAD automatically updates the shape in the drawing to reflect those changes.

Shape-Description Elements

A single shape file can contain as many as 255 individual shape descriptions. Each shape description in a shape file contains at least two lines of ASCII text: a header line containing general information about the shape, and a numerical description containing numbers that correspond to the movements of an imaginary pen. These pen movements create the final shape. The numbers describing the pen movements are called the *elements* of the numerical description. Each element in the shape description is separated from the others by a comma.

There is a limit of 2,000 elements in each numerical description in the shape file. Because so many elements are allowed per shape, a shape's numerical description can occupy many lines of text in the shape file.

No line of text in a shape-description file can extend past column 128 (column 80 in earlier versions). If any line in your shape file is longer than this, the file will not compile.

It is easy to continue a long numerical description on multiple lines of text in the file. Simply end each line with the usual comma that follows an element and continue the description on the next line.

Hexadecimal Numbers

In order for the shape file to function as fast as possible, it uses a special numerical counting system, called *hexadecimal*. While a decimal system is based on counting cycles of 10, a hexadecimal system is based on counting cycles of 16.

For example, in hexadecimal counting, the first ten integers are the same as decimal integers: 0, 1, 2, 3, 4, 5, 6, 7, 8, and 9. The hexadecimal system, however, substitutes the letter A for 10, B for 11, C for 12, D for 13, E for 14, and F for 15. After it reaches F, it continues with number 10. Number 10 in hexadecimal notation, therefore, has the same value as 16 in decimal notation.

Hexadecimal notation can become complex with such numbers as DD, 3F, and so on. Fortunately, only the numbers 0 through F are necessary when writing shape descriptions.

Why bother using a hexadecimal number system? The reason has to do with the way in which MS-DOS computers handle bits of data, which is normally in groups of 16. A numbering system based on 16 rather than 10 is much more memory-efficient and

Shape Files

increases computer speed, making the insertion of shapes as fast as possible and reducing the overall size of the AutoCAD drawing file. You can substitute the decimal equivalent for a hexadecimal value when doing so makes the source code easier to understand.

Standard Line Lengths

Shape descriptions use other means to achieve speed and efficiency. AutoCAD shape descriptions can use 15 standard lengths for straight lines. These line lengths are expressed as whole numbers ranging from 1 drawing unit to 15 drawing units. Lines that have fractional lengths or lengths longer than 15 are considered nonstandard lines and are discussed separately in this chapter.

Standard Angles

AutoCAD shape files recognize sixteen standard angles at which line segments may be drawn. Figure 3.1 shows these standard angles. You will notice that angle zero in Figure 3.1 is AutoCAD's standard orientation for angle zero. The angle numbers increase in a counterclockwise direction, from zero through F. It is possible to produce nonstandard angles; they are discussed separately in this chapter.

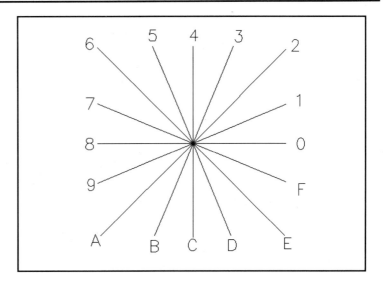

FIGURE 3.1:
AutoCAD shape file standard angles.

Signal Elements

Certain elements in a shape description have special meanings and are reserved for that purpose. These numbers are called *signal elements,* because they are a signal to AutoCAD that it must do something other than move the pen parallel to the drawing surface. They are as follows:

- 001 Brings the imaginary pen down. Pen movements that follow this element produce visible lines. This is the default at the start of each shape.

- 002 Brings the pen up. Pen movements that follow this element will not produce visible lines. This allows for the production of complex shapes with many line segments.

- 003 Scales down (*shrinks*) the overall size of the shape. It must be followed by an additional element, a whole number by which all line lengths in the shape are divided. This allows for some additional flexibility while working with standard line lengths.

- 004 Scales up the overall size of the shape. It must be followed by a single element, a whole number by which all line lengths in the shape are multiplied.

- 005 Causes AutoCAD to store the current pen location in memory for quick recall later. If you are using Release 12, you can store up to four pen locations in this manner. Using signal element 006, you can recall the locations in "first-in, last-out order." If you are using an earlier version, only one pen location at a time can be stored in this manner. Signal element 005 is often used for generating several line segments from a single reference point.

- 006 Causes AutoCAD to recall a previously noted pen location and position the pen there. Signal element 005 must have been previously issued.

Shape Files

007	Causes AutoCAD to include another shape in the current shape description. It is followed by the header line number of the additional shape to be drawn, starting at the current pen location. The referenced shape must be a member of the same shape file.
008	Causes AutoCAD to draw a single nonstandard line segment. It is followed by two elements indicating movement along an X-axis and then along a Y-axis.
009	Causes AutoCAD to draw a series of nonstandard line segments. It is followed by a series of pairs of elements, indicating pen movement along an X-axis and a Y-axis. The series is terminated with a special element pair: 0,0.
00A	Causes AutoCAD to produce a standard arc. It is followed by two elements. The elements following this element define the radius of the arc, whether the arc is clockwise or counterclockwise, the starting angle, and the arc length measured in octants. (An arc spanning eight octants is a full circle.)
00B	Causes AutoCAD to produce a nonstandard arc. It is followed by elements that define the starting point, endpoint, starting angle, and length.
00C	Causes AutoCAD to draw a different type of nonstandard arc, called a *bulge arc*. It is followed by three elements. The first two define X and Y movement of the pen, producing a straight line. The third element adds a *bulge factor*, which bends the line into an arc.
00D	Causes AutoCAD to draw a series of bulge arcs. The series is terminated by the special element pair 0,0.
0	This single zero signals the end of the numerical description. All shape descriptions end with a single zero.

USING SHAPES AND FONTS
CH. 3

Creating a Shape Description

To demonstrate how these signal codes work together in a shape description, here is an example of a simple shape description that might be included in an AutoCAD shape file.

```
*1,6,EDGE
010,013,02D,013,010,0
```

Figure 3.2 shows the kind of shape this shape description produces:

The Header Line

The first line in the example shape description

```
*1,6,EDGE
```

is the header line. This line employs a rigid and consistent structure. It contains four elements in the following order:

1. An asterisk. This symbol identifies the start of a new shape description in AutoCAD shape files.

2. A unique shape number followed by a comma. In our example, the shape number is 1, . No two shapes may have the same shape number in the same file. If they do, the file will not compile. Shape numbers, since they are unique to individual shapes, may be arbitrarily assigned. They need not be in sequence (although that is usually the most reasonable arrangement).

3. The number of numerical elements that define the shape. In this example, there are six numerical elements on the next line; therefore, the number placed here is 6.

4. The shape's unique name. You will use this name to call the shape into your drawing. It must be in uppercase letters in the shape description, or the shape will not be usable. Keep the shape name short for easy typing during the drawing session. The example shape has been named EDGE.

The Numerical Description

The second line, the numerical description

```
010,013,02D,013,010,0
```

Shape Files

FIGURE 3.2:
The EDGE shape.

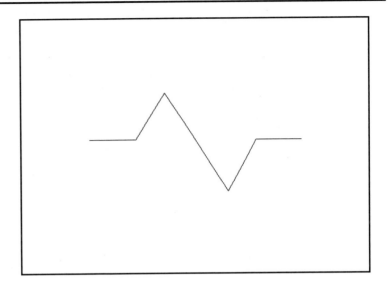

first describes a line segment one unit in length, drawn at AutoCAD's standard angle 0. Next, another one-unit line segment was drawn at AutoCAD's standard angle 3. A two-unit line segment was drawn at AutoCAD's standard angle D. Another one-unit line was drawn at angle 3. Finally, the last line segment was drawn, one unit long, at AutoCAD's standard angle 0. A single zero signals the end of the shape description.

Notice that, except for the zero at the end, the elements in this numerical description consist of groups of three numbers separated by commas.

Each element begins with a zero. This informs AutoCAD that we are dealing with hexadecimal numbers. If we were to skip the leading zero, AutoCAD would assume that we were using decimal numbers, and the resulting shape would be different than what you expected.

The second number in each element describes the length of a single line segment, expressed in drawing units. The first line segment in this shape, for example, is one drawing unit long; the third line segment is two drawing units long.

The third number in each element describes the standard angle at which the line segment is drawn. The first line segment in this shape, for example, is drawn at the

USING SHAPES AND FONTS
CH. 3

angle zero. The third segment is drawn at angle D. Figure 3.3 shows the example shape in AutoCAD, with each element code placed along the line it creates.

Creating and Compiling the Shape File

To place this shape description into a shape file, do the following:

1. Enter your text editor.
2. Create a new file called EXAMPLE.SHP.
3. Enter the example shape description exactly as shown above. Place a carriage return at the end of each line, including the second line of text.
4. Save the file to your AutoCAD system subdirectory to guarantee its accessibility to other drawings.
5. Compile the shape file according to the instructions given previously in this chapter. AutoCAD will respond

   ```
   Compiling shape/font description file
   ```

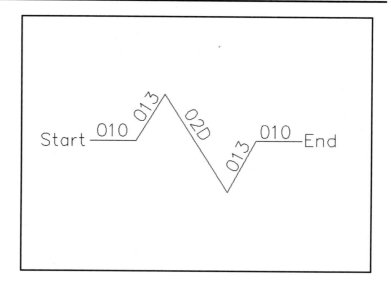

FIGURE 3.3:
The EDGE shape with description elements added.

Shape Files

6. You will soon see the message

   `Compilation successful. Output file EXAMPLE.SHX contains 48 bytes`

   If not, you will see an error message; check your original EXAMPLE.SHP file for errors and compile it again.

7. When the file is successfully compiled, issue the LOAD command at the AutoCAD command prompt. AutoCAD prompts for the name of a shape file to load; enter **EXAMPLE**.

8. Next, issue the AutoCAD SHAPE command followed by the name of the shape, EDGE. You can now insert the shape anywhere in the drawing.

Complex Shape Descriptions

Some shape descriptions require more than movements of a pen. If the shape consists of several line segments, it will be necessary to change the pen's location without producing a line. In addition, the relationships between the line segments of a more complex shape may require that the shape be drawn very large and then scaled down to fit within a drawing.

Pen Up, Pen Down, and Scaling

Figure 3.4 illustrates a more complex shape that requires up and down movements of the pen as well as scaling. As mentioned earlier, you are required to express standard line segments in whole numbers. The XBOX shape description contains two short line segments surrounded by larger line segments. The smallest standard line segment available to us is one drawing unit. Therefore, the sides of the box must be larger than one drawing unit—in fact, three drawing units. To simplify the process of scaling the shape at insertion time, this shape description will be scaled down by a factor of three, resulting in overall dimensions of one drawing unit by one drawing unit.

Here is the shape description for the XBOX shape, shown in Figure 3.4:

```
*2,15,XBOX
003,3,030,034,038,03C,002,012,001,012,002,01C,001,016,0
```

FIGURE 3.4:
The XBOX shape.

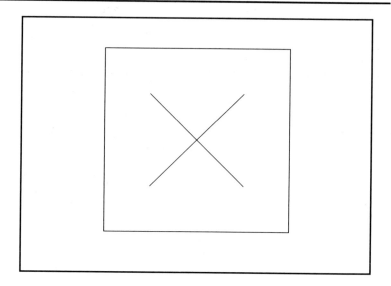

The header line for XBOX follows the same structure as all header lines in shape descriptions: its shape number is 2, the number of elements in the numerical description is 15, and its name is included in uppercase letters. The numerical description begins with these two elements:

003,3,

The first element in the numerical description is a signal element, 003, which means, "Divide all the lengths of the shape by the number that immediately follows." The element that follows, the number 3, reduces the overall size of the shape by a factor of three. Because this factor of three in the second element is not describing any pen motion, it can be a simple decimal integer, and a leading zero is not necessary. This distinguishes it from the signal element 003.

The next four elements

030,034,038,03C,

describe a square, starting at the lower left and proceeding counterclockwise along standard angles for zero, 90, 180, and 270 degrees. AutoCAD's pen finishes at its starting position.

To get the X in the center, the next element, signal element 002, lifts AutoCAD's pen. The element following 002 moves the pen without creating a visible line:

002,012,

The element 012 moves the pen one drawing unit at standard angle 2; that is, up and to the right at a 45-degree angle.

The next two elements lower the pen and draw one line:

001,012

The signal element 001 lowers AutoCAD's pen. The element 012 draws a line one drawing unit long at 45 degrees.

The next two elements raise and move the pen again:

002,01C

This time the pen is moved one drawing unit straight down, at standard angle C.

The last three elements finish the numerical description:

001,016,0

The pen is lowered again and a line is drawn diagonally at standard angle six, 135 degrees. Last, but certainly not least, the shape description finishes with a single zero.

At this point, you may rightly wonder how this shape description was able to move diagonally one drawing unit, and yet draw an X in the exact center of the square. After all, if the sides of the square are three drawing units each, the distance between opposite corners must be greater than three drawing units.

The answer lies in AutoCAD's special way of handling standard line lengths when drawn diagonally. AutoCAD automatically compensates by drawing these lines longer than corresponding horizontal or vertical lines. For shapes like XBOX, this can be very handy and can greatly simplify the shape description. However, as you might suspect, there are times when such automatic compensation can interfere with your intentions. Generating nonstandard lines is the way around such difficulties.

Octant Arcs

Curved lines are added to shapes using standard arc segments, also known as *octant arcs*. An octant arc is a 45-degree arc. Larger arcs can be created by combining octant

USING SHAPES AND FONTS
CH. 3

arcs. Eight octant arcs form a full circle. You may combine octant arcs with line segments and scaling, also pen-up and pen-down motions, to produce a variety of useful shapes. The radius of an octant arc may be any whole number from 1 to 255, and octant arcs may be drawn either clockwise or counterclockwise. Figure 3.5 illustrates these arcs.

FIGURE 3.5:
Standard octant arcs.

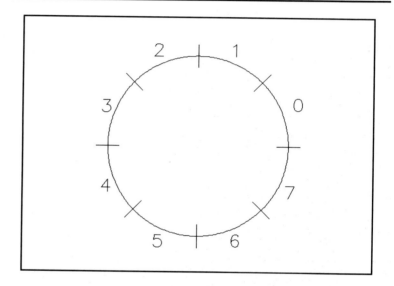

An octant arc begins at one of eight standard starting angles. These starting angles, called *octant angles,* are numbered zero through seven, moving counterclockwise from AutoCAD's standard angle zero. They are illustrated in Figure 3.6. Notice that the numbers for octant angles are different from those for the standard angles used to draw line segments (shown in Figure 3.1).

Figure 3.7 illustrates an octant arc drawn at starting angle 1, with a radius of one drawing unit. Octant arcs may span any number of 45-degree octants. Figure 3.8 shows an octant arc starting at angle one and spanning four 45-degree octants. This yields an arc of 180 degrees.

Shape Files

FIGURE 3.6:
Octant-arc starting angles.

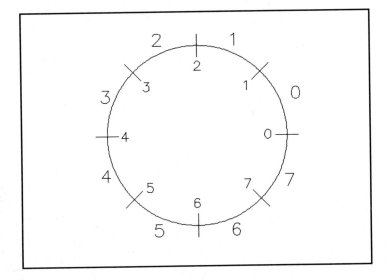

FIGURE 3.7:
An octant arc beginning at starting angle 1.

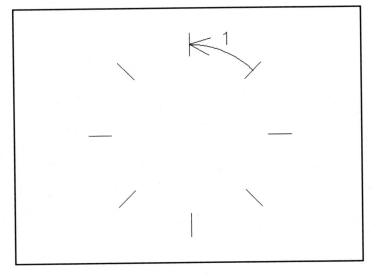

FIGURE 3.8:
An octant arc beginning at starting angle 1 and spanning four octants.

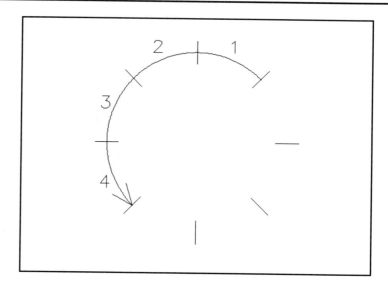

A special signal element, 00A, is used in the shape description to show that an octant arc is to be drawn. The next two elements will describe the arc. Use the first element as the radius of the arc. Use the second element to decide the direction of the arc (clockwise or counterclockwise), the starting angle of the octant arc (angle numbers zero through even), and the number of octants that the arc spans (one through eight). For example, here is the syntax for drawing a 90-degree octant arc beginning at octant angle 1:

00A,1,-012

In this example, 00A signals the octant arc and 1 describes the radius.

The third element, -012, begins with a negative-zero, indicating that the arc is to be drawn clockwise. (If this element were positive—zero without a minus sign—the arc would then be drawn counterclockwise.) The second number in this element, 1, indicates that the arc begins at octant angle one. The third number, 2, indicates that the octant arc will span two octants.

Combining Elements of a Shape Description

You can use AutoCAD to design and draw the original sketch of a proposed shape, and help learn whatever dimensions you require to translate line segments and arcs

Shape Files

into elements of the shape description. The following example demonstrates this.

Figure 3.9 illustrates a shape called INSUL, which combines octant arcs and line segments. This shape could be arrayed between parallel wall lines to add texture, indicating the presence of an insulated wall.

Begin the construction of this shape by sketching a rough version using AutoCAD elements. You will observe that the shape is simple: two semicircles joined by some straight lines.

For the sake of simplicity, draw the lines and semicircles using a length of one drawing unit as the radius of the arcs and the length of the line segments, and see how it works out. Figure 3.10 shows the preliminary drawing.

If you use AutoCAD's automatic dimensioning feature to discover the overall area of this basic design, you'll receive some good news: the design covers an area of four drawing units by four drawing units. If for any reason you don't like this overall size, you can adjust the lines and arcs until you have the exact shape you desire. Figure 3.11 shows the example sketch with AutoCAD's automatic dimensioning added.

FIGURE 3.9:
The INSUL shape.

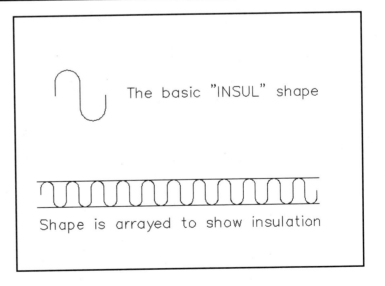

FIGURE 3.10:
The basic INSUL construction.

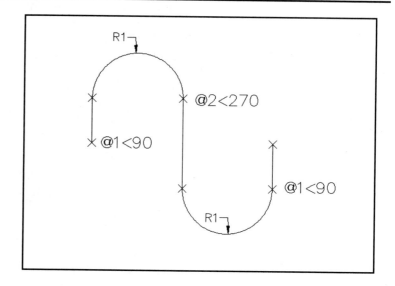

FIGURE 3.11:
INSUL with dimensioning added.

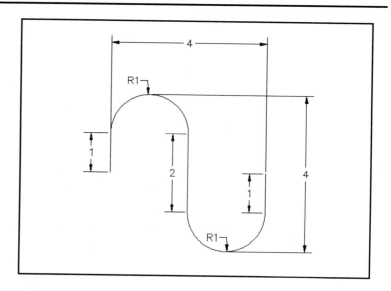

Shape Files

It is fortunate that the basic overall dimension of this shape is four by four drawing units, because you can then scale down the overall shape description by a factor of four. By scaling the shape down in this fashion, you will create a shape with overall dimensions of one drawing unit by one drawing unit.

One-by-one shapes are very flexible. You can scale them up to any dimension as needed at drawing time. For example, if you wish to insert the shape between wall lines that are 6½ inches apart, you could specify a shape height of 6.5 drawing units at insertion time. The one-by-one shape would then fit nicely between the wall lines. You can insert the same shape between thicker or thinner walls just by specifying a shape height equal to the thickness of the wall.

Here is the shape description for INSUL:

```
*3,12,INSUL
003,4,014,00A,(001,-044),02C,00A,(001,044),014,0
```

The first two shape-description elements are scaling instructions:

```
003,4,
```

These two elements will reduce the final shape by a factor of four. The next element

```
014,
```

describes the first line segment, which is one drawing unit in length, and drawn at AutoCAD's standard angle four (90 degrees).

The next element is the signal element 00A, followed by the elements that describe a single octant arc:

```
00A,1,-044,
```

The number 1 tells AutoCAD that the octant arc has a radius of one drawing unit. The next element describes the arc. It begins with −0, which will produce a clockwise arc. The first 4 is the starting angle for the octant arc. The second 4 tells AutoCAD that this octant arc spans four octants, which makes it a 180-degree arc.

To make these octant-arc elements more readable at a later time, you can, if you choose, include them in parentheses:

```
00A,(1,-004),
```

The parentheses are optional, and AutoCAD ignores them when the shape file is compiled.

The next element is another straight line segment:

02C,

Notice that it is two drawing units long, and drawn straight down (standard angle C). The next element describes another 180-degree arc:

00A,(001,044),

This arc is drawn counterclockwise; therefore, the second element following 00A is positive. The last line segment is one drawing unit long at angle 4 (90 degrees):

014,

The shape description concludes with a single zero:

0

Try compiling the new EXAMPLE.SHP file with this description added. Then, insert it into a drawing. Notice that you can change the height of the shape.

Adjusting the Insertion Point

There is a drawback to this shape as it stands: if you want to insert it between two parallel wall lines, you must select an insertion point that is exactly midway between them, because the insertion point of the shape is the starting point of the shape description.

A better starting position for this shape would be its lower-leftmost point. By starting there, you could use AutoCAD's OSNAP to snap the shape to the endpoint of one wall line, thus making it easier to insert.

You can change the insertion point of the shape easily by lifting AutoCAD's pen before actually creating visible lines. The extra elements to do this are added to the INSUL shape description below (they are in boldface type here for emphasis only):

*3,15,INSUL
3,4,**002,024,001**,014,00A,(001,-044),02C,00A,(001,044),014,0

These extra elements lift the pen, move it two drawing units at angle 4, and lower the pen again to draw the shape. By lifting the pen and moving it two drawing units, you create an insertion point that is different from the start of the shape drawing.

Notice that you must change the total number of elements as shown in the header line. Three extra elements change the header from twelve to fifteen.

Shape Files

Add these extra elements to your description and notice how the shape drags across the screen at insertion time. Next, draw two parallel lines, each twenty drawing units long. Place them one drawing unit apart. Then try using OSNAP ENDP to snap the shape into position between the two horizontal lines. (Snap to the left endpoint of the lower line.) Accept the height of the shape as one drawing unit. The shape should settle neatly into position. Figure 3.12 illustrates this.

Next, use the AutoCAD ARRAY command to fill in the insulation pattern between the two lines. You will need to create an array with a single row and enough columns to extend the length of the lines. Here is where the overall shape dimensions of one-by-one again work to your advantage. To calculate the correct number of columns, follow these steps:

1. Divide the length of the wall lines in drawing units by the width of the shape. In this example, the result is twenty columns (20 divided by 1).

2. Determine the distance between the columns as equal to the width of the shape—in this case, one drawing unit. (The width of this shape is always equal to its height.)

FIGURE 3.12:
The INSUL shape after snapping it into position.

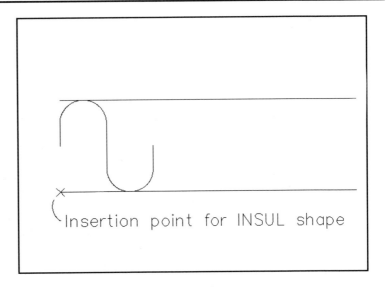

USING SHAPES AND FONTS
CH. 3

This example works well because the lengths of the walls are divisible by even multiples of one drawing unit. But what happens when walls have fractional lengths? There are a couple of ways to handle this problem. One way is to move the final pattern slightly within the wall lines after the array is made. This may seem like cheating (it is), but it often works very well, especially when two walls intersect and the patterns might otherwise overlap. Another solution is to create a couple of INSUL shapes with different height-width ratios. For example, by using a smaller arc radius and compensating with longer line lengths, you can create a similar shape that is one drawing unit tall and only half a drawing unit wide. This kind of shape will fit many fractional wall lengths. Here is the shape description of this narrow version of the shape, called INSUL2:

```
*4,15,INSUL2
003,008,002,044,001,034,00A,(001,-044),06C,00A,(001,044),034,0
```

Figure 3.13 shows this shape with AutoCAD dimensioning added. Compare this with the shape description for the original INSUL shape. Remember that the original size of the INSUL2 shape (before it is scaled down) is eight units high and four units wide, in order to give you the proper ratio of one drawing unit to one-half drawing unit after scaling.

FIGURE 3.13:
The INSUL2 shape.

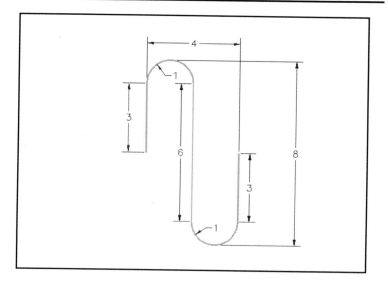

Shape Files

If you were to compile this shape and insert it between the wall lines used in the previous example, your parameters for the array would be different. With your inserted shape now one drawing unit tall, its width is only one-half drawing unit. Therefore, you would create a rectangular array with one row, 40 columns instead of 20, and 1/2 drawing unit distance between columns.

If you change your wall lengths to 21 drawing units, the parameters of your array would be the same, except that you would now need 42 columns in your array instead of 40.

This may seem complex when explained in words, but a little experimentation and practice with these shapes will make the concept clear. Try different wall lengths and widths to get the hang of creating these textured walls.

Shapes Using Nonstandard Lines and Arcs

Using standard line angles and lengths, octant arcs, and octant angles to create shapes conserves memory space and drawing size, but at times it is very limiting. For cases where standard lines and arcs simply can't be used, there are ways to draw shape lines and move the pen in nonstandard ways. These nonstandard lines and arcs use up additional memory and slow down the process slightly.

Nonstandard Lines

AutoCAD shape files allow for nonstandard pen movement by means of a special signal element that instructs AutoCAD to move its pen to specific coordinate points. The coordinates are referenced by combining pen movements along the X-axis and Y-axis. Lines of any length and any direction may be created by this means.

The signal element for this X-Y pen movement is 008. This signal element is always followed by two additional elements, which tell AutoCAD how much movement takes place along the X-axis and then the Y-axis. For example, the following sequence of elements tells AutoCAD to move the pen 16 drawing units to the right and 2 drawing units up:

008,16,2

Note that leading zeros were omitted here, so that AutoCAD will read the numbers as decimals, not hexadecimals. You can use hexadecimal numbers if you want; remember, however, that sixteen units in hexadecimal is expressed as 010.

USING SHAPES AND FONTS
CH. 3

The range of pen movement for nonstandard lines is −127 through +127 drawing units. If the value of movement along the X-axis is negative, the pen moves to the left. If it is positive, the pen moves to the right. If the value of movement along the y-axis is negative, the pen moves down. If it is positive, the pen moves up.

Note that for positive numbers, the + symbol is optional; it is not included in the above example. Also, as is true with octant arcs, you may include parentheses for readability. With parentheses added, the example elements are as follows:

```
008,(16,2)
```

Although two motion elements are used, only one line is generated using these elements. The line that results from this nonstandard motion will extend from the location of the pen when the 008 element is invoked to the point where the pen is located when the motion is complete. If the pen has been lifted by means of signal element 002, no line is drawn, and the pen is merely relocated.

Figure 3.14 shows a simple shape that includes two nonstandard diagonal lines. Here is the shape description that draws the LIGHT shape shown in Figure 3.14:

```
*5,18,LIGHT
003,8,040,05C,008,(4,-14),08C,00A,(8,-4),
084,008,(4,14),054,040,0
```

All of these elements have been demonstrated in earlier examples. After the header line, the numerical description begins with the element to scale down the shape by a factor of eight. Next, two line segments are drawn, beginning at the shape's insertion point. Then comes the 008 element and, within parentheses, the element to move the pen to the right four drawing units and down fourteen drawing units. Again, notice that this movement simply locates the endpoint of the resulting line segment.

The shape continues: another standard line is drawn, followed by an octant arc and two more standard lines. Then another nonstandard line is drawn. The syntax for this line is the same, although one value is different. Here the X-Y movement is four drawing units to the right and fourteen drawing units up. Two more standard lines finish off the shape and, as always, the shape description concludes with a single zero.

It is possible to draw a shape that consists entirely of nonstandard lines. Rather than reissue the 008 signal element repeatedly, you can use another signal element (009) to indicate a series of nonstandard X-Y pen movements.

Shape Files

FIGURE 3.14:
A theatrical lamp symbol drawn with nonstandard lines.

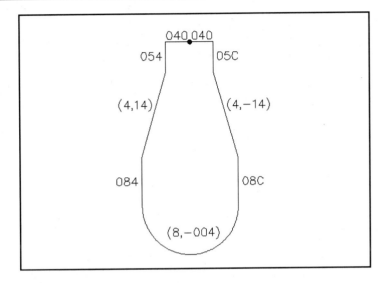

When this signal element is issued, a series of pairs of X-axis and Y-axis movement elements follows. Any number of pairs of X-Y movement elements can follow, but they must terminate with the special X-Y movement elements, 0,0.

Here is an example shape description that contains a series of four nonstandard line movements, beginning with element number 4. This example creates a simple narrow-diamond shape:

```
*6,21,DIAMD
003,12,020,009,(-1,-6),(-1,6),(1,6),
(1,-6),(0,0),002,008,(-1,6),
001,0CC,0
```

This example includes a little bit of everything. It is scaled down by a factor of twelve to reduce its overall height from twelve drawing units to one drawing unit. First, a single standard line segment is drawn, two drawing units long at standard angle zero. A series of four nonstandard lines follows, using the appropriate X-Y pen movement elements, which are terminated as required with the elements 0,0. Notice how each pair of X-Y pen-movement elements is contained within a set of parentheses.

Following the nonstandard movement, the pen is lifted, and it backtracks by reversing its last movement. The 008 element works for this single nonstandard line movement. The element 001 lowers the pen again and a single standard vertical line is drawn, 12 drawing units in length.

The next-to-last element includes the hexadecimal number for 12 (C) to describe both the length of the line and its angle. (Notice that, in this example, the numerical description extends to more than a single line of text.)

Nonstandard Arcs

It is possible to create shape descriptions using arcs that do not begin on an octant angle, or whose total degrees are not a multiple of 45. There are two methods for doing this. One method creates an *offset arc;* the other method creates a *bulge arc.*

Offset Arcs   An offset arc references the two nearest standard offset angles and draws the arc in relation to those angles. Offset arcs are signaled by element 00B, which is followed by five special elements that describe the offset arc.

The first three of these describe how the nonstandard arc is offset from the standard arc. The last two elements are the standard arc-description elements we have seen before.

For example, here are the numerical elements that describe a small, nonstandard arc that begins at 52 degrees and ends at 127 degrees, has a radius of five drawing units, and is drawn counterclockwise:

`00B,(40,210,0,5,012)`

The first element is 00B, signaling AutoCAD that an offset arc is to be described. The next two elements indicate the starting and ending offsets for this arc. These elements are calculated using the following formula:

$$(((\text{Offset} - \text{Octant}) \times 256) / 45)$$

You can apply this formula as follows:

1. Determine the starting angle of the offset arc. In our example, this is 52 degrees.

2. Determine the next lowest standard octant angle from the starting angle of the octant arc. In this example, this would be octant angle 1, 45 degrees.

Shape Files

3. Determine the difference in degrees between the starting angle of the offset arc and the octant angle. In this case, the difference is 7 degrees.

4. Having calculated this difference, multiply it by 256. In our example, this results in 1,792.

5. Divide the result by 45. In our example, this result is 40.82.

6. Drop the decimal portion of the number, because the shape compiler automatically adjusts for rounding differences. In our example, the result is 40.

Therefore, the starting offset for our example arc is 40. This is the numerical element that immediately follows element 00B.

Apply the same formula for calculating the offset for the endpoint of the arc:

1. Determine the ending angle of the nonstandard arc. In our example, this is 127 degrees.

2. Determine the next lowest standard octant angle from the ending angle of the octant arc. In this example, it would be octant angle 2, or 90 degrees.

3. Determine the difference in degrees between the ending angle of the offset arc and the octant angle. In this case, the difference is 37 degrees.

4. Having calculated this difference, multiply it by 256. In our example, this results in 9,472.

5. Divide the result by 45. In our example, this results in 210.48.

6. Drop the decimal portion of the number. In our example, this is 210.

Therefore, the ending offset for the offset arc is 210. This is the second element in the offset-arc description.

The third element in the offset-arc description will always be zero. This zero simply indicates that the radius of the offset arc is less than the maximum allowable 255 drawing units.

The fourth and fifth elements in the offset-arc description are the same as a standard arc. In this case, the radius is 5 drawing units, so the fourth element is 5. The arc is drawn counterclockwise, begins in octant one, and spans a total of two octants, so the fifth element is 012.

USING SHAPES AND FONTS
CH. 3

Figure 3.15 illustrates a simple shape, called CAP, that includes this offset arc. This is the complete shape description for CAP:

```
*7,24,CAP
003,10,002,008,(-1,5),001,0AC,002,020,
001,0A4,002,008,(2,-1),001,
00B,(40,210,0,5,012),0
```

1. This shape is scaled by a factor of ten (**003,10,**).

2. The pen is lifted and moved one drawing unit to the left, five drawing units up (**002,008,(−1,5),**).

3. The pen is lowered and a standard line segment is drawn ten drawing units at angle C (**001,0AC,**).

4. The pen is again lifted, and moved two drawing units at angle 0 (**002,020,**).

5. The pen is lowered and a standard line segment is drawn ten drawing units at angle 4 (**001,0A4,**).

FIGURE 3.15:
The CAP shape, including a nonstandard arc.

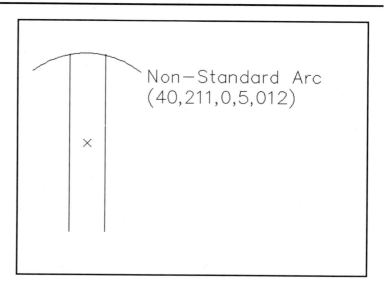

Shape Files

6. The pen is lifted and moved two drawing units to the right and one drawing unit down (**002,008,(2,–1),**).

7. Finally, the pen is lowered and the offset arc is generated (**001,00B,(40,210,0,5,012),0**).

The secret to designing nonstandard shapes like this is to use AutoCAD in the sketching and design process. In this example, the insertion point of the shape was used as the center point of the arc. The radius of the arc was determined by measuring from the insertion point to the endpoint of one of the vertical lines. After the arc was drawn, this center point was again referenced, using AutoCAD's angular dimensioning feature, to determine its starting and ending angles.

When AutoCAD first measured the radius, starting angle, and ending angle of the arc, these measurements were fractional. However, for purposes of calculating offsets, these fractional dimensions were rounded to the nearest whole number without problems.

Bulge Arcs   If all this calculating of offset arcs seems daunting, there is another method for producing a nonstandard arc of 180 degrees or less. You can create a bulge arc. The following example uses this means to make a change in the theatrical lamp shape shown in Figure 3.14.

The process of creating a bulge arc involves drawing a nonstandard straight line segment using X-Y movement as we have seen before, and then *bulging* it from its center point. The signal element for a single bulge arc is 00C.

The 00C element is followed by three elements:

1. The X-axis movement
2. The Y-axis movement
3. The *bulge factor,* the amount of bulge to be applied to the line

The following is an example of a bulge arc:

`00C,(5,5,60)`

In this example, first the line is drawn by moving the pen five drawing units to the right and five drawing units up. Then a bulge factor of sixty is applied to the line. Because this number is positive, the final arc will be drawn counterclockwise. If 60 had been negative, the final arc would have been drawn clockwise.

USING SHAPES AND FONTS
CH. 3

You can apply a bulge factor within a range from –127 to +127. Using the maximal or minimal value will result in a 180-degree arc. Arcs larger than 180 degrees will have to be drawn as standard arcs, as nonstandard arcs using offset calculations, or as a series of bulge arcs.

For a working example of a bulge arc, the following is the shape description of the LIGHT shape again, drawn using a standard 180-degree octant arc (the elements for the octant arc are boldfaced for emphasis):

```
*5,18,LIGHT
003,8,040,05C,008,(4,-14),08C,
00A,(8,-004),084,008,(4,14),054,040,0
```

The next shape description substitutes a bulge arc, for a less rounded effect:

```
*5,19,LIGHT
003,8,040,05C,008,(4,-14),08C,00C,(-16,0,-60),
084,008,(4,14),054,040,0
```

Notice that because an extra element was used to generate the bulge arc, the number of elements in the header line is increased by one, from eighteen to nineteen. Notice also that the bulge factor is negative, which results in the necessary clockwise arc. In Figure 3.16, the two shapes are compared.

FIGURE 3.16:
Octant-arc theatrical lamp compared to bulge-arc theatrical lamp.

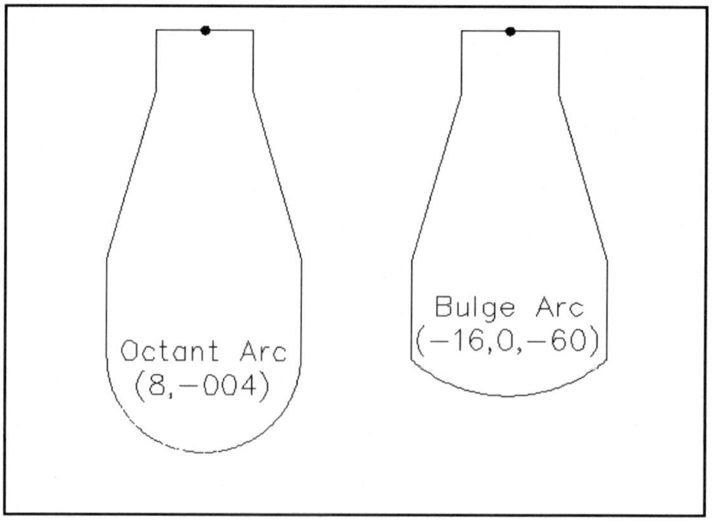

Shape Files

As with nonstandard lines, there is a special signal element, 00D, for defining a series of bulge arcs. As with a series of nonstandard lines, any number of bulge-arc descriptions can follow this signal element, but the series must be terminated with the special elements 0,0. The following is an example of a shape description using a series of bulge arcs:

```
*8,18,CURLS
003,10,00D,(10,10,60),(10,10,-60),
(3,14,120),(3,14,-120),(0,0),0
```

If you wish, you can apply a bulge factor of zero, which results in a straight line. This is very useful when connecting a continuous series of straight lines and bulge arcs into a continuous line. By using the zero bulge, you are spared the trouble of going back and forth between the various special elements to call nonstandard lines and bulge arcs. The following is an example of this:

```
*9,21,CURLS2
003,5,00D,(5,5,60),(5,5,-60),(5,0,0),
(5,5,60),(5,5,-60),(0,0),0
```

Note how a straight line element is added within the series of bulge arcs (5,0,0,) simply by supplying a bulge factor of zero.

How to Calculate the Correct Bulge Factor Once you have designed and dimensioned your shape using AutoCAD, you can continue to use AutoCAD to determine the correct bulge factor. The formula for determining a bulge factor is as follows:

$$((\text{Angle} / 180) \times 127)$$

You can apply this formula as follows:

1. Determine the angle of your arc. AutoCAD's autodimensioning feature is invaluable here. Draw scratch lines to connect the endpoints of the arc with the center of the arc, as shown in Figure 3.17.

2. After drawing your scratch lines, use AutoCAD's DIM ANG command to measure the angle formed by them. Figure 3.18 adds dimensions to the example drawing.

3. Divide the arc angle by 180, and multiply the result by 127. This yields the correct bulge factor.

FIGURE 3.17:
Connecting the arc center and endpoints.

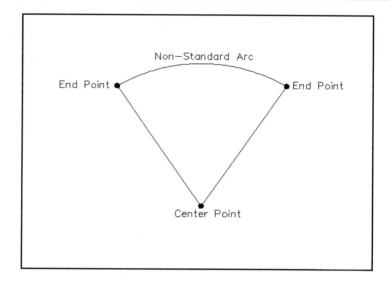

FIGURE 3.18:
Arc angle determined by AutoCAD.

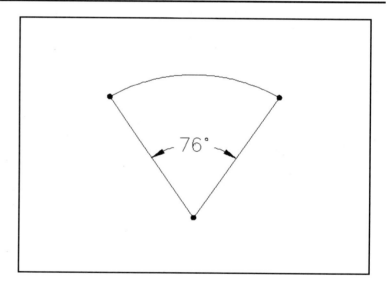

If you choose to draw the arc clockwise, apply the bulge factor as a negative number; otherwise apply the bulge factor as a positive number.

This combination of autodimensioning and calculation can be made considerably easier and faster by using a short AutoLISP routine. For those who intend to design a lot of shapes using bulge arcs, such a routine is provided in Appendix B, "Example Functions and Routines."

Text-Font Files

AutoCAD produces text in a drawing by means of a special shape file called a *text-font file*. Text-font files are large and complex, because each letter, number, and punctuation mark must be defined as a single shape. If you own a unique proprietary font and you want to create AutoCAD text in that font, you can draw the letters and define them as shapes individually. The process will be time-consuming.

Fortunately, for any standard text font, this process is unnecessary. AutoCAD is supplied with a variety of predefined text fonts, and many third-party developers have created additional text fonts for you. Most drafters will prefer to purchase third-party text fonts rather than design their own.

In addition, AutoCAD Release 12 provides you with the capability of reading Adobe Type 1 (Format Version 1.1) PostScript fonts. Hundreds of these fonts are available, and Autodesk supplies a few with its Release 12 package. After standard installation, they can be found on your hard disk in the subdirectory \ACAD\FONTS. They have the file extension .PFB. This capability vastly increases the number of text fonts available in Release 12.

If you find that you must create your own text fonts, the information in the following pages will help you get started. In addition, the following pages discuss how to convert .PFB files to AutoCAD's standard .SHX files, and how to convert text entities into line entities.

Comparing Text-Font Files to Shape Files

As mentioned earlier, text-font files are similar to ordinary shape files. Like shape files, they have the file extension .SHP. They are created and edited using your text editor, and must be compiled into .SHX files before they can be used.

Text-font files, however, contain certain special shape descriptions that distinguish them from ordinary shape files. Unlike ordinary shape files, the shape numbers in the header line of a text-font file correspond to ASCII codes used to generate those text characters via the screen or printer. Table 3.1 contains the ASCII codes for text characters.

TABLE 3.1: ASCII Codes for Text Characters

32	(space)	54	6	76	L
33	!	55	7	77	M
34	"	56	8	78	N
35	#	57	9	79	O
36	$	58	: (colon)	80	P
37	%	59	; (semicolon)	81	Q
38	&	60	<	82	R
39	'(apostrophe)	61	=	83	S
40	(	62	>	84	T
41	)	63	?	85	U
42	*	64	@	86	V
43	+	65	A	87	W
44	,(comma)	66	B	88	X
45	-(hyphen)	67	C	89	Y
46	.(period)	68	D	90	Z
47	/(forward slash)	69	E	91	[
48	0	70	F	92	\ (backslash)
49	1	71	G	93	]
50	2	72	H	94	^ (caret)
51	3	73	I	95	_ (underscore)
52	4	74	J	96	' (rev. apostrophe)
53	5	75	K	97	a

Text-Font Files

TABLE 3.1: ASCII Codes for Text Characters (continued)

98	b	108	l	118	v
99	c	109	m	119	w
100	d	110	n	120	x
101	e	111	o	121	y
102	f	112	p	122	z
103	g	113	q	123	{ (opening brace)
104	h	114	r	124	I (vertical bar)
105	i	115	s	125	} (closing brace)
106	j	116	t	126	~ (tilde)
107	k	117	u		

Because you use these standard ASCII codes, all text-font files are, in effect, prenumbered. For example, the shape number for an uppercase A is always 65.

The shape names in shape descriptions of text-font files are entered in lowercase (unlike the shape names in ordinary shape files, which are entered in uppercase). Because the standard numbering system in text-font files eliminates the need to name the shapes, when the text-font file is compiled, AutoCAD will ignore the lowercase shape names, thus conserving space in the compiled file. The only reason to include shape names is to make individual text characters easier to locate for subsequent editing.

Scaling is handled differently in text-font files. In ordinary shape files, scaling is handled on a shape-by-shape basis. In text-font files, the entire file is scaled by means of a special shape description. Characters in a text-font file are often designed using a large scale, which allows complex characters to be rendered using whole numbers. Afterwards, the entire text-font file is scaled down to allow more flexibility in establishing text height at insertion time.

Special Shape Descriptions in a Text-Font File

Two special shape descriptions signal AutoCAD that the file is a text-font file. The first identifies scaling, letter positioning, and orientation of the characters in the font,

USING SHAPES AND FONTS
CH. 3

and the second is the line-feed description. Here is an example of the first special shape description in a text-font file:

```
*0,4,fontname
38,7,0,0
```

The header line contains the required shape number (zero), the number of numerical description elements (there are always four), and the name of the text font, always entered in lowercase. AutoCAD uses the numerical elements in this shape description to learn the scaling and orientation of the font:

1. The first element describes the maximum number of drawing units the uppercase letters extend above the baseline of the text. In this case the number is 38. This number may be different in your text-font file.

2. The second element describes the maximum number of drawing units that the lowercase letters may extend below the baseline of the text. In this case the number is 7. Again, this number may be different in your text-font file.

3. The third element is the orientation mode element. This number is zero if the text font is only horizontal. If the font contains optional pen motions for vertical orientation, the mode element is 2. No other numbers are used in this position.

4. The fourth element is the standard zero that finishes all shape descriptions.

Here is the second special shape description in a text-font file:

```
*10,5,lf
002,008,(0,-46),0
```

This is the line-feed shape description. It is always shape number 10. This shape description represents the downward motion of the pen when more than one line of text is entered. The motion is described by the signal element 002 and a nonstandard pen motion moving down the Y-axis. It causes the pen to drop one line without drawing. In this example, the total pen motion required to drop one line is 46 drawing units. This motion includes 38 drawing units to account for the maximum height of the letters, plus 7 drawing units for the amount that lowercase letters may extend below the baseline, plus an additional drawing unit to allow for space between multiple lines of text.

Text-Font Files

Designing Text-Character Shapes

The process of creating a text-font file from scratch is time-consuming. The first step is to create a shape description for each letter, number, punctuation mark, and symbol to be used in the font. All the shape-designing and describing techniques you have seen so far may be used to generate these text-character shape descriptions.

Figure 3.19 shows a bold-outlined uppercase A, including the description elements needed to produce it. The following is the equivalent shape description:

```
*15,38,uca
009,(14,38),(6,0),(14,-38),(-7,0),(-4,11),(-12,0),(-4,-11),(-7,0 ),(0,0),
002,008,(13,17),001,009,(4,9),(4,-9),(-8,0),(0,0),002,008,(27,-1 7),0
```

Notice that this shape description consists entirely of nonstandard line segments. The pen is lifted twice: first to draw the triangle in the center of the A and again to move the pen to its standard finishing position, which is six drawing units to the right of the lower-right corner of the letter. This allows space between the A and whatever letter may follow it.

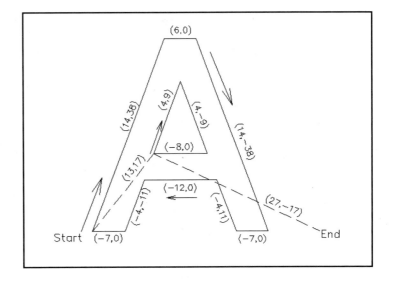

FIGURE 3.19:
Uppercase A showing AutoCAD pen movements.

Dual-Orientation Text-Font Files

Once each character's shape description has been created and tested, special signal elements may be added to the description that will allow the font to be entered in either vertical or horizontal orientation. Text-font files that can be entered with either vertical or horizontal orientation are called *dual-orientation text-font files*.

In a dual-orientation text-font file, each shape description contains special optional pen-motion elements. AutoCAD ignores these optional elements unless the user specifies vertical text orientation when the font file is loaded into the drawing. These optional pen-motion elements are usually found at the beginning and end of each shape description. Their purpose is to lift and relocate the pen to the correct starting and finishing positions that orient the text vertically.

Figure 3.20 illustrates the extra pen motions necessary to adapt the uppercase A to vertical orientation. The optional pen-motion elements shown in Figure 3.20 are preceded by the special signal element 00E. Unless the user chooses vertical orientation when loading the text-font file, AutoCAD ignores the first element that follows this special signal element. Subsequent elements are processed normally.

FIGURE 3.20:
Uppercase A with optional vertical pen motion.

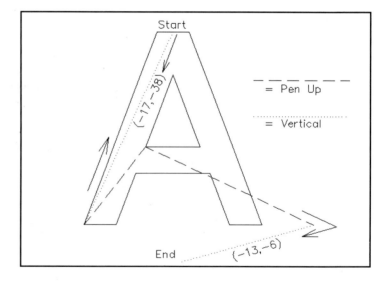

There is no special signal element for a series of optional pen motions. If you need to use such a series, each optional element must be preceded by the code 00E.

The following is the shape description for an uppercase A with optional vertical pen-motion elements added (boldface is for emphasis only):

```
*65,49,uca
00E,002,00E,008,(-17,-38),001,009,(14,38),(6,0),
(14,-38),(-7,0),(-4,11),(-12,0),(-4,-11),
(-7,0),(0,0),002,008,(13,17),001,009,
(4,9),(4,-9),(-8,0),(0,0),002,008,(27,-17),
00E,008,(-13,-7),0
```

Notice that the total number of elements in the header line has been increased to account for these additional elements.

At the end of this shape description, more optional pen motions relocate the pen to the lower-center position of the shape. Each shape description in the text-font file will begin, as this one does, with an optional pen motion straight down the height of the character. This causes the characters to line up vertically.

The optional pen motions required by your font file will depend on how you want your text characters to line up vertically: centered, left justified or right justified. In the above example, the pen motion is set to line up the characters along a vertical centerline.

Reading a PostScript Font in Release 12

Following are some of the more common PostScript fonts that ship with AutoCAD Release 12:

Abbreviation	Font
RO	Roman
ROB	Roman Outline Bold
ROI	Roman Outline Italic
SAS	Sans-Serif
SASB	Sans-Serif Outline Bold
SASBO	Sans-Serif Outline Bold Oblique

USING SHAPES AND FONTS
CH. 3

Abbreviation	Font
SASO	Sans-Serif Outline Bold Oblique
TE	Leroy Techic
TEB	Leroy Techic Bold
TEL	Leroy Techic Light

Compiled font files will load more rapidly in a drawing. If you intend to use a PostScript font frequently, compile it into a .SHX file first. To do this, invoke the COMPILE command. Select the name of the .PFB file you want to compile. Notice that the names of the files are heavily abbreviated; for example, ROB.PFB is the PostScript file for Times-Roman Outline Bold. Bear in mind that when bold PostScript fonts are compiled, they produce text in an outline format.

After AutoCAD compiles ROB.PFB into ROB.SHX, invoke the STYLE command and make ROB the current text style. Subsequent calls to the TEXT command will produce Times-Roman outline bold text.

Turning Text into Line Entities

Outline text in particular presents opportunities for clever hatching and editing. Unfortunately, AutoCAD does not permit you to edit text entities in this fashion. However, you can convert text into line entities if you so desire.

The process of conversion involves exporting the text entities into a special binary format file and importing the binary file back into AutoCAD. When you import the binary file, the text is converted into hundreds of tiny line segments that can be edited like any other AutoCAD line entity.

In order to create the binary file, you must first create a new plotting configuration for AutoCAD. The following steps describe this technique for Release 12, which allows multiple plotting configurations. Earlier versions require that you create a separate configuration file. Refer to Chapter 1 for more information on maintaining multiple AutoCAD configurations in earlier versions. In Release 12:

1. Open a new AutoCAD drawing named DXBTEST.
2. Invoke the CONFIG command.

Turning Text into Line Entities

3. At AutoCAD's Configuration menu, select Configure Plotter.
4. At AutoCAD's Plotter Configuration menu, select Add a Plotter Configuration.
5. At AutoCAD's Available Plotters menu, select AutoCAD File Output File Formats.
6. At AutoCAD's Supported Models menu, select AutoCAD DXB File.
7. Press ↵ to accept the default maximum number of horizontal drawing units, or change to an appropriate number of your choosing.
8. Accept the default number of plot steps per drawing unit by pressing ↵, or change to an appropriate number of your choosing.
9. Press ↵ to accept the default maximum number of vertical drawing units, or change to an appropriate number of your choosing.
10. Enter **N** to indicate no change to the other plot defaults listed, unless you have reason to adjust them.
11. Enter **DXB Output** as the description of this plotter configuration.
12. Return to the Plotter Configuration menu.
13. Return to the main Configuration menu.
14. Exit to the drawing editor, entering **Y** to save your configuration changes.

These steps allow you to use AutoCAD to produce a DXB-format output file from your drawing. To change text entities to lines, do the following:

1. Invoke AutoCAD's TEXT command, and enter some text.
2. Invoke the PLOT command.
3. When the Plot Configuration dialog box appears, select Device and Default Selection.
4. When the default selection dialog box appears, select DXB Output.
5. Pick the OK button, and when the previous dialog box reappears, pick the OK button again.

These steps produce a file on disk whose name is the same as the current drawing, with the extension .DXB. To import the file:

6. Invoke the NEW command.

7. Save or discard the changes to the current drawing, and enter a new drawing file name.

8. When the drawing editor reappears, invoke the DXBIN command.

9. Select the DXB file that you just created.

The text will appear in the new drawing, and you may now edit it as a series of AutoCAD lines. For example, if the text font was an outline font, you may now fill the text with a hatch pattern.

When using this technique, it is best to create the text separately and insert it into existing drawings using the INSERT command, to avoid exporting and importing unwanted entities. Of course, once you have imported the text as line entities, AutoCAD no longer recognizes these entities as text. If you want to edit the text itself, you will have erase the lines and create new text, or use AutoCAD line editing commands. Finally, be aware that modifying long text entities this way can dramatically increase the size of your drawing file.

Editing Compiled Shape and Font Files

When you use AutoCAD to compile PostScript font files, AutoCAD creates only machine-readable files with the .SHX extension. To edit these files, you must first decompile them into ASCII files. Look for a public-domain program called SHX2SHP, found on many electronic bulletin boards that contain AutoCAD-related material. This small program will convert the machine-readable files to their ASCII equivalent for editing purposes. If you do not have access to an electronic bulletin board, ask your dealer or a member of your local user's group to assist you. This utility is also included on the companion disk available for this book (see the disk offer on the last page).

CHAPTER FOUR

Creating Custom Menus

CREATING CUSTOM MENUS
CH. 4

The custom menu is a powerful tool at your disposal for improving your AutoCAD drawing productivity. Custom menus enable you to eliminate unnecessary menu selections and repetitive keyboard entry. You can easily create and modify them using your text editor.

Custom menus are used for the following purposes:

1. Grouping frequently used AutoCAD commands together on the screen, so that you no longer need to jump between screen menus to find them or type them out at the keyboard. For example, a custom menu might include LINE, ZOOM, and ERASE commands on the same screen. Another custom menu might combine the PLINE drawing command with specific PEDIT options. You may also wish to place frequently used commands together on the digitizing tablet.

2. Clarifying the on-screen or tablet command display by eliminating commands that are rarely (if ever) used. For example, if your editing consists almost entirely of ERASE, MOVE, COPY, BREAK, and CHANGE, you could create a special editing menu that displays only those commands. Perhaps you would like to add your most frequently used OSNAP overrides for extra convenience. Condensing the menu in this fashion can save significant amounts of drawing time.

3. Combining several commands and features into a macro, so that a single menu pick can execute the series in sequence. A macro can include your own names of blocks, shapes, layers, and so forth. For example, a custom menu might include a special series of layer-changing macros that automatically make any layer current with a single mouse or tablet pick.

This chapter presents basic techniques for accessing and changing the AutoCAD standard menu. Chapter 5 will examine the construction of custom menu macros in detail.

Creating the Custom Menu

The purpose of a custom menu is to have a special version of AutoCAD dedicated to your particular drawing needs and area of specialization. Besides the fundamental principles discussed here, there is no right or wrong way to organize the menu—only ways that are useful, that work, and that produce beneficial results for you.

Knowing What You Want

Your most important asset when creating a custom menu is your knowledge of how you use AutoCAD. This may require some analysis, especially if you have been too busy creating drawings to spend much time watching and making notes on how you use the program. However, this knowledge is essential. A well-organized custom menu must be thought-out thoroughly. You could develop the custom menu by trial and error if you wish, but there are more efficient ways.

Get into the habit of making notes. For example, note which commands you use together frequently. You might be able to join these commands together in a macro and save time, especially if they are on different submenus or located far apart on the tablet. Do you use many scratch lines? Do you usually select objects by windowing? Do you often zoom in once and then zoom back out again? You can make these processes more efficient by using custom menu macros. The more complete your notes and the more thorough your knowledge of how you use AutoCAD, the more powerful your custom menu will be.

When you are stringing together a sequence of commands for a custom menu macro, carefully run through the command sequence step by step, preferably from the keyboard. Make a note of each step, the prompt, and the type of input required. Leave nothing out. Although this process is tedious, it will save you much time overall because you will not have to make several journeys between AutoCAD and your word processor as you correct an improperly entered command sequence.

There is little reason to attempt writing a custom menu until you have a good working knowledge of AutoCAD. When writing these menus, all the characters, punctuation marks, and even spaces become extremely important. There is simply no room for error. Without a working understanding of AutoCAD, you could write a custom menu that did not work and never figure out why.

Once you have acquired some experience in this area, don't be afraid to experiment; a custom menu, even if it does not work, will not hurt AutoCAD. Keep your notebook handy even after your custom menu has been created and seems to be working properly. Little surprises may still pop up from time to time. Note where they occur, under what circumstances, and what needs to be done.

Making a Copy of the AutoCAD Standard Menu

Use a copy of AutoCAD's standard menu as a model upon which modifications can be made. Under no circumstances should you make any changes to the original menu that was supplied with AutoCAD. You will want to have an unchanged copy of the original menu available always, in case your editing goes awry and you need to return to a tried-and-true version of the menu.

Depending on your version of AutoCAD, look for the file ACAD.MNU on the source or support files directory of your hard disk after installing the software.

After logging onto the directory containing ACAD.MNU, copy it to a new file in AutoCAD's support files directory, using a DOS command such as the following:

COPY ACAD.MNU \ACAD\SUPPORT\CUSTOM.MNU

The above command works when AutoCAD has been installed using standard installation defaults. You may have to use different command parameters if you have not installed AutoCAD in the standard way.

If you are using Release 12, you also should make a copy of the file ACAD.MNL. This file contains AutoLISP routines used together with AutoCAD's standard menu. Log onto the support files directory and copy the file using a DOS command such as the following:

COPY ACAD.MNL CUSTOM.MNL

After you have copied this file, you can be sure that AutoCAD's menu-specific AutoLISP routines will work with your custom variation.

Once you have created the file CUSTOM.MNU from the original ACAD.MNU and placed it among AutoCAD's support files, you can use that copy to make changes and edits, knowing that you will not affect your original ACAD menu. This file should remain on a directory where AutoCAD can find it, compile it, and load it easily.

Loading the Custom Menu

To load CUSTOM.MNU, start a new drawing and enter the AutoCAD command MENU, followed by CUSTOM. The first time you do this, AutoCAD will compile the menu before it appears on the screen. This may take a minute or so. After compiling, a new file, called CUSTOM.MNX, is stored on the hard disk. This is the file that AutoCAD displays in the drawing editor.

At this point, your custom menu looks exactly like AutoCAD's standard menu. AutoCAD will not recompile this menu until you make a change to the original source-code file, CUSTOM.MNU. When you edit the source code, AutoCAD will detect the change and automatically recompile the file the next time it loads the menu.

To return to the AutoCAD standard menu, simply enter **MENU**, followed by **ACAD**. The standard menu will immediately return.

Whatever menu was active at the time a drawing is last saved to disk is the menu that will be active the next time you edit that drawing. Eventually, you may wish your custom menu to become the default menu for new drawings that you create. To do this, edit your prototype drawing (ACAD.DWG), load the custom menu, and then save the drawing.

There is no limit on the number of custom menus you may have. However, to prevent one menu from overwriting another, be certain that each custom menu has a unique name. Do not name any custom menu ACAD.MNU. To do so may result in the loss of AutoCAD's standard menu.

The Screen Menu Structure

The source-code files for AutoCAD menus are ASCII files comprising many lines. When you first load the menu source code into your word processor, you will see a long list of AutoCAD commands and various symbols aligned on the leftmost column.

Each line in a custom menu contains a specific command sequence, using one or more AutoCAD commands and appropriate options. Each sequence begins at the extreme leftmost position, and can continue to the right indefinitely. Later in this chapter, you'll learn how to wrap around long command sequences so that they are visible in their entirety on the screen.

CREATING CUSTOM MENUS
CH. 4

Major Sections

AutoCAD menus are organized into several *major sections*, identified by specific *section labels*. Each major section contains commands that relate to a particular hardware device or screen display area. They are:

- ***Comment**—This section contains notes and other explanatory text that does not appear on the screen and is intended for use by persons who view and edit the ASCII file. You can have as many comment sections as you like in your custom menu. AutoCAD's standard menu begins with a comment section that includes copyright and distribution information.

- ***BUTTONS1–***BUTTONS4**—These sections contain commands and functions that are executed by pressing buttons on the pointing device. Prior to Release 12, there was only a single BUTTONS section.

- ***AUX1–***AUX4**—These sections contain commands that are executed by pressing the buttons of an auxiliary function box (an external hardware device with buttons that can be configured to execute AutoCAD commands). Prior to Release 12, there was only a single AUX1 section.

- ***POP0–***POP16**—Sections labeled POP0 through POP16 contain commands that can be accessed from AutoCAD's pull-down menus, if your display device supports these menus. In Release 12, POP0 is a cursor menu, which appears at the crosshair intersection when you press a button on the pointing device. Versions prior to Release 12 have pull-down menus only in the range POP1–POP10. Pull-down menus are available beginning with Release 9.

- ***ICON**—This section contains AutoCAD slide information and commands that can be accessed by means of *icon menus*, if your hardware display device supports them. Icon menus are available beginning with Release 9.

- ***SCREEN**—This section contains commands that appear in the screen menu area. This section is by far the largest major section in the AutoCAD standard menu. Because this major section is very large and contains lots of AutoCAD commands, it is broken into dozens of *menu subsections*.

- ***TABLET1–***TABLET4**—Four sections labeled TABLET1 through TABLET4 contain command sequences executed by touching specific areas of the digitizing tablet.

The Screen Menu Structure

Major sections of the menu are not commands. A custom menu is not required to have all these major sections.

Subsections

Major sections of the menu can contain many subsections. This is normally the case with the SCREEN section, whose many subsections help control which part of the menu appears at any given moment. Each menu subsection contains a list of the specific command sequences that will be executed when picked with the pointing device. These command sequences can include special syntax to control the screen display of menu subsections.

Subsections of SCREEN can contain as many text lines as there are lines available in your monitor's screen menu area. If any subsection is longer than the maximum displayed on your monitor, the extra lines are wasted—they will not appear.

When a menu subsection has fewer lines than its maximum, the contents of the menu subsection are displayed, and any previous commands not overwritten by the new menu subsection will continue to appear on the screen. These previous commands will function normally if selected.

You can cause the display of a menu subsection to begin on any line you choose. By using this display feature, you can keep frequently used command sequences on the screen while different menu subsections are displayed.

Syntax

Your custom menus use special syntax to define how they will appear on the screen and how the command sequences will work. The elements of this syntax are summarized below.

Section Labels

As you've seen, three asterisks identify the major sections. The asterisks are followed by the major section *label*. The major section labels in an AutoCAD menu will appear in the leftmost margin of the menu file, heading their respective groups of commands.

CREATING CUSTOM MENUS
CH. 4

Two asterisks identify menu subsection labels, which contain related sets of command sequences. These labels act as pointers for the AutoCAD menu processor. For example:

**ERASE

This menu subsection, called ERASE, would probably contain commands, optional features, and/or likely prompt responses related to AutoCAD's ERASE command. The subsection label itself is not an ERASE command. It will not appear on the monitor screen. Every line that follows this subsection marker will appear in the screen menu area until either another menu subsection label or a major section label is encountered, the maximum number of lines is used, or the menu file ends.

The subsection label can contain an optional number that will instruct the AutoCAD menu processor to begin the display of this subsection on a particular line. For example:

**ERASE 3

would show that this subsection begins on the third line of the screen menu area, leaving the first two lines intact. Any command sequences found on these two lines would remain active and accessible to the pointing device after the ERASE subsection is displayed.

The Subsection Reference

The syntax that controls which menu subsection appears on the screen takes the following form:

$<key>=<subsection label>

When AutoCAD encounters this special set of characters in processing any command sequence, it will call the named menu subsection.

For example, if you wanted the ERASE subsection to appear on the screen, at the appropriate point in the menu, you would include the following characters:

$S=ERASE

You can see from the above example that the command syntax for bringing up a screen menu subsection is $S= followed by the name of the subsection. The letter S that appears after the dollar sign indicates that the subsection is part of the SCREEN major section. The character S is the SCREEN section's *key character*, and is supplied between the dollar sign and the equal sign.

The Screen Menu Structure

As SCREEN menu subsections are displayed, AutoCAD keeps track of them, up to a maximum of eight. You can backtrack through these screen menu references by means of the following syntax:

$S=

In this case, S is always used as the key character between the dollar sign and the equal sign. Each time these characters are issued without a subsection name, AutoCAD will recall the previous menu subsection and display it, until the maximum number of saved subsections (depending on your version) have been recalled. Once AutoCAD has backtracked through the previous eight subsections (or it runs out of previous subsections, whichever comes first), this syntax has no effect.

Other key characters are used for other major menu sections:

- **$B1=** through **$B4=** will access the BUTTONS major sections.
- **$A1=** through **$A4=** will access the AUX major sections.
- **$T1=** through **$T4=** will access tablet menu sections 1 through 4.
- **$P0=<subsection>** through **$P16=<subsection>** will access subsections within pull-down menu sections POP0 through POP16. However, the selection subsection will not automatically appear on the screen. To force display of a particular pull-down menu, use the special syntax, $P*n*=*, where *n* is the number of the pull-down menu section to be displayed. This process is explained in more detail later in this chapter.
- **$I=<subsection>** will access icon menu subsections. However, they will not automatically appear on the screen. To access a particular icon menu and have it appear on the screen, the syntax must be followed by $I=*.

It is frequently useful to change the on-screen menu display while an AutoCAD command sequence is in progress. The above syntax will not interrupt a command sequence in progress.

As you debug your custom menu, you may discover that you have inadvertently created a menu subsection that offers no way to reference a needed menu subsection, or perhaps does not allow you to return to the root menu. In this case, your only recourse is first to make a note of what happened (so you can find the problem

CREATING CUSTOM MENUS
CH. 4

area quickly and correct it using your word processor), and then type the AutoCAD command MENU followed by either the default name of the current menu or a new menu. When the menu is loaded, you will be at the top of the menu file again.

Brackets

Normally, the part of the menu that appears on the screen is enclosed in brackets. In standard installations of AutoCAD, you may include up to eight characters, including spaces, within these brackets. If you are using Release 12, you can choose to enlarge this area when you configure AutoCAD. Refer to AutoCAD's *Installation and Performance Guide* for details on configuration.

The AutoCAD menu processor will display what it finds within brackets on the screen for you to pick. For example:

```
[ERASE:]
[FILLET: ]
[ZOOM ALL]
```

The brackets are followed by the sequence of commands and prompt responses to be executed when the characters within brackets are selected with the pointing device.

Brackets are not absolutely required, although they usually make things easier to understand. If brackets are not used, the characters on each command line will be displayed on the screen, up to the width of the screen menu area (eight characters by default). When such characters are picked by the pointing device, it has the same effect as if the characters were typed at the keyboard. For example, suppose the following lines appeared in a custom menu:

```
zoom w 0,0 12,12
```

This would have the same effect as entering that exact line from the keyboard, character for character, space for space. AutoCAD would respond by zooming in on a window with opposite corners at points 0,0 and 12,12. This macro might be useful; however, when the line is displayed in the standard screen menu area, only the following characters would be visible:

```
zoom w 0
```

The Screen Menu Structure

You cannot see what the command sequence does. The command might be easier to understand if it were preceded by a short tag enclosed in brackets, as in the following example:

`[Zoom0/12]zoom w 0,0 12,12`

In this example, `Zoom0/12` would appear on the screen, and when picked with the pointing device, the command sequence after the brackets would be issued.

The Space and the Semicolon

The AutoCAD menu processor reads and interprets every letter, punctuation mark, and space in a custom menu. A space character in the command sequence will nearly always function the same as if you pressed ↵. This function of a space in the menu is just the same as the function of the spacebar key in AutoCAD.

The semicolon can also be used to indicate a ↵ keystroke. In this book, all custom menu examples use a semicolon rather than a space to indicate a ↵, to eliminate ambiguity.

Sometimes it may be necessary to *force* AutoCAD to read ↵ in a custom menu. For example, if you select something from the menu in response to a prompt for text entry (for example, the contents of a block attribute), AutoCAD will type the selected string including any spaces it finds. In this case, a simple space will not be read as ↵ but as part of the text string. In cases where ↵ must be forced in this fashion, you are required to use a semicolon.

AutoCAD's menu processor usually supplies an automatic ↵ at the end of each line in the menu file. Generally, this is what you want, but there are exceptions: if the line ends with a semicolon, a backslash, a control character, or a plus sign, AutoCAD does not supply the automatic ↵.

Usually, this is a convenience. However, in cases where a line ends with one of these special characters and a ↵ is necessary as well, simply force the ↵ by adding a semicolon to the end of the line.

The Backslash

The backslash character is used whenever the command sequence must pause to accept input from the user. The backslash can accept input that is either digitized or typed at the keyboard. For example:

`[ZOOM IN]ZOOM;W;\\`

CREATING CUSTOM MENUS
CH. 4

This simple macro invokes the ZOOM command, issues ↵, invokes the Window option with the W, issues another ↵ (as you would if you were typing these commands at the keyboard), and finally pauses twice to get the coordinates of the corners of the zoom window from the user.

No space or semicolon follows the backslash, as no ↵ is necessary after the window corner picks.

The Caret

The caret, or control character, identifies an AutoCAD control sequence within the menu. For example, ^C will be read by the AutoCAD menu processor as a Cancel command, and ^O will be read as the orthogonal mode toggle. Any control sequence recognizable by AutoCAD can be used as part of a custom menu command sequence. Like menu subsection references, control characters do not interrupt a command sequence in progress.

^P is a common control sequence in AutoCAD menus. This character toggles off the display of menu commands in the command prompt area. This is a convenience, since the menu commands tend to flash by rapidly and can be very distracting.

For a complete listing of AutoCAD control sequences, see the inside front cover of this book.

The Underscore Character

The underscore character is used in menus beginning with Release 12. This character serves an important purpose in menus that might be used with foreign-language versions of AutoCAD. When an English-language command is preceded by an underscore, it will automatically call its equivalent in any foreign-language version. AutoCAD commands in this book's example menus are not preceded by an underscore, although the character is used throughout the standard menu. If you intend to use a custom menu with more than one language version of AutoCAD, you should add an underscore character before each English AutoCAD command.

The Plus Sign

To extend a single menu command sequence over several lines in a custom menu, use the plus sign (+) at the end of the line that is to be continued. It can be inserted anywhere in the line, even in the middle of a word if necessary. It is invisible to the AutoCAD menu interpreter, and can make the menu much easier to read and edit by allowing a long sequence of commands to appear on several lines in the menu file. There is no limit to the length of a command sequence.

When a long command sequence occupies many lines in this fashion, it is said to be *wrapped around*. Command sequences that are wrapped around do not reduce the maximum number of display lines available for use within that subsection. In other words, although they occupy several text lines in the menu file, the AutoCAD menu processor sees wrapped-around command sequences as a single line. Thus, your maximum number of available display lines remains the same.

Examining the AutoCAD Standard Menu

Once you have made a copy of the AutoCAD standard menu, CUSTOM.MNU, enter your word processor and look at it. At this point, CUSTOM.MNU looks just like ACAD.MNU. You will find that it is a long document. Following the initial comment section (if you are looking at a menu for Release 11 or later), you will see the following section:

```
***BUTTONS1
;
$p0=*
^C^C
^B
^O
^G
^D
^E
^T
```

The first line signals the start of the BUTTONS section. The first button on the pointing device is always the Pick button; there is no way to change this. Therefore, the lines that follow the BUTTONS section label indicate the AutoCAD commands that are executed when you press the remaining buttons on the pointing device.

If you are using a three-button mouse, only the first two lines of this section are operable. The remaining lines are ignored. With a four-button digitizing puck, only the first three lines of this menu are operable.

In this menu, the second line (button 2) is a semicolon. Therefore button 2 on the pointing device is the same as the ↵ key.

CREATING CUSTOM MENUS
CH. 4

The third line (button 3) invokes a menu subsection reference that will display another menu subsection. The characters $p0=* will cause the Release 12 cursor menu to appear on the screen near the location of the crosshairs, if your display hardware supports pull-down menus.

The pull-down menu sections appear a little further on in the file. The first pull-down menu begins with the label POP0 in Release 12, or POP1 in earlier versions. The first few lines in Release 12's standard POP1 menu are as follows:

```
***POP1
[File]
[New...]^C^C_new
[Open...]^C^C_open
[Save...]^C^C_qsave
[Save As...]^C^C_saveas
[Recover...]^C^C_recover
[--]
[Plot...]^C^C_plot
[--]
```

The first line after the POP1 section label contains a *keyword* that will appear on the top line of the AutoCAD screen display, known as the status line. When a pointing device is used, such as a digitizer or a mouse, and the crosshairs are moved onto the status line, the menu bar will appear with up to ten keywords on it. The first line under each pull-down menu section is reserved for keywords. The keyword is enclosed in brackets. It is not followed by a command sequence. In this case, the word File will be displayed on AutoCAD's menu bar.

Commands to open and save drawing files appear in the lines below File. Following each set of brackets, the referenced command is invoked. (Notice the underscore character, as this example comes from AutoCAD's standard menu.) If the user highlights and selects one of the bracketed prompts, the command is invoked and the pull-down menu will automatically disappear from the screen.

Notice the control sequence that appears before each command: the symbol for Control-C, ^C, is invoked and then repeated. The repetition of the Cancel control sequence is a safety device. If this menu subsection were referenced from inside the AutoCAD dimensioning feature, for example, a single CANCEL command might not be enough to return to AutoCAD's Command prompt. But two CANCELs will always work. In cases where a single CANCEL would be enough, repeating the control sequence has no effect.

Examining the AutoCAD Standard Menu

Note also that no space appears between these control characters and the command. This is because a ↵ at this point is not necessary; if you attempted to place a space here, you could generate unintended results, since AutoCAD will read that space as ↵.

When you write your own custom command sequences, begin each with this double Control-C. In this way you can be sure that you are beginning each command sequence from the AutoCAD Command prompt, and not accidentally from inside another AutoCAD command.

The next major section in the AutoCAD standard menu is the ICON section. These lines will look something like the following:

```
***icon
**poly
[Set Spline Fit Variables]
[acad(pm-quad,Quadric Fit Polymesh)]'surftype 5
[acad(pm-cubic,Cubic Fit Polymesh)]'surftype 6
[acad(pm-bezr,Bezier Fit Polymesh)]'surftype 8
[acad(pl-quad,Quadric Fit Polyline)]'splinetype 5
[acad(pl-cubic,Cubic Fit Polyline)]'splinetype 6
```

Unlike the other major section labels, the ICON label in your version of the menu may appear in lowercase letters; this is simply an idiosyncrasy of the menu; major section labels are not case-sensitive.

The icon menu section contains several subsections, each corresponding to a particular icon menu display. As in pull-down menus, the first line of a subsection is a keyword (or words) that will appear at the top of the icon menu when it is displayed on the screen. Below the keyword are the names of AutoCAD slide files, enclosed in brackets. Up to 16 of these slides (20 in Release 12) may appear in a single icon menu. Following the slide name is the sequence of commands that will be executed when the individual slide is highlighted and picked by the user.

The next major section of the menu is the SCREEN section:

```
**Comment
     Begin AutoCAD Screen Menus
***SCREEN
**S
[AutoCAD]^C^C^P(ai_rootmenus) ^P
[* * * *]$S=OSNAPB
```

CREATING CUSTOM MENUS
CH. 4

```
[ASE]^C^C^P(ai_aseinit_chk) ^P
[BLOCKS]$S=X $S=BL
[DIM:]^C^C_DIM
[DISPLAY]$S=X $S=DS
[DRAW]$S=X $S=DR
[EDIT]$S=X $S=ED
[INQUIRY]$S=X $S=INQ
[LAYER...]$S=LAYER '_DDLMODES
[MODEL]$S=X $S=SOLIDS
[MVIEW]$S=MVIEW
[PLOT...]^C^C_PLOT
[RENDER]$S=X $S=RENDER
[SETTINGS]$S=X $S=SET
[SURFACES]$S=X $S=3D
[UCS:]^C^C_UCS
[UTILITY]$S=X $S=UT

[SAVE:]^C^C_QSAVE
```

Immediately following the SCREEN major section label is a menu subsection label named S, which identifies the AutoCAD Root menu. Whenever you wish to jump immediately to the Root menu, the following syntax will do the trick:

$S=S

The first line after the subsection label causes "AutoCAD" to appear, and if you select it at any time, the command line will invoke an AutoLISP function, (ai_root-menus), that has the effect of resetting the opening screen menu. This function is found in the ACAD.MNL file (or in copies of ACAD.MNL that you create for other custom menus).

The second line displays four asterisks on the screen. The AutoCAD menu interpreter will not confuse them with a label, because they are within brackets. When these asterisks are selected, the command sequence will display the OSNAPB menu subsection.

Notice how the next line, BLOCKS, references two menu subsections. The first menu subsection, X, can be found immediately following a series of header subsections. Menu subsection X is 18 lines long, only the last three of which contain command sequences:

```
**X 3
[__LAST__]$S= $S=
```

Examining the AutoCAD Standard Menu

```
[  DRAW  ]^C^C$S=X $S=DR
[  EDIT  ]^C^C$S=X $S=ED
```

The number 3 follows the subsection label, X. This indicates that subsection X will begin its display on line three of the menu display area. When referenced, this menu subsection will effectively clear any previously referenced menu subsections, except the top two lines, and display its three command sequences on the lower part of the screen menu area.

The second menu subsection referenced by BLOCKS is subsection BL. It looks like this:

```
**BL 3
[ATTDEF:]^C^C_ATTDEF
[BASE:]^C^C_BASE
[BLOCK:]^C^C_BLOCK
[INSERT:]^C^C_INSERT
[MINSERT:]^C^C_MINSERT
[WBLOCK:]^C^C_WBLOCK

[XBIND:]^C^C_XBIND
[XREF:]^C^C_XREF
```

This menu subsection also begins its display on line three, again leaving the two top lines alone. This menu subsection is only nine lines long, so the three lines at the bottom of menu subsection X will remain on the screen.

Returning to menu subsection S, notice how a reference to menu subsection X combines with several different menu subsections. Using this technique, you do not have to copy the command sequences that form menu subsection X onto many different menu subsections.

Sometimes there are too many options to fit on a single menu subsection. In such cases, AutoCAD uses a simple expedient, an example of which is found in the DR menu subsection:

```
[next]$S=X $S=DR2
```

Although the brackets say [next], all that occurs is a reference to a menu subsection that contains related commands. As you might expect, the menu subsection DR2 contains the following line:

```
[previous]$S=X $S=DR
```

CREATING CUSTOM MENUS
CH. 4

Skipping to the BLOCK subsection of CUSTOM.MNU, you will find the following:

```
**BLOCK 3
[BLOCK:]^C^C_BLOCK
?

[Select]$S=OSELECT1 \$S=
[Objects]$S=OSELECT1 \$S=


[Yes]_YES
[OOPS]^C^C_OOPS


[__LAST__]$S=
[  DRAW  ]^C^C$S=X $S=DR
[  EDIT  ]^C^C$S=X $S=ED
```

Here the BLOCK menu subsection contains the AutoCAD BLOCK command. The ? option (for obtaining a list of referenced block names) appears on the following line. This simple response is not enclosed in brackets. Brackets are not necessary here, since selecting this option has the same effect as typing it at the keyboard. Nor is a semicolon necessary; AutoCAD's menu processor automatically supplies ↵ at the end of each line in the menu file.

An alternate method for displaying this response would be:

```
[?]?;
```

This method would yield the same result, with AutoCAD typing only the question mark followed by ↵. In this example, a semicolon forces ↵. Because a semicolon was included at the end of the line, AutoCAD's menu processor does not supply an automatic ↵.

Neither of the above two display methods has any significant advantage over the other. AutoCAD's standard menu generally reserves use of the simpler form for entering keywords in response to prompts from invoked AutoCAD commands.

First Changes to the Custom Menu

In this section, you will practice making changes to CUSTOM.MNU that are designed to clarify the on-screen display and group together commands that are used more

First Changes to the Custom Menu

frequently. The following example demonstrates this technique by making some changes to the menu subsections that contain AutoCAD's entity drawing commands. These subsections are labeled DR and DR2. In their original form in the Release 12 menu, they look like this:

```
**DR 3
[ARC]$S=ARC
[ATTDEF:]^C^C_ATTDEF
[BHATCH:]^C^CBHATCH
[CIRCLE]$S=CIRCLE
[DONUT:]^C^C_DONUT
[DTEXT:]^C^C_DTEXT
[ELLIPSE:]^C^C_ELLIPSE
[HATCH:]^C^C_HATCH
[INSERT:]^C^C_INSERT
[LINE:]^C^C_LINE
[MINSERT:]^C^C_MINSERT
[OFFSET:]^C^C_OFFSET

[next]$S=X $S=DR2
**DR2 3
[PLINE:]^C^C_PLINE
[POINT:]^C^C_POINT
[POLYGON:]^C^C_POLYGON
[SHAPE:]^C^C_SHAPE
[SKETCH:]^C^C_SKETCH
[SOLID:]^C^C_SOLID
[TEXT:]^C^C_TEXT
[TRACE:]^C^C_TRACE
[3DFACE:]^C^C_3DFACE

[3D Surfs]$S=X $S=3D
[MODELER]$S=X $S=SOLIDS

[previous]$S=X $S=DR
```

This example will change the order in which these drawing commands are displayed, placing more frequently used commands on the first subsection DR, less frequently used commands on the second subsection DR2, and eliminating commands that are either never used or found elsewhere on the menu.

CREATING CUSTOM MENUS
CH. 4

Begin by listing the drawing commands, grouping them under four headings: Often Selected, Seldom Selected, Never Selected, and Found Elsewhere. A list of this type might look like the following:

Often Selected:	Seldom Selected:	Never Selected:	Found Elsewhere:
Arc	Attdef	Minsert	Insert (BLOCKS)
Circle	Donut	Sketch	Offset (ED2)
Line	Dtext	Solids	3Dline (3D)
Hatch	Ellipse	Trace	3Dface (3D)
Pline	Shape		3D Surfs (3D)
Point			
Polygon			
Solid			
Text			

Having thus determined priorities for selecting entity drawing commands, your next step is to note which lines in the menu currently contain references to other menu subsections. You will want to keep these menu subsection references on their original lines as you delete and move commands around. However, you can move them if there is a good reason and you don't disturb the operation of the menu file.

In the above example, [next] occurs on line 14 of subsection DR, and [previous] occurs on line 14 of subsection DR2.

Commands from other subsections can be added here to good effect. For example, it may be useful to place the ERASE command on line 13 of both DR and DR2, just before the menu subsection references. (Placing the command on the same line in both subsections will allow you to find it in a consistent position in the display.) This will allow you to erase entities a little more quickly. You won't need to first access the editing commands subsection and then return to the entity drawing commands subsection. The ERASE command can be found on the menu subsection labeled ED. Copy it (don't move it) to line 13 of DR and DR2.

First Changes to the Custom Menu

After you have deleted the commands that are Never Selected or Found Elsewhere, and have moved the Often Selected commands to DR and the Seldom Selected commands to DR2, the menu subsections should look something like the following:

```
**DR 3
[ARC]$S=X $S=ARC
[CIRCLE]$S=X $S=CIRCLE
[LINE:]$S=X $S=LINE ^C^CLINE
[PLINE:]$S=X $S=PLINE ^C^CPLINE
[POINT:]$S=X $S=POINT ^C^CPOINT
[POLYGON:]$S=X $S=POLYGON ^C^CPOLYGON
[TEXT:]$S=X $S=TEXT ^C^CTEXT
[HATCH:]$S=X $S=HATCH ^C^CHATCH
[ERASE:]$S=X $S=ERASE ^C^CERASE
[next]$S=DR2
**DR2 3
[ATTDEF:]$S=X $S=ATTDEF ^C^CATTDEF
[DONUT:]$S=X $S=DONUT ^C^CDONUT
[DTEXT:]$S=X $S=DTEXT ^C^CDTEXT
[ELLIPSE:]$S=X $S=ELLIPSE ^C^CELLIPSE
[SHAPE:]$S=X $S=SHAPE ^C^CSHAPE
[SOLID:]$S=X $S=SOLID ^C^CSOLID
[ERASE:]$S=X $S=ERASE ^C^CERASE
[previous]$S=DR
[__LAST__]$S=DR
```

Besides placing the more frequently used commands up front in the menu structure, you have saved some drawing time by locating an extra ERASE command in a more convenient location. Figures 4.1 and 4.2 show how these new entity drawing menus might appear on the screen.

This technique can be applied to any given menu subsection; editing commands, display commands, and utility commands are all candidates for this kind of treatment. As you consolidate your custom menu, seconds of time saved will begin to add up to significant savings. There are ways to save even more time by means of custom menu macros, discussed in the next chapter.

FIGURE 4.1:
Customized version of DR menu subsection.

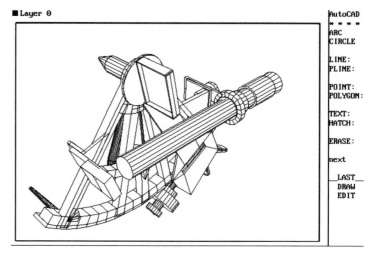

FIGURE 4.2:
Customized version of DR2 menu subsection.

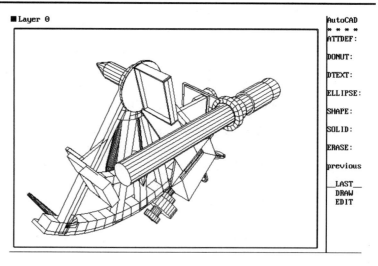

Customization Using the Digitizer

If you use a digitizing tablet as your input device, you can make the process of drawing much more efficient by means of custom tablet menus. AutoCAD allows you to specify up to four separate areas of your tablet as menu areas, plus a remaining area to be used as the screen pointing area. These menu areas are rectangular, but they may be arranged on the tablet in any way you choose. With a well-organized set of tablet menus, you can bypass the hierarchical screen menu altogether.

After you have defined each tablet menu area, you may partition it to contain as many smaller rectangular boxes as you choose. (There is a theoretical limit of 32,766 items, but in practice you would not want more than a couple of hundred.) AutoCAD automatically numbers the boxes within a tablet menu area, beginning with number one in the upper left, and continuing horizontally, row by row, ending with the box in the lower right. Each of the boxes can be designated as a particular AutoCAD command, setting, or macro.

Figure 4.3 shows a typical arrangement of a digitizer tablet divided into four tablet menus and a screen pointing area, and Figure 4.4 shows a tablet menu area partitioned into thirty boxes (five columns by six rows).

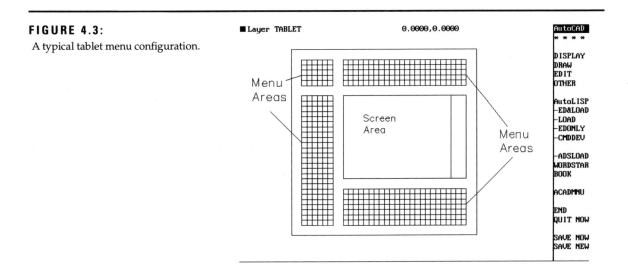

FIGURE 4.3:
A typical tablet menu configuration.

CREATING CUSTOM MENUS
CH. 4

FIGURE 4.4:
Tablet menu area with numbered boxes.

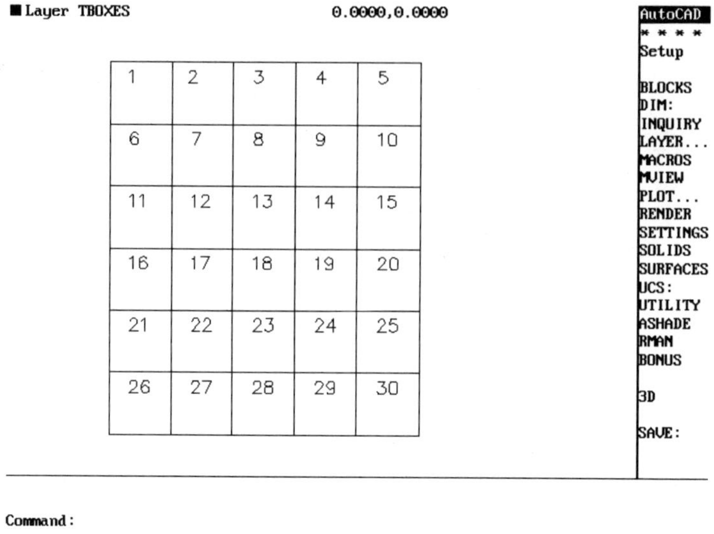

Designing the Template

The first step in creating a custom digitizing tablet is to design a model of your tablet menu areas, their location on the digitizing tablet, the number of boxes in each, and the location of the screen pointing area.

Once you have settled on an arrangement of tablet menu areas and commands, you can create a *template*, a drawing of your arrangement. Label each box in the menu area with its intended AutoCAD command or command sequence. You can, if you wish, make some boxes larger than others by having the same command apply to adjacent boxes.

Arrange the commands on your template drawing so that a minimum of pen motion is required to move from command to command, and group related commands together. Commands frequently used in sequence should be located near each other, if not actually strung together in macros.

Of course, use AutoCAD to draw the template. When your template design is satisfactory, plot it out at the correct scale. Fasten the template onto the surface of your digitizing tablet.

Customization Using the Digitizer

To prevent your template from wearing out too quickly, you may consider laminating it. If you don't want to laminate it, another trick is to use AutoCAD's MIRROR command to flip the finished template, plotting it in reverse on sturdy clear vellum. Then reverse the vellum when fastening the template to your digitizing tablet.

Configuring the Tablet

When your template is in place, you are ready to configure AutoCAD to respond to your custom tablet menus. You tell AutoCAD about your arrangement of tablet menu areas by issuing the TABLET CFG command. When you do, AutoCAD will prompt:

`Enter number of tablet menus desired (0-4)<0>:`

After you enter the appropriate number of tablet menus, AutoCAD prompts you to enter the upper-left corner, lower-left corner, and lower-right corner of each tablet menu area. Respond by digitizing the requested points on your template drawing. The set of three points must form a 90-degree angle, or AutoCAD will request a new set of points. The tablet menu areas must not overlap.

After you enter the location of each tablet menu area, AutoCAD prompts:

`Enter the number of columns for menu area n:`

Respond with the number of vertical columns in the menu area. AutoCAD next prompts:

`Enter the number of rows for menu area n:`

Respond with the number of horizontal rows in the menu area. Continue this process until you have defined all your tablet menu areas. AutoCAD then prompts:

`Digitize lower left corner of screen pointing area:`

Respond by digitizing the appropriate point. AutoCAD prompts:

`Digitize upper right corner of screen pointing area:`

Respond by digitizing the appropriate point. Do not overlap the screen pointing and tablet menu areas.

CREATING CUSTOM MENUS

CH. 4

Placing Commands on the Digitizing Tablet

Once you have configured the digitizing tablet, you may assign AutoCAD commands, settings, macros, and so on to the labeled menu area boxes. Do this by editing the TABLET1 through TABLET4 major sections of CUSTOM.MNU.

CUSTOM.MNU, because it is a copy of AutoCAD's standard menu, has TABLET sections already assigned various AutoCAD commands and settings. These entries correspond to a standard template provided with AutoCAD. If you are using AutoCAD's standard template, only TABLET1 should be edited. Leave the others alone. If you are using your own template, you will probably want to overwrite at least some others.

In AutoCAD's standard menu, TABLET1 you have room for 200 user-definable commands. Figure 4.4 illustrates a considerably smaller tablet menu area with five columns and six rows. Boxes in this tablet menu are numbered from 1 to 30. Using this example, menu section TABLET1 will contain thirty text lines. The first line corresponds to box number 1, the second line to box 2, and so on.

Figure 4.5 illustrates a possible arrangement of AutoCAD LAYER commands and options in the example tablet menu area.

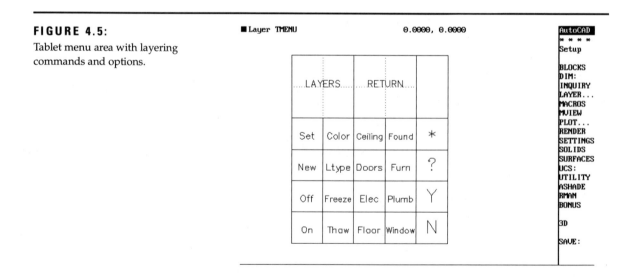

FIGURE 4.5:
Tablet menu area with layering commands and options.

Customization Using the Digitizer

To correspond to the illustrated menu area, the TABLET1 section of the menu file should look as follows:

```
***TABLET1
^C^CLAYER;
^C^CLAYER;
;
;
[ ]
^C^CLAYER;
^C^CLAYER;
;
;
[ ]
S;
COLOR;
CEILING;
FOUNDATION;
[ ]*;
New;
LTYPE;
DOORS;
FURNITURE;
?;
OFF;
FREEZE;
ELEC;
PLUMB;
Y;
ON;
THAW;
FLOOR;
WINDOW;
N;
```

In this example, notice how some command boxes in the tablet menu were enlarged simply by repeating the same command in adjacent boxes.

Lines 5 and 10 of this section contain empty brackets. This is a convenient way of indicating an empty box, although a blank line will do just as well. On a tablet menu, if AutoCAD encounters a pair of brackets at the beginning of a line, the brackets plus anything contained within them are ignored.

CREATING CUSTOM MENUS
CH. 4

Line 15 contains a pair of brackets followed by an asterisk. These brackets are necessary to move the asterisk off the leftmost column of the file. The asterisk is an appropriate response to some prompts within the layer command, but if it appears on the menu file's leftmost column, the menu processor will misinterpret it as the beginning of a new subsection. The brackets solve the problem.

Boxes in a tablet menu area can contain macros, such as those described in the next chapter. Long command sequences are wrapped around several text lines for easier editing, and all custom menu syntax (for example, screen menu changes) can be used where desired in the tablet sections of the custom menu file.

Multiple template designs are possible as well. AutoCAD stores the configuration of the digitizing tablet as part of the drawing, so if you wish to use more than one template design, you will need a prototype drawing for each. If you use a consistent template design, you can change commands assigned to the boxes by loading different custom menus.

Creating a New Menu Subsection

In the next chapter you will create lengthy macros. This section demonstrates the technique for creating a new menu subsection in the SCREEN major section of CUSTOM.MNU. The subsection created here will be called MACROS; you can use it to store the custom menu macros discussed in the next chapter.

With your word processor, return to the beginning of the SCREEN major section of CUSTOM.MNU. The first menu subsection in the SCREEN major section is subsection S.

Once you have found this menu subsection, place the cursor on any convenient blank line. (The 19th line in the S menu subsection is usually blank. If it is, place the cursor there.) Once you are on a blank line in the S menu subsection, type in the following, beginning at the leftmost column:

```
[MACROS]^C^C$S=X $S=MACROS
```

This now-familiar syntax will cause the word MACROS to appear on the screen. Next, a double Cancel is invoked to cancel any command that might be active when MACROS is picked. Finally, the menu subsection references for the X menu subsection followed by the MACROS menu subsection are invoked.

The next step is to create the MACROS menu subsection. Go to the end of the SCREEN major section. The major section after SCREEN is TABLET1. Therefore, you can find the TABLET1 major section label using your word processor and skip to the right end of the line just above this label. Press ↵. This should open up a new line just above TABLET1, with the cursor positioned in the leftmost column. If this is so, type the following:

**MACROS 3

Now, press ↵ two or three times, save the new menu file, and you are finished.

As your macros become more numerous, you may wish to move or copy them to other menu subsections in the custom menu file. This is fine, but remember not to exceed the maximum number of lines your screen allows, and remember that menu subsections can be combined. When adding lines to a menu subsection, be careful that you don't accidentally overwrite any necessary command sequence displayed from a previous menu subsection.

Creating New Pull-Down Menus

Figure 4.6 illustrates the standard menu bar as supplied by Autodesk. In this illustration, the user has moved the crosshairs into the upper-left corner of the screen, activating the horizontal menu bar, and highlighted the keyword Draw. When the user pushed the Select button, the pull-down menu below that keyword appeared on the screen.

This pull-down menu will remain in place until the user takes one of four possible actions:

1. Selects a command or option from any displayed on the screen in any menu area.
2. Selects any point on the graphics screen.
3. Types anything at the keyboard.
4. Moves the pointing device into the rightmost screen menu area.

Any of the above will cause the pull-down menu to disappear from the screen.

FIGURE 4.6:

AutoCAD's pull-down menu bar.

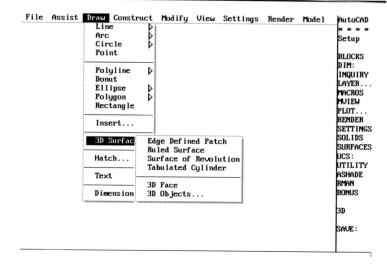

Although the appearance and behavior of the pull-down menu is different from the AutoCAD standard screen menu, the techniques for creating or modifying it are similar to the techniques for creating standard AutoCAD screen menus and menu macros.

The Structure of Pull-Down Menus

AutoCAD automatically adjusts pull-down menus to be as wide as the longest word they contain. All words in a pull-down menu are left-justified within the display. They appear just below the selected keyword in the horizontal menu bar.

You can create pull-down menus that are as wide as your screen, but as you add pull-down menus and the number of keywords increases, you will be forced to use ever-narrowing menu displays. If you use all of the possible pull-down menu keywords in your horizontal menu bar, the keywords should average no more than a few letters each, so as to fit. If the keywords cannot fit, the rightmost ones will be ignored, and thus inaccessible.

Creating New Pull-Down Menus

The following list contains the menu items found in Release 12's POP4 (Construct) section:

```
***POP4
[Construct]
[Array]^C^C_array
[Array 3D]^C^C3darray
[Copy]$M=$(if,$(eq,$(substr,$(getvar,cmdnames),1,4),GRIP),+
_copy,^C^C_copy)
[Mirror]$M=$(if,$(eq,$(substr,$(getvar,cmdnames),1,4),GRIP),+
_mirror,^C^C_mirror)
[Mirror 3D]^C^Cmirror3d
[--]
[Chamfer]^C^C_chamfer
[Fillet]^C^C_fillet
[--]
[Divide]^C^C_divide
[Measure]^C^C_measure
[Offset]^C^C_offset
[--]
[Block]^C^C_block
```

The first line after the POP4 menu section label contains the keyword Construct enclosed in brackets. AutoCAD places that word into the horizontal menu bar. When the user selects that menu item, the commands that follow it in the menu section are displayed as a pull-down menu. If no menu commands appear below the keyword, the menu will not be usable.

The command sequences in pull-down menus are structured in the same way as commands in the screen menu. When the user selects one of these commands, the command sequence following the brackets will be executed by AutoCAD as if it had been typed at the keyboard. The command sequence can include changes in the display of the original screen menu.

Controlling the Pull-Down Menu Display

You do not need to select the word displayed in the horizontal menu bar to cause a pull-down menu to appear. As mentioned earlier, you can use a special command syntax to cause the appearance of a pull-down menu:

$Pn=*

CREATING CUSTOM MENUS
CH. 4

When using this syntax, substitute the number of the desired POP*n* menu section label for *n*. For example, to cause the appearance of the POP3 menu, use this syntax:

P3=*

Swapping Menus (Release 11 and Earlier)

You can create different pull-down menus to appear in the same place along the menu bar. This technique was the only way to create submenus in AutoCAD versions prior to Release 12. It has been supplanted by a new Release 12 submenu technique, described just ahead.

Still, if you are using an earlier version of AutoCAD, you may want to swap pull-down menus. The syntax for displaying these secondary menus is similar to that used to display menu subsections in the original screen menu.

For example, consider the following simple custom pull-down menu, which contains display commands:

```
***POP10
[Display]
[Redraw]'redraw
[--]
[Pan:]'PAN
[View:]'VIEW;
[Zoom:]'ZOOM;
[--]
[DView]^C^C$S=X $S=DVIEW dview
[Vpoint 3D        >]^C^C$S=X $S=VPOINT3D $i=3dviews $i=*
```

This will work fine, but if the user selects Zoom from this pull-down menu, the options for this command (Window, Dynamic, Previous, All, and so on) will have to be entered manually. You could, if you wish, include all the various Zoom options on the same pull-down menu, or you could decide to place the Zoom options in a menu of their own, which would replace the current menu when Zoom is selected. In the following example, notice the lines that have been added to this pull-down menu:

```
***POP4
**P4A
[Display]
[Redraw]'redraw;
[--]
[Pan:]'PAN;
[View:]'VIEW;
```

Creating New Pull-Down Menus

```
[Zoom:]$P4=P4B;$P4=*;
[--]
[DView]^C^C$S=X;$S=DVIEW;dview;;ca;
[Vpoint 3D  >]^C^C$S=X;$S=VPOINT3D;vpoint;;
**P4B
[Zoom]
[Window]$P4=P4A;'zoom;w;
[Previous]$P4=P4A;'zoom;p;
[Dynamic]$P4=P4A;'zoom;d;
[All]$P4=P4A;'zoom;a;
[--]
[Display]$P4=P4A;$P4=*;
```

In the above example, two subsections of POP4 have been created, labeled P4A and P4B. These subsection labels are preceded by two asterisks, to differentiate them from the Pop4 menu section label, which is preceded by three asterisks. The first subsection, P4A, will appear on the screen when the word Display is selected from the menu bar.

Figure 4.7 illustrates how this new Display menu appears on the screen.

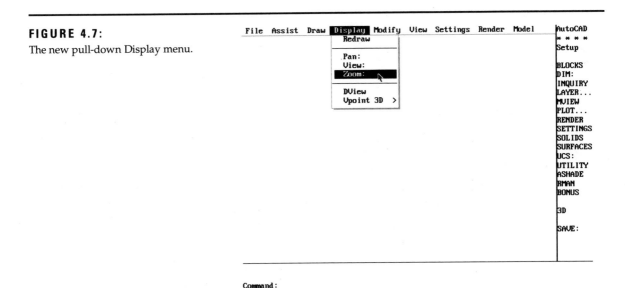

FIGURE 4.7:
The new pull-down Display menu.

111

CREATING CUSTOM MENUS
CH. 4

Notice the command following [Zoom:]. This sequence will change the default subsection from P4A to P4B:

$P4=P4B

In order for this new subsection to appear immediately on the screen, this syntax is followed by:

$P4=*

Figure 4.8 illustrates the appearance of the second menu subsection after Zoom is selected.

This new menu subsection (including the word Zoom displayed in the horizontal menu bar) will remain active until the drawing session is ended or the original menu subsection is made active again.

In this example, the menu subsection syntax is repeated when the user selects an option found on the new subsection P4B. This time the syntax references the original subsection, P4A:

$P4=P4A

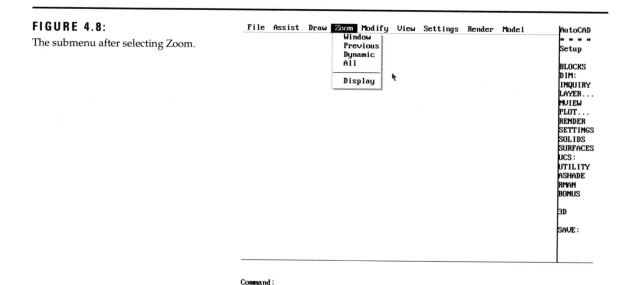

FIGURE 4.8:
The submenu after selecting Zoom.

Creating New Pull-Down Menus

This time it is not necessary to force the immediate display of the P4A subsection. It will appear when the user next highlights the horizontal menu bar.

However, in case the user has selected the Zoom command by accident, or if the Zoom menu subsection is left active, the following command sequence is added to the P4B menu subsection:

`[Display]$P4=P4A $P4=*`

This sequence insures that the user will always be able to return to the original default menu subsection. As you build more complex menu structures, be certain that you always leave an escape hatch such as this for the user.

Pull-Down Submenus (Release 12)

Release 12 includes a more elegant way to access submenus within pull-down menus. Release 12 submenus are accessed by means of a special syntax within the bracketed prompts: a hyphen followed by a greater-than symbol (->). In an ASCII file, this symbol looks like an arrow pointing to the right.

This special symbol shows that subsequent command lines in the pull-down menu section are part of a submenu, which will appear when you select the bracketed prompt with the pointing device.

All command lines within the section that appear below this special symbol will be included in the submenu. To cause subsequent command lines to appear in the main pull-down menu instead, place a different symbol inside the brackets for the last submenu command line. This symbol consists of a less-than sign followed by a hyphen (<-), which resembles an arrow pointing to the left. When the menu processor encounters this symbol, subsequent command lines revert to the original pull-down menu. Following is a short example of this technique:

```
***POP10
[Display]
[Redraw]'redraw;
[--]
[Pan:]'PAN;
[View:]'VIEW;
[->Zoom]
    [Window]^C^C'zoom;w;
    [Previous]^C^C'zoom;p;
    [Dynamic]^C^C'zoom;d;
    [<-All]^C^C'zoom;a;
```

CREATING CUSTOM MENUS
CH. 4

```
[--]
[DView]^C^C$S=X;$S=DVIEW;dview;;ca;
[Vpoint 3D  >]^C^C$S=X;$S=VPOINT3D;vpoint;;
```

In the above example, the Zoom options will appear when you select Zoom from the pull-down menu. You can then select the option you like, and AutoCAD invokes the command.

You can nest pull-down submenus as many levels as you like, although too much nesting (more than one or two levels) can look cluttered and may detract from the overall ease-of-use of your interface.

For clarity, submenu command lines are indented in the ASCII file. This indentation has no effect on how the menu is compiled and displayed, but it helps make the overall menu organization a little easier to understand when you are reading or editing the ASCII file.

Other Pull-Down Menu Features

Two minor features are available to help with the appearance of your pull-down menus. The first is a symbol composed of two hyphens surrounded by brackets:

```
[--]
```

When this symbol occupies a line in a pull-down menu, it will display a series of hyphens separating the items in the pull-down menu.

You can adjust the display of the words within the brackets using the second feature: when a tilde (~) precedes a bracketed item, the item will appear at a lower intensity than a normal bracketed item. This display technique can be used to identify short prompts or symbols that are not intended to represent commands, or for any other display purpose you wish.

Creating Icon Menus

Icon menus are likely to be more exciting to the experienced user of AutoCAD, because they represent a significant improvement when selecting blocks, shapes, text styles, or other forms of graphic input. After all, it is sometimes difficult to remember the exact difference between blocks or shapes with names like Part51A3 and Part52A3.

Creating Icon Menus

An *icon menu* is a means to preview graphic input selections before inserting them into a drawing. When an icon menu is displayed on the screen, up to 16 graphic options (20 in Release 12) can be presented to the user, along with a special arrow character that moves to select the desired option. In addition, icon menus can reference other icon menus, making it possible to review any number of options in sequence.

Figure 4.9 illustrates an icon menu created using the standard ES shape file supplied with AutoCAD.

There are three steps to creating an icon menu:

1. Create an AutoCAD slide file for each option to be displayed in the icon menu.

2. Optionally, use AutoCAD's SLIDELIB.EXE utility to combine the slides into a slide library file on the hard disk.

3. Add the syntax for displaying the icon menu to ACAD.MNU.

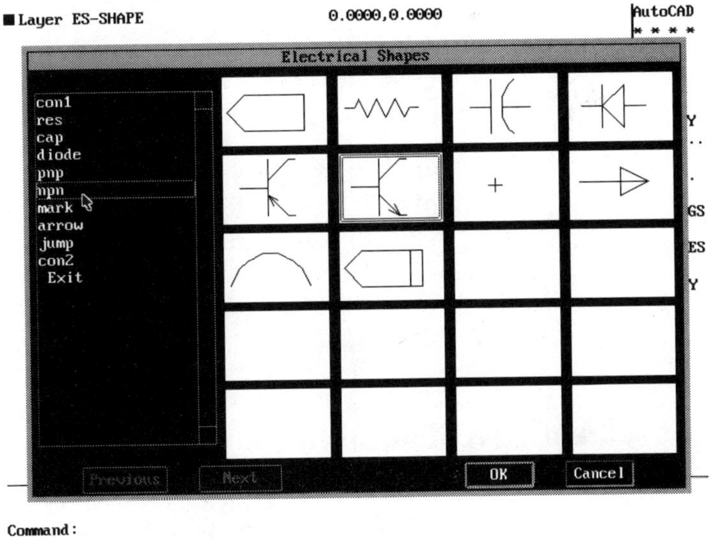

FIGURE 4.9:
ES shapes displayed in an icon menu.

CREATING CUSTOM MENUS
CH. 4

Once you have created the slide and ACAD.MNU is changed, AutoCAD automatically handles the display of the icon menu. Fortunately, the icon menu syntax is easy to learn, and in most respects follows conventions similar to other custom menu displays.

Creating the AutoCAD Slide Files

Create slides to be used in icon menus the same way you would create any other AutoCAD slide, using the MSLIDE command and giving the slide file a unique name. Here are two tips to keep in mind:

- Keep the drawings as simple as you can. Don't use filled lines, solids, or complicated drawings. The resulting display of your icon slide will be very small, and tiny details will be lost anyway. The simpler the slides, the faster the display of the icon menu.
- When making the slide, enlarge the graphic image to fill the entire drawing editor. If the image cannot fill the editor, center the drawing in the editor as much as possible.

To create the above example icon menu, slides were made of each shape in the AutoCAD standard shape file, ES.SHX. Each slide file was given the same name as the shape it represented.

Once your slide files are created, you are ready to incorporate them into an icon menu. However, in order for your icon menu to work, all the slides must be on disk and available to AutoCAD. If you create many icon menus, the dozens (or even hundreds) of slides can be quite cumbersome to manage. You can make it easier to manage groups of related slide files by combining them into a single disk file called a *slide library*, using a special utility, SLIDELIB.EXE.

Creating a Slide Library File

To create a slide library file, first use your word processor or text editor to create an ASCII file that contains a single-spaced list of the slide file names you intend to combine into the library file.

Creating Icon Menus

To create the library file used in the example icon file, the following list of slide file names was entered into an ASCII file named ESNAMES:

```
c:\acad\CON1
c:\acad\RES
c:\acad\CAP
c:\acad\DIODE
c:\acad\PNP
c:\acad\NPN
c:\acad\MARK
c:\acad\ARROW
c:\acad\JUMP
c:\acad\CON2
```

Notice that the file extension SLD is assumed for each of these slide file names. The directory path name for each slide (in this example, C:\ACAD) is included, although the path name will not be saved in the library file. (Collecting the slides into a single library file makes individual slide path names unnecessary.)

You can, if you wish, combine slides from several subdirectories into a single slide library file. Also, if you know that all the slides will be contained on the default directory when you create the library file, you can safely omit the path name from the list.

The ASCII file containing the list of slide names was arbitrarily assigned the file name ESNAMES. You can name your own list of slide names anything you like.

After you have created ESNAMES, be certain that it is copied onto the same directory as the file SLIDELIB.EXE. Log onto that directory and enter the following command at the DOS prompt:

```
SLIDELIB ES < ESNAMES
```

The first parameter on this command line is the name of the library file to create. In this case, the library file that results will be named ES, and AutoCAD will give it a file extension of SLB. You need not specify the file extension in the command line. You may name your library files anything you like, but it will be to your advantage to keep the names short to simplify subsequent typing.

The second parameter on the command line is the name of the ASCII list of slide names to be combined into the library file. It is preceded by the symbol <, indicating to DOS that the file ESNAMES is to be used as input by SLIDELIB.EXE.

CREATING CUSTOM MENUS
CH. 4

Once SLIDELIB.EXE has completed execution, the library file ES.SLB will be created, containing all the slides in the list. You can then copy the original slide files and the list of slide names onto a backup disk and erase them from the hard disk.

Do not erase the slide files without backing them up first. If you wish to add slides to the library, the only way to do so is to create a brand-new slide library to replace the old one. Thus, you may need to use those original slide files and the list of names again. There is no procedure for simply adding slides to an existing library file, nor is there any procedure for deleting individual slides from the library file.

To view slides from the library, use AutoCAD's VSLIDE command. At the prompt, simply reference the library as part of the slide name, as in the following example:

```
ES(CON1)
```

Note that the library name is followed by the slide name contained in parentheses. No spaces are used to separate the names. A path name can be included as well in response to the VSLIDE prompt:

```
C:\ACAD\SLIDES\ES(CON1)
```

Any slide that is part of a library may be referenced using the above *library(slide name)* syntax.

Creating the Icon Menu in ACAD.MNU

After you have created your slides and placed them in a library file of your choosing, you are ready to modify ACAD.MNU to include a reference to the new icon menu.

All icon menus are contained within a menu section labeled ICON. Each icon menu is a unique menu subsection within ICON. In the standard version of ACAD.MNU supplied by Autodesk, the ICON menu section follows the POP*n* menu sections.

To add the ES icon menu to ACAD.MNU, first locate the ICON menu section. Next, insert a new subsection label, ES, just underneath the ICON menu label, as follows:

```
***icon
**ES
```

Notice that the subsection label is preceded by two asterisks, to distinguish it from the menu section label. The next step is to add the title of the icon menu in brackets, on the line just below ES, as follows:

```
***icon
```

Creating Icon Menus

```
**ES
[Electrical Shapes]
```

Each line that follows this title line begins with the name of a slide in brackets. Following the names of the slides, you may type in any command sequence of your choosing, to be executed when that particular slide is picked off the icon menu. The following example illustrates this. Here, the command sequence is the SHAPE command, followed by the selected shape name:

```
***icon
**ES
[Electrical Shapes]
[es(con1)]^C^CSHAPE;CON1;
[es(res)]^C^CSHAPE;RES;
[es(cap)]^C^CSHAPE;CAP;
[es(diode)]^C^CSHAPE;DIODE;
[es(pnp)]^C^CSHAPE;PNP;
[es(npn)]^C^CSHAPE;NPN;
[es(mark)]^C^CSHAPE;MARK;
[es(arrow)]^C^CSHAPE;ARROW;
[es(jump)]^C^CSHAPE;JUMP;
[es(con2)]^C^CSHAPE;CON2;
[ Exit]^C^C
```

Finally, notice that the last line of the icon menu contains the word Exit in brackets followed by a cancel sequence. This line is required only in versions prior to Release 12, which automatically adds an OK button to the icon menu; this has the same effect. In earlier versions, this line will remove the icon menu from the screen if the user has selected it by accident. There is no Exit slide; this is not a problem. The first character within the brackets is a space; when AutoCAD reads the initial space inside the brackets, it understands that there is no slide to be displayed and the word within the brackets is displayed on the icon menu instead.

Icon menus are flexible. You can combine different libraries of slides in the same icon menu. You can combine slides that are not in library files with slides that are in library files. You can, if you choose, reference slide names including a full path name, as in the following example:

```
[res2]^C^CINSERT;RES2;
[c:\acad\slides\insul2]^C^CINSERT;INSUL2;
[es(con1)]^C^CSHAPE;CON1;
[es(res)]^C^CSHAPE;RES;
```

119

CREATING CUSTOM MENUS
CH. 4

In the above example, custom slide files named RES2 (on the default directory) and INSUL2 (on the C:\ACAD\SLIDES directory) have been referenced along with slides that are part of the ES.SLB library file (also on the default directory).

Remember that the command sequences following the slide names must be valid AutoCAD menu command sequences, and are subject to all the rules pertaining to custom menu commands and macros.

You can include up to 16 individual command sequences (20 in Release 12) on a single icon menu. (A technique for using more than one icon menu to handle larger numbers of command sequences is discussed in the following section.)

Displaying the Icon Menu on the Screen

Once the icon menu has been set up in ACAD.MNU, the only step that remains is to include a reference to it in another command sequence of your choosing. The reference may be placed in a pull-down menu section, an original screen menu section, or both. The following is a typical icon menu reference, using the ES icon menu:

`[ESHAPES]$i=es $i=*`

Notice the similarities to the pull-down menu references. The first reference causes the icon menu subsection ES to become active:

`$i=es`

Notice that the letter i follows the dollar sign, and no number is used because there can be only one icon menu section. An equal sign follows the letter i, followed by the name of a particular icon menu subsection; in this case, subsection ES. This syntax alerts AutoCAD that icon menu subsection ES is now *active*, or capable of being displayed.

In icon menus, after a menu subsection is referenced, it will almost always be immediately displayed on the screen. The reference that does this is similar to the pull-down menu reference for display, thus:

`$i=*`

When AutoCAD reads this syntax, the active icon menu subsection is immediately displayed, and the user is free to choose one of its options.

To test your modified menu, enter AutoCAD's drawing editor and enter the command MENU, followed by your menu file name. AutoCAD will recompile your

Creating Icon Menus

custom menu and in a moment or so, your new menu will appear. Try selecting your new commands. If things don't work out smoothly, enter your word processor and check to see that your command sequences were entered correctly. Then return to the drawing editor, enter the MENU command again, and after AutoCAD recompiles your menu, try selecting your new commands again.

Remember, you can never hurt AutoCAD with a custom menu. Sometimes you can get into trouble with command sequences that don't operate as you anticipate, but you are never far from help. In case of absolute disaster, you can always get back to AutoCAD's standard menu by entering the command MENU ACAD at the keyboard. Thus, don't be afraid to experiment. Experimentation is your best learning device.

CHAPTER FIVE

Custom Menu Macros

CUSTOM MENU MACROS
CH. 5

A *macro* is a series of commands and options that will execute in sequence from a single menu or tablet selection. Using macros can save time and promote drawing efficiency. For example, a macro based on AutoCAD's layer commands might set any existing layer as current without going through all the keystrokes required to change a layer at the keyboard.

When do you need a macro? Whenever you find yourself jumping around between menus on the same screen or typing the same things repeatedly at the keyboard, you are looking at an opportunity to create a powerful, time-saving macro.

This chapter presents some examples of general-purpose macros that you can add to the screen menu or include in a command box on a tablet menu. Use them as the basis for constructing more specific macros geared to your own individual needs.

Utility Macros

Among the most useful macros you can create are those related to the process of managing your drawing files. Layers, blocks, named entities, and the like often require a series of commands and laborious keyboard input to process. Placing these "management" command sequences and named entities within a macro can save considerable time and improve overall drawing efficiency.

Layer Macros

Layer changing is one of those things that can seem to take forever. Here are some macros that speed up the movement between layers. These examples use layers named Red, Yellow, Blue, and Green.

To begin, place the following subsection reference on your drawing or editing menu:

```
[LayerSet]^C^C$S=LSET
```

This macro cancels any current operation and references a menu subsection named LSET, which contains macros that set any one of the example layers current:

```
**LSET 3
[red]LAYER;S;RED;;$S=
[yellow]LAYER;S;YELLOW;;$S=
[blue]LAYER;S;BLUE;;$S=
[green]LAYER;S;GREEN;;$S=
```

Utility Macros

```
[0]LAYER;S;0;;$S=

[LASTMENU]$S=
[ROOTMENU]$S=S
```

Using this menu subsection, you can pick the layer of your choice from the screen menu; AutoCAD sets the layer current, and you are returned to the menu subsection you came from. This is a lot faster than using off-the-shelf AutoCAD. When you use this technique, the drawing must already contain the referenced layers. This technique works best for layers found in a prototype drawing.

Notice the need for the double semicolon in these macros. AutoCAD requires an extra ↵ at the conclusion of the LAYER command to restore the AutoCAD prompt.

You can easily compose variations on this theme, such as the following:

```
[LayerOn]^C^C$S=LSON
[LayerOff]^C^C$S=LSOFF
```

These macros transfer you to menu subsections for turning layers on and off, respectively.

The following is the menu subsection for turning layers off (compare it to the LSET subsection):

```
**LSOFF 3
[red]LAYER;OFF;RED;;$S=
[yellow]LAYER;OFF;YELLOW;;$S=
[blue]LAYER;OFF;BLUE;;$S=
[green]LAYER;OFF;GREEN;;$S=

[0]LAYER;OFF;0;;$S=
[ALL]LAYER;OFF;*;;;$S=
[LayerOn]^C$S=LSON
[LASTMENU]$S=
[ROOTMENU]$S=S
```

Besides the commands for turning off individual layers, notice the ALL command on the eighth line; it turns off all the layers except the one that is current. The macro labeled ALL can tell which layer is current because AutoCAD's default answer to the prompt

`Really want to turn the current layer off?`

is No. An extra ↵ is added in the macro as the response to this prompt. The result is that the current layer is left on while all the others go off. The reference to the LSON subsection is repeated on this display for convenience.

The following is the LSON subsection, which uses the same general technique:

```
**LSON 3
[red]^CLAYER;ON;RED;;$S=
[yellow]^CLAYER;ON;YELLOW;;$S=
[blue]^CLAYER;ON;BLUE;;$S=
[green]^CLAYER;ON;GREEN;;$S=

[0]^CLAYER;ON;0;;$S=
[ALL]^CLAYER;ON;*;;$S=
[LayerOff]^C$S=LSOFF
```

On each of these layer menu subsections, the names of the layers appear in the same position. This provides consistency when the menu is displayed and reduces the chance of selection error.

If you have more layers in your drawing than a single menu subsection can accommodate, include additional subsection references labeled *next* and *previous*. Examples of these references can be found in Chapter 4. In such a case, you may wish to alphabetize the layer names or display the names with the most-often selected first and the least-often selected last. Choose an arrangement that helps you locate the layer names as quickly as possible.

When using multiple displays of layer names, remove $S= from the command sequence on succeeding lists of layer names. Instead, show a direct reference to appropriate originating menu subsections on each menu subsection, such as

```
[DRAW]^C^C$S=DRAW
[EDIT]^C^C$S=EDIT
[ROOTMENU]^C^C$S=S
```

Using the $S= syntax on succeeding lists of layer names will only return you to the previous list of layer names, which could prove inconvenient.

Menu Subsections to Save Keystrokes

Listing names on menu subsections is a technique that can be applied to several commands that require typing names. For example, the following is a command sequence for the HATCH command. It invokes the command and immediately references the

Utility Macros

Hatch menu subsection:

`[HATCH:]^CHATCH $S=HATCH`

In the following example, the subsection reference is changed to a custom subsection label:

`[HATCH:]^C^CHATCH $S=HP`

When you invoke the HATCH command, the first prompt displayed is

`Pattern (? or name/U,style):`

While AutoCAD displays this prompt, the new menu subsection, HP, lists favorite hatch-pattern names:

```
**HP 3
[angle   ]angle;$S=HATCH
[brick   ]brick;$S=HATCH
[concrete]concrete;$S=HATCH
[cork    ]cork;$S=HATCH
[cross   ]cross;$S=HATCH
[dots    ]dots;$S=HATCH
[escher  ]escher;$S=HATCH
[grate   ]grate;$S=HATCH
[honeycmb]honey;$S=HATCH
[houndsth]hound;$S=HATCH
[net3    ]net3;$S=HATCH
[stars   ]stars;$S=HATCH
[triang  ]triang;$S=HATCH
[trihex  ]trihex;$S=HATCH
[tweed   ]tweed;$S=HATCH

[continue]$S=HATCH
[ROOTMENU]^C^C$S=S
```

This subsection makes it easy to select from a group of frequently used hatch-pattern names and eliminates the need to type them out. Each pattern name on the list includes a reference to the standard Hatch menu subsection; thus, after you select the name, you can continue through the remaining prompts as usual. Also included on this subsection is a special reference, [continue], which takes you to the Hatch menu subsection without making a selection from the list. This is needed for those times when the desired pattern does not appear on the list. An additional reference cancels everything and returns you to the root menu, in case you selected the HATCH command by accident.

Quick Undo

If you are using AutoCAD Version 2.5 or later, you have a quick way of recovering when a command accidentally goes awry. You can place the following simple UNDO macro, which will immediately undo the last command sequence, all over your menu landscape. This macro will even undo complex macro sequences.

```
[UNDO]^C^CUNDO;;
```

Quick Zoom In and Out

Here are two simple but extremely useful "quickies" that can be used with many drawing and editing commands:

```
[ZOOMIN]^C^CZOOM;W;\\
[ZOOMOUT]^C^CZOOM;P;
```

They first cancel any current command that might be in place and then invoke the ZOOM command. ZOOMIN goes on to select the Window option with a W, and then pauses twice for the user to mark the window. ZOOMOUT takes the user to the previous view. You can add these to your drawing and editing menu subsections, as appropriate. They can save you time if you zoom in and out a lot.

As your experience with custom menus grows, try placing these macros on their own menu subsection, similar to the X menu subsection, as well as combining this one menu subsection with various short drawing and editing menus.

ZOOMIN and ZOOMOUT are examples of the best kinds of macros. They are quick, easy to implement, and they do an effective and time-saving job. You will find that, in many ways, simple macros like these are more valuable than complex, specialized macros.

You can use this technique to replace any sequence of commands that requires repeated typing of standard data, such as shape names, saved views, and block names.

Quickly Clear the Screen

The following macro erases all the visible entities in a drawing that measures 1,020 drawing units horizontally and 780 drawing units vertically:

[ZAP]^C^CERASE;W;0,0;1020,780;;REDRAW;
[OOPS!!!]^C^COOPS;

This macro first invokes a window erase, and then references the coordinates of the drawing area automatically. It then issues a redraw. The AutoCAD OOPS command can recover the screen, so it is a worthwhile companion macro.

The next example is a safer variation of ZAP:

[SAVE-ZAP]^C^CSAVE;;ERASE;W;0,0;1020,780;;REDRAW;

This macro takes a little longer, but the SAVE command before the screen erase, followed by two ↵ keystrokes, first saves the drawing to disk under the current name, then clears the screen.

The following macro will pause to accept a name for the file to be saved before the screen clears:

[SAVE-ZAP]^C^CSAVE;\ERASE;W;0,0;1020,780;;REDRAW;

On occasion this macro can be quite handy; for instance, by saving a series of simple drawings under different file names and clearing the screen automatically, you can quickly create a series of several blocks written to outside drawing files. This is much faster than using the BLOCK and WBLOCK commands.

Rotating the Crosshairs

The following macro will rotate the crosshairs to any user-specified angle, using the point 0,0 as the base point of rotation:

[+ ANGLE]^C^CSNAP;R;0,0;\

If you rotate the crosshairs to standard reference angles, you can do it quickly by placing macros like the following in their own menu subsection:

*CHRSHRS 3
[ROTATE]
[CROSS]

[HAIRS]

```
[ANG-10]^C^CSNAP;R;0,0;10;
[ANG-25]^C^CSNAP;R;0,0;25;
[ANG-30]^C^CSNAP;R;0,0;30;
[ANG-45]^C^CSNAP;R;0,0;45;
[ANG-60]^C^CSNAP;R;0,0;60;
[ANG-80]^C^CSNAP;R;0,0;80;
```

The following macro quickly resets the crosshairs to normal position:

`[+ RESET]^C^CSNAP;R;0,0;0;`

Word Processor Macros

If you have already modified ACAD.PGP to include a command to call your word processor (as discussed in Chapter 1), the following macros will make using that command easier:

`[WORDPROC]^C^CWP;`

The word WORDPROC will appear in the screen menu area. The command sequence cancels any current command and issues the command for accessing the word processor (WP, in this case).

If your word processor allows document names at the command line, the following variation on this macro helps edit CUSTOM.MNU:

`[EDITMENU]^C^CWP;CUSTOM.MNU;MENU;CUSTOM;`

This macro invokes the WP command and follows it immediately with the answer to the "File to Edit?" prompt. Then, upon your return to the drawing editor, the macro picks up where it left off, invoking the MENU command followed by the menu name. Using this macro, you can complete the entire editing cycle with a single menu selection.

If your word processor command does not allow file names at the command line, the following macro will help when editing CUSTOM.MNU:

`[EDITMENU]^C^CWP;MENU;CUSTOM;`

Macros That Aid the Editing Process

The editing process in AutoCAD frequently involves several commands in sequence—selecting the editing command, selecting the object (and sometimes selecting the means by which objects can be selected for edits), plus various editing parameters that must be specified after you complete the selection process. As you develop your own style for using AutoCAD, you will notice that certain sequences of commands repeat themselves. These repeating sequences can and should be combined into macros.

Quick Selection Macros

The following macro from AutoCAD's standard menu invokes the ERASE command and references the Erase subsection:

`[ERASE:]^C^CERASE;$S=ERASE`

If you often select objects to erase by means of a window, or if you often wish to erase the last object drawn, the following macros will save you considerable time. They can be added underneath the standard ERASE command on your custom menu:

```
[ window]^C^CERASE;W;\\;
[ last]^C^CERASE;L;;
```

These macros do not reference the Erase subsection, because it is not necessary. Instead, they invoke the desired selection mechanism along with the command. If you select

`window`

you return to the screen and can window the objects you wish to erase, which will then immediately vanish. If you select

`last`

the last entity drawn will disappear from the screen immediately.

Since both macros cause selected objects to disappear from the screen immediately, they require a bit of caution. If you ever do erase more than you intended, the OOPS or UNDO command will reverse the effect of these macros.

Notice that two semicolons are needed after the L (for last); they indicate the extra ↵ keystrokes needed to end the object selection process. It is easy to forget these extra ↵ characters.

The following macros apply the same principle to the MOVE and COPY commands:

```
[COPY:]^C^CCOPY;$S=COPY
[ window]^C^CCOPY;W;\\;\\
[ last]^C^CCOPY;L;;\\

[MOVE:]^C^CMOVE;$S=MOVE
[ window]^C^CMOVE;W;\\;\\
[ last]^C^CMOVE;L;;\\
```

Extra backslashes in these macros pause and accept user input for the points of displacement. The display words

window

and

last

are indented within their brackets when they are added underneath the standard versions of these commands to improve the screen appearance. Figure 5.1 shows how these additions might look on a custom menu.

If you are using AutoCAD 2.18 or earlier, you can add syntax to these macros that will invoke the dynamic dragging feature automatically, as shown in the following lines:

```
[ window]^C^CCOPY;W;\\;\DRAG;\
[ last]^C^CCOPY;L;;\DRAG;\

[ window]^C^CMOVE;W;\\;\DRAG;\
[ last]^C^CMOVE;L;;\DRAG;\
```

Notice that DRAG; appears immediately after the backslash that lets the user select the base point of displacement. A ↵ keystroke, in the form of a semicolon, is required after the word DRAG to switch on AutoCAD's dragging mode.

In AutoCAD Version 2.5 and later, commands such as COPY or MOVE drag automatically, by default. If you like, you can still include the DRAG; syntax in the macro, but it will have no visible effect.

FIGURE 5.1:
A custom menu including editing macros.

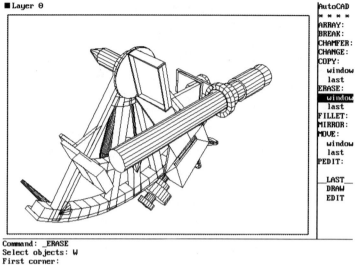

Macros That Combine Drawing and Editing Commands

The following macro draws a line segment and then makes a copy of it immediately (it helps draw parallel lines):

`[PARALINE]^C^CLINE;\\;COPY;L;;\\`

It combines some unrelated commands. After the standard cancel, the LINE command is invoked and two backslashes are inserted for the user to input the endpoints of the line. The COPY command is then invoked, and the L option (for last) is selected automatically. Next, an extra ↵ tells AutoCAD that no more selection is necessary. Finally, the macro pauses to get the points of displacement from the user. This macro can seem remarkably fast if you're used to performing this process with off-the-shelf AutoCAD.

If you are using AutoCAD Version 2.18 or earlier, you may wish to invoke the dynamic dragging feature, as in the following macro:

`[PARALINE]^C^CLINE;\\;COPY;L;;\DRAG;\`

If you are using AutoCAD Version 2.5 or later, you can rework the macro using AutoCAD's OFFSET command:

[WALL]^C^CLINE;\\;$S=OFFSET;OFFSET;

This macro will draw a single line segment and immediately invoke the OFFSET command. When the macro ends after invoking the OFFSET command, all normal command options will be prompted as usual, so a menu subsection reference to the Offset menu subsection is included within the macro.

The next macro takes advantage of the multiple-copy option of the COPY command in AutoCAD Versions 2.5 and later:

[MANYLINE]^C^CLINE;\\;COPY;L;;M;

Notice here that the macro ends at the selection of the base point of displacement. This allows the user to make any number of copies immediately after drawing the line.

The following variation on the theme uses block insertion with multiple copies:

[MANYBLKS]^C^CINSERT;\\\\\COPY;L;;M;

Notice the series of five backslashes after the INSERT command. These backslashes allow for user input to select

1. The block name
2. The insertion point
3. The X-scale factor
4. The Y-scale factor
5. The rotation angle

All five of these backslashes are required. No ↵ is necessary to end the INSERT command, so the COPY command is issued immediately after the fifth backslash, followed by the L option (for last), the extra finishing ↵, and the M option (for multiple). The macro ends after the selection of the M option, so that the user is free to select as many copies of the inserted block as needed.

Macros That Combine Editing and Display Commands

Any series of AutoCAD commands and references can be combined into macros, not just those that are intuitively related. In the examples that follow, editing and display commands are combined, eliminating the need to move between screen menus.

Cleaning Corners

After drawing some intersecting sets of parallel lines, you can use macros to help clean up the corners. The following macro uses the FILLET command to clean a simple corner formed by intersecting sets of parallel lines. It works with AutoCAD versions that have OSNAP capability. In Release 12, the macro looks like this:

[CORNER1]^C^CFILLET;R;0;;C;INT;\INT;@;;C;INT;\INT;@;

In earlier versions, it takes the following form:

[CORNER1]^C^CFILLET;R;0;;INT;\@;;INT;\@;

Figures 5.2 and 5.3 illustrate how this command might work. This macro sets the fillet radius to zero automatically, just in case it is not already zero. The macro then repeats the FILLET command by means of an extra ↵. Next, OSNAP INTER is invoked, and a backslash pauses the macro for the user to select an intersection. Once the intersection is selected, AutoCAD automatically reselects the same point to complete the fillet, using the @ symbol, which references the last selected point. The FILLET command is again invoked by means of an extra ↵, and the process repeats, filleting the second intersection.

If you need to fillet lines that are not intersecting, you can, using a slightly different macro. The following macro will work for both intersecting and nonintersecting wall lines, but it requires two line picks per fillet, four picks altogether.

[CORNER2]^C^CFILLET;R;0;;NEAR;\NEAR;\;NEAR;\NEAR;\

This macro sets the fillet radius to 0 and uses the OSNAP NEAR object-selection override to help pick the lines to be filleted. Four lines need to be selected, but NEAR makes the selection easier by not requiring quite so much exactitude. Notice how the semicolon is used to repeat the FILLET command after the second backslash in this macro. Figures 5.4 and 5.5 show how intersecting and nonintersecting lines can be picked using this alternate corner clean-up macro.

FIGURE 5.2:
Selecting points for the CORNER1 clean-up macro.

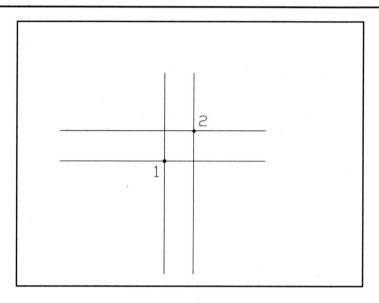

FIGURE 5.3:
The corner after running the clean-up macro.

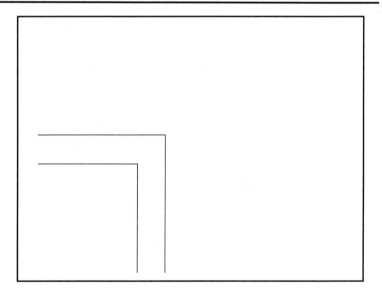

Macros That Aid the Editing Process

FIGURE 5.4:
Cleaning up both intersecting and nonintersecting wall lines with a macro.

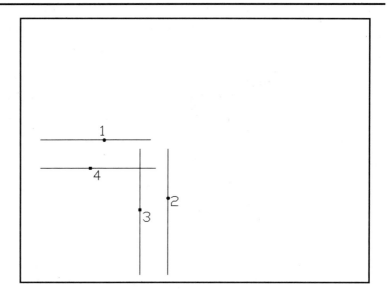

FIGURE 5.5:
The results of the clean-up using CORNER2.

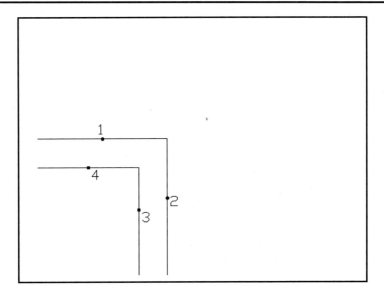

For those cases where the lines and corners are close together and the intersections are difficult to pick, the following macros begin with an automatic window zoom, which enables you to get close to the corner you wish to clean up:

```
[CORNER1]^C^CZOOM;W;\\FILLET;R;0;;C;INT;\INT;@;;+
C;INT;\INT;@;ZOOM;P;
[CORNER2]^C^CZOOM;W;\\FILLET;R;0;;NEAR;\NEAR;\+
;NEAR;\NEAR;\ZOOM;P;
```

The CORNER1 macro looks slightly different in Release 11 and earlier versions:

```
[CORNER1]^C^CZOOM;W;\\FILLET;R;0;;INT;\@;;INT;\@;ZOOM;P;
```

When finished, these macros automatically zoom back out to the previous view.

When editing a large, complex drawing, you may wish to use the zoom feature of these macros only occasionally. In that case, instead of placing the zooms within the macro, you can place the ZOOMIN and ZOOMOUT macros (presented earlier in this chapter) on the same menu subsection as your corner clean-up macros. With this configuration, you may zoom as you wish or not use it at all.

An alternative approach for selecting objects in a complex drawing is to reduce the size of the Osnap aperture box temporarily. Use AutoCAD's APERTURE command within the macro to shrink the aperture temporarily and then restore it to normal again.

The following macros demonstrate this principle. They assume that the current Osnap aperture size is ten pixels; they reduce the aperture size to five pixels temporarily, execute the macro normally, and then reinstate the previous ten-pixel aperture size:

```
[CORNER1]^C^CAPERTURE;5;FILLET;R;0;;C;INT;\INT;@;;+
C;INT;\INT;@;APERTURE;10;
[CORNER2]^C^CAPERTURE;5;FILLET;R;0;;NEAR;\NEAR;\+
;NEAR;\NEAR;\APERTURE;10;
```

In Release 11 and earlier versions, CORNER1 looks slightly different:

```
[CORNER1]^C^CAPERTURE;5;FILLET;R;0;;INT;\@;+
;INT;\@;APERTURE;10;
```

You may wish to experiment with different size values.

Cleaning an Open-T

Macros that clean up open-T intersections use the same fundamental techniques as described in the previous section.

[OPEN-T]^C^CBREAK;NEAR;\@;FILLET;R;0;;+
C;INT;\INT;@;;C;INT;\INT;@;

This macro invokes the BREAK command so that you can break the line segment that must disappear for the open-T. OSNAP NEAR again helps by requiring less exactitude. Two points on this line are needed, but notice that the second break point is automatically invoked using the @ symbol, followed by a ↵. (This technique can be used to split any breakable entity into two or more segments.) After making the line break, the macro sets the fillet radius to 0. The filleting process used is the same as that described in the previous section. Figure 5.6 shows the point selections that will clean up an open-T intersection.

If your lines are close together and you find the segments are hard to select, even using OSNAP, you could easily add zooms or change the aperture size as described

FIGURE 5.6:
Cleaning up an open-T with a macro.

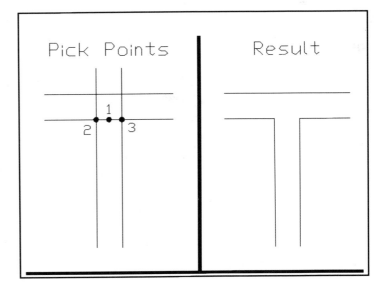

in the previous section. In the following examples, the open-T macro is repeated, once using added zooms and a second time with added aperture changes:

```
[OPEN-T]^C^CZOOM;W;\\BREAK;NEAR;\@;FILLET;R;0;;+
C;INT;\INT;@;;C;INT;\INT;@;ZOOM;P;
[OPEN-T]^C^CAPERTURE;5;BREAK;NEAR;\@;FILLET;R;0;;+
C;INT;\INT;@;;C;INT;\INT;@;APERTURE;10;
```

Notice that both macros use the plus sign to wrap the command sequence to the text line underneath.

Cleaning a Cross Intersection

The next two macros clean up an open-cross intersection. The first example will work in AutoCAD Version 2.5 and later.

```
[CROSS]^C^CTRIM;C;\\;NEAR;\NEAR;\NEAR;\NEAR;\;
```

This macro combines the TRIM command with the crossing window option to select four wall lines. Following that, a touch of each inner line segment causes it to disappear. The final semicolon in the macro ends the TRIM selection process, since no more points need to be selected. Figure 5.7 shows the point picks the macro requires.

FIGURE 5.7:
Cleaning up an open-cross intersection.

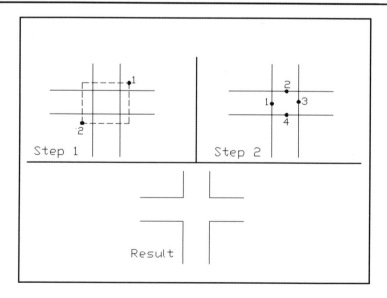

In the following examples, the same macro is repeated, once using added zooms and a second time using added aperture changes:

```
[CROSS]^C^CZOOM;W;\\TRIM;C;\\;NEAR;\NEAR;+
\NEAR;\NEAR;\;ZOOM;P;
[CROSS]^C^CAPERTURE;5;TRIM;C;\\;NEAR;\NEAR;+
\NEAR;\NEAR;\;APERTURE;10;
```

Macros for Block Operations

Block insertion is always command-intensive, requiring a block name and insertion parameters. Macros can be very helpful in this regard, as the examples in this section demonstrate.

Inserting Blocks

Macros are helpful when inserting standard blocks or shapes. The following example shows a subsection labeled Furn, which contains a few macros that insert blocks. This example assumes that the drawing file contains some blocks named for a few standard pieces of furniture (door1, window, sofa, table, and chair). Substitute your own block names to use these macros:

```
**FURN 3
[door1]^C^CINSERT;door1;NEAR;
[window]^C^CINSERT;window;
[sofa]^C^CINSERT;sofa;
[table]^C^CINSERT;table;
[chair]^C^CINSERT;chair;
```

The first macro displays the name of the block, door1, on the screen. The INSERT command is invoked and the door1 block is spelled out within the command sequence, as if typed at the keyboard. OSNAP NEAR ensures that the door is seated on a point on the wall line. The X- and Y-scale factors are automatically dragged, but if you wish, you can enter exact values for the door dimensions.

The door1 block uses much the same scaling technique we used in Chapter 3. When the block was originally created, it was drawn to measure one drawing unit by one drawing unit. The block is illustrated in Figure 5.8.

FIGURE 5.8:
The door1 block, with dimensioning added.

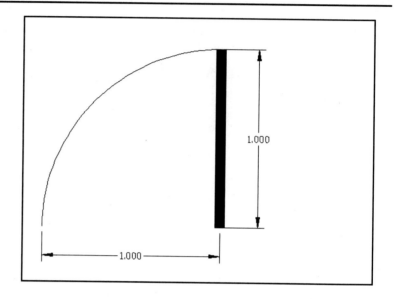

That's a very small door, but it's also very easy to scale to a variety of door widths. For example, using this one-unit door, if you enter X- and Y-scales of 32, you will insert a 32-inch door. Later, if you use X- and Y-scales of 28, you will insert a 28-inch door. Different scale factors will always result in an equal number of door-inches when the block is inserted. This process is illustrated in Figure 5.9.

After the door is inserted, it may be rotated to any angle. Whenever you insert door1 using this macro, you have the choice of either dragging the rotation of the block or entering the exact angle of the wall at the keyboard.

This same technique can be used to insert any frequently called block, as in the previous examples from the Furn menu subsection. All these blocks are originally one drawing unit by one drawing unit; you can therefore enter whatever specific lengths and widths you wish. The chair and table blocks are illustrated in Figure 5.10.

FIGURE 5.9:
The door1 block at scales of 28 and 32

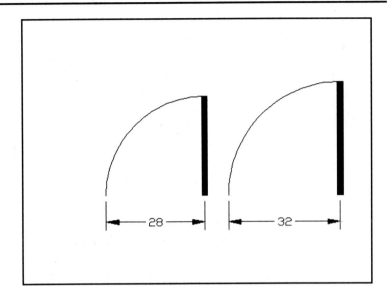

FIGURE 5.10:
Furniture blocks, original size and scaled.

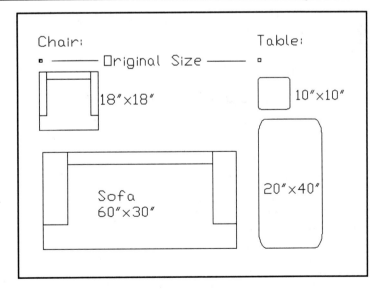

Inserting Blocks with Attributes

You can take this block insertion routine a step further. What if the door1 block included attributes? Suppose you find that you enter the same kinds of attribute data frequently. Why not use a menu subsection to select attribute data instead of typing it out?

In the following example, assume that the door1 block has three attributes: 1) door frame specifications, 2) door materials specifications, and 3) hardware specifications. Further assume that you have standard codes for this data that you enter each time you insert a door block.

The first step is to add an additional menu subsection reference to the DOOR insertion macro:

```
[DOOR]^C^CINSERT;door1;NEAR;\\\\$S=DSPECS
```

Now the macro inserts the door and immediately references a new menu subsection named Dspecs. This new menu subsection might look something like the following:

```
**DSPECS 3
[Hardw:]
[BRASS]brass;
[ALUMINUM]aluminum;
[STAINLSS]stainless steel;
[Door:]
[ALUMINUM]Aluminum;
[OAK]Oak;
[MAPLE]Maple;
[PLYWOOD]Plywood;
[Frame:]
[ALUMINUM]Aluminum;
[OAK]Oak;
[MAPLE]Maple;
[PINE]Pine;
[FURNMENU]^C^C$S=FURN
```

This menu allows you to pick standard specifications regarding the door's hardware, material specifications, and frame specifications. You simply use your pointing device to highlight the specific attribute you wish to apply to any particular door and pick it. The standard data is entered into each attribute without typing. Figure 5.11 illustrates this process.

Macros for Block Operations

FIGURE 5.11:
Picking attributes from a screen menu.

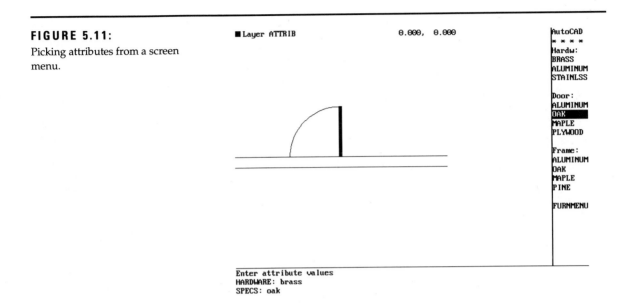

The technique illustrated here will work for any set of standard attribute data attached to any block. If any block contains nonstandard attribute data, you can enter that data using the keyboard and move on to the next attribute.

In this example, when you have picked the last attribute (frame specifications), a menu subsection reference returns you automatically to the original Furn menu subsection that contains your original insertion macro, setting you up to insert more blocks if you wish.

When different block attributes are listed on the same menu subsection, they should be listed in the *reverse order of their original setup,* because AutoCAD will prompt for attribute data beginning with the last attribute and ending with the first. You will want to include the menu subsection reference that returns you to your original subsection only after your response to the last prompt. In this example, the frame specifications attribute was the first attribute created for the door1 block. Therefore, on the attribute data menu, it is the last set of attribute data. The menu subsection reference to return to the Furn subsection comes immediately after the response to this last entry.

145

You may sometimes need to place a series of attribute data on more than one menu subsection. This is fine; simply include the appropriate menu subsection reference on any attribute data line that requires it.

At the bottom of each attribute data menu subsection, be sure to include an independent menu subsection reference that does not insert attribute data, but simply references the next menu subsection. This technique is like the "next" and "previous" references you saw earlier. In this way, the user will be able to move through the menu structure even when typing nonstandard data from the keyboard. It is also worthwhile to include an independent reference to the original block-inserting menu on each attribute data menu subsection, in case you decide to cancel the process altogether.

Finally, notice that the semicolons following the attribute data are not optional; they are required. Because AutoCAD allows spaces to be considered as part of the attribute data, the menu processor will not read spaces as ↵ characters. The semicolon is always considered a ↵ when it appears in any menu command sequence. This also means that you cannot include a semicolon as part of your standard attribute data unless you skip the menu and type it at the keyboard.

Editing around the Inserted Block

Once the door has been placed on the wall line, you can use another macro to help trim the wall around the door:

```
[TRIMDOOR]^C^CLINE;INT;\PERP;\;;+
INT;\PERP;\;TRIM;\\;\\;
```

This macro may look complex, but it only combines techniques you have seen before. First, it invokes the LINE command to draw two short line segments perpendicular to the original wall lines. OSNAP INT helps find a point on one wall line, and PERP helps locate the perpendicular point on the opposite wall line. This process is repeated; hence the two semicolons before the second INT: the first finishes the LINE command, and the second repeats it. Figure 5.12 illustrates the process.

After the lines are drawn, the macro employs the TRIM command. First the two small line segments just drawn are selected by the user as the cutting edges. Then the wall line segments are selected and trimmed out.

Macros for Block Operations

FIGURE 5.12:
Trimming the wall around the door.

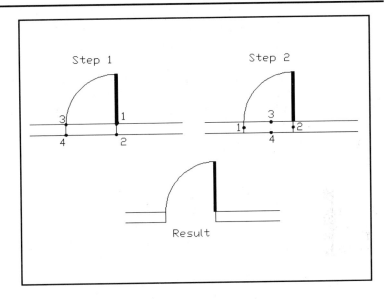

As with the previous macros, you can add zooms or aperture size changes to make the selection process easier:

```
[TRIMDOOR]^C^CZOOM;W;\\LINE;INT;\PERP;\;;+
INT;\PERP;\;TRIM;\\;\\;ZOOM;P;
[TRIMDOOR]^C^CAPERTURE;5;LINE;INT;\PERP;\;;+
INT;\PERP;\;TRIM;\\;\\;APERTURE;10;
```

Other Editing and Display Macros

In AutoCAD Releases 9 and later, the process of changing an entity's color and/or thickness is an example of an editing request that involves stepping through a series of command options. The following macros allow you to change the color or thickness of a single entity by first selecting the entity, then immediately entering the new value:

```
[NEWCOLOR]^C^CCHPROP;\;C;\;
[THICKEN]^C^CCHPROP;\;TH;\;
```

If you wish to change an entire group of entities in this fashion, you can add a window selection mechanism to these macros, as follows (for a crossing window, substitute the letter C for W):

```
[NEWCOLOR]^C^CCHPROP;W;\\;C;\;
[THICKEN]^C^CCHPROP;W;\\;TH;\;
```

Anytime you make global changes like these, you may change more entities than you intended. It would be helpful to keep the UNDO macro nearby, to reverse the results of any mistaken edits.

The following macros also demonstrate the principle that little macros, designed to do simple things (in this case, speeding up simple edits that involve command options) can sometimes be the most useful. These macros instantly turn a selected polyline into a spline-curve or fit-curve. When you invoke these macros, you simply pick the polyline and the appropriate curve is immediately drawn:

```
[S-CURVE]^C^CPEDIT;\S;;
[F-CURVE]^C^CPEDIT;\F;;
```

A similar macro will undo the curve:

```
[UNCURVE]^C^CPEDIT;\D;;
```

In AutoCAD Release 10 and later versions, management of the correct User Coordinate System is a top priority. The following macro will change the User Coordinate System to that of any existing entity:

```
[UCS PICK]^C^CUCS;E;\
```

The following macro will quickly return you to the plan view of the world coordinate system:

```
[GO HOME]^C^CSETVAR;ELEVATION;0;UCS;W;PLAN;;
```

If you establish a standard set of named User Coordinate Systems in your drawings (via ACAD.DWG, or a custom menu attached to a particular drawing), you may place these named User Coordinate Systems on a special submenu, as in the following example, which assumes the existence of User Coordinate Systems named Left, Right, Front, Back, Top, and Bottom:

```
***UCSNAMES 3
[USER]
[COORD.]
[SYSTEMS]
[LEFT]^C^CUCS;R;LEFT;
```

Macros for Block Operations

```
[RIGHT]^C^CUCS;R;RIGHT;
[FRONT]^C^CUCS;R;FRONT;
[BACK]^C^CUCS;R;BACK;
[TOP]^C^CUCS;R;TOP;
[BOTTOM]^C^CUCS;R;BOTTOM;
```

The following macro quickly sets the origin point of the current UCS to any point the user selects:

```
[ORIG-PT]^C^CUCS;ORIGIN;\
```

The following macros turn the UCS icon on and off:

```
[ICON-ON]^C^CUCSICON;ON;
[ICON-OFF]^C^CUCSICON;OFF;
```

The following macro moves the UCS icon to the lower-left corner of the screen (regardless of origin):

```
[ICON-LL]^C^CUCSICON;N;
```

The following macro moves the UCS icon to the origin point:

```
[ICON-ORG]^C^CUCSICON;OR;
```

The following macros rotate the current User Coordinate System 30 degrees along the selected axis. Reselecting a macro increments the rotation. If you have configured AutoCAD to increment angle measures in a counter-clockwise direction, the positive value will rotate the User Coordinate System counter-clockwise; the negative value will rotate clockwise. You may substitute any degree of angle rotation you wish. These macros will execute most efficiently if you first turn the grid display off. Try selecting these macros repeatedly while the UCS icon is displayed on the screen:

```
[UCS-X+30]^C^CUCS;X;30;
[UCS-Y+30]^C^CUCS;Y;30;
[UCS-Z+30]^C^CUCS;Z;30;
[UCS-X-30]^C^CUCS;X;-30;
[UCS-Y-30]^C^CUCS;Y;-30;
[UCS-Z-30]^C^CUCS;Z;-30;
```

CHAPTER SIX

Introduction to AutoLISP

INTRODUCTION TO AUTOLISP
CH. 6

AutoLISP is a programming language used to write instructions carried out by AutoCAD. A set of instructions written in AutoLISP is called a *LISP routine*. LISP routines are contained in ASCII files called *LISP files*. LISP files can have any name that is a valid DOS file name, and by convention they have the file extension LSP.

If you are an AutoCAD user, as opposed to a developer of AutoCAD applications, AutoLISP is your most powerful tool for optimizing AutoCAD performance. It enables you to "automate" AutoCAD even beyond what you can accomplish using macros. AutoLISP routines have many possible applications, including the creation of new and unique AutoCAD commands, the insertion of special drawing and calculating functions in custom menu macros, and the development of applications that automatically carry out detailed graphics analysis and drawing inside AutoCAD's drawing editor.

LISP routines can quickly calculate and analyze data used to generate drawing entities on the monitor screen. They analyze existing drawing entities or create new entities by invoking AutoCAD commands directly. The entities created by LISP routines are the same as any created by the user, except that with AutoLISP, the process is faster and easier. LISP routines greatly enhance the production of complex drawings, and they also eliminate unnecessary menu selections and repetitive keyboard entries.

Since AutoLISP is a small language and limited in scope, it is easy for nonprogrammers to learn. Nonprogrammers learning AutoLISP need to learn only the more basic programming concepts; for example, storing data during processing with memory variables; processing data in a series of sequential steps; organizing steps within a routine by defining new functions; choosing between alternative steps (branching); and repeating a sequence of steps until a specific condition is met (looping).

In addition, AutoLISP works only within AutoCAD. This means that the process of designing and debugging an AutoLISP routine is made considerably easier and faster by the robust nature of the AutoCAD environment in which it performs.

Is it profitable to learn AutoLISP? It certainly can be. A small LISP routine that may take a beginner 10 hours to develop can save several minutes of drawing time per day, and pay for itself very quickly in terms of increased productivity and a higher quality of product.

It's true that programming can occasionally be frustrating. Often the development of an AutoLISP routine is marked by a grinding process of *debugging*—getting rid of problems that interfere with the routine's ability to achieve its intended results. The solution to one problem can reveal another problem waiting underneath. A program may have to be tested several times before it runs correctly. This process notwithstanding, it is still overwhelmingly advantageous for everyday users to avail themselves of the power of AutoLISP.

Planning an AutoLISP Routine

Once you have learned the *syntax*, or language rules, of AutoLISP, LISP routines are fairly easy to create and modify with your word processor. However, a useful LISP routine must be thought out in advance.

The process of developing a LISP routine is similar to that of developing a custom menu macro. In one sense, a LISP routine is really a complex macro. The instructions contained in a LISP routine are executed in sequence; they build on each other, the results of previous instructions being used to carry out subsequent instructions. A LISP routine, however, can handle more sophisticated instruction sets than a simple macro.

As in the development of macros, the first step in writing any LISP routine is to sit down with a pencil and paper and describe in plain English exactly what you would like the LISP routine to do. This exercise is extremely important as a time-saving and error-preventing device. It will help you organize your thoughts and wishes, and by referring to it later, you can keep yourself on track as you work out the details. Programmers refer to this plain-English version of a routine as *pseudocode*. It's simply good organization; no other single step will save you more time or prevent more errors.

When developing the pseudocode for your LISP routine, you should manually go over the process from the keyboard, as much as possible. You can enter most AutoLISP instructions from the AutoCAD command prompt. This pretesting procedure will help you spot problems early in the developmental process and save you lots of time in debugging. Make notes of every step you take and how it was accomplished. Note what calculations were involved and on what the figures were based; in short, note everything that relates to the drawing you wish to produce or the process you wish the LISP routine to accomplish.

You can collect ideas for useful LISP routines by keeping a notepad handy during your drawing sessions. Keep a record of how you use AutoCAD. Note where you are slowing down to make mathematical calculations, for instance. Note any types of objects you find yourself drawing repeatedly. Can this drawing process be automated, at least in part? These notes will be the seedbed for your LISP routines. They will tell you exactly how you can benefit from AutoLISP.

Even after your LISP routines seem to be working perfectly, keep the notepad handy to jot down any little surprises that might pop up days or even weeks later, perhaps when a new user tries out the same routines. Note where they occurred, under what circumstances, and what needs to be done to correct the problem. Don't rely on memory alone to guide you as you move between AutoCAD and your word processor. As you learn and acquire more experience, the number of bugs in your LISP routines will certainly diminish.

Syntax Conventions

The syntax of AutoLISP is built on certain conventional ways of organizing computer instructions in ASCII files. These structures make it possible for AutoCAD, by way of the AutoLISP interpreter, to read the ASCII files and execute the instructions contained in them. These syntax structures are relatively few, especially when compared to ordinary spoken languages. They also tend to be more rigid, with fewer exceptions and little tolerance for slight variances. AutoLISP syntax structures are summarized in this section.

Functions

The fundamental instruction format in AutoLISP is called the *function*. A function carries out a series of processes on data and generally returns some result.

For example, imagine that you are drawing a complex mechanical part; to draw the next curve, you need to know the quotient of 84.037 divided by 2.56. You have several options. You could do it in your head if you're mathematically inclined, you could stop what you're doing and work it out on paper, or you could turn to that trusty little calculator you keep next to the computer keyboard. Perhaps you could

Syntax Conventions

call up some memory-resident calculator utility, if you have one that works with AutoCAD. If you are using Release 12, you could try AutoCAD's own CAL command. Another option is to use AutoLISP, by typing the following at the command prompt:

```
(/ 84.037 2.56)
```

After you press ↵, AutoCAD will instantly provide the answer (rounded to three decimal places): 32.827.

When you use AutoCAD to perform math like this, you are accessing AutoCAD's *AutoLISP interpreter* and offering it a *function*, which it then *evaluates*. After the AutoLISP interpreter evaluates the function, it returns a *result*—in this example, 32.827.

AutoCAD can recognize AutoLISP functions when they follow certain general rules. These general rules are:

- AutoLISP functions are contained within parentheses. All parentheses in LISP routines must be matched, or *balanced;* that is, a pair of parentheses must surround each individual function.
- The function reads from left to right.
- The first thing inside the parentheses is the *function operator,* which is a command to the AutoLISP interpreter to do something. In the example, the command was to perform a division. The function operator for this command is the forward slash symbol (/).
- The function operator is followed by any necessary function *arguments*. Arguments are individual items of information that are required by the AutoLISP interpreter to accomplish the purpose of the function. In the example, the AutoLISP interpreter needs two numbers in order to perform a division, so the forward slash is followed by these two arguments.
- The function operator and its arguments are separated by at least one space, so the AutoLISP interpreter can tell where one ends and the next one begins.
- Extra spaces and carriage returns within and between functions are not required and are therefore ignored by the AutoLISP interpreter. This means that a function can occupy many lines in an ASCII file.

- Functions use standard ASCII characters. They are not case-sensitive; when typing out AutoLISP functions you can use either upper- or lowercase characters, or mix upper- and lowercase together. Over time, some conventions have evolved regarding the use of capitalization in AutoLISP. In general, predefined functions are written in lowercase, with variable names in uppercase.

The above example of an AutoLISP function, translated into English, says, "Perform a division. Take 84.037 and divide it by 2.56." In all division functions, the first number is divided by the second; in mathematical terms, the first number following the operator is the dividend, and the second number is the divisor.

The following is the function for addition, using the same numbers for its arguments:

`(+ 84.037 2.56)`

In English this means, "Perform an addition. Take 84.037 and add 2.56 to it." If you type this out at the AutoCAD command prompt, AutoCAD will return the result, 86.597.

The following function performs subtraction. Notice how the subtraction is carried out:

`(- 84.037 2.56)`

In English this means, "Perform a subtraction. Take 84.037 and subtract 2.56 from it." In all subtraction functions, the second number is subtracted from the first. In this case, the result returned by AutoCAD is 81.477.

The following function performs multiplication:

`(* 84.037 2.56)`

AutoCAD returns 215.135.

AutoLISP contains dozens of useful predefined functions. Different functions require different types and quantities of arguments; many functions have arguments that are optional. The next chapter examines several of these functions.

Memory Variables

Memory variables are the basic means by which a computer can organize, store, and later recall information. All programming languages depend on the manipulation of memory variables.

AutoLISP memory variables work in the following way:

1. A portion of the computer's random-access memory is set aside as a place to hold AutoLISP's memory variables.

2. When a memory variable is created, it is given a *variable name*.

3. When the memory variable has been created and named, it can then receive a *value*, the specific piece of information that is associated with its name. When the name of a memory variable has a value, the variable is said to be *bound* to that value.

4. When a memory variable is bound to a value, a function can make use of the value by using the memory-variable name. As the function is evaluated, whenever the name is encountered, the AutoLISP interpreter substitutes the value for the name.

Memory variables allow one set of general instructions to be used on many different sets of data. Without memory variables, LISP routines would have to be edited each time the data changed.

AutoLISP uses a special function, SETQ, to create memory variables and bind them to values. This function requires a minimum of two arguments. The first argument is the name of the memory variable. The second is the value to which the memory variable is bound. Here is an example:

```
(setq x 2)
```

Translated into English, this function means, "Create a memory variable. Give it the name x. It contains the integer 2."

Once AutoLISP has evaluated this function, the following function becomes valid:

```
(* 2.36 x)
```

AutoLISP will substitute 2 for x in this function, and will multiply 2.36 by 2, returning the result, 4.72.

If you wish, you can use the SETQ function to assign a new value to x:

`(setq x 3)`

The memory variable x has already been created. Repeating the function with the same name and a new value does not create a second memory variable with the same name, but merely binds x to a new value, 3. Now the multiplication function will return a new result:

`(* 2.36 x)`

AutoLISP will substitute 3 for x in this function and then return the result, 7.08.

A single SETQ function can be used to bind a group of memory variables to values. The following function binds memory variables a, b, and c to values of 1, 2, and 3:

`(setq a 1 b 2 c 3)`

When used in this fashion, SETQ's arguments are always presented in pairs: first the variable name, followed by the value, another variable name, another value, and so on.

You can find out the value of a memory variable quickly if you type an exclamation point followed by the memory-variable name at the AutoCAD command prompt. For example, if you have assigned a value to the memory variable x, type the following at the AutoCAD command prompt:

`!x`

AutoCAD will return with the current value of the memory variable x.

Memory-variable names contain no spaces, periods, quotation marks, or parentheses. They always begin with a letter (not a number) and can have as many characters as you like, up to the limit of available memory. However, your LISP routines will be processed more quickly and you will conserve computer memory space if you keep them short, preferably six characters or fewer.

Generally, memory-variable names are mnemonic descriptions of the value to which they are bound. For example, you might choose to store angle information in memory variables with names like ang (such as x_ang, y_ang, ang_1, or ang_2). Likewise, you may choose to store coordinate-point information using memory variables with names like pt (such as x_pt, y_pt, pt_1, or pt_2).

Syntax Conventions

A memory variable whose value never changes is called a *constant*. AutoLISP makes use of only one predefined constant, *pi*. The value of pi is always approximately 3.1415926. The advantage of designating this value as a constant is that **pi** is easier to type than **3.1415926**. Also, because the actual value of the constant pi computes to an infinite number of decimal places, using the constant is more accurate than using the decimal value.

Nesting

The results returned by functions can be used as the arguments of other functions in a process called *nesting*. For example, here is a valid AutoLISP function:

(+ 1 1)

As you have seen, the plus sign is the function operator for addition, and the arguments are 1 and 1. The function will return a value of 2. Now observe the following nested function:

(* 2.36 (+ 1 1))

Note how the addition function is nested within a multiplication function. These combined functions return a result of 4.72. The function that adds 1 and 1 exists on what is called the *second level* of nesting, because it is nested within only one other function. Notice how the parentheses that surround the multiplication function also surround the entire addition function, including its set of parentheses.

You can build deep levels of functions within functions. The AutoLISP command interpreter can trace nested functions up to 100 levels deep. The AutoLISP interpreter will evaluate nested functions beginning with the deepest level. Here is an example of the addition function nested three levels deep:

(− (* 2.36 (+ 1 1)) 2)

This function returns the result 2.72 after a three-level computation. First, the integer 1 is added to 1, returning the result 2. Next, 2 is multiplied by 2.36, which returns the result 4.72. Finally, 2 is subtracted from 4.72, which returns the final result, 2.72.

The parentheses are arranged in matched pairs surrounding each function. Careful arrangement of these parentheses requires a little practice and alertness, as it can become quite complex in more involved routines.

INTRODUCTION TO AUTOLISP
CH. 6

LISP routines often perform a calculation and store the result in a memory variable. For example, consider the following AutoLISP function:

`(setq m (/ 4 2))`

This function divides four by two and assigns the result of this computation to the new memory variable m. This example demonstrates a fairly common structure for basic AutoLISP functions.

System Variables

AutoLISP makes use of certain special memory variables called *system variables*. These contain values related to the AutoCAD drawing environment and the state of the current drawing. AutoLISP comes supplied with dozens of predefined system variables.

For example, the system variable ORTHOMODE contains a value of either 0 or 1. When the value of ORTHOMODE is 0, AutoCAD's orthogonal mode is off. When the value of ORTHOMODE is 1, AutoCAD's orthogonal mode is on.

System variables can be changed by means of the AutoLISP function SETVAR. For example,

`(setvar "ORTHOMODE" 1)`

sets the value of ORTHOMODE to 1. When ORTHOMODE has a value of 1, AutoCAD's orthogonal mode is toggled on, just as if you toggled on Ortho mode with a keyboard function key (F8 on most systems).

The AutoLISP function GETVAR is related to SETVAR; it reports the current value of a system variable. For example,

`(getvar "ORTHOMODE")`

will return the current value of AutoCAD's ORTHOMODE system variable but will not change it. This is handy when a LISP routine needs to find out the value of a system variable.

System variables are extremely valuable when you are creating LISP routines that change AutoCAD drawing parameters. A list of all the current AutoCAD system variables can be found in Appendix A of the *AutoCAD Reference Manual*.

Radians

AutoLISP does not use degrees for measuring angles; instead, it uses a system of *radians*. Fortunately, angle degrees can be converted to radians using a simple formula: divide the angle degrees by 180 and multiply the result by pi. In AutoLISP, the mathematics are expressed as follows:

```
(* pi (/ angle 180))
```

Converting a large set of angle degrees to radians is not as cumbersome as it first seems, because you can define a special AutoLISP function that will do it automatically. Chapter 7 presents functions that convert angle degrees to radians and radians to angle degrees. Many of the example routines in this book depend on such a function.

Fundamental AutoLISP Data Types

The data used by AutoLISP can be grouped into *data types*, categories of data distinguished by what they can and cannot do when used within LISP routines. The following are brief descriptions of AutoLISP data types.

Entity Names

Each drawing entity created in AutoCAD is listed in a special database along with all information required to reproduce that entity. A straight line, for example, is stored as a *line entity* along with information that describes its starting point, ending point, and drawing-layer location. More complex entities have longer lists of information associated with them.

Using AutoLISP, you can select an entity from the drawing database. The *entity name* is a data type reserved for handling the list of definition data and distinguishing it from other selected entities. Once an entity has been selected and assigned a name, any item in the list of information can be extracted and manipulated by AutoLISP. This technique is demonstrated in Chapter 8.

File Descriptors

AutoLISP has functions that can open a file on disk for information storage or read the information contained in disk files. When a file is opened under AutoLISP, it is assigned a special data type, called a *file descriptor,* which acts as a pointer to that file, keeping track of its physical location on the disk for storage and access, and distinguishing it from any other selected files.

Integers and Real Numbers

AutoLISP recognizes two forms of numerical data: *integers* and *real numbers.* Integers never include decimal points. They can be processed quickly but are limited in range. The range of valid integers depends on the system you are using. On a 16-bit system, integers are whole numbers from −32,768 to +32,767. On a 32-bit system, integers range from −2,147,483,648 to +2,147,483,647. Although AutoCAD uses 32-bit internal processing, AutoLISP only passes 16-bit integers to AutoCAD. Therefore, if you are moving integer values from AutoLISP to AutoCAD, be sure these values stay between −32,768 and +32,767.

The result of using integers is also an integer. For example, the following function uses integers:

(/ 35 2)

The result returned by this function is 17, not 17.5. This is because both 35 and 2 are expressed as integers, and therefore the result can only be another integer.

Real numbers are more flexible, although they process a bit more slowly. Here, the same function uses two reals instead of two integers:

(/ 35.0 2.0)

The result returned by this function is mathematically correct: 17.5, another real number.

Real numbers are easily identified because they always include a decimal point; integers never do. If a real has a value of less than 1, its decimal point must be preceded by a leading zero. For example, 0.5 is a valid real number, and .5 is not.

You can combine integers and reals in the same function:

(/ 35.0 2)

Fundamental AutoLISP Data Types

The result returned by this function is also 17.5. When integers and reals are combined in the same function, the result is always a real number.

A good rule of thumb regarding integers and reals is this: Use integers when you are sure that you need only whole numbers in your processing, and that these numbers (as well as the results of calculations using these numbers) will stay within the allowed range for integers. Do this for speed and memory efficiency. In all other cases, or when in doubt, use real numbers.

Lists

In AutoLISP, a *list* is any group of individual items of information enclosed by a matched set of parentheses. The items are separated from each other by at least one space. Items on a list can be numbers, characters, function operators, arguments, or even other lists. They derive their meaning from the nature of their contents and the context in which they appear. Thus, a function is a list composed of a function operator and its arguments. The length of a list is the number of individual items it contains. Lists can be any length.

Although a function can be seen as one kind of a list, not all lists are functions. AutoLISP treats X-Y coordinate information as a list of two numbers, indicating a coordinate point. For example, given the list

```
(1.25 2.75)
```

AutoLISP assumes that the first number is the X-coordinate and the second number is the Y-coordinate. In AutoCAD Version 2.6 and later, a third number on the list would be recognized as the Z-coordinate of a 3-D point.

Strings

Strings are sequences of one or more characters (letters, numbers, and punctuation marks) that do not require mathematical processing. A string is always surrounded by quotation marks. For instance, consider the following AutoLISP SETQ function:

```
(setq x "This is a string")
```

This function takes the sequence of characters "This is a string" and stores it in memory variable x.

You can place a maximum of 132 characters between a set of quotation marks. If necessary, you can create strings of any length by joining shorter strings together. AutoCAD allocates memory for them as needed. Long strings can really slow down processing, because they occupy a lot of computer memory that might otherwise be available for processing. Keep your strings as short as possible.

Strings are often used as prompts for the user, which is why such prompts can be so cryptic at times. Computer programs attempt to strike a balance between processing speed and ease of use, often with mixed results.

Try typing the above example function at the AutoCAD command prompt. Then type !x and press ↵. Notice that AutoCAD returns the value of the variable. You can use the exclamation point plus the variable name to return the contents of any AutoLISP variable at the command prompt. Try using various strings. Remember to include the quotation marks.

Symbols

The term *symbol* is used to describe ASCII characters that stand for something else. Memory-variable names are symbols; so are function operators. A string is different from a symbol because it is literal, representing only itself. Likewise, a number is different from a symbol because it can only represent its own value.

The characters that make up a symbol can include any combination of ASCII letters, numbers, and punctuation marks except the following:

( ) . ' " ;

These punctuation marks have special meaning in AutoLISP, and will be discussed later on.

Selection Sets

AutoLISP allows you to select groups of drawing entities. A group of entities can be given a name, called a *selection set,* and can then be acted upon as a group. The manipulation of selection sets is demonstrated in Chapter 8.

Managing AutoLISP Routines in AutoCAD

AutoLISP routines are contained in separate files on disk; thus, they require some simple management before they can be used within AutoCAD. The file contents must be loaded before they can be executed, and sufficient memory must be allocated for their use.

Loading AutoLISP Routines

A LISP routine can be executed when its file is loaded into an area of memory reserved for that purpose by AutoCAD. To load a file, use the AutoLISP function LOAD, as in the following example:

(load "filename")

This function would cause AutoCAD to look for the file FILENAME.LSP on the default subdirectory. If found, the entire contents of FILENAME.LSP would be loaded into memory and the expressions it contains would be evaluated. If you need to load a LISP routine from a different subdirectory, use the full path name of the file. For example, if the file FILENAME.LSP is located on foreign subdirectory \ACAD\LISPFILE, it could be loaded as follows:

(load "c:/acad/lispfile/filename")

Notice that in the above syntax, the forward slash (/) is used to separate subdirectory names in the full path name of the LISP file. This is because the backslash (\) has a special meaning in AutoLISP; it is reserved for designating special control characters in strings.

Memory Management

Later versions of AutoCAD have increasingly automated its allocation of memory. If you are using Release 11 or later with a standard hardware and operating system set-up, there is little need for you to tinker with AutoCAD's methods for handling available memory.

For example, memory for AutoLISP is allocated as new functions and routines are loaded. Functions and routines are stored in 12-byte memory structures called *nodes*. Nodes are allocated in groups, called *segments*. Each segment contains 514 nodes, or 6,168 bytes. The more AutoLISP routines you load, however, the less memory is left available for AutoCAD's other processes. At some point, depending on the amount of memory in your system, the size of your drawing file, and the number of external routines you have loaded, AutoCAD will begin using your hard disk as *virtual memory* (temporary storage for data in random-access memory). Virtual memory slows down AutoCAD's processing a great deal.

Although DOS 386 AutoCAD will work with as little as four megabytes of random-access memory, your custom system with many AutoLISP or ADS routines may work more efficiently with a practical minimum of eight megabytes.

The area of available memory allocated to AutoLISP is used to store variable names, functions, prompt strings, as well as data generated during the processing of AutoLISP routines. If you attempt to execute a routine that requires more total memory space than is available, you will receive error messages such as the following from the AutoLISP interpreter:

```
error: insufficient node space
error: insufficient string space
error: LISPSTACK overflow
```

Sometimes these errors arise from a problem in the source code. This is especially true for messages regarding string space. If you get a message indicating a problem with string length, first check to be sure you haven't inadvertently left out a closing quote. Unbalanced parentheses and quotation marks can sometimes appear to be memory problems.

If you are using Release 10 or earlier, you can make more room for your LISP routines by including the following two DOS commands in your AUTOEXEC.BAT file or in a batch file you use to start AutoCAD:

```
SET LISPHEAP=40000
SET LISPSTACK=5000
```

The total of these two numbers cannot exceed 45,000. You may not need to use numbers this big, or you may eventually find that you have to juggle these values around. The value of LISPHEAP is usually set as the larger of the two, especially if you define lots of functions and memory variables. If you nest your functions very deeply, you may need to increase the LISPSTACK number. The same is true if your LISP routines repeat the same calculation many times before returning a final result, or if you have defined functions that require a long list of arguments.

Managing AutoLISP Routines in AutoCAD

Setting up these values in DOS has no effect on programs other than AutoCAD, and no effect at all on Release 11 and later.

Extended AutoLISP (Release 10 286)

If you are using AutoCAD Release 10 and have at least 500K of extended memory that is not currently in use by virtual disks or other software, you may take advantage of Release 10's *Extended AutoLISP* feature. Extended AutoLISP works only with extended memory; it will not work with expanded memory. Check your hardware documentation or with your dealer if you are not sure which type of extra memory you have.

To use Extended AutoLISP, you must have the following three files on your hard disk: 1) ACADLX.OVL (place this file on your AutoCAD system subdirectory); 2) EXTLISP.EXE; and 3) REMLISP.EXE.

AutoCAD must be specially configured to use Extended AutoLISP. To do this, select option 5, Configure AutoCAD, from AutoCAD's main menu. From the configuration menu, select option 8, Configure Operating Parameters. Then select option 7, AutoLISP Feature. Answer Y to both questions, *Do you want AutoLISP enabled?* and *Do you want to use Extended AutoLISP?* Then exit AutoCAD.

Once you have configured AutoCAD to use Extended AutoLISP, enter the command EXTLISP at the DOS prompt before you enter AutoCAD. You may enter this command from the keyboard or place it in a batch file. You need to enter EXTLISP once each time you reboot or turn on the computer. You can erase EXTLISP from RAM by entering the command REMLISP.

Using Local Memory Variables

When you create AutoLISP functions and routines, you have the option of defining your memory variables as either *local* or *global*. The technique for doing this is explained fully in Chapter 7.

Both types of memory variables have their advantages. Local variables are always reset at the conclusion of the function in which they are bound to a value. If they were bound to a value before the function was called, they are reset to that value. Otherwise, they are reset to nil (meaning "no value" in AutoLISP), thus releasing the memory they occupied. Global variables, on the other hand, are never reset;

their values can be passed between separate functions and routines. To reset a global variable to nil requires a specific SETQ function, for example:

`(setq X nil)`

You will make additional memory space available for AutoLISP processing by resetting variables to nil when they are no longer needed. Therefore, use local variables whenever you can.

Writing Efficient Code

Your AutoLISP routines will take up less memory space if you keep the following principles in mind:

- **Keep your character strings as short as possible**. This is often easier said than done. A cryptic prompt or error message is not particularly useful and can be pretty annoying as well; on the other hand, long character strings require a lot of memory. If your AutoLISP routines will be used and/or studied by others, you may have to work out a trade-off between clarity, user-friendliness, and needed node space. On the other hand, if you are writing routines strictly for your own use, you can make those strings as short as you like.

- **Undefine functions when they are no longer needed**. If you have no further use for a particular function in a drawing session, you can recover the node space used by that function by binding the function name to a null value, as follows:

    `(setq FUNCTION nil)`

- **Keep your variable names six characters or less in length**. AutoLISP allocates a fixed amount of memory for each variable name; variable names more than six characters in length require additional string space to hold the name. Thus, it is very important that you keep the names short. Abbreviated variable names may make your code less understandable to others, or even to yourself if you attempt to modify the code after leaving it alone for a few weeks. To help you remember what the names mean, you may consider making two copies of your code, one with long variable names for easier reading and debugging, and a second one with abbreviated variable names for loading and processing. Most word processors have a global replacement feature that can simplify the process of converting variable names. Another possibility is to list the meaning of all your variable names in a comment section within the LISP file. (See "Comments," ahead.)

- **Share variable names whenever possible**. Within a particular routine, variables must be given unique names. However, it is good practice to reuse a variable name when the variable is no longer needed within a routine, or for local variables among unrelated routines.

    Recycling memory variables requires the programmer to track the value of a variable throughout all phases of a given AutoLISP routine. This can be tedious and time-consuming, and it can open your routine to unforeseen errors. However, given that the amount of available memory is so often limited, this technique may be the only way you can cram a long routine into memory without a major performance hit. Cramped memory is the reason for using duplicate local variable names. If the clarity of your code is more important than overall performance, or if you are blessed with large amounts of RAM, you need not recycle variable names.

    At present there is no standard system for naming AutoLISP variables, but if you adopt a consistent variable-naming system of your own, you will be rewarded with more compact code. Again, if your code will be read by others, you may find yourself trading off between reading clarity and node space.

- **Share functions whenever possible**. In Chapter 7 you will learn how to create your own AutoLISP functions. If two or more of your routines use the same sequence of processes, you can define the sequence as a separate function, and call that function from any routine that needs it. This not only speeds up loading of the individual routines, but also prevents inadvertent waste of node space that can occur when routines use identical processing sequences.

    You should only load those shared functions that you are certain will be called frequently. You can load infrequently called functions on an as-needed basis. As you will learn in subsequent chapters, AutoLISP provides the means for testing to see if a function is currently loaded, and loading it if required.

Making a LISP File More Readable

The AutoLISP interpreter will read and execute any LISP routine as long as the function syntax is correct. However, the user reading a listing of the routine must also be able to understand what it intends to accomplish; it is not always easy to decipher what is going on among the various AutoLISP functions, arguments, symbols, and parentheses. Fortunately, there are two ways to make a LISP routine more easily understandable to the human reader, as well as to the AutoLISP interpreter: comments and indentation.

Comments

You can place plain-English explanations and comments within your LISP routines that will be ignored by the AutoLISP interpreter. To do this, simply precede each line of comment with a semicolon. Here is an example:

```
; This function assigns a value of 2 to the memory variable x:
(setq x 2)
```

AutoLISP will read the function, but ignore the comment above it because a semicolon precedes the comment. Comments may begin anywhere on a line; everything following a semicolon on any one line is ignored.

As a general rule, place comments in the LISP file to explain the meanings and operations of functions that are not readily apparent, and as an aid to yourself for editing or debugging the LISP file at a later date. There is no limit on the number of comments in a LISP file, but they do enlarge the file and slow the process of loading it into the computer's memory. Again, you may wish to work with two copies of your LISP file, one with extensive comments (as well as more descriptive variable names) for editing and debugging, and one without comments for loading and executing.

Indentation

When several nested functions are strung together in a LISP file, it can become difficult to read. One way to sort things out is to arrange parentheses within the LISP file so as to isolate specific functions, as in the following valid AutoLISP functions:

```
(setq m
   (/ (+ x y)
      2
   )
)
```

When arranged in this fashion, the right parenthesis of the outermost function has been placed on a separate line, directly underneath its corresponding left mate. The deeper function has been indented on the page, and its corresponding right parenthesis has also been indented below its left mate. The deepest function has been left alone. By having mates share the same degree of indentation, this layout helps the eye to isolate specific functions and their arguments and to see which sets of parentheses belong together. If a parenthesis had been accidentally left out, it would be fairly easy to spot, making debugging much easier.

The AutoLISP interpreter has no trouble with this arrangement as long as at least one space separates data items on any given text line. The following example repeats the previous example, showing required spaces as underlines:

```
(setq_m
   (/
     (+_x_y)
     2
   )
)
```

This kind of arrangement of functions is optional and somewhat subjective. For example, you may not wish to indent your LISP files unless the function is more than two or three levels deep or involves some special, complex analysis. The key issue here is to make the files as easy to read and analyze as possible. As you acquire more experience, you will undoubtedly settle on a layout method that works best for you. However, if your LISP files are going to be read by someone else, you should make every possible effort to keep them clear.

Getting Out of Trouble

Not every LISP routine works the first time. Some routines will function but achieve unintended results; others may simply fail to function. The AutoLISP documentation provides a complete list of error messages and their meanings. The following two techniques, the console break and the unbalanced function prompt, help you handle a LISP routine that performs in an unexpected way.

Console Break with Ctrl-C

In the midst of executing a lengthy LISP routine, you may wish to abort the process if, for instance, the routine is offering incorrect or unintelligible results, or if it appears to stop processing altogether. You can abort a LISP routine by pressing Ctrl-C or Ctrl-Break. This will cause the LISP routine to cease execution after it has evaluated the current function. AutoCAD will also display a message like one of the following:

```
Error: Console Break
Error: Function Canceled
*Cancel*
```

Once you have aborted a LISP routine, you are returned to the AutoCAD command prompt, where you may take any corrective action required.

The Unbalanced Function Prompt

As you build more and more complex functions with deeper and deeper levels of nesting, you may accidentally leave out a parenthesis or two. This will cause your AutoLISP routine to produce strange results. In such an event, the following prompt may replace the familiar AutoCAD command prompt:

n>

The *n* will be the number of right parentheses that are still needed in order to have an equal number of left and right parentheses in the LISP routine.

If you ever encounter this strange and persistent little prompt, there is only one way to get rid of it and return to the AutoCAD command prompt: type the same number of right parentheses at the keyboard and press ↵. From the AutoCAD command prompt, return to your word processor, and add right parentheses or delete left parentheses as necessary. Then return to AutoCAD and reload the LISP file. This will ensure that your LISP routine runs properly.

If you find that this prompt persists even after you have typed the correct number of right parentheses, the cause is probably a missing quotation mark. Once the AutoLISP interpreter encounters a quotation mark, everything that follows, including right parentheses, is treated as part of a string. This includes the parentheses that you type at the keyboard. To get back to the standard AutoCAD prompt so you can correct the problem, type a set of quotation marks followed by the correct number of right parentheses.

Getting Out of Trouble

It will help if you use nesting levels sparingly at first until you have the AutoLISP routine working. Once the file is working, you can go back and nest functions to reduce the number of needed memory variables and use your computer's memory more efficiently.

CHAPTER SEVEN

Creating AutoLISP Routines

CREATING AUTOLISP ROUTINES
CH. 7

As you learned in Chapter 6, a LISP routine is a set of related AutoLISP functions that, when evaluated in sequence, perform a given task. This set of AutoLISP functions is contained in an ASCII file called a *LISP file*. LISP files can be named with any valid DOS file name. By convention, they have the extension LSP. Using your word processor, you can create LISP files as you would any other ASCII file.

LISP files are loaded into a part of memory reserved by AutoCAD for that purpose. Once loaded, AutoCAD's AutoLISP interpreter evaluates all the functions in the LISP file. The functions are evaluated one after another, from top to bottom within the file. As each function is evaluated, its deepest level of nesting is evaluated first, the next-deepest level next, and so on to the shallowest level.

A good LISP routine should accomplish its tasks as quickly and efficiently as possible. It should also be well organized and structured, so that any subsequent modifications can be made easily. Although all functions in the file are evaluated when it is loaded, it is good practice to structure a LISP routine so that instead of simply executing functions, it defines brand new functions, which then can be called at any time during the drawing session. As you will see in this chapter, it is possible to define functions that can be called from AutoCAD's command prompt just like any AutoCAD command.

There are several good reasons to write LISP routines that are based on defining new functions:

- Defining functions results in better program organization, with a complex process broken down into simple steps, each step handled by a defined function.
- Defined properly, a function is *portable*—functions defined in one LISP routine can be used in other LISP routines that are loaded later.
- When a LISP routine is based on defined functions, its problems are easier to locate, making the process of debugging faster.
- Defined functions are kept in memory and can be accessed repeatedly, without reloading the LISP file each time.

Defun

AutoLISP uses a special function, Defun, to create new functions from predefined ones. Defun uses the following structure:

```
(defun function_name( arguments / local_variables)
    ...(other_functions)...
)
```

Defun requires that you supply a unique name for the new function, which is followed by a list of arguments and local variables. *Arguments* are variables that are supplied when the function is called. *Local variables* are used within the body of the new function. The body of the new function contains other functions that are processed in sequence when the new function is called. For example, consider the following simple function:

```
(defun example(x)
    (1+ x)
)
```

This function accepts a number and uses a predefined AutoLISP function, 1+, to increment that number by one. Once it is defined and loaded, you can call this function with the syntax

```
(example 1)
```

and the function will return 2.

The functions that you define will be more complicated than this. For example, the following function tests to be sure that the function argument is really a number, and returns nil if the argument is not a number:

```
(defun example(x)
    (if (or (= (type x) 'INT)
            (= (type x) 'REAL)
        )
        (1+ x)
    )
)
```

This example tests for the data type in the argument x. If the data type is either an integer or a real number, it is incremented by one. Otherwise, nothing happens and the function returns nil. Thus,

```
(example 1)
```

177

still returns 2, but

`(example "X")`

returns nil. If you defined the function without testing for the data type, the last example would cause an AutoLISP error message, and processing would stop.

Global and Local Variables

AutoLISP treats newly-declared variables as global, unless you indicate that they are local when you define the function. For example, consider the following simple function:

```
(defun example()
    (setq G:X 1)
)
```

This simple function has the effect of creating a variable named G:X and giving it a value of 1. The variable G:X is global in this case, and can be used by other functions invoked after this one. Now consider the following:

```
(defun example( / X)
    (setq X 1)
)
```

In the second example, the variable X is local, because it is listed within the parentheses following the function name. When a variable is local, it is visible only while the function is active, and other functions will not be able to make use of it. If a variable named X existed before this function was called, the local function exists separately from it. The previous value of X is retained when the example function completes processing.

Notice also the backslash that appears within the parentheses before the local variable declaration. Since the variable name is declared following the backslash, the AutoLISP interpreter knows that this local variable is not a required argument for the function. Compare the previous example to the following:

```
(defun example(Z / X)
    (setq X Z)
)
```

Both variables Z and X are local, because they are declared in the parentheses following the function name. However, the variable Z is required as an argument to the function, because it is declared before the backslash. The variable X is not a function argument. In order to execute this function, you must invoke the function with an argument, such as:

`(example 1)`

This would cause the value 1 to be stored to the local variable X.

In general, local variables are more efficient and safer to use. There is less likelihood of conflict between variables of the same name in different routines when variables are declared local. Unless you have a good reason to make variables global, try to make them local as a general rule.

It is helpful to adopt a consistent naming approach for global variables, so that they can be distinguished easily in your code. The functions in this chapter identify global variables by the prefix G:, which causes them to stand out clearly in the code. Be extremely careful when manipulating global variables, and keep close track of all global variables on the loose in your system's memory. Be especially cautious that your global variable values are not inadvertently overwritten by other AutoLISP routines.

Parametric Programming

At first, your AutoLISP routines will probably follow a *parametric* model. The parametric model involves three basic steps:

1. The routine prompts the user to supply needed information, or program parameters. Alternatively, these parameters may come from another source, such as a file on disk. This file is normally another ASCII file, created by a database, speadsheet, or other third-party program.

2. The routine uses these parameters to complete some form of internal processing, such as making complex calculations, applying data to formulas, or choosing between alternate steps based on the type of information supplied.

3. After completing its processing, the routine supplies some form of finished output, such as AutoCAD drawing entities, some set of meaningful data for the user, or other information that can be displayed on the screen, printed, or stored on disk in another file.

CREATING AUTOLISP ROUTINES
CH. 7

Each of these steps should be accomplished in accordance with certain basic principles of good organization:

1. When the user must supply parameters, the routine should pause and display clear and concise prompts for them. The routine should contain as much processing as possible so that it rejects and reprompts when clearly erroneous data is entered. The routine should ask for the minimum amount of information necessary. Since the point of a LISP routine is to save time and simplify AutoCAD, the less information the user is required to supply, the better. AutoLISP's predefined functions for inputting points, distances, angles, and so on make the process of writing this part of a LISP routine fairly simple.

2. The internal processing should be based on predefined functions. These functions break processing down into simple, discrete steps. To whatever extent possible, you should create small, simple functions for each step in processing. Simple, straightforward functions have the best chance of being reused as building blocks in other routines you write.

3. If the routine reads or writes disk files, those files should be opened just before reading or writing, and closed immediately when they are no longer needed. This minimizes any possibility of damage to data from unforeseen problems with hardware (for example, a power failure while reading or writing to a file). File access and internal processing should be done in separate steps whenever possible.

4. When processing is lengthy, it is helpful to display some information during processing that allows the user to see that progress is being made. Without this kind of feedback, the user may wonder if the computer is still working or if processing is actually suspended because of some internal error.

5. Any good routine will account for the possibility of a premature end to processing, either because the information supplied is not adequate for completion, or because the user voluntarily canceled the processing. Users can abort an AutoLISP routine by entering Ctrl-Break or Ctrl-C before the routine has a chance to complete.

As exacting an art as programming is, it is also a matter of individual style. Different programmers often take unique approaches to the solution of the same problem. Exceptions to the general rules often arise based on individual circumstances and the goals of any particular routine. But the principles listed above are a good basis for sound programming practice, and should not be violated without some compelling reason.

A Basic LISP Routine

The following example demonstrates how a LISP routine is put together. This fundamental routine creates a new AutoCAD command that draws a gear, based on formulas found in the machinist's handbook. Bear in mind that this example is not intended to be a complete application for producing gears in AutoCAD, but rather an example of how a parametric program can be used to produce an object that would be much more difficult to produce without AutoLISP. As you go through the steps involved in producing this routine, notice how the general principles are applied to the problem's solution.

If parts of your own drawing are based on mathematical calculations, building them into a LISP routine will make your job much simpler. Generally speaking, if you are using a calculator to help create AutoCAD drawings, consider placing those calculations in a LISP routine instead.

At first, the GEAR.LSP routine will produce the gear by prompting the user for necessary information in sequence, in AutoCAD's command prompt area on the screen. For Release 12 users, the routine is then enhanced by adding a custom dialog box that requests the same parameters.

Stating the Problem

Begin producing an AutoLISP routine by first writing a clear and concise statement of the *problem*; in other words, what specific goal you intend to address using the routine. GEAR.LSP, for example, attempts to solve the following problem: The need to draw a gear shape, based on certain fundamental information supplied by the user:

1. The center point
2. The pitch circle radius

3. The number of teeth

4. The radius of the center hole, if any

5. The dimensions of a notch added to the center hole, if any

After the user has answered prompts for this information, the routine will check to see if a gear is possible, and if so, will draw the gear in AutoCAD. Examples of some criteria that should be checked before drawing are:

1. The center point must be a valid AutoCAD point.

2. The number of teeth must be at least 14.

3. The center hole radius, if supplied, must be less than the overall gear radius.

4. The notch dimensions, if supplied, must be proportionate to the radius of the center hole.

Writing the Pseudocode

As you saw in Chapter 6, the next development step after stating the problem is to specify, in plain English, the steps taken by the routine to solve the problem. Recall that this specification is called *pseudocode,* because it follows the logical track of AutoLISP code without actually writing AutoLISP. This step is important because it helps clarify the logical processes involved in solving the problem. Pseudocode breaks down the overall task into a series of small, simple steps that lead to the desired result. It is much better to break down the task in this way before you become involved with the intricacies of the language, debugging, and testing. Pseudocode will prevent many problems and generally leads to a cleaner, more reliable and efficient routine. It also saves time in the long run.

Here is one possible way to write the pseudocode for GEAR.LSP.

Pseudocode for GEAR.LSP

The GEAR.LSP routine is defined in English by these steps:

1. Prompt the user for the center point. If a center point was given previously, use the previous point as the default.

Writing the Pseudocode

2. Prompt the user for the pitch circle radius. If given previously, use the previous response as the default.

3. Prompt the user for the number of gear teeth. Repeat the prompt while the number of teeth is less than 14. If given previously, use the previous response as the default.

4. Prompt the user for the radius of the center hole. Allow zero, indicating no center hole. Repeat the prompt while the center hole radius is equal to or greater than the pitch circle. If a radius was given previously, use the previous response as the default.

5. If the user indicates a center hole, prompt for the depth and width of a notch. Allow zero, indicating no notch. Check that the depth and width of the notch are possible, given the current pitch circle and center hole parameters. Repeat the prompt while the notch dimensions are greater than or equal to the center hole diameter. If notch dimensions were given previously, use the previous response as the default.

6. Calculate the diametral pitch of the gear.

7. Calculate the length of half the end of a tooth.

8. Calculate the distance between the pitch circle and the end of a tooth.

9. Calculate the length of the side of a tooth.

10. Draw half of a tooth using the results of these calculations.

11. Mirror what was drawn to create a whole tooth.

12. Perform a circular array based on the user-specified number of teeth.

13. Add the center hole, if not zero radius.

14. Add the notch, if dimensions are not zero. Trim the center hole to the notch, if required.

Figures 7.1 and 7.2 illustrate the process of drawing a 6-inch gear with 36 teeth.

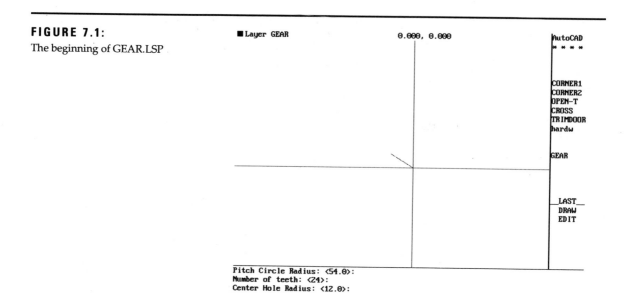

FIGURE 7.1:
The beginning of GEAR.LSP

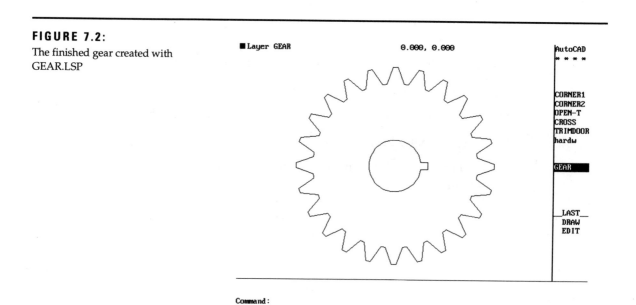

FIGURE 7.2:
The finished gear created with GEAR.LSP

The GEAR.LSP Routine

The entire GEAR.LSP routine is shown in Listing 7.1. The routine begins with the Getp function, which asks for the necessary parameters. Interaction with the user is a key element in many AutoLISP routines, so several features of this function are worth examining in detail.

Listing 7.1: The GEAR.LSP Routine

```
; FILE NAME:     GEAR.Lsp - AutoCAD Release 9+
; Written by:    Bob Thomas
;
;------------------------------------------------------------------
; G:DTR function:
;
(defun g:dtr(a)
   (* pi (/ a 180.0))              ; convert degrees to radians
)
;
;------------------------------------------------------------------
; G:STR function:
;
(defun g:str( string default )     ; format string w/default variable
   (princ string)
   (princ " <")
   (princ default)
   (princ ">:")
   (princ "")
)
;
;------------------------------------------------------------------
; G:PT function: - Formatted Getpoint
;
(defun g:pt(pt prmpt default / temp)
   (if default                                    ; if default exists
      (if pt                                      ; if pt exists
         (setq temp (getpoint pt (g:str prmpt default)))   ; prompt
         (setq temp (getpoint (g:str prmpt default)))
      )                                           ; if default doesn't exist
      (if pt                                      ; if pt exists
         (setq default (getpoint pt prmpt))       ; prompt
         (setq default (getpoint prmpt))
      )
```

```
        )
        (if temp                                ; if temp exists (response was given)
            (setq default temp)                 ; set new default
            default                             ; otherwise, return existing default
        )
)
;
;------------------------------------------------------------------------
; G:DIST function: - Formatted Getdist
;
(defun g:dist(pt prmpt default / temp)
    (if default                                              ; if default exists
        (if pt                                               ; if pt exists
            (setq temp (getdist pt (g:str prmpt default))) ; prompt
            (setq temp (getdist (g:str prmpt default)))
        )
                                                             ; if default doesn't exist
        (if pt                                               ; if pt exists
            (setq default (getdist pt prmpt))     ; prompt
            (setq default (getdist prmpt))
        )
    )
    (if temp                                ; if temp exists (response was given)
        (setq default temp)                 ; set new default
        default                             ; otherwise, return existing default
    )
)
;
;------------------------------------------------------------------------
; G:INT function: - Formatted Getint
;
(defun g:int(prmpt default / temp)
    (if default                                              ; if default exists
        (setq temp (getint (g:str prmpt default)))        ; prompt
        (while (not default)                                 ; while default doesn't exist
            (setq default (getint prmpt))        ; prompt
        )
    )
    (if temp                                ; if temp exists (response was given)
        (setq default temp)                 ; set new default
        default                             ; otherwise, return existing default
    )
)
;
;------------------------------------------------------------------------
; GETP function: - Get gear parameters
```

The GEAR.LSP Routine

```
;
(defun getp( / temp)
   (if g:cp                        ; if global center point
       (setq g:cp (g:pt nil "\nCenter of Gear:" g:cp)) ; prompt
       (while (not g:cp)           ; while not global
          (setq g:cp (g:pt nil "\nCenter of Gear:" g:cp))  ; prompt
       )
   )
   (if g:pc                        ; if global pitch circle
       (setq g:pc (g:dist g:cp "\nPitch Circle Radius:" g:pc)) ; prompt
       (while (not g:pc)           ; while not global
          (setq g:pc (g:dist g:cp "\nPitch Circle Radius:" g:pc)) ; prompt
       )
   )
   (while (< temp 14)              ; while teeth (temp) is less than 14
      (setq temp (g:int "\nNumber of teeth:" g:teeth)) ; prompt
      (if (>= temp 14)             ; if valid
          (setq g:teeth temp)      ; set global
      )
   )

   ; Prompt for center hole:

   (setq g:hole (g:dist g:cp "\nCenter Hole Radius:" g:hole))
   (if (not g:hole) (setq g:hole 0))   ; if not given, reset to zero

   ; Prompt for notch:

   (cond ( (/= g:hole 0)           ; case: center hole given
           (setq g:nd (g:dist g:cp "\nNotch Depth:" g:nd)) ; get notch depth
           (if (not g:nd) (setq g:nd 0)) ; if not given, reset to zero

           (if (/= g:nd 0)  ; if notch depth given,
               (setq g:nw (g:dist g:cp "\nNotch Width:" g:nw)) ; get width
           )
           (if (and (/= g:nd 0) (/= g:nw 0)) ; if notch data was given
               (setq g:setn 1)             ; set notch flag on
               (setq g:setn 0)             ; otherwise, set off
           )
         )
         ( T (setq g:setn 0))      ; default case: set notch flag off
   )                               ; end case

   (if (or (not g:nd) (not g:nw))  ; if notch data still doesn't exist
       (setq g:setn 0) )           ; set notch flag off
```

```
)
;
;-----------------------------------------------------------------
; CALCP function:
;
(defun calcp()
       (setq pcpt   (polar g:cp 0 g:pc)          ; pitch circle point
             dpitch (/ g:teeth (* 2.0 g:pc))     ; diametral pitch
             htooth (/ 0.32 dpitch)              ; tooth height
             xtooth (/ 1.0 dpitch)               ; tooth extension
             side   (* (/ 2.257 dpitch) 1.0642)  ; length of a tooth side.
       )
)
;
;-----------------------------------------------------------------
; DRAW function:
;
(defun draw()
   (command "ZOOM" "C" g:cp (* 2.5 g:pc)         ; move view to gear center
            "PLINE" (polar pcpt 0 xtooth) "A"    ; draw half-tooth
            "CE" g:cp "L" htooth "L"
            (polar (getvar "lastpoint") (g:dtr 160) side)
            "Arc" "CE" g:cp "L" htooth "")

   (setq ss1 (ssadd (entlast)))                  ; create to selection set

   (command "MIRROR" ss1 "" pcpt g:cp "n" )      ; mirror half-tooth

   (setq ss1 (ssadd (entlast) ss1))              ; add to selection set

   (command "ARRAY" ss1 "" "polar" g:cp g:teeth "360" "yes") ; array teeth

   (if (/= g:hole 0)                             ; if center hole not zero
       (progn
          (command "CIRCLE" G:CP G:HOLE)         ; draw center hole
          (setq ss1 (ssadd (entlast)))           ; create new selection set

          (if (and (= g:setn 1) (/= g:nd 0) (/= g:nw 0)) ; if notch data OK
             (notch)                             ; create notch
          )
       )
   )
)
;
;-----------------------------------------------------------------
;
```

The GEAR.LSP Routine

```
; NOTCH function:
;
(defun notch(/ np1 np2 np3 np4 np5)

   (setq np1 (polar g:cp (g:dtr 270) (/ g:nw 2.0))    ; define points for notch
         np2 (polar np1 0 (+ g:hole g:nd))
         np3 (polar g:cp (g:dtr 90) (/ g:nw 2.0))
         np4 (polar np3 0 (+ g:hole g:nd))
         np5 (polar g:cp 0 g:hole)
   )
   (command "PLINE" np1 np2 np4 np3 "")              ; draw notch

   (setq ss1 (ssadd (entlast) ss1))                  ; add to selection set

   (command "TRIM" ss1 "" np1 np3 np5 "")            ; trim excess
)
;
;-----------------------------------------------------------------
; COMMAND FUNCTION: GEAR
;
(defun C:GEAR (/ oldblp oldech olderr oldpbx pcpt dpitch htooth
                 xtooth side ss1)

   (setq oldblp (getvar "BLIPMODE")    ; Set up environment
         oldech (getvar "CMDECHO")
         oldpbx (getvar "PICKBOX")
         olderr *ERROR*
   )
   (setvar "BLIPMODE" 0)
   (setvar "CMDECHO" 0)
   (setvar "PICKBOX" 0)

   (defun *ERROR* (msg)                 ; define new error handler
      (princ " \n") (princ msg)         ; print message
      (setvar "BLIPMODE" oldblp)        ; restore environment
      (setvar "CMDECHO"  oldech)
      (setvar "PICKBOX"  oldpbx)
      (setq *ERROR* olderr)
      (princ)
   )

   (getp)                 ; get gear information
   (calcp)                ; calculate
   (draw)                 ; draw gear
```

```
    (setvar "BLIPMODE" oldblp) ;  Restore environment
    (setvar "CMDECHO"  oldech)
    (setvar "PICKBOX"  oldpbx)
    (setq *ERROR* olderr)
    (princ)
)

; Eof: GEAR.lsp.    223 lines.    Bob Thomas
```

Remembering Default Values

One of the features of GEAR.LSP is its ability to "remember" previous responses to the user prompts and offer them as defaults for the next time. This is helpful when the user is drawing more than one object and some of the parameters will remain unchanged. Global variables are used to store this information.

The global variables in GEAR.LSP are as follows:

G:CP	Default Center point
G:PC	Pitch Circle Radius
G:HOLE	Center Hole Radius
G:ND	Notch Depth
G:NW	Notch Width

Be certain that these variables do not conflict with any other global variables used by other AutoLISP routines in your system. If they do, you must rename them.

Global Functions

Five functions in GEAR.LSP are designed to be used in a wide variety of routines. One converts degrees to radians; the other four prompt the user for information: points, distances, and integers. They can be loaded separately, if you wish, and can be used in your other routines that require user input.

G:DTR

G:DTR is a common function that converts degrees to radians. It is used to make development easier by allowing you to accept angle information in degree format and convert it to the format required by AutoLISP. It also can be used to clarify the source code, if you are used to reading angles as degrees rather than radians. This is how it is used in GEAR.LSP. It is called with the syntax

```
(g:dtr degrees)
```

where *degrees* is a number representing angle degrees. It is defined as follows:

```
(defun g:dtr(a)
   (* pi (/ a 180.0))
)
```

Although not used in GEAR.LSP, a counterpart to this function is also common. This function converts radians into degrees. The syntax is

```
(g:rtd radians)
```

where *radians* is a number representing radians, such as the output of AutoLISP's Angle function. The function is defined as

```
(defun g:rtd(a)
   (* (/ a pi) 180.0)
)
```

Both of these functions are used so often you may wish to include them in ACAD.LSP, loading them each time you begin AutoCAD. More information about ACAD.LSP appears at the end of this chapter.

G:STR

G:STR is a function that formats a prompt string to include a default response. It can be used in any function that has a prompt string as one of its arguments. It is called with the syntax

```
(g:str string default)
```

where *string* is the prompt string displayed to the user, and *default* is a default value inserted after the string in angle brackets. For example,

```
(g:str "\nEnter a number" 1)
```

CREATING AUTOLISP ROUTINES
CH. 7

will return

```
Enter a number <1>:
```

This function is useful since the default argument may be bound to a variable, and therefore might change during the course of a drawing session. You can insert this function as the prompt argument in AutoLISP's various GET functions. For example, consider the following function:

```
(defun example( / TEMP)
   (if (not G:X)
      (setq G:X 1)
   )
   (setq TEMP (getint (g:str "\nEnter an integer" G:X)))
   (if TEMP
      (setq G:X TEMP)
   )
   G:X
)
```

This function will pause, display the formatted prompt, and offer the default response. If the user does not enter a value, Temp is nil, and G:X remains unchanged. If the user enters a value, G:X is set to that value. The function always returns the value of G:X. If you enter a new value for G:X, the prompt string will change the next time you call the function during the drawing session.

Notice that the G:STR function is simply a series of Princ functions, and returns a space, so that it can be accepted as a string argument to an AutoLISP Get function.

G:INT

The G:INT function is a slightly more elaborate version of the previous example. It prompts for an integer, and allows for variations in the prompt string depending on whether a default has yet been established:

```
(defun g:int(prmpt default / temp)
   (if default
      (setq temp (getint (g:str prmpt default)))
      (while (not default)
         (setq default (getint prmpt))
      )
   )
   (if temp
      (setq default temp)
```

Global Functions

```
      default
   )
)
```

This function returns either the default or a response entered by the user. In GEAR.LSP, this function is used to prompt the user for the number of teeth in the gear. Additional code is used to test whether the user has entered at least 14:

```
(while (< temp 14)
   (setq temp (g:int "\nNumber of teeth:" teeth))
   (if (>= temp 14)
      (setq teeth temp)
   )
)
```

Defining Temp as local at the start of the function ensures that the Temp variable is always bound to nil before the start of the loop. The While function creates a loop that causes the G:INT function to repeat, until the user enters a valid response (or accepts the default). If a default response exists, it is not changed until the user enters a valid new response.

G:DIST

The G:DIST function is a more elaborate version of G:INT. It prompts for a point, and allows for variations in the prompt string depending on whether a default has yet been established. It also checks to see if a base point variable exists, and uses it to create a rubberband line on the screen if it is found:

```
(defun g:dist(pt prmpt default / temp)
   (if default
      (if pt
         (setq temp (getdist pt (g:str prmpt default)))
         (setq temp (getdist (g:str prmpt default)))
      )
      (if pt
         (setq default (getdist pt prmpt))
         (setq default (getdist prmpt))
      )
   )
   (if temp
      (setq default temp)
      default
   )
)
```

193

G:PT

The G:PT function is an even more elaborate version of the previous example. It prompts for a point, and allows for variations in the prompt string depending on whether a default has yet been established. It also checks to see if a base point variable exists, and uses it if it is found:

```
(defun g:pt(pt prmpt default / temp)
   (if default
      (if pt
         (setq temp (getpoint pt (g:str prmpt default)))
         (setq temp (getpoint (g:str prmpt default)))
      )
      (if pt
         (setq default (getpoint pt prmpt))
         (setq default (getpoint prmpt))
      )
   )
   (if temp
      (setq default temp)
      default
   )
)
```

In GEAR.LSP, the base point variable is always set to nil, because the rubberband line feature of AutoLISP's Getpoint function is not required in this routine.

GETP

These global functions are called within a separate function that is unique to GEAR.LSP, named GETP, which asks for the parameters necessary to draw the gear. For example, notice how GETP uses the G:PT function to ask for the gear's center point:

```
(if g:cp
   (setq g:cp (g:pt nil "\nCenter of Gear:" g:cp))
   (while (not g:cp)
     (setq g:cp (g:pt nil "\nCenter of Gear:" g:cp))
   )
)
```

Global Functions

If a default exists (bound in the variable G:CP), the routine prompts normally. If a default is not yet established, the prompt will repeat until a valid response is given, thus establishing a default for next time.

When GETP asks for the value of the center hole, it must allow the user to enter no value if no center hole is desired. Thus the line

```
(setq g:hole (g:dist g:cp "\nCenter Hole Radius:" g:hole))
```

is followed by code that sets the G:hole variable to zero if no value was entered:

```
(if (not g:hole) (setq g:hole 0))
```

If a default was previously set, the user must enter a zero if no center hole is desired. If a center hole value is given, GETP prompts for an optional notch in the hole:

```
(cond ( (/= g:hole 0)
       (setq g:nd (g:dist g:cp "\nNotch Depth:" g:nd))
```

If a notch depth is given, the GETP function prompts for a notch width. Otherwise, the function sets the notch width value to zero and bypasses the notch width prompt:

```
        (if (not g:nd) (setq g:nd 0))
        (if (/= g:nd 0)
            (setq g:nw (g:dist g:cp "\nNotch Width:" g:nw))
        )
```

GEAR.LSP uses an additional global variable, named G:SETN, to test whether valid notch values are input. If valid notch values exist, G:SETN is bound to 1; otherwise, it is bound to 0 (zero):

```
        (if (and (/= g:nd 0) (/= g:nw 0))
            (setq g:setn 1)
            (setq g:setn 0)
        )
)
```

If the user entered no value for the center hole, G:SETN is automatically set to zero:

```
        ( T (setq g:setn 0))
```

It is worth digressing for a moment to notice how the symbol T is used in the above example: In the Cond function, this line will be a default case, because it will always evaluate. This line will always evaluate because the logical condition that triggers it is the symbol T. This symbol always evaluates to a non-nil value in AutoLISP, and the functions that follow it will therefore always execute, provided that no previous case within the Cond function had already evaluated to non-nil. If a previous condition within the Cond function evaluated to a value other than nil, this default line would then be skipped.

When you use conditional functions in your own routines, you can, when appropriate, use this technique to add a default as the last case; that is, use the symbol T as the case's last conditional function.

Alternatively, there may be times when you don't want to create a default case within a Cond function. In some situations, it may be appropriate that the Cond function have no default and return nil, after all its conditional functions have returned nil.

If the user has entered a value for the center hole but manually reset the notch values to zero, the G:SETN variable still must be adjusted:

```
(if (or (not g:nd) (not g:nw))
   (setq g:setn 0) )
```

The G:SETN variable will become more useful when you add a dialog box to this routine later in this chapter.

CALCP

Once the user has entered the parameters, the routine is ready to calculate necessary values based on some of these parameters. This job is handled by the CALCP function:

```
(defun calcp()
   (setq pcpt   (polar g:cp 0 g:pc)         ; pitch circle point
         dpitch (/ teeth (* 2.0 g:pc))      ; diametral pitch
         htooth (/ 0.32 dpitch)             ; tooth height
         xtooth (/ 1.0 dpitch)              ; tooth extension
         side   (* (/ 2.257 dpitch) 1.0642) ; tooth side.
   )
)
```

These variables are not defined as local to the CALCP function, because they will be used by another function in the routine. Instead, they are defined as local to the C:GEAR function, which calls CALCP. They will cease to exist when the C:GEAR command completes processing.

DRAW

The DRAW function produces the gear in the drawing editor. It invokes the Pline command, using the calculated variables to draw the gear. As it creates entities, it builds a selection set, stored in a variable named SS1. It references that selection set when calling the Mirror and Array commands to build the gear.

If the radius of the center hole is not zero, the function calls the Circle command. If G:SETN (the notch flag) equals 1 and notch values aren't zero, Draw calls the Notch function.

NOTCH

The Notch function is called only if G:SETN equals 1 and non-zero values exist for a notch in the center hole. The Notch function calculates the location of needed points based on the global variables for the center point, and notch depth and width, then draws lines. It adds the lines to a selection set, and references that set within the Trim command to cut away the excess. The function is useful for study as it is simple in scope, and it shows how to calculate points using the Polar command and then execute AutoCAD commands after all points are calculated:

```
(defun notch(/ np1 np2 np3 np4 np5)
   (setq np1 (polar g:cp (g:dtr 270) (/ g:nw 2.0))
         np2 (polar np1 0 (+ g:hole g:nd))
         np3 (polar g:cp (g:dtr 90) (/ g:nw 2.0))
         np4 (polar np3 0 (+ g:hole g:nd))
         np5 (polar g:cp 0 g:hole)
   )
   (command "PLINE" np1 np2 np4 np3 "")

   (setq ss1 (ssadd (entlast) ss1))

   (command "TRIM" ss1 "" np1 np3 np5 "")
)
```

C:GEAR

Finally, when all the functions are defined, they are ready to be assembled into an AutoCAD command. AutoCAD commands are defined just like functions, but their name always begins with C:. This special naming technique indicates to AutoCAD that these functions can be called directly from the command prompt.

Therefore, by defining a function named C:GEAR, you will create a new command called Gear.

In its simplest form, C:GEAR could be defined as:

```
(defun C:GEAR (/ dpitch htooth xtooth side ss1)
    (getp)
    (calcp)
    (draw)
)
```

Notice that the variables used in the CALCP function are defined as local to C:GEAR. This allows them to be used both by CALCP and DRAW, and still be discarded when C:GEAR concludes processing. Also, bear in mind that there are a number of ways to make this command more efficient and elegant.

Enhancements to GEAR.LSP

Many AutoLISP routines, including GEAR.LSP, make changes to the drawing environment. These changes improve the screen appearance during processing, as well as make the command more accurate and reliable.

In general, environmental changes within AutoLISP routines follow these general principles:

1. Save the current environmental settings in variables local to the command.

2. Reset the environment as desired.

3. At the conclusion of processing, reset the environment to the stored settings.

4. End the new command with a call to the Princ function (no arguments), which will cause the command prompt to return without displaying any function return values.

GEAR.LSP makes the following changes:

```
(setq oldblp (getvar "BLIPMODE") ; screen blips
      oldech (getvar "CMDECHO") ; echoing of commands on screen
      oldpbx (getvar "PICKBOX") ; pick box size
)
```

Then, it sets the following values:

```
(setvar "BLIPMODE" 0)    ; turn off screen blips
(setvar "CMDECHO" 0)     ; turn off command echoing
(setvar "PICKBOX" 0)     ; set the pick box to zero
```

Turning off screen blips and command echo reduces unnecessary clutter on the screen. Setting the pick box to zero improves the accuracy of entity selection when entities are close together in the display. For study, you might try editing GEAR.LSP with other valid values for these system variables, to observe the effect such changes have.

Error Trapping in GEAR.LSP

GEAR.LSP uses AutoLISP's Get functions to obtain parameters, and these functions include some error trapping to prevent bad data (for example, Getpoint will not allow integer or string input). It is also possible for the user to enter data which will produce an "impossible" gear; for example, a notch that is bigger than the gear itself. These types of errors will be apparent when the gear is drawn.

A more serious consideration is the possibility that the user may want to cancel the processing early, by pressing Ctrl-C at the keyboard. Normally, this will cause AutoCAD to display a long list of functions, indicating at which point processing was aborted. This information is useful when debugging the routine, but you may want to spare yourself or your users the necessity of sitting through this process once the function is fully debugged. You can change the error behavior of AutoLISP by redefining a special function, called *Error* (the asterisks are part of the function name). This redefinition process uses the following general principles:

1. Store the current function in a local variable
2. Redefine *Error* using the Defun function
3. Restore the original *Error* function at the conclusion of processing

GEAR.LSP adds the following lines to its environmental changes:

```
(setq oldblp (getvar "BLIPMODE")
      oldech (getvar "CMDECHO")
```

```
        oldpbx (getvar "PICKBOX")
        olderr *ERROR*
)
```

This stores the current *Error* function to the Olderr variable. Next, GEAR.LSP creates a new error routine, which will execute if the user enters Ctrl-C:

```
(defun *ERROR* (msg)
  (princ " \n") (princ msg)
  (setvar "BLIPMODE" oldblp)
  (setvar "CMDECHO" oldech)
  (setvar "PICKBOX" oldpbx)
  (setq *ERROR* olderr)
  (princ)
)
```

This new *Error* function prints a simple error message that is automatically returned by the AutoLISP interpreter, then restores the environmental settings that were changed by GEAR.LSP. It also restores the previous version of the *Error* function. Notice that these same changes are made at the end of the C:GEAR function, so that all original settings are returned when the function concludes normally.

Study the code for the C:GEAR function closely, as shown in Listing 7.1. The location of the line restoring the original *Error* function is important. It is always the second to last function called in the routine, just before the final call to Princ, for quiet exiting.

Entering Parameters Using Dialog Boxes (Release 12 Only)

It is nearly axiomatic that, when you are programming, the easier you make things for the user, the harder your job as a programmer. Such is the case when you choose to add a dialog box to your routine, as Release 12 allows. A dialog box makes it much easier for the user to set up a long list of program parameters, but you must add extra code to your routine to provide for it.

Entering Parameters Using Dialog Boxes (Release 12 Only)

There are two extra development steps required for adding dialog boxes to AutoLISP routines:

1. You must write a separate ASCII file of instruction code, called a *DCL file*. These files can have any name, and include the extension .DCL. DCL (Dialog Control Language) is a separate language, different from AutoLISP. A DCL file contains design specifications that instruct AutoCAD on the format of your custom dialog box. Fortunately, the language is sparse and, with a little practice, much easier to master than AutoLISP.

2. Once you have created the design specification, you must add extra functions to your AutoLISP routine that initiate the display of your dialog box, control its behavior while on the screen, manage the way it accepts information from the user, validate entered data, and store it in variables for use by your routine.

Dialog boxes are composed of sections, called *tiles*, which are stacked in rows and columns within the dialog box. A tile can contain any one of several types of standard data-entry mechanisms, depending on which is the easiest mechanism for handling any individual item. You can "mix and match" the various mechanisms at will.

Fortunately, AutoCAD handles all the design details involved in transferring your design specification in the DCL file to the screen display. You need only specify the arrangement of the tile, the mechanisms they contain, and any optional features you may wish to attach to a given tile.

Data validation is extremely important when using dialog boxes. For example, AutoCAD handles data entered via dialog boxes only as character strings. If your routine uses numeric data, the character strings taken from the dialog box must be converted to numbers before they are passed to the processing portion of your routine. If the user can accidentally enter characters that cannot be converted to numbers, your routine must account for the error in a way that makes corrections easy and intuitive.

The best way to learn how to design good dialog boxes is to study the standard dialog boxes in AutoCAD. AutoCAD's standard dialog boxes are excellent models to follow when you are working out your custom design specifications. In addition, the Dialog Control Language contains several standard tile configurations that you can include with a single line of code in your DCL file. You should make use of these

CREATING AUTOLISP ROUTINES
CH. 7

standard configurations (called *widgets*) whenever possible, to simplify your design process and keep your specifications consistent with the rest of AutoCAD.

Designing a Dialog Box

Listing 7.2 is a DCL file that contains the specification for the dialog box illustrated in Figure 7.3.

FIGURE 7.3:
The dialog box displayed by GEAR.DCL

Listing 7.2: A DCL file for GEAR.Lsp - GEAR.DCL

```
// GEAR.DCL - Dialog box for DDGEAR.LSP
// Written by: Bob Thomas

gear : dialog {

    label = "Gear Parameters";

    : row {                                 // Row 1

        : boxed_column {                    // Column 1 of 3:

            : button {                      // Button for picking points
                key = "pickpoint";
                label = "Pick Point <";
                mnemonic = "P";
                fixed_width = true;
                alignment = left;
            }
```

Entering Parameters Using Dialog Boxes (Release 12 Only)

```
            : edit_box {                 // Edit box for X coordinate
                key = "x_pt";
                label = "X:";
                mnemonic = "X";
            }
            : edit_box {                 // Edit box for Y coordinate
                key = "y_pt";
                label = "Y:";
                mnemonic = "Y";
            }
        }                                // End Column 1
        : boxed_column {                 // Column 2 of 3:
            : edit_box {                 // Edit box for pitch circle
                key = "pitch";
                label = "Pitch Circle:";
                mnemonic = "P";
                edit_width = 8;
            }
            : edit_box {                 // Edit box for number of teeth
                key = "teeth";
                label = "Teeth:";
                mnemonic = "T";
                edit_width = 8;
            }
            : edit_box {                 // Edit box for center hole
                key = "hole";
                label = "Center Hole:";
                mnemonic = "C";
                edit_width = 8;
            }
        }                                // End Column 2
        : boxed_column {                 // Column 3 of 3:
            : toggle {                   // Toggle for notch data
                label = "Notch";
                mnemonic = "N";
                key = "notch";
            }
            : edit_box {                 // Edit box for notch depth
                key = "depth";
                label = "Depth:";
                mnemonic = "D";
```

```
                }
            : edit_box {                     // Edit box for notch width
                key = "width";
                label = "Width:";
                mnemonic = "W";
            }
        }                                    // End Column 3
    }                                        // End Row 1

    spacer_1;                                // Row of space for appearance
    ok_cancel;                               // Widget - OK and Cancel buttons
    errtile;                                 // Widget - Error message line

}                                            // End Gear Dialog

// EOF: GEAR.DCL   Lines: 80
```

The first line of GEAR.DCL initializes the dialog box and gives it a key name; in this case, gear:

```
gear : dialog {
```

The opening bracket at the end of this line will be matched by a closing bracket at the end of the file. Throughout the file, matched pairs of brackets are used to separate the various building blocks that make up the overall specification. These building blocks can be nested within one another as necessary.

The first specification in the dialog is a label. This label will be automatically highlighted and centered on the top line of the dialog box when it is displayed on the screen. The command line to establish the label is as follows:

```
label = "Gear Parameters";
```

This line, like all command lines in a DCL file, is followed by a semicolon, indicating that it is a single unit of design information to be processed by AutoCAD when it reads the DCL file. Notice how semicolons are used to mark command lines throughout the file. (Lines ending in brackets do not use semicolons.)

Because tiles are arranged in rows and columns, the next line indicates the content of the first row in the dialog box. In fact, this dialog box has only one row, with three

Entering Parameters Using Dialog Boxes (Release 12 Only)

columns of information. Notice how the opening bracket is matched by a closing bracket near the end of the file. Also, notice how the syntax for the specification begins with a colon:

```
: row {
```

The first column in the dialog box is of a special type, called a *boxed column*. A boxed column is simply a column of data-entry tiles with a line drawn around it for emphasis. Again, an opening bracket will be matched by a closing bracket after the list of data-entry tiles in the column:

```
: boxed_column {
```

The first data-entry tile is a *button*, a mechanism that appears on the screen as a small highlighted rectangle. When the user moves the pointer to it on the screen and picks it with the pointing device, the controlling AutoLISP routine will activate a specified function:

```
: button {
    key = "pickpoint";
    label = "Pick Point <";
    mnemonic = "P";
    fixed_width = true;
    alignment = left;
}
```

The command lines within the brackets marking the button specification link certain control elements to the button. These elements are:

- *key*—A character string that is used to identify this data-entry tile within the controlling AutoLISP routine.

- *label*—A character string that will be displayed on screen as a label on the button

- *mnemonic*—A single character in the label that, when pressed at the keyboard while the dialog box is displayed, will highlight the button. When the button is highlighted, pressing the Spacebar is the same as picking it with the pointing device. Not all platforms support mnemonics; check the AutoCAD documentation for your platform to be sure.

- *fixed_width*—Set to *true,* this indicates that the button's size is controlled by the size of the label, not the column.

- *alignment*—This element indicates that the button is lined up to the left within the column, as opposed to the other possible alignments, *centered* or *right*.

The next two data-entry mechanisms in the column are *edit_boxes.* An edit box allows the user to enter data by typing it at the keyboard. Labels are used as prompts to indicate what data should be entered. Like other data-entry mechanisms, they are given a unique key, and an optional mnemonic:

```
: edit_box {
    label = "X:";
    mnemonic = "X";
    key = "x_pt";
}
: edit_box {
    label = "Y:";
    mnemonic = "Y";
    key = "y_pt";
}
}
```

The extra closing bracket matched the boxed_column specification's open bracket, indicating that there are no more tiles in this particular column.

The next boxed_column specification indicates three more edit boxes, similar to those found in the first column. They have their own labels, unique identifying keys, and optional mnemonics.

The last boxed_column specification contains more edit boxes, but also a special tile called a *toggle*. A toggle is a small square in which an X will appear or disappear as the user selects it with the pointing device (or by highlighting it using the mnemonic character and pressing the Spacebar). When the X appears in the square, the toggle is considered active. When the square is empty, the toggle is considered inactive. Certain controlling AutoLISP functions can be invoked or ignored depending on the status of the toggle:

```
: toggle {
    label = "Notch";
    mnemonic = "N";
    key = "notch";
}
```

Additional closing brackets (in the lines following this example) indicate the end of the third boxed column, as well as the end of the first row in the dialog box. Finally, the DCL file concludes with three self-contained specifications, each invoked with a single line of code:

```
spacer_1;
ok_cancel;
errtile;
```

These specifications are called *widgets*. A widget is a predefined standard set of tiles that AutoCAD will add to the dialog box. These tiles include their own keys, labels, and mnemonics.

Spacer_1 displays a blank line of text. Use it to help balance the appearance of the elements in the dialog box by inserting a space between defined tiles.

Ok_cancel displays a row with two buttons centered in the dialog box: an OK button and a Cancel button. The OK button's key is "accept" and the Cancel button's key is "cancel."

Errtile displays a blank line, but unlike the blank line created by spacer, this line can be used to display text messages as situations warrant. The key for this tile is "error."

Widgets are extremely useful. Notice how complex, standard specifications can be handled with only a single command line in the DCL file. Standard DCL widgets are:

Widget	Includes
errtile	Blank line (key: "error") for displaying text
ok_only	OK button (key: "accept")
ok_cancel	OK button, plus Cancel button (key: "cancel")
ok_cancel_help	OK and Cancel button, plus Help button (key: "help")
ok_cancel_help_info	OK, Cancel, and Help button, plus Info button (key: "info")
ok_cancel_help_errtile	OK, Cancel, Help buttons, plus blank line for text (key: "error")

Controlling Data Input via a Dialog Box

The AutoLISP routine DDGEAR uses the functions found in GEAR.LSP to draw the gear, plus additional functions to handle dialog box input, convert data as necessary, and verify that correct data has been entered. Listing 7.3 contains the complete routine. Notice that, because it shares functions with GEAR.LSP, it requires that GEAR.LSP also be loaded before DDGEAR is run.

Listing 7.3: DDGEAR.LSP routine

```
; FILE NAME:     DDGEAR.Lsp - AutoCAD Release 12
; Written by:    Bob Thomas
;
;-----------------------------------------------------------------
; SETLOC function:
;
(defun setloc()
   (if g:cp                                   ; Center point exists
      (setq x_pt (rtos (car g:cp) 2 4)        ; create X-Y variables
            y_pt (rtos (cadr g:cp) 2 4)
      )
      (setq g:cp (list                        ; otherwise,
                  (distof (setq x_pt "0.0000")) ; create new X-Y
                  (distof (setq y_pt "0.0000"))
            )
      )
   )
   (set_tile "x_pt" x_pt)                     ; place X-Y in tiles
   (set_tile "y_pt" y_pt)
   (if (not g:pc)                             ; if no pitch circle,
      (setq g:pc 1.0) )                       ; create
   (set_tile "pitch" (setq pc (rtos g:pc 2))) ; set tile

   (if (not g:teeth)                          ; if no teeth value,
      (setq g:teeth 14) )                     ; create
   (set_tile "teeth" (setq teeth (itoa g:teeth))) ; set tile

   (if (not g:hole)                           ; if no center hole,
      (setq g:hole 0.0) )                     ;   set default 0
   (set_tile "hole" (setq hole (rtos g:hole 2 4))) ; set tile

   (if (not g:setn)                           ; if no notch flag,
      (setq g:setn 0) )                       ;   set default 0
   (set_tile "notch" (itoa g:setn))           ; set tile
```

Entering Parameters Using Dialog Boxes (Release 12 Only)

```
    (get_notch)                                 ; adjust dialog tiles

    (if (not g:nw)                              ; if no notch width;
        (setq g:nw 0.0) )                       ; set default 0
    (set_tile "width" (setq nw (rtos g:nw 2)))  ; set tile

    (if (not g:nd)                              ; if no notch depth;
        (setq g:nd 0.0) )                       ; set default 0
    (set_tile "depth" (setq nd (rtos g:nd 2)))  ; set tile

    (verify)                                    ; verify data
)
;
;----------------------------------------------------------------
;
; RS_ERROR function:
;
(defun rs_error()
   (set_tile "error" "")    ; erase error tile
)
;
;----------------------------------------------------------------
;
; OK_REAL function:
;
(defun ok_real (var vartype)
    (cond ( (distof var 2)       ; case: tile variable converts to real
            (rs_error)           ; clear error tile
            var )                ; return tile variable

          ( T                                             ; otherwise,
            (set_tile "error"                             ; display message
                (strcat "Invalid " vartype " value.") )
            nil )                                         ; return nil
    )                            ; end case
)
;
;----------------------------------------------------------------
;
; OK_INT function:
;
(defun ok_int (var)
    (cond ( (atoi var)           ; case: tile variable converts to integer
            (rs_error)           ; clear error tile
            var )                ; return tile variable
          ( T  nil)              ; otherwise, return nil
    )                            ; end case
```

```
)
;
;----------------------------------------------------------------
; GO function:
;
(defun go()
   (cond ( (verify)             ; case: data verifies OK
           (calcp)               ; calc gear parameters
           (draw)                ; draw gear
         )
         ( T (setq what_next 3) )  ; otherwise, bind what_next to 3
   )                                ; end case
)
;
;----------------------------------------------------------------
; VERIFY function:
;
(defun verify( / ok_para)
   (rs_error)                                     ; clear error tile
   (if (and (setq ok_para T)
            (/= (type g:cp) 'LIST) )              ; if no valid
       (progn (set_tile "error"                   ; center point,
              "Invalid center point.")            ; display message and
              (setq ok_para nil) ) )              ; disable further checks

   (if (and ok_para (not (> g:pc 0)))             ; if no valid
       (progn (set_tile "error"                   ; pitch circle,
              "Invalid pitch circle.")            ; display message and
              (setq ok_para nil) )  )             ; disable further checks

   (if (and ok_para (< g:teeth 14))               ; if no valid
       (progn                                     ; teeth value,
         (set_tile "error"                        ; display message and
         "Invalid value for teeth (14 or more).")
         (setq ok_para nil)  )  )                 ; disable further checks

   (if (and ok_para
            (or (>= g:hole g:pc)                  ; if center hole too big,
                (< g:hole 0)                      ; or less than zero,
                (and (= g:hole 0) (= g:setn 1)))) ; or zero w/ notch flag up,
       (progn (set_tile "error"                   ; display message and
              "Invalid center hole parameter.")
              (setq ok_para nil)  )  )            ; disable further checks

   (if (and ok_para (= g:setn 1)                  ; if notch flag is up and
```

```
                  (> g:nw (* 2 g:hole)))         ; notch width too big,
         (progn
             (set_tile "error"                    ; display message and
                "Invalid notch width parameter.")
             (setq ok_para nil) ) )               ; disable further checks

     (if (and ok_para (= g:setn 1)                ; if notch flag is up and
              (>= g:nd (- g:pc g:hole)))          ; notch depth too big,
         (progn
             (set_tile "error"                    ; display message and
                "Invalid value for notch depth.")
             (setq ok_para nil) ) )               ; disable further checks

     ok_para                                      ; return ok_para value
)
;
;-----------------------------------------------------------------------
;
; GET_X function:
;
(defun get_x()
    (rs_error)                                    ; clear error tile
    (if (ok_real                                  ; if converted to real
           (setq x_pt (get_tile "x_pt"))
              "X coordinate")
        (setq g:cp (list (distof x_pt) (distof y_pt)))  ; set G:CP to point
    )
    nil                                           ; return nil
)
;
;-----------------------------------------------------------------------
;
; GET_Y function:
;
(defun get_y()
    (rs_error)                                    ; clear error tile
    (if (ok_real                                  ; if converted to real
           (setq y_pt (get_tile "y_pt"))
              "Y coordinate")
        (setq g:cp (list (distof x_pt) (distof y_pt)))  ; set G:CP to point
    )
    nil                                           ; return nil
)
;
;-----------------------------------------------------------------------
;
; GET_PC function:
;
```

```
(defun get_pc()
   (rs_error)                                       ; clear error tile
   (if (ok_real                                     ; if converted to real
           (setq pc (get_tile "pitch"))
           "pitch radius")
       (setq g:pc (distof pc))                      ; set G:PC to pitch circle
   )
   nil                                              ; return nil
)
;
;------------------------------------------------------------
; GET_TEETH function:
;
(defun get_teeth()
   (rs_error)                                       ; clear error tile
   (if (or (not (ok_int                             ; if converted to
                   (setq teeth (get_tile "teeth"))))  ; integer
           (< (setq g:teeth (atoi teeth)) 14)       ; and valid number,
       )
       (verify)                                     ; verify data
   )
   nil                                              ; return nil
)
;
;------------------------------------------------------------
; GET_HOLE function:
;
(defun get_hole()
   (rs_error)                                       ; clear error tile
   (if (ok_real                                     ; if converted to real,
           (setq hole (get_tile "hole"))
           "center hole")
       (setq g:hole (distof hole))                  ; set G:HOLE to center hole
   )
   (if (and (> g:hole 0) (>= g:hole g:pc))          ; if valid data,
       (verify)                                     ; verify data
   )
   nil                                              ; return nil
)
;
;------------------------------------------------------------
; GET_NOTCH function:
;
(defun get_notch()
   (rs_error)                                       ; clear error tile
```

```
    (cond ( (= 0 (setq g:setn (atoi (get_tile "notch"))))    ; notch flag up?
            (mode_tile "width" 1)                            ; activate
            (mode_tile "depth" 1)                            ; tiles
          )
          ( T                                                ; otherwise,
            (mode_tile "depth" 0)                            ; deactivate
            (mode_tile "width" 0)                            ; tiles
          )
    )
    (verify)                                                 ; verify data
)
;
;------------------------------------------------------------------------
;
; GET_WIDTH function:
;
(defun get_width()
    (rs_error)                                               ; clear error tile
    (if (ok_real                                             ; if converted to real
            (setq nw (get_tile "width"))
            "notch width")
        (setq g:nw (distof nw))                              ; set G:NW to notch width
    )
    (if (and (> g:hole 0) (> g:nw (* 2 g:hole)))             ; if valid data,
        (verify)                                             ; verify data
    )
    nil                                                      ; return nil
)
;
;------------------------------------------------------------------------
;
; GET_DEPTH function:
;
(defun get_depth()
    (rs_error)                                               ; clear error tile
    (if (ok_real                                             ; if converted to real
            (setq nd (get_tile "depth"))
            "notch depth")
        (setq g:nd (distof nd))                              ; set G:ND to notch depth
    )
    (if (and (> g:hole 0) (>= g:nd (- g:pc g:hole)))         ; if valid data,
        (verify)                                             ; verify data
    )
    nil                                                      ; return nil
)
;
;------------------------------------------------------------------------
;
```

```
; RESTORE function:
(defun restore()
    (setvar "BLIPMODE" oldblp)          ; restore environment
    (setvar "CMDECHO"  oldech)          ; on normal exit or early abort
    (setvar "PICKBOX"  oldpbx)
    (setq *ERROR* olderr)
)
;
;---------------------------------------------------------------
; COMMAND FUNCTION: DDGEAR
;
(defun C:DDGEAR (/ oldblp oldech oldpbx olderr pcpt dpitch htooth xtooth
                   ss1 side what_next dcl_id pc x_pt y_pt teeth hole nd nw)

    (setq oldblp (getvar "BLIPMODE")    ;  Set up environment
          oldech (getvar "CMDECHO")
          oldpbx (getvar "PICKBOX")
          olderr *ERROR*
    )
    (setvar "BLIPMODE" 0)
    (setvar "CMDECHO"  0)
    (setvar "PICKBOX"  0)

    (defun *ERROR* (msg)                ; define custom error message
        (princ " \nERROR: ") (princ msg) ; print message
        (unload_dialog dcl_id)          ; unload dialog
        (restore)                       ; restore environment
        (princ)                         ; traditional "quiet" exit
    )

    (if (or (not g:str) (not g:dtr)     ; load Gear.Lsp functions
            (not g:pt)  (not calcp)     ; if required
            (not draw)  (not notch)
        )
        (if (findfile "gear.lsp")                   ; display error if not
            (load "GEAR")                           ; loaded
            (progn (princ "\nGEAR.LSP not found.")
                   (restore)                        ; restore environment
                   (exit)  )                        ; abort processing
        )                                           ; end if
    )                                               ; end if
```

214

Entering Parameters Using Dialog Boxes (Release 12 Only)

```
(setq dcl_id (load_dialog "gear.dcl"))        ; load dialog

(setq what_next 5)                            ; initialize loop

(while (< 2 what_next)

   (if (not (new_dialog "gear" dcl_id))       ; exit if no dialog found
       (progn (restore)                       ; restore environment
              (exit)   )                      ; abort processing
   )

   (setloc)                                   ; set defaults or current data

   (action_tile "pickpoint" "(done_dialog 4)")  ; link functions to tiles
   (action_tile "x_pt"      "(get_x)")
   (action_tile "y_pt"      "(get_y)")
   (action_tile "pitch"     "(get_pc)")
   (action_tile "teeth"     "(get_teeth)")
   (action_tile "hole"      "(get_hole)")
   (action_tile "notch"     "(get_notch)")
   (action_tile "depth"     "(get_depth)")
   (action_tile "width"     "(get_width)")
   (action_tile "accept"    "(done_dialog 1)")
   (action_tile "cancel"    "(done_dialog 0)")

   (setq what_next (start_dialog))            ; start dialog, return value to
                                              ; what_next

   (cond ( (= what_next 1)                    ; case: "accept" button picked,
           (go)                               ; create gear
         )
         ( (= what_next 4)                    ; case: "pickpoint" button picked,
                                              ; prompt for center point
            (if g:cp
              (setq g:cp (g:pt nil "\nCenter of Gear:" g:cp))
              (while (not g:cp)
                (setq g:cp (g:pt nil "\nCenter of Gear:" g:cp))
              )
            )
         )
   )                                          ; end Case
)                                             ; end what_next loop

(unload_dialog dcl_id)
```

CREATING AUTOLISP ROUTINES
CH. 7

```
    (restore)                           ; restore environment
    (princ)                             ; traditional "quiet" exit
)
;
;------------------------------------------------------------------
; EOF: DDGEAR.LSP      354 Lines
```

Several functions in DDGEAR.LSP are worth examining in greater detail.

Setloc

The Setloc function is designed to initialize local variables that contain either default values for the gear parameters the first time the routine is run, or the current global values from previous processing. Notice that a series of If functions test for the existence of global values, and initialize the local variables accordingly. Also, notice how numeric data is converted to string data, using the Rtos and Itoa functions, before assigning the data to the local variables.

Rs_error

The Rs_error function is a useful global function that sets any tile with the key "error" to a blank line. It simply calls the standard AutoLISP Set_tile function with fixed arguments.

Ok_real

The Ok_real function is another general function, extremely useful in checking string data before converting it to real-number data. If the string cannot be converted, it displays an error message on the errtile line. It requires two arguments: the data to be converted, and a string indicating the parameter type (for example, "pitch circle," "center hole," and other data required to draw the gear). This second argument is inserted into the error message, if one is to be displayed. It returns the first argument unchanged if successful.

Ok_int

Ok_int is a simplified version of Ok_real, which checks that string data can convert to an integer, but does not display an error message if unsuccessful. It requires only a single argument, and returns the argument unchanged if successful. Otherwise, it returns nil.

Verify

The Verify function sifts through the data that has been entered until it encounters some form of invalid data. It displays a message in the errtile if invalid data is found. A special local variable, Ok_para, is set to nil when an error is found, which bypasses subsequent error checking. Otherwise, it remains set at T (a symbol indicating "True" in AutoLISP). This function returns the value of Ok_para. The DDGEAR.LSP routine will not draw a gear until this function returns the "True" value.

Get_ Functions

Several functions that begin with the characters "Get_" are designed to be activated when the user selects various data-entry tiles in the dialog box. They reset the errtile line; control the entry of string data; check that it can be converted, when appropriate, using the Ok_real or OK_int functions; and return nil. For example, the Get_pc function is activated when the user selects the Pitch Radius edit box. It checks the entry, stores it to a local variable, and if the entry is convertible to a real number, sets the global variable G:pc to that numeric value. When the gear is drawn, this value is used for the pitch circle.

Get_notch

The Get_notch function is of special interest. It checks the status of the notch toggle, and if active, binds the global variable G:setn to 1 and activates the notch parameter tiles. Notice how the Mode_tile function is used to accomplish this. If the toggle is not active, it binds the global variable G:setn to zero and deactivates the notch parameter tiles. If G:setn is bound to zero, the notch is not drawn, even if defaults are stored in the G:nw and G:nd variables.

Go

The Go function executes the Verify function, and if it returns true, executes the Calcp and Draw functions, which produce the Gear. If Verify returns nil, there are errors in the data, and the Go function sets the variable What_next to 3. This variable is used to control the main loop of the routine, which continues as long as What_next has a value greater than zero. Thus, when What_next is set to 3, the program will redisplay the dialog box.

C:DDGEAR

The main function, C:DDGEAR, uses many of the functions found in GEAR.LSP, with some important extra elements added. First, code is added to load the DCL file in memory:

```
(setq dcl_id (load_dialog "gear.dcl"))
```

The Load_dialog function returns a unique integer ID number when the load is successful, and nil otherwise. In your own routines, you should store this value in a variable and use the variable to test whether the load was successful.

The next line initializes a variable used to control the program loop:

```
(setq what_next 5)
(while (< 2 what_next) ...
```

What_next will be bound to various values depending on the action of the user. Each time through the loop, the routine tests for the existence of the correct dialog box specification:

```
(if (not (new_dialog "gear" dcl_id))
    (progn (restore)
           (exit)  )
)
```

The routine aborts if anything has gone wrong.

If the routine does not abort, the routine sets up the initial values for the dialog box using the Setloc function. Then, it indicates which functions are to be called when the user selects various tiles. Notice how tiles are identified by their key expression from the GEAR.DCL file. Also, notice how the functions to be called are passed as *string arguments*, not simply as functions, to each Action_tile function:

```
(setloc)
(action_tile "pickpoint" "(done_dialog 4)")
(action_tile "x_pt"      "(get_x)")
(action_tile "y_pt"      "(get_y)")
(action_tile "pitch"     "(get_pc)")
(action_tile "teeth"     "(get_teeth)")
(action_tile "hole"      "(get_hole)")
(action_tile "notch"     "(get_notch)")
(action_tile "depth"     "(get_depth)")
(action_tile "width"     "(get_width)")
(action_tile "accept"    "(done_dialog 1)")
(action_tile "cancel"    "(done_dialog 0)")
```

Entering Parameters Using Dialog Boxes (Release 12 Only)

Finally, you are ready to display the dialog box on-screen. The Start_dialog function handles the display. At the conclusion of the dialog, the function returns an integer, which is stored in the What_next variable:

```
(setq what_next (start_dialog))
```

The user has several methods of ending the dialog: Press the OK button, the Cancel button, Ctrl-C, or ESC. The last two have the same effect as the Cancel button. Notice how pressing the Cancel button (action_tile: "cancel") calls the Done_dialog function with an argument of zero. This has the effect of exiting the Start_dialog function, and passing that zero to the What_next variable. Pressing Ctrl-C or ESC also returns a value of zero to the What_next variable.

Pressing the OK button will execute the Done_dialog function, passing 1 to the What_next variable. Notice that picking the "pickpoint" tile will pass 4 to What_next. The next lines of code evaluate the value of What_next, and branch accordingly:

```
(cond ( (= what_next 1)
        (go)
      )
      ( (= what_next 4)
        (if g:cp
          (setq g:cp (g:pt nil "\nCenter of Gear:" g:cp))
          (while (not g:cp)
            (setq g:cp (g:pt nil "\nCenter of Gear:" g:cp))
          )
        )
      )
)
```

If What_next is bound to 1, the Go function executes.

Notice how this function is invoked only *after* a call to Done_dialog. Go cannot be invoked while Start_dialog is still active, because the Command function called within Go cannot be invoked while Start_dialog is active. After Done_dialog, however, it becomes a legal function again.

(As an aside, notice that several predefined AutoLISP functions are not "legal" calls from within Start_dialog; these include Command, Prompt, and interactive Ssget, plus all the Get*xxxx* functions, display control functions, screen graphics functions, and the entity-handling functions. Consult the AutoCAD customization manual for a complete list of functions that are not permitted while Start_dialog is active.)

If the What_next variable is bound to a value of 4, the user picked the "pickpoint" tile. If this is the case, the routine issues the functions from GEAR.LSP that ask for the gear's center point. Because the value of What_next is 4, the loop will continue, and the dialog box will be redisplayed after the user picks a point. Notice how, when the loop continues, the Setloc function and Verify functions are called again, and this action places the X and Y coordinates of the selected point in their respective edit tiles.

Summary—GEAR.LSP

The work you've done with the GEAR and DDGEAR routines, hammering out all the code necessary to produce a gear using programmable dialog boxes, will give you, as a beginner, the fundamentals you need to construct useful dialog-box interfaces for your AutoLISP routines. It will also give you an effective context for further exploration and experimentation with AutoCAD's other custom dialog box features. After exploring the code in GEAR.DCL and DDGEAR.LSP, you will find that AutoCAD's custom dialog box documentation is much easier to understand, and it will greatly enhance your customization abilities.

Placing LISP Routines on a Custom Menu

You can simplify the process of loading LISP routines if you include the LOAD function as part of a custom menu macro:

```
[GEAR]^C^C(if (not C:GEAR) (load "GEAR"));GEAR;
```

The NOT function will return true if the command name C:GEAR is not bound to any value. If so, GEAR.LSP has not been loaded, and the LOAD function is evaluated. After GEAR.LSP is loaded, the command is executed. The next time this macro is selected, the loading function will not be evaluated, because C:GEAR has a value, and the NOT function will return nil.

Sharing Functions—ACAD.LSP

Whenever possible, you can conserve memory, and reduce development and loading time, by having routines share common functions. It is helpful, if you use these routines regularly, to place their common functions in the file ACAD.LSP. This special file will load automatically at the beginning of each drawing session. This may increase the time you must spend at the beginning of each drawing session, while the message "loading acad.lsp..." appears in the command prompt area. However, you needn't include these common functions in other routines that use them. Specific routines can then load only those functions that are unique to the routine, which will save time overall.

It is helpful, however, to test for the existence of common functions before calling them, as is demonstrated in DDGEAR.LSP. For example:

```
(if (not g:str)       ; function not found
    (load "GEAR")     ; load file containing function
)
```

This safety factor prevents any unwanted effects of calling routines if required functions, for whatever reason, are not present.

CHAPTER EIGHT

Entity Association Lists

AutoCAD stores all entities in a specialized entity database. AutoCAD Releases 10 and later include several powerful AutoLISP functions that allow you direct access and modification of AutoCAD's entity database, selecting items to be modified either individually or in groups. This can speed up your work by reducing the time spent in the selection process, or free you to do other work while AutoCAD performs complex selection and editing routines for you.

Entity Names and Association Lists

During a drawing session, AutoCAD assigns a unique entity name to each entity in the database. The entity name is an eight-digit number in hexadecimal notation. The internal structure of entity names and their assignment to entities is completely transparent to the user.

An entity name is a unique AutoLISP data type. When you retrieve an entity name from the underlying database by means of various predefined functions, it will be displayed in the format

<Entity name: *nnnnnnnn*>

where *nnnnnnnn* represents the numbers that make up the entity name. Several functions accept an entity name as an argument, but it either must be bound first to a memory variable or, if it is not necessary to store the entity name in memory, you may use a function that returns an entity name as an argument to a function that accepts one.

Linked to each entity name is the information required to produce that entity on the screen or plotting device. AutoCAD extracts this information for your use as an *association list*. An association list is a list composed of other, smaller lists, called *sublists*.

For example, a new line drawn in AutoCAD would automatically be given a unique entity name, and associated with that name would be an association list containing sublists that indicate:

1. The type of entity it is ("LINE").
2. The name of the layer the entity is on.
3. The line type (if not the default for the layer).

Entity Names and Association Lists

4. The start point.
5. The end point.
6. The elevation (if any, in Release 10 and earlier).
7. The Z-orientation thickness (if any).
8. The color (if not the default for the layer).
9. The extrusion vector point (used for 3D manipulation).

The first member of each sublist is a special integer called a *group code*, which identifies a particular property of the entity. For example, the first sublist in any association list is the entity name itself. The entity name always has a group code of –1. Given an entity name of 60000014, the sublist for that entity name would look like the following:

```
(-1 . <Entity name: 60000014>)
```

As a further example, the group code for the layer location of any entity is 8. Therefore, if the entity existed on layer 0, the sublist for the layer location would appear as follows:

```
(8 . "0")
```

Most association-list sublists, like the above example, contain only two members: the group code and the specific item of drawing information associated with that group code. When the sublist contains only two members, it will be displayed showing the members separated by a space, a period, and another space, as in the above examples. Such sublists are called *dotted pairs*. Association lists use dotted pairs because they use less memory than ordinary lists.

Sublists that contain coordinate point information cannot be dotted pairs, because they contain either three or four members: the group code, an X-coordinate, a Y-coordinate, and often a Z-coordinate. A dotted pair will not work here, so these sublists appear as ordinary data lists. The group codes currently used for coordinate point information are codes 10 through 16. Such coordinate-point sublists appear as in the following example, which shows a point at 12,12,0 (the trailing zeros may or may not appear on your display configuration):

```
(10 12.000000 12.000000 0.000000)
```

ENTITY ASSOCIATION LISTS
CH. 8

The use of group codes allows AutoCAD to identify any particular sublist, no matter the order in which it appears in the association list. The following group codes are common to all entities:

−1	Entity Name
0	Entity Type
5	Handle (if enabled using Handles command)
6	Line Type (if not default for layer)
8	Layer Name
38	Elevation (when not zero, in Release 10 and earlier)
39	Thickness parallel to Z-axis (when not zero)
62	Color (if not default for layer)
210	Extrusion Direction Vector (used in 3D work, to translate the entity's coordinate system to the world coordinate system)

Entity Handles

Entity handles are another means for identifying entities, available in Release 10 and later. While an entity name may change from editing session to editing session, an entity handle is permanently associated with a particular entity for as long as it exists in the drawing. Entity handles are alphanumeric strings that are assigned to entities when they are created, and placed within the association list for each entity. Entity handles are useful when creating AutoLISP functions that must automatically access the same set of entities in a drawing across many editing sessions. To use entity handles, you must explicitly instruct AutoCAD to assign them by means of the Handles command. Entity handles should not be used unless required by an AutoCAD application (such as the SQL interface), because they can significantly increase the size of AutoCAD's underlying drawing database.

Entity Access Functions

As mentioned earlier, association lists are long lists containing sublists, all enclosed within matched sets of parentheses. Because they all adhere to this structure, they can be used and modified by AutoLISP functions. Some functions have been predefined to act exclusively upon association lists. Predefined AutoLISP functions that act on entity association lists begin with the letters "ENT," and are summarized in this chapter.

Creating Entities with Entmake

It is possible to create entities directly, without resorting to AutoCAD drawing commands. The following code fragment creates a line segment between two points and adds it to the drawing:

```
(entmake (list (cons 0 "LINE")
               (cons 10 '(0 0 0))
               (cons 11 '(5 5 0))
         )
)
```

Notice that the argument for the Entmake function is an association list, created by AutoLISP's List function. The list function has three arguments, each a sublist created using the Cons function:

1. The argument

    (cons 0 "LINE")

    returns

    (0 . "LINE")

    a dotted pair indicating the entity type.

2. The argument

    (cons 10 '(0 0 0))

    returns

    (10 0.000 0.000 0.000)

    a list indicating the starting point.

ENTITY ASSOCIATION LISTS
CH. 8

3. the argument

   `(cons 11 '(5 5 0))`

   returns

   `( 11 5.000 5.000 0.000 )`

   a list indicating the ending point.

The above sublists combine to form the minimum information required by AutoCAD to create a line. This example produces a line in the drawing editor from points 0,0,0 to 5,5,0. Because other information such as a layer name or color was not included, AutoCAD assumes default values for these items when it creates the line segment; they include the current layer plus the current layer's color and linetype, and the default line thickness along the current Z-axis.

AutoCAD automatically assigns the line's entity name (group code –1), entity handle (group code 5 if handles are enabled), and extrusion direction vector (group code 210). Therefore, these group codes are never used in a List function being passed to Entmake. You can include the other optional information associated with the line by providing the necessary arguments to List. For example,

```
(entmake (list (cons 0 "LINE")
               (cons 10 '(0 0 0))
               (cons 11 '(5 5 0))
               (cons 62 3)
               (cons 8 "Floor_Plan")
         )
)
```

would create the same line, green color (group code 62; color code 3) on layer "Floor_Plan" (group code 8, plus the layer name).

Keep the following tips in mind when using Entmake to create entities:

1. Construct sublists, especially dotted pairs, using the Cons function, to guarantee readability by AutoCAD.

2. Enclose all sublists within an overall list, using the List function. This creates an association list.

3. All group codes and associated values must be valid for the type of entity you create.

Entity Access Functions

4. For greatest accuracy, include Z-coordinates for points passed to Entmake, even if they are zero.

When AutoCAD is able to create the entity successfully, the Entmake function returns the new entity's association list (not including the new entity name or handle). If AutoCAD cannot create the entity for any reason, Entmake returns nil.

The following list shows the minimum information required to create standard AutoCAD drawing entities with Entmake. Additional group code sublists may be added to make entity definitions more complete. For additional sublists, follow the format as illustrated here. Boldface indicates values you must supply, such as strings, points, or angles. String values are indicated by quotes. Numeric values are real numbers, except where specifically indicated as integers. Angles are expressed in radians.

1. To create a Point, the Entmake function requires the following syntax:

```
(entmake (list (cons 0 "POINT")
               (cons 10 point)
         )
)
```

2. To create a Line, Entmake requires the following:

```
(entmake (list (cons 0 "LINE")
               (cons 10 start point)
               (cons 11 end point)
         )
)
```

3. To create an Arc, Entmake requires the following:

```
(entmake (list (cons 0 "ARC")
               (cons 10 center point)
               (cons 40 bulge factor)
               (cons 50 start angle)
               (cons 51 end angle)
         )
)
```

4. To create a Circle, Entmake requires the following:

```
(entmake (list (cons 0 "CIRCLE")
               (cons 10 center point)
               (cons 40 radius)
         )
)
```

5. To create a Trace, Entmake requires the following:

   ```
   (entmake (list (cons 0 "TRACE")
                  (cons 10 1st corner point)
                  (cons 11 2nd corner point)
                  (cons 12 3rd corner point)
                  (cons 13 4th corner point)
            )
   )
   ```

6. To create a Shape, Entmake requires the following:

   ```
   (entmake (list (cons 0 "SHAPE")
                  (cons 2 "shape name")
                  (cons 10 insert point)
            )
   )
   ```

7. To create a Solid, Entmake requires the following (if the figure is three-sided, two adjacent points must be the same point):

   ```
   (entmake (list (cons 0 "SOLID")
                  (cons 10 1st corner point)
                  (cons 11 2nd corner point)
                  (cons 12 3rd corner point)
                  (cons 13 4th corner point)
            )
   )
   ```

8. To create a 3D Face, Entmake requires the following (if the figure is three-sided, two adjacent points must be the same point):

   ```
   (entmake (list (cons 0 "3DFACE")
                  (cons 10 1st corner point)
                  (cons 11 2nd corner point)
                  (cons 12 3rd corner point
                  (cons 13 4th corner point)
            )
   )
   ```

9. To create a Text entity, Entmake requires the following:

   ```
   (entmake (list (cons 0 "TEXT")
                  (cons 1 "Text String")
                  (cons 10 start point)
                  (cons 40 text height)
            )
   )
   ```

Entity Access Functions

10. To create a Block Definition, Entmake requires the following (group code sublists for a Block Definition should be supplied in this order: 0, 2, 70, 10):

    ```
    (entmake (list (cons 0 "BLOCK")
                   (cons 2 "block name")
                   (cons 70 integer block flag)
                   (cons 10 insertion point)
             )
    )
    ```

11. To create an Attribute Definition, Entmake requires the following:

    ```
    (entmake (list (cons 0 "ATTDEF")
                   (cons 1 "Default Value")
                   (cons 2 "Attribute Tag")
                   (cons 3 "Prompt")
                   (cons 10 insert point)
                   (cons 40 text height)
                   (cons 70 attribute flag)
             )
    )
    ```

12. To create a Block End-of-Definition, Entmake requires the following:

    ```
    (entmake (list (cons 0 "ENDBLK")
             )
    )
    ```

13. To create a Normal Block Insertion, Entmake requires the following:

    ```
    (entmake (list (cons 0 "INSERT")
                   (cons 2 block name)
                   (cons 10 insert point)
             )
    )
    ```

14. To create an Insert with attributes, Entmake requires the following:

    ```
    (entmake (list (cons 0 "INSERT")
                   (cons 2 block name)
                   (cons 10 insert point)
                   (cons 66 1)
             )
    )
    ```

ENTITY ASSOCIATION LISTS
CH. 8

15. To create an Insert Block Attribute, Entmake requires the following:

```
(entmake (list (cons 0 "ATTRIB")
               (cons 1 "Attribute Value")
               (cons 2 "Attribute Tag")
               (cons 10 insert point)
               (cons 40 text height)
               (cons 70 integer attribute flag)
         )
)
```

16. To create a 2D Polyline header, Entmake requires the following:

```
(entmake (list (cons 0 "POLYLINE")
         )
)
```

17. To create a 2D Polyline vertex, Entmake requires the following:

```
(entmake (list (cons 0 "VERTEX")
               (cons 10 point)
         )
)
```

18. To create a 3D polyline header, Entmake requires the following:

```
(entmake (list (cons 0 "POLYLINE")
               (cons 70 8)
         )
)
```

19. To create a 3D Polyline vertex, Entmake requires the following:

```
(entmake (list (cons 0 "VERTEX")
               (cons 10 point)
               (cons 70 32)
         )
)
```

20. To create an End-of-Sequence, Entmake requires the following:

```
(entmake (list (cons 0 "SEQEND")
         )
)
```

Entity Access Functions

Retrieving Entities from the Database

Once entities are stored within the database, you can retrieve them and modify their properties. Retrieving and acting upon entity association lists is a three-step process:

1. The entity name is retrieved from the drawing database.
2. Sublists associated with that entity name are retrieved and modified by referencing the appropriate group code.
3. The entire association list is updated in the drawing database to include the changed entities.

Several functions can be used to retrieve entities. Consider the following example, which will retrieve the last entity in the database, storing it in the variable Ent:

`(setq ent (entlast))`

You can ask AutoCAD to pause and wait for the user to select an individual entity:

`(entsel)`

This function displays AutoCAD's "Select objects:" prompt. When the user selects an entity, it returns in a list containing the entity name and the point used to select it. For example:

`( (-1 . <Entity name: 60000014>) (5.000000 5.000000 0.000000) )`

This structure is useful within routines that require both items of information. To isolate the entity name, place the Entsel function with the Car function:

`(car (entsel) )`

Also, since you are likely to want to store the entity in a variable, add the Setq function:

`(setq ent (car (entsel) ) )`

Once you have bound a variable to an entity name, you can loop through the database using the Entnext function, with the entity name as an argument. The following function takes the entity to which Ent is bound, and stores the following entity in the database back into Ent:

`(setq ent (entnext ent))`

ENTITY ASSOCIATION LISTS
CH. 8

You could loop through the database, starting with a selected entity, using the following code:

```
(setq ent (car (entsel)))
(while ent
   ; add some code here to process the entity bound to Ent
   (setq ent (entnext ent))  ; loop to the next entity
)
```

In the above example, after you have selected an entity in the database, the While loop will cause AutoCAD to access each following entity, until no more were found, at which point Ent would be bound to nil, and the loop would end.

Once an entity name is retrieved from the database, you can extract the association list and modify it, using a series of functions. The Entget function returns the association list for a selected entity:

```
(setq alist (entget ent))
```

For example, suppose the drawing contains a green line that begins at point 0,0,0 and ends at point 5,5,0. It is located on layer Zero. If this entity is bound to the variable Ent, the above example would return an association list similar to the following, and bind it to the Alist variable:

```
(
    (-1 . <Entity name: 60000014>)
    ( 0 . "LINE")
    ( 8 . "0")
    (10   0.000000   0.000000   0.000000)
    (11   5.000000   5.000000   0.000000)
    (210  0.000000   0.000000   1.000000)
    (62 . 3)
)
```

If you try this using AutoCAD, you will find that the association list is returned in a continuous stream of characters. Here it is indented and formatted for clarity's sake.

Having extracted the association list for an entity, you may now isolate one or more of its sublists, referencing them by their group codes. For example,

```
(setq color (assoc 62 alist) )
```

returns the color code sublist

```
(62 . 3)
```

Entity Access Functions

and binds the sublist to the Color variable. If no color code sublist exists, the entity is the color assigned to its layer, and the Assoc function returns nil.

If the color variable is not nil, you can further isolate the color value from the sublist using the Cdr function:

```
(setq cvalue (cdr color))
```

(Cdr color) returns 3, storing it to the variable Cvalue. Suppose you want to use AutoLISP to change the color of the selected entity from 3 (green on most systems) to 1 (red on most systems). After extracting the color sublist using the above sequence, use the Subst function to change the entire association list:

```
(setq alist          ; Alist will be rebound to the modified list
  (subst              ; This function returns modified lists
    (cons 62 1)       ; New sublist for color value (62 . 1)
    color             ; The current sublist, (62 . 3)
    alist             ; The current association list
  )
)
```

After you execute this function, the Alist variable contains a modified association list, almost identical with the one previously bound to Alist, except that it now contains the new color value sublist. Next, invoke the function

```
(entmod alist)
```

which updates the entity in the drawing database.

This sequence works well when a sublist you intend to change already exists in the association list. The sequence is different if the new sublist must be added to the association list.

In the following example, assume that you created a value for Alist as you did in the previous example, except that Alist does not contain a sublist for color. Instead of the Subst function, use the Append function to add the new sublist to the association list:

```
(setq alist        ; a new value will be bound to Alist
  (append          ; merge lists into one list. Include:
    alist                 ; the current association list,
    (list (cons 62 1)) ; with a list containing the new sublist
  )
)
```

235

ENTITY ASSOCIATION LISTS
CH. 8

In the above example, the Alist variable is bound to a modified association list. Notice that the Append function accepts only lists as arguments, and it combines the members of each list into one list. Although the dotted pair returned by the Cons function is a list, it cannot be supplied directly as an argument to the Append function. If you did so, only the paired data would be appended, instead of the sublist as a unit. Therefore, the dotted pair returned by the Cons function must be contained within a list before you can pass it as an argument to Append. This way, the whole dotted pair is appended as a unit, not just its member data.

If you want to change colors frequently using AutoLISP, all the functions in the above sequence could be combined into a compact function:

```
(defun newcolor( ent newc / alist)
   (if         ; test for existence of a current color sublist
     (setq sublst                        ; set sublst variable
        (assoc 62                        ; seek color sublist
           (setq alist (entget ent))     ; set current assoc list
        )
     )
     (entmod    ; if there's a current color sublist, modify
        (subst
           (cons 62 newc)                ; create new color sublist
           sublst                        ; instead of current sublist
           alist                         ; in current assoc list
        )                                ; end Subst function
     )                                   ; end Entmod function
     (entmod    ; if there's no current color sublist, modify
        (append                          ; Append function merges lists
           alist                         ; take current assoc list
           (list (cons 62 newc))  ; combine new color sublist
        )                                ; end Append function
     )                                   ; end Entmod function
   )                                     ; end If function
)                                        ; end Defun function
```

After defining this function, try the following syntax:

```
(newcolor (car (entsel)) 1)
(newcolor (entlast) 1)
```

The first example will have the effect of changing the color of a single entity you pick, unless it is already the color represented by color code 1 on your system. The second example will cause the last entity in the database to change color to 1.

This model can be applied to changing any sublist in the drawing, except entity names and handles.

WALLS.LSP

Extracting association lists and acting upon them, as well as adding new entities to the drawing via Entmake, takes some practice. In this section you will study a complex parametric routine that makes use of entity access functions for speed and reliability.

WALLS.LSP is a routine that draws walls in three dimensions using 3D faces. It has the added feature of allowing you to enter parameters for giving the walls a specific thickness, and placing rectangular openings in the walls, for windows and doors, as you create them.

In a manner similar to the Line and Pline commands, you can create a series of connected walls, and as you add additional wall sections, the intersecting corners are beveled. Finally, you can close up the wall segments by entering "C" or "Close" when prompted for a new wall segment.

This presents several problems to the AutoLISP routine. First, the routine must store all the necessary entity information about the first wall section, in case the user enters "C" or "Close." The routine must, in that circumstance, bevel the corner formed by the starting and ending wall sections. Next, the routine must always record not only the current wall section, but also the previous section, so that it may make the necessary changes to the corners, depending on the angle formed by the two sections.

Finally, the routine must account for multiple openings in a single section. It does so by the simple expedient of requiring only one opening per wall, but allowing the user to enter wall sections that are adjacent to one another, and modifying their appearance on the fly, to present the illusion of a single wall containing multiple openings.

Following is the pseudocode for WALLS.LSP:

1. Prompt for wall thickness and wall height.
2. Prompt for a starting point and ending point of the wall section.
3. Draw a reference line for the wall segment at floor level.

4. Prompt for the side of the reference line on which to offset the wall thickness.
5. Prompt for a window insertion point on the reference line.
6. If no window point is entered, skip steps 7 and 8.
7. Prompt for a window width and height.
8. Prompt for a window elevation above floor level. An elevation of zero indicates that a door is being drawn.
9. Erase the reference line.
10. Calculate all necessary points to draw intersecting 3D faces that represent the wall section (and opening, if present).
11. Create the faces using the calculated points, including selected invisible edges to provide the illusion that the wall is a single segment.
12. Save necessary information about the faces, to modify the intersection of this wall and the next wall section in the series, if any.
13. If this is the first wall in the series, store information about its faces, in case the wall sections are closed at the end.
14. If this is not the first wall in the series, upon completion of the current wall section, determine if the current and previous wall sections are at an angle, or adjacent.
15. If at an angle, modify the faces in both wall sections so they intersect at the corner.
16. If adjacent, modify the intersecting edges so that they are invisible, thus giving the illusion of an extended wall section.
17. For each new wall section in the series, repeat steps 2 through 16.
18. If at least two walls are drawn and the user enters "C" or "Close" in response to a prompt for the next wall section, draw the reference line from the end point of the previous wall section to the start point of the first wall section. Prompt for an opening as before, and update the corners on both ends of the final wall section.

WALLS.LSP

Figure 8.1 illustrates a typical output of WALLS.LSP.

FIGURE 8.1:
Output of WALLS.LSP

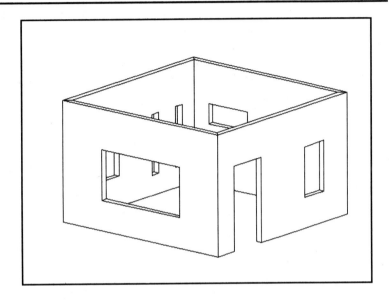

Listing 8.1 contains the complete source code for the routine.

Listing 8.1: WALLS.LSP Source Code

```
; FILE NAME:      WALLS.Lsp
; Written by:     Bob Thomas
(Prompt "\nLoading WALLS.LSP (2.0) ... ")    ; standard loading prompt
;--------------------------------------------------------------------
; C:WALLS Function:
(defun C:WALLS(/ c_sp c_ep o_sp o_ep z_sp z_osp z_ep z_oep    ; local vars
                 l_left wll wlr wul wur o_wll o_wlr o_wul o_wur
                 np z_np i_sp i_osp i_oep i_zosp i_zoep
                 c_osp c_oep c_zosp c_zoep p_osp p_oep p_zosp p_zoep
                 ent1 uline c_top i_top p_top f1 f2 f3 f4 i_f1 p_f3
                 i_of1 i_of2 i_of3 p_of1 p_of2 p_of3 p_of4
                 c_of1 c_of2 c_of3 c_of4 t_angl wset)

    (setq oldblp (getvar "BLIPMODE"))          ; store current environment
```

```
                oldech  (getvar "CMDECHO")    oldos  (getvar "OSMODE")
                ce      (getvar "ELEVATION")  olderr *ERROR*
                wset    (ssadd)

                start T          ; set flag to indicate starting wall section
        )                        ; end setq
(setvar "CMDECHO" 0)                          ; set up environment
(command ".undo" "g")
(setvar "BLIPMODE" 0)

(defun *ERROR* (msg)                          ; define error-handler
   (setvar "BLIPMODE" oldblp) (setvar "OSMODE" oldos)
   (command ".undo" "e") (command ".u")
   (setvar "CMDECHO" oldech)
   (princ msg) (setq *ERROR* olderr)
   (princ)
)
cond ( (or (not G:STR)           ; check for global functions
           (not G:DIST)
       )
       (prompt
           "\n*ERROR*: Global functions G:STR or G:DIST not loaded.\n")
       (exit)
     )
)

(setq g:ww (g:dist nil "\nWall width: " g:ww))    ; prompt for wall width
(while (not g:ww)
   (setq g:ww (g:dist nil "\nWall width: " g:ww))
)

(setq g:wh (g:dist nil "\nWall height: " g:wh))   ; prompt for wall height
(while (not g:wh)

   (setq g:wh (g:dist nil "\nWall height: " g:wh))
)

(initget 1)
(setq c_sp (getpoint    "\nStart point: "))  ; prompt for start point
(initget 1)
(setq c_ep (getpoint c_sp "\nTo point: "))   ; and first end point
```

WALLS.LSP

```
    (setq uline (makeline c_sp c_ep) )          ; draw first reference line
                                                ; save it to erase later

(getoffset)                                     ; get wall offset side

(wdraw)                                         ; draw the first wall

(setq i_sp c_sp                                 ; update drawing variables
      c_sp c_ep)

(while (and (not (equal c_ep nil))              ; loop while user enters
            (not (equal c_ep i_sp))             ; new wall points
            (not (equal c_ep "Close"))
       )

    (initget "Close")
    (setq c_ep (getpoint c_sp "\nTo Point: "))  ; prompt for wall end

    (cond
        ( (equal c_ep nil)                      ; Enter key pressed (no close)
          (makeface c_sp o_ep z_oep             ; draw end face only
              (list (car c_sp)
                    (cadr c_sp)
                    (+ ce g:wh)
              )
              0
          )
        )                                       ; end case no close

        ( (or (equal c_ep i_sp)                 ; closing walls up
              (equal c_ep "Close")
          )
          (closeup)
        ) ; end case closing

        ( T                                     ; otherwise, continue
          (if (< tang pi)
                             (wallpt '+)
              (wallpt '-)
          )
          (wdraw)
          (wedit)
          (setq c_sp c_ep)
        )                                       ; end case continuing
```

ENTITY ASSOCIATION LISTS
CH. 8

```
            )                               ; end cond

        )                                   ; end while

    (setvar "BLIPMODE" oldblp) (setvar "OSMODE" oldos)  ; restore environment
    (command ".undo" "e")      (setvar "CMDECHO" oldech)
    (setq *ERROR* olderr)

    (princ)                    ; quiet

)                              ; End C:WALLS

;----------------------------------------------------------------------
; WDRAW function:

(defun wdraw()

    (if (< tang pi)                 ; calculate offset points for wall
        (wallpt '+)
        (wallpt '-)
    )
    (setq z_sp  (list (car c_sp) (cadr c_sp) (+ ce g:wh))
          z_ep  (list (car c_ep) (cadr c_ep) (+ ce g:wh))
          z_osp (list (car o_sp) (cadr o_sp) (+ ce g:wh))
          z_oep (list (car o_ep) (cadr o_ep) (+ ce g:wh))
    )

; if not the first wall, draw a reference line for the user:

    (if (not start)
        (setq uline (makeline c_sp c_ep) )
    )

    (getwindow)

    (entdel uline)

; if this is not the first wall in the series, test the angle formed
; by the walls to determine if beveling is necessary:

    (if (not start)
        (if (< (setq t_angl (- (angle c_sp c_oep) (angle c_sp o_sp))) 0)
            (setq t_angl (+ t_angl (* 2 pi)))
        )
```

WALLS.LSP

```
        )
    (cond ( start                                   ; drawing walls -- setup
            (setq ent1 (makeface c_sp o_sp z_osp z_sp 0))
            (addset wset)
          )
    )
    (if (not l_left)                    ; if plain wall (no window)
        (d_pwall)                       ; draw plain wall faces
        (d_wwall)                       ; draw wall faces with opening
    )

    (setq c_top (makeface z_sp z_ep z_oep z_osp 0))   ; top off
    (addset wset)
    (if start (setq i_top c_top p_top c_top start nil))
)
) ; End WDRAW

;----------------------------------------------------------------------
; WEDIT Function:

(defun wedit()

   (cond ( (>= t_angl 0.003)                  ; if angle is wide enough, bevel
           (prompt "\nBeveling walls...")
           (setq np   (inters p_osp p_oep c_osp c_oep nil)
                 z_np (inters p_zosp p_zoep c_zosp c_zoep nil)
           )
           (modify p_of3 11 np)
           (modify p_of3 12 z_np)
           (modify c_of1 10 np)
           (modify c_of1 13 z_np)
           (modify p_top 12 z_np)
           (modify c_top 13 z_np)
           (if c_of2
               (modify c_of2 13 z_np)
           )
           (if c_of4
               (modify c_of4 10 np)
           )
           (if p_of2
               (modify p_of2 12 z_np)
           )
           (if p_of4
```

```
                    (modify p_of4 11 np)
                )
                (rdwset wset)
            )
            ( T                  ; otherwise, hide edges to look like one wall
                (accum p_of3 70 2)
                (accum c_of1 70 8)
                (accum p_top 70 2)
                (accum c_top 70 8)
                (accum f1 70 8)
                (accum p_f3 70 2)
            )
        ) ; end cond

        (setq p_top c_top        ; update entities that may be edited next time
              p_f3 f3
              p_of2 c_of2
              p_of3 c_of3
              p_of4 c_of4
              p_osp c_osp
              p_oep c_oep
              p_zosp c_zosp
              p_zoep c_zoep
        )
) ; End WEDIT

;--------------------------------------------------------------------
; ** UTILITY FUNCTIONS:
; ADDSET Function:

(defun addset( s_set )
    (if (= (type s_set) 'PICKSET)      ; add entity to selection set
        (ssadd (entlast) s_set)
    )
)

;--------------------------------------------------------------------
; WALLPT Function:

(defun wallpt( x )        ; calculate base offset points
    (if (= x '+)
        (setq o_sp (polar c_sp (+ (angle c_sp c_ep) 1.570796) g:ww)
              o_ep (polar c_ep (+ (angle c_sp c_ep) 1.570796) g:ww))
        (setq o_sp (polar c_sp (- (angle c_sp c_ep) 1.570796) g:ww)
              o_ep (polar c_ep (- (angle c_sp c_ep) 1.570796) g:ww))))
```

```
;------------------------------------------------------------------
; MODIFY Function:

(defun modify( ent code nvalue / cvalue alist)
   (if (and (= (type ent) 'ENAME)
            (= (type code) 'INT)
       )
      (if (setq cvalue
                  (assoc code                        ; if sublist exists,
                     (setq alist (entget ent))
                  )
          )
          (entmod (subst (cons code nvalue)          ; change existing sublist
                     cvalue
                     alist
                  )
          )
          (entmod (append alist                      ; otherwise, add new sublist
                     (list (cons code nvalue))
                  )
          )
      )
   )
)

;------------------------------------------------------------------
; RDWSET Function:

(defun rdwset( s_set / i ss_len)
   (cond ( (and (= (type s_set) 'PICKSET)
                (= (type (setq ss_len (sslength s_set))) 'INT)
           )
           (setq i -1)
           (repeat ss_len                            ; loop through set
              (redraw (ssname s_set                  ; redrawing each entity
                         (setq i (1+ i))             ; update index
                      )
              )
           )
         )
   )
)

;------------------------------------------------------------------
```

```
; ACCUM Function:

(defun accum( ent code acc / x )
    (if (and (= (type ent) 'ENAME)                  ; if existing sublist
             (setq x (cdr (assoc code (entget ent))))) ; get current value
        )
        (modify ent code (+ x acc))                 ; modify, adding new value
    )
)

;------------------------------------------------------------------
; MAKEFACE Function:

(defun makeface(p0 p1 p2 p3 edges)
    (if (< edges 0)                                 ; set edges=0 if nil
        (setq edges 0)
    )
    (if (entmake (list (cons 0  "3Dface")           ; Build the face.  IF built,
                       (cons 10 p0)
                       (cons 11 p1)
                       (cons 12 p2)
                       (cons 13 p3)
                       (cons 70 edges)
                 )
        )
        (entlast)                                   ; return the entity name
    )
)

;------------------------------------------------------------------
; MAKELINE Function:

(defun makeline(p0 p1)
    (if (entmake (list (cons 0 "LINE")              ; Build the line. IF built,
                       (cons 10 p0)
                       (cons 11 p1)
                 )
        )
        (entlast)                                   ; return the entity name
    )
)

;------------------------------------------------------------------
; GETLL Function:
```

WALLS.LSP

```
(defun getll()
   (setvar "OSMODE" 512)          ; set Osnap "Near" on
   (setq l_left                   ; get insertion point for window
     (getpoint "\nWindow insert point on wall line (RETURN=no window): ")
   )
   (setvar "OSMODE" 0)            ; set Osnap "None"
   l_left                         ; return point value
)

;------------------------------------------------------------------
; GETWINDOW Function:

(defun getwindow( / valid)

   (while (not valid)                        ; while valid response flag=nil

      (while ( and (getll)                              ; get insertion point
               (not (inters c_sp c_ep l_left l_left) )  ; check if on
           )                                            ; reference line
         (prompt
            "\n*ERROR*: Window insert point not on wall line.")
      )

      (cond ( l_left                          ; OK insertion point
              (setq g:w_wid (g:dist l_left "\nWindow width: " g:w_wid ))
              (while (not g:w_wid)
                 (setq g:w_wid (g:dist l_left "\nWindow width: " g:w_wid ))
              )
              (if (> (+ (distance c_sp l_left) g:w_wid) (distance c_sp c_ep))
                  (prompt (strcat "\n*ERROR*: Window width is greater "
                          "than wall length,\nor insert point "
                          "is too close to wall end point. "))

                  (setq valid T)    ; set flag if window insert OK
              )
            )
            ( T (setq valid T) )              ; otherwise, no insertion point
      )                             ; end case window insert picked

   )                                ; end while not valid response

   (cond ( l_left                   ; continue, if insert point was picked
```

```
            (setq valid nil)          ; set valid response flag nil
            (while (not valid)

                (setq g:w_ht (g:dist l_left "\nWindow height: " g:w_ht ))
                (while (not g:w_ht)
                    (setq g:w_ht (g:dist l_left "\nWindow height: " g:w_ht ))
                )
                (setq g:w_el (g:dist l_left "\nWindow elevation: " g:w_el ))
                (while (not g:w_el)
                    (setq g:w_el (g:dist l_left "\nWindow elevation: " g:w_el ))
                )

                (if (> (+ g:w_ht g:w_el) g:wh)
                    (prompt (strcat "\n*ERROR*: Window height+elevation "
                        "exceeds wall height."))
                    (setq valid T)
                )

            )                         ; end while

; set window point variables:

            (setq lr (polar l_left (angle c_sp c_ep) g:w_wid)
                  wll (list (car l_left) (cadr l_left) (+ ce g:w_el))
                  wlr (list (car lr) (cadr lr) (+ ce g:w_el))
                  wur (list (car lr) (cadr lr) (+ ce g:w_el g:w_ht))
                  wul (list (car l_left) (cadr l_left) (+ ce g:w_el g:w_ht))
            )
            (if (< tang pi)
                (setq o_wll (polar wll (+ (angle c_sp c_ep) 1.570796) g:ww)
                      o_wlr (polar wlr (+ (angle c_sp c_ep) 1.570796) g:ww)
                      o_wul (polar wul (+ (angle c_sp c_ep) 1.570796) g:ww)
                      o_wur (polar wur (+ (angle c_sp c_ep) 1.570796) g:ww))
                (setq o_wll (polar wll (- (angle c_sp c_ep) 1.570796) g:ww)
                      o_wlr (polar wlr (- (angle c_sp c_ep) 1.570796) g:ww)
                      o_wul (polar wul (- (angle c_sp c_ep) 1.570796) g:ww)
                      o_wur (polar wur (- (angle c_sp c_ep) 1.570796) g:ww)
                )
            )
        )                      ; end case window insert picked
    )                          ; end cond
)

;------------------------------------------------------------------------
; D_PWALL Function:
```

WALLS.LSP

```
(defun d_pwall()

    (prompt "\nDrawing plain wall...")
    (setq f1 (makeface c_sp c_ep z_ep z_sp 0)     ; draw and store faces
          f3 f1
    )
    (addset wset)
    (if start (setq i_f1 (entlast)                ; store if first section
                    p_f3 i_f1
              )
    )
    (setq c_of1 (makeface o_sp o_ep z_oep z_osp 0))  ; draw and store offset
    (addset wset)
    (if start (setq i_osp o_sp                    ; store points if first
                    i_oep o_ep                    ; wall section
                    i_zosp z_osp
                    i_zoep z_oep
                    i_of1 c_of1
                    i_of2 nil
                    i_of4 nil
                    p_osp o_sp
                    p_oep o_ep
                    p_zosp z_osp
                    p_zoep z_oep
              )
    )
    (setq c_osp o_sp                              ; store points for
          c_oep o_ep                              ; current wall section
          c_zosp z_osp
          c_zoep z_oep
          c_of3 c_of1
          c_of2 nil
          c_of4 nil
    )
    (if start (setq p_of3 c_of3) )
)

;----------------------------------------------------------------
; D_WWALL Function:

(defun d_wwall()

    (prompt "\nDrawing window/wall...")
    (setq f1 (makeface c_sp wll wul z_sp         ; draw and store face
```

ENTITY ASSOCIATION LISTS
CH. 8

```
              (if (<= g:w_el 0) 4 5 )      ; set invisible edge(s)
       )                                   ; based on window elevation
)
(addset wset)                              ; add to selection set
(if start (setq i_f1 f1))                  ; store face if first wall

(makeface wul wur z_ep z_sp 10)            ; draw and store face
(addset wset)                              ; add to selection set
(setq f3 (makeface wlr c_ep z_ep wur       ; draw and store face
              (if (<= g:w_el 0) 4 5 )      ; set invisible edge(s)
       )                                   ; based on window elevation
)
(addset wset)                              ; add to selection set
(if start (setq p_f3 f3))                  ; store face if first wall

(cond ( (> g:w_el 0)                       ; if window elevation not zero
        (makeface c_sp c_ep wlr wll 10)    ; draw and store last face
        (addset wset)                      ; add to selection set
      )
)

(setq c_of1 (makeface o_sp o_wll o_wul z_osp ; draw and store offset face
              (if (<= g:w_el 0) 4 5 )      ; set invisible edge(s)
       )                                   ; based on window elevation
)
(addset wset)                              ; add to selection set

(if start
    (setq i_osp o_sp                       ; store points if first wall section
          i_oep o_ep
          i_zosp z_osp
          i_zoep z_oep
          i_of1 c_of1
          p_osp o_sp
          p_oep o_ep
          p_zosp z_osp
          p_zoep z_oep
    )
)
(setq c_osp o_sp                           ; store points for current wall section
      c_oep o_ep
      c_zosp z_osp
      c_zoep z_oep
)
(setq c_of2                                ; draw and store
```

WALLS.LSP

```
                (makeface o_wul o_wur z_oep z_osp 10)   ; offset face
        )
        (addset wset)                                   ; add to selection set
        (if start                                       ; store face if first wall
            (setq i_of2 c_of2
                  p_of2 c_of2
            )
        )

        (setq c_of3
              (makeface o_wlr o_ep z_oep o_wur         ; draw and store offset face
                        (if (<= g:w_el 0) 4 5 )        ; set invisible edge(s)
              )                                        ; based on window elevation
        )
        (addset wset)                                  ; add to selection set
        (if start (setq p_of3 c_of3))                  ; store face if first wall

        (cond ( (> g:w_el 0)
                (setq c_of4                            ; draw and store
                      (makeface o_sp o_ep o_wlr o_wll 10)  ; last offset face
                )
                (addset wset)                          ; add to selection set
              )
              ( T (setq c_of4 nil) )   ; otherwise, set last face variable nil
        )
        (if start
            (setq i_of4 c_of4                          ; store face if first wall
                  p_of4 c_of4
            )
        )
        (makeface wll o_wll o_wul wul 0)               ; draw window faces
        (makeface wul o_wul o_wur wur 0)
        (makeface wlr o_wlr o_wur wur 0)
        (if (> g:w_el 0)                               ; if window elevation not zero
            (makeface wll o_wll o_wlr wlr 0)           ; draw bottom window face
        )
)

;------------------------------------------------------------------------
; GETOFFSET Function:

(defun getoffset( / op)

    (initget 1)
    (setq op (getpoint "\nPick side to offset: "))
```

```
    (setq tang (- (angle c_sp op)          ; setup test angle
                  (angle c_sp c_ep)
            )
    )
    (if (< tang 0)                          ; correct angle to determine offset
        (setq tang (+ tang (* 2 pi)))       ; if less than zero
    )
)

;------------------------------------------------------------------
; CLOSEUP Function:

(defun closeup()
   (if (equal c_ep "Close")                 ; if entered "C" or "Close"
       (setq c_ep i_sp)                     ; set current end point=initial start point
   )

   (if (< tang pi)                          ; calculate base offset points
       (wallpt '+)
       (wallpt '-)
   )

   (wdraw)                  ; draw wall
   (wedit)                  ; update faces

   (if (< (setq t_angl                      ; check angle of new wall.
                (- (angle i_sp o_ep)        ; If not tangent,
                   (angle i_sp i_osp)       ; angle trim is in order...
                )
          )
          0
       )
       (setq t_angl (+ t_angl (* 2 pi)))
   )                                        ; end if

   (entdel ent1)                            ; delete starting face

   (cond ( (< t_angl 0.003)                 ; if angle indicates wall extension,
           (accum i_f1 70 8)                ; hide edges to smooth wall
           (accum i_of1 70 8)
           (accum f3 70 2)
           (accum c_of3 70 2)
           (accum c_top 70 2)
```

WALLS.LSP

```
            (accum i_top 70 8)
         )                             ; end case: not beveling
         ( T            ; otherwise, bevel closing intersection
            (setq np
               (inters i_osp i_oep c_osp c_oep nil)      ; calc intersection
            )
            (setq z_np
               (inters i_zosp i_zoep c_zosp c_zoep nil)
            )
            (modify i_of1 10 np)             ; update initial faces
            (modify i_of1 13 z_np)
            (if i_of2
               (modify i_of2 13 z_np)
            )
            (if i_of4
               (modify i_of4 10 np)
            )
            (modify i_top 13 z_np)
            (modify c_top 12 z_np)
            (modify c_of3 11 np)
            (modify c_of3 12 z_np)
            (if c_of2
               (modify c_of2 12 z_np)
            )
            (if c_of4
               (modify c_of4 11 np)
            )
            (rdwset wset)                ; redraw selection set
         ) ; end case beveling
      ) ; end cond
)

;----------------------------------------------------------------------------

(princ " Loaded.")          ; prompt indicates file was loaded
(princ)                     ; quiet: finished loading

;----------------------------------------------------------------------------
; EOF: WALLS.LSP Ver 2.0
```

Drawing the Faces

As many as thirteen faces may be required to draw a wall section with a window opening. To simplify matters, each 3D face in WALLS.LSP is constructed consistently. If you were facing the wall section with the starting point to your left and ending point to your right, the face points are always entered starting with the lower-left corner, then the lower-right, then upper-right, and finally upper-left. Figure 8.2 illustrates how faces are constructed around a window opening and door opening. Notice that when the window elevation is zero, face number 4 is not drawn.

FIGURE 8.2:
Drawing faces around a window and door opening

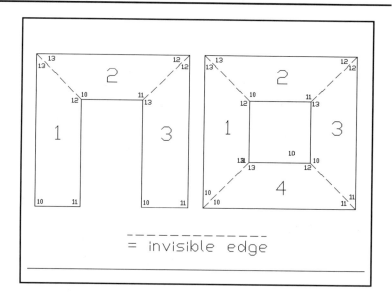

Managing Variable Names

Much of the code in WALLS.LSP is taken up with handling data from the user and shifting data between memory variables. Certain conventions are observed in

WALLS.LSP

naming variables, to make the code as readable as possible. The following are lists of the global and local variable names in WALLS.LSP, and their meanings:

Global Variable	Meaning
g:ww	Wall Width (same as wall thickness, or offset distance)
g:wh	Wall Height
g:w_wid	Window Width
g:w_ht	Window Height
g:w_el	Window Elevation

If these global names conflict with global names in other routines of yours, you must change them to unique names that do not conflict. Use your text editor's search-and-replace feature and modify the source code carefully.

Local Variable	Meaning
c_sp	Current wall start point
c_ep	Current wall end point
c_osp	Current wall offset start point
c_oep	Current wall offset end point
c_zosp	Current wall elevation offset end point
o_sp	Offset start point for calculating
o_ep	Offset end point for calculating
z_sp	Elevation start point for calculating
z_ep	Elevation end point for calculating
z_osp	Elevation offset start point
z_oep	Elevation offset end point
l_left	Window insert point (lower-left facing wall) at floor level
wll	Window lower-left point at elevation
wlr	Window lower-right point at elevation

ENTITY ASSOCIATION LISTS
CH. 8

wul	Window upper-left point at elevation
wur	Window upper-right point at elevation
o_wll	Offset window lower-left point
o_wlr	Offset window lower-right point
o_wul	Offset window upper-left point
o_wur	Offset window upper-right point
np	Floor level intersection point for walls
z_np	Wall height intersection point
i_sp	Store first wall start point
i_osp	Store first wall offset start point
i_oep	Store first wall offset end point
i_zosp	Store first wall elevation start point
i_zoep	Store first wall elevation end point
p_osp	Store previous wall offset start point
p_oep	Store previous wall offset end point
p_zosp	Previous wall elevation offset start point
p_zoep	Previous wall elevation offset end point
uline	Reference line at floor level
ent1	End face on first wall
c_top	Current wall top face
i_top	First wall top face
p_top	Previous wall top face
f1	Current wall face number 1
f2	Current wall face number 2
f3	Current wall face number 3
f4	Current wall face number 4
i_f1	First wall face number 1
p_f3	Previous wall face number 3
c_of1	Current wall offset face number 1

Entity-Access Functions in WALLS.LSP

c_of2	Current wall offset face number 2
c_of3	Current wall offset face number 3
c_of4	Current wall offset face number 4
i_of1	First wall offset face number 1
i_of2	First wall offset face number 2
i_of3	First wall offset face number 3
i_of4	First wall offset face number 4
p_of1	Previous wall offset face number 1
p_of2	Previous wall offset face number 2
p_of3	Previous wall offset face number 3
p_of4	Previous wall offset face number 4
t_angl	Test angle for offset direction
wset	Selection set of 3D faces for redrawing

Global Functions

Since WALLS.LSP prompts the user for distances (wall and window parameters), and offers defaults for each, it uses the global functions G:DIST and G:STR, discussed in Chapter 7. You may load GEAR.LSP to activate these functions, or load them separately. In any event, WALLS.LSP will not work without them.

Entity-Access Functions in WALLS.LSP

The most important functions in WALLS.LSP are those that create and modify entities by directly manipulating the drawing database.

Makeline

The simplest of these is the Makeline function, which draws the reference line used by WALLS.LSP. The syntax is

(makeline **point point**)

ENTITY ASSOCIATION LISTS
CH. 8

Makeline is defined within WALLS.LSP, and the definition is repeated here for quick reference:

```
(defun makeline(p0 p1)
   (if (entmake (list (cons 0 "LINE")
                      (cons 10 p0)
                      (cons 11 p1)
                )
       )
       (entlast)
   )
)
```

Makeline creates a single line segment and requires two points as arguments. It returns the entity name of the line, which may be stored to a variable.

Makeface

Makeface creates 3D faces with optional invisible edges. All five arguments are required. If no edges are invisible, the fourth argument, Edges, must be either zero or nil. The syntax is

(makeface **point point point point edges**)

The definition for Makeface is repeated here:

```
(defun makeface( p0 p1 p2 p3 edges )
   (if (< edges 0)
      (setq edges 0)
   )
   (if (entmake (list (cons 0   "3Dface")
                      (cons 10 p0)
                      (cons 11 p1)
                      (cons 12 p2)
                      (cons 13 p3)
                      (cons 70 edges)
                )
       )
       (entlast)
   )
)
```

The *edges* argument is combined with group code 70 to determine invisible edges on the face. The 70 group code value in the 3Dface association list is a bit-code that determines which edges are invisible. You can create any combination of invisible edges by totaling any of the following values:

  1 = First Edge (point p0 to p1)

  2 = Second Edge (point p1 to p2)

  4 = Third Edge (point p2 to p3)

  8 = Fourth Edge (point p3 to p0)

Makeface uses additional code that allows the edges argument to be nil. If it is nil, it is reset to zero within the function, making all edges visible. The function returns the entity name of the newly created face.

Modify

The Modify function changes entity association lists and updates the drawing. It is a more generalized version of the Newcolor function, described earlier in this chapter. When successful, it returns the revised association list. The syntax is

```
( modify entity group code new value )
```

WALLS.LSP uses this function to fillet the corners of the walls as new wall sections are added. WALLS.LSP uses this function exclusively for 3-D faces. Within the routine, the syntax is

```
(modify <face> <point group code> <new point> )
```

using only valid group codes for 3D face points: 10, 11, 12, or 13.

Modify is written generally, with only a minimum of error trapping. Any entity may be passed to Modify, but if you pass incorrect values for either the group code or the associated value, Modify will fail, returning either nil or an AutoLISP error message. If the specified group code is not found in the current association list, Modify will attempt to add it to the entity's association list.

Before calling Modify, WALLS.LSP uses the Inters function to calculate the intersection points for lines formed by the horizontal edges of the current and previous offset faces. After that, it is easy to use the Modify function to update the necessary faces in the drawing, using the calculated intersection points as arguments for Modify.

Modify is defined as follows:

```
(defun modify( ent code nvalue / cvalue alist)
   (if (and (= (type ent) 'ENAME)
            (= (type code) 'INT)
       )
       (if (setq cvalue (assoc code
                    (setq alist (entget ent))
              )
           )
           (entmod (subst (cons code nvalue)
                      cvalue
                      alist
                   )
           )
           (entmod (append alist
                    (list (cons code nvalue))
                   )
           )
       )
   )
)
```

Accum

In WALLS.LSP, when added wall sections are adjacent, additional face edges must be made invisible. The Accum function is a variation on Modify, and its purpose is to add to, rather than merely substitute for, the existing bit-code value for invisible edges in 3D faces. It requires that the Modify function be loaded in memory. The syntax is

(accum **face group code added bit-code value**)

Accum is defined as follows:

```
(defun accum( ent code acc / x )
   (if (and (= (type ent) 'ENAME)
            (setq x (cdr (assoc code (entget ent))))
       )
       (modify ent code (+ x acc))
   )
)
```

Entity-Access Functions in WALLS.LSP

Accum is written to apply to any entity for which you may want to accumulate values in association lists. It will return the revised association list when successful, and will return nil if the group code is not explicitly present in the entity's association list.

Addset

Addset is a quick function that adds the last-drawn entity in the database to an existing selection set. It is useful when you are drawing entities and adding them to selection sets simultaneously. The selection set argument to Addset must exist before Addset is called. The syntax is

(addset **selection set**)

It is easy to create a selection set without entities in AutoLISP. Simply invoke:

(setq wset (ssadd))

The above code fragment stores an empty selection set in the variable Wset. Once created, it can be passed as an argument to Addset:

(addset wset)

Addset is defined as follows:

```
(defun addset( s_set )
     (if (= (type s_set) 'PICKSET)
          (ssadd (entlast) s_set)
     )
)
```

Rdwset

Rdwset is a quick function that redraws only those entities in a selection set. It is a convenience to the user because, depending on the viewing angle, overlapping lines may disappear as 3D faces are modified. This screen image is misleading—the faces will appear normally after invoking a Redraw or Regen command.

WALLS.LSP continually adds entities to a selection set using the Addset function, then redraws them after modification, using this function. The function always returns nil. The syntax is

(rdwset **selection set**)

Rdwset is also useful as a demonstration of a fast way to loop through a selection set in AutoLISP:

```
(defun rdwset( s_set / i ss_len)
   (cond ( (and (= (type s_set) 'PICKSET)
                (= (type (setq ss_len (sslength s_set))) 'INT)
           )
           (setq i -1)
           (repeat ss_len
                (redraw (ssname s_set (setq i (1+ i))))
           )
         )
   )
)
```

Rdwset first tests to be sure that the argument is a selection set. Then it tests to be sure that there are no more than 32,535 entities in the set. If there are too many entities, the number returned by Sslength is a real number, not an integer, and for the sake of speed the function uses integers, not real numbers. It returns nil if it cannot process the selection set. This function would probably be of little use on selection sets with more than 32,000 entities, anyway.

Notice how the Repeat function is called using the number of entities in the selection set as its first argument (the number of repeats). Each time the Redraw function is repeated, the selection set index is incremented by one.

The selection set index variable is initialized as minus one, so that the first time through repeat-redraw, the index would be updated to zero, the index value for the first entity in the set.

Other Functions in WALLS.LSP

The other functions in WALLS.LSP are used to organize the code and handle the user interface. They are briefly summarized here.

C:WALLS

C:WALLS is the function that brings all the other functions together into a command that can be invoked from AutoCAD's command prompt. It uses techniques much like those used in GEAR.LSP, described in the previous chapter. This function

Other Functions in WALLS.LSP

establishes the local variables shared by the other functions, sets up the drawing environment, defines a mechanism for handling errors, and starts prompting for the general wall parameters (wall width and height). It sets up a main loop during which the user can continue to add wall sections onto the section previously drawn. The loop ends when the user does one of the following:

- Presses ↵ instead of entering a new wall extension point.
- Picks the original starting point.
- Enters "C" or "Close" in response to the prompt for a new wall extension point. This has the same effect as entering the original starting point.

Wdraw

The Wdraw function prompts for wall opening parameters, calculates the points necessary for producing either plain walls or walls with openings, and calls another function for the specific wall type. It adds a horizontal covering face to the top of the wall after the vertical faces are drawn.

Wedit

The Wedit function organizes the editing functions that change faces as new wall sections are added. It performs tests that determine what changes are needed. After editing, it transfers point values into existing variables, to make use of them for additional changes, which may be required the next time it is called.

Wallpt

The Wallpt function is a small utility function that calculates base offset points for the more complex calculations done by Wdraw and Wedit. It can offset to either side of the existing reference line depending on the argument (+ or −) passed to it. A plus sign offsets clockwise, a minus sign offsets counterclockwise.

Getll

The Getll function prompts for a point on the reference line, on or above which the lower-left corner of the door or window opening will be positioned. When successful, it returns the point selected, to be used as a base point for subsequent point calculations.

Getwindow

The Getwindow function first tests that the point returned by the Getll function is on the reference line. Notice how it uses the Inters function within a while loop to accomplish this. Then it prompts for a window width, height, and elevation above floor level (if any). It contains error-checking mechanisms to prompt the user if the window parameters will cause the door or window opening not to fit in the wall. If the window parameters are correct, this function calculates the points necessary to draw the door or window.

D_pwall and D_wwall

The D_pwall function uses calculated points to draw a wall without a door or window opening. The D_wwall function uses calculated points to draw the wall with a door or window opening. Both functions keep track of faces stored in variables, and initialize special variables if this is the first wall drawn.

Getoffset

The Getoffset function prompts the user to pick one side of the first reference line. It uses the relationship between the picked point and the line to calculate the base angle for determining subsequent wall offsets.

Closeup

The Closeup function is similar to the Wdraw function, but it recalls the editing functions additionally, to account for the extra editing needed to close the first and last wall sections when the user enters "C" or "Close," or picks the original starting point.

Direct Entity Access versus the Command Function

WALLS.LSP, in addition to providing a useful application, demonstrates how to create entities, store them in memory, add them to selection sets and modify them after they have been added to the database. Direct database manipulation is usually faster and more accurate than calling AutoCAD commands from within an AutoLISP routine; however, the programming job is more complex.

When should you use the Command function to call AutoCAD commands, and when should you manipulate the database directly? Use the Command function when the alternative leads to enormous development overhead. For example, making a polar array or trimming curved lines requires complex math. It is not necessary to "reinvent the wheel" when commands like Array and Trim are at your disposal. As you experiment and gain experience, you will arrive at a balance between the time you are willing to take in developing and debugging, and the elegance and speed of your routines.

Using WALLS.LSP

The following AutoCAD exercise will produce the walls shown in Figure 8.1. Boldface indicates AutoCAD prompts; normal type indicates your keyboard entries. Some prompts and defaults may vary, depending on your display configuration and AutoCAD version. Notice that architectural units are used throughout. Be careful when entering values for feet and inches.

Command: (load "WALLS")

Loading WALLS.LSP (2.0) ... Loaded.

Command: SPLFRAME

New value for SPLFRAME: 0

Command: UNITS

Enter choice 1 to 5: 4

(Note: All default responses may be used for the remaining AutoCAD prompts in the UNITS command.)

Command: LIMITS
ON/OFF/<Lower left corner>: 0,0
Upper right corner: 26',30'
Command: VPOINT
Rotate/<View point>: 3,-3,1

Command: WALLS

ENTITY ASSOCIATION LISTS
CH. 8

```
Wall width: 6"
Wall height: 10'
Start point: 6',12'
To point: 22',12'
Pick side to offset: 13',14'
Window insert point on wall line (RETURN=no window): 10',12'
Window width: 8'
Window height: 50"
Window elevation: 30"
Drawing window/wall...

To point: 22',20'
Window insert point on wall line (RETURN=no window): 22',14'
Window width: 40"
Window height: 80"
Window elevation: 0
Drawing window/wall...
Beveling walls...

To point: 22',28'
Window insert point on wall line (RETURN=no window): 22',22'
Window width: 30"
Window height: 50"
Window elevation: 30"
Drawing window/wall...

To point: 6',28'
Window insert point on wall line (RETURN=no window): 12',28'
Window width: 48"
Window height: 20"
Window elevation: 60"
Drawing window/wall...
Beveling walls...

To point: C
Window insert point on wall line (RETURN=no window): (press ↵)
Drawing plain wall...
Beveling walls...

Command: HIDE
Regenerating drawing.
Hiding lines: done
```

CHAPTER NINE

Introduction to ADS

INTRODUCTION TO ADS
CH. 9

The AutoCAD Development System (ADS) is a special library of predefined functions, macros, and constants that gives professional developers and AutoCAD users the ability to add custom extensions to AutoCAD using the more powerful capabilities of the C programming language. This chapter presents an introduction to and overview of the ADS development process.

Who This Chapter Is For

This chapter's material is intended for AutoCAD users who:

- Thoroughly understand AutoCAD's fundamental features and its underlying database structure.
- Have a practical understanding of the C programming language, and have experience writing and compiling C programs.
- Want a concrete overview of the ADS development process to help them understand the particular requirements and pitfalls of the ADS development process.
- Want a descriptive overview of the ADS development process to assess whether it will be cost-effective to invest additional time and resources in private ADS program development.

If you have looked at the ADS documentation provided with AutoCAD, and find it difficult to understand, this chapter may help. Although this chapter will not turn you into an expert C programmer overnight, you will get a solid feel for how ADS programming works. After working your way through the sample source code for an ADS application and reading the text explaining various functions, you will find that you can return to AutoCAD's ADS documentation and it will be much easier to understand.

ADS Features

ADS offers three major advantages to the user seeking to customize AutoCAD's feature set:

- Because ADS programs are written in C and compiled, they tend to run at measurably faster speeds than comparable AutoLISP programs. This makes ADS suitable for larger and more complex programs that must perform elaborate calculations.
- The C language offers special functions that can directly access a machine's memory, storage, and peripheral devices. This means that applications written in ADS can do anything that a C-language program can do, along with controlling the AutoCAD drawing editor.
- Because ADS programs are compiled, you can distribute working ADS programs and keep the original source code secure from unwanted access; you can also prevent unauthorized revisions of your distributed material.

The additional power, flexibility, and security of an ADS application comes at a price, however. You must spend additional money to purchase a C compiler and linker, as well as optional debuggers and builders to help speed up the development process. This additional software can easily cost you a thousand dollars or more, depending on the compiler you select.

ADS programs are more difficult to write and debug because you, as the program developer, are responsible for programming the critical resource management tasks that are the foundation of a reliable and robust program. ADS provides several predefined functions and a strong framework for linking your program with AutoCAD. However, responsibility for your program's use of memory and storage, plus the integrity of your data, is entirely in your hands.

Thus, you should consider programming in ADS if your particular customization needs are unusual enough to justify the time and cost of self-development. If you are not experienced and can find a third-party product that fills your needs, this option is likely to be more cost-effective.

If you cannot find an existing product that adequately addresses your needs and AutoLISP lacks sufficient speed or power to get the job done adequately, consider hiring an experienced outside developer to do the work for you. If your project is at all complex and you are not an experienced C programmer, there is a good chance that your in-house development cost will eventually run higher than that of contracting a responsible and experienced outside developer.

Consider private in-house ADS development if you have plenty of time in which to develop, debug, test, and refine your solution, and can assimilate the development cycle into your daily working routine. The decision is similar to what you would face if you decided to make major renovations on your home: Can you accept the time, expense, and work quality of hiring yourself as a remodeler, or is it better to go with the services of a more experienced professional? Are you prepared to accept whatever results you may achieve in return for the benefit of acquiring valuable experience and additional skills? There is no right or wrong answer; either approach has its advantages and disadvantages, and it is up to you to examine your circumstances, make the comparison, and finally decide.

Programming for Productivity, Profit, and Fun

You may want to consider private ADS development if you feel confident that there is a sufficiently large market for your proposed solution, and you have a reason to believe you can recoup your development costs, or maybe turn a profit, by selling your solution to others. For part-time developers, this is a risky enterprise. To improve your chances for success, do some careful market analysis before investing your resources. Make certain that your solution offers an original and unique approach to solving the problem, that it has a readily identified market, and that you have sufficient additional resources to spend promoting your solution effectively to that market. The commercial software field is not an easy one, and you must have something really special to succeed.

To sell your work profitably, you must keep your market as large as possible. ADS programs are portable between different AutoCAD platforms only at the source-code level. Unless you intend to distribute source code (not recommended), you may want to invest in compilers for AutoCAD platforms other than your own.

These caveats and warnings may sound dire and discouraging, but they aren't meant to be. Like do-it-yourself home remodeling, do-it-yourself software development can be exciting, as well as personally and professionally rewarding. If you are interested, don't hesitate to try it out; but avoid rushing the process. It cannot be done recklessly.

Finally, be aware that there are a host of different ways to write the same program; that no one has all the answers;and that there are only a few absolutes to learn, and only a few guidelines for what makes a good program, from an end-user's perspective:

1. A good program should be reliable, simple, and focused on performing specific, concrete tasks.
2. It should be easy for others to learn and use.
3. It should be as fast as possible.
4. It should manage memory and storage space efficiently.

As you attempt to create a program that complies with these general ideals, remember that you are absolutely free to experiment as much as you like or your resources will allow. The best way to learn is by digging in and making lots of mistakes. Protect your data by making lots of backups.

Requirements for ADS Development

Besides the necessary additional software, you must have a practical working knowledge of the C programming language and your machine's operating system before you try your hand at ADS development. In particular, you should be familiar with data types, pointers, and structures, as ADS relies heavily on these. If data types, pointers, and structures are not clear to you, it is better that you study C some more before diving into ADS.

It is hard to imagine learning or programming any form of C without a thorough knowledge of your operating system, but at the very least, you will want to fine-tune your operating system to make the compiling and linking process as efficient as possible. This involves procedures such as changing your file search path, setting up operating system variables, and writing batch files. If you don't know your operating system already, take time out to learn the basics before proceeding. Consider a SYBEX book such as *Mastering DOS*, by Judd Robbins, *Understanding UNIX*, by Stan Kelly-Bootle, or any one of several other good books available at bookstores and libraries.

Books on C Programming

There are many good books on the C language. Here are some recommendations:

- Kernighan and Ritchie; *The C Programming Language,* 2nd Edition; Prentice Hall, 1988. This book is considered a classic. Most C Programmers turn to it eventually. It is one of the clearest and most concise texts available, handy as both a learning device and a reference tool.

- Lafore, Robert; *Microsoft C Programmming for the PC.* Howard W. Sams, 1989. An accessible and readable book on all phases of programming in C.

Ask for other recommendations from programmers at conventions, user group meetings, or on computer bulletin boards.

Supported Compilers for ADS

Theoretically, ADS can support any high-level language if the library function definitions are available. For all practical purposes, however, the following C-language compilers are supported:

- In OS/2 and UNIX-based systems, you can use the compiler, linker, and debugger provided with your operating system.

- For 80386 and 80486 DOS-based systems, you can use MetaWare High C Version 1.7, MetaWare High C/C++ (which includes special libraries and options for ADS development), WATCOM C 386 compiler, or Zortech C++ compiler version 3.0. The protected-mode object files produced by these compilers should be linked using the Phar Lap 386 linker. This linker is available from Phar Lap as part of a special package called the Phar Lap 386 | DOS Extended Developer's Kit.

- For developing 80386 and 80486 DOS-based systems, you may find other optional tools useful. These include the Phar Lap 386-DEBUG debugger; Phar Lap 386-VMM virtual memory manager; and Phar Lap 386-ASM Assembler.

- Also for 80386 and 80486 DOS-based systems, you can use Microsoft C versions 5.1 or later, or Borland C versions 2.0 or later. These compiler/linker packages can produce 16-bit real mode ADS object files, using special libraries provided with AutoCAD. These 16-bit compilers sacrifice protected-mode performance, since they can execute only in the first 640K of RAM. However, they are more economical than their protected-mode counterparts.

- The VAX or 80286 versions of AutoCAD do not support ADS.

Compiling AutoCAD's Sample ADS Programs

AutoCAD is shipped with source code for several illustrative ADS sample programs. Although AutoCAD provides executable versions of these programs, you should compile them yourself using the compiler you have chosen. Since the code for the sample programs has been thoroughly tested and debugged, you can use it to test whatever configuration switches and options you must include to compile and link ADS programs for your system. Once you have successfully compiled a sample program, you will be ready to compile programs of your own.

In particular, consult the ASCII text file provided with AutoCAD for your chosen ADS compiler. Files for supported compilers can be found in the subdirectory \ADS\DOCS, which is nested below your AutoCAD system subdirectory.

The sample programs in this chapter were compiled and tested using MetaWare High C/C++, and linked using the Phar Lap 386-Link linker, on a 80386 DOS machine running AutoCAD Release 12. The MetaWare and Phar Lap products were installed using all default options, and operating system variables were set according to the products' documentation. Every effort has been made to write code that is portable across existing ADS platforms, but if you are using a different compiler and linker, you may need to make slight modifications to accommodate your chosen platform.

Using MetaWare High C/C++, the following command was invoked to compile and link an ADS application:

```
hc386 filename -I\highc\inc -Hloclib -Hads -lads.lib
```

Here, *filename* is the name of the C source code file.

INTRODUCTION TO ADS
CH. 9

Notice that this command is different from the standard command used to compile and link ADS applications in MetaWare High C version 1.7:

```
hc386 -Hads filename -f287 -I\highc\inc -Hpro=sample.pro -lads.lib
```

ADS programs are compiled using four header files:

File Name	Purpose
adslib.h	Defines general-purpose constants, macros, and system-dependent program controls.
adscodes.h	Defines manifest constants for standard integer control codes used by ADS. Although the code values may change with different platforms or versions of ADS, use of these constants ensures that ADS code is as portable as possible.
ads.h	Defines ADS library functions and data type declarations.
ol_errno.h	Defines manifest constants for integer error codes returned by the library functions and stored in AutoCAD's system variable ERRNO. This file is optional. It is included in applications that analyze ERRNO for program flow control and debugging purposes.

All ADS applications incorporate the following directive:

```
#include <adslib.h>
```

This directive automatically includes the related files ads.h and adscodes.h.

It is not necessary to know the contents of these files to program in ADS, but it is helpful to look through them after you have acquired some familiarity with ADS programming. Knowing the contents of these files can deepen your understanding of ADS.

All ADS programs are linked with a special ADS object library file. The name and contents of this file are system dependent. Refer to the instruction text in the \ADS\DOCS subdirectory for more information on the library file for your system.

The ADS Development Process—Basic Steps

Development of an ADS program incorporates the basic programming steps you have seen in previous chapters, plus a few added techniques for handling the specialized ADS environment. As with any programming project, you should begin with a clear statement of the application's objectives, and you should keep the design as simple as possible. Then, translate your design into pseudocode, breaking it down into a step-by-step process.

After detailing the discrete steps in your pseudocode, write C-language functions to perform these steps. As functions are written, incorporate them into your ADS program using the sample file TEMPLATE.C as your model for fitting them into an ADS application. This process will be described in greater detail later in this chapter.

It is likely that your development process will include several passes through your compiler, as you correct problems and add refinements and enhancements. To whatever extent you are able, try to test your application on a function-by-function basis, adding new functions after current ones pass muster. This is much more efficient in the long run than writing several functions and testing the whole application all at once.

This process should be flexible. Some functions will depend upon each other, and must be tested together. You may find it worthwhile, as you develop the application, to write separate functions whose sole purpose is to measure the results of the working function you are developing.

Although this process can seem long and tedious, it is generally more efficient in the long run, especially when working with such a highly structured language as C.

Creating an ADS Function from Scratch—FPROMPT.C

In this section you will step through each stage of developing a simple ADS function.

Many AutoCAD commands pause and request input from the user. This example function is designed to display a prompt, then pause and wait for character input.

275

INTRODUCTION TO ADS
CH. 9

The function will accept only a limited set of valid responses from the operator, and store the most recent response as a default for the next time. If the operator presses ↵, the function will return the default response to AutoLISP, and an integer code indicating its success or failure to ADS.

Finally, the function will format the prompt string in a consistent way. Thus, if you use this function for a variety of input strings and prompts, you can use only the minimum requirements for a prompt string in your programming, and be certain that your prompt messages will show a consistent style on the screen.

Name the function *fprompt*, for "formatted prompt." If you prefer to use some other name, you are free to do so.

As you will see, most of the ADS code for this function is devoted to overhead—that is, managing the links between AutoCAD and ADS. The code for the function itself is comparatively small.

To begin, here is a pseudocode description of the function:

- If this is the first time the function is invoked, a default response will not be established yet. In this case, display only the prompt message.
- If a default response has been established, include that default in the prompt message, between angle brackets, and display the message.
- If a default response has been established, allow the operator to enter the default by pressing ↵ only.
- If the operator enters a valid response other than the default, store this response as the default to be used the next time.

A few other features are included for convenience when including this code in your programs:

- If the user enters a valid response, the function returns the RTNORM integer.
- If the operator cancels by pressing Ctrl-C, the function returns the RTCAN integer.

Having outlined the function's features, you are ready to translate the function into C code. Here is the prototype:

```
int fprompt(char *keywds, char *mess, char *defresp);
```

Listing 9.1 contains code for the ADS fprompt() function.

Listing 9.1: The fprompt() function

```
int fprompt( keyw , message , defres)  {
    int val;
    char temp[6];
    char prmt[35];
    strcpy( temp, defres);
    strcat( strcpy( prmt , "\n" ) , message );
    if ( strcmp( temp , "" ) != 0 ) {
       strcat( strcat( strcat( prmt , " <" ) , temp ) , ">" );
       ads_initget( 0 , keyw );
    } else
       ads_initget( 1 , keyw );
    if ( (val=ads_getkword( strcat( prmt , ": " ) , defres )) == RTCAN ) {
       ads_printf("\nFunction cancelled.");
       ads_retvoid();
    } else {
       if ( strcmp( defres , "" ) == 0 ) {
           val=RTNORM;
           strcpy( defres , temp );
       }
       ads_retstr(defres);           /* Send response to AutoLISP */
    }
    return val;                      /* Function return code     */
}
```

The function code begins by declaring some necessary variables: an integer variable for storing codes returned by ADS library functions and the fprompt() function, and two local arrays for storing character strings. The first array, temp, is six characters long, large enough to hold the longest possible response from the operator in this example. The second is 35 characters long, more than enough to hold the longest prompt string in this example, including default and format characters.

As the programmer, you should declare character arrays that are large enough to hold the longest strings the function may generate, or use character pointers to avoid tedious declarations of arrays. If you rewrite the function using longer string arguments, be certain you increase available memory space for these arrays. If you rewrite the function using longer string arguments, be certain you increase the size of these arrays. (The theoretical limit on character arrays—used by the ads_init() and ads_getkword() library functions—varies from system to system, but it is around five hundred characters. For most practical purposes, a figure less than this should be enough.)

The response variable, defres, should be declared externally and be large enough to store the longest possible user response from any call to this function, for example:

```
char defres[6]="No";
```

This ensures that sufficient memory is set aside for the response string before the function is called. In this example, the default response is initialized as No, but possible are Yes, No, and Maybe. Therefore, the default response variable should be at least an array of six characters, large enough to hold "Maybe," plus the null ending character.

When fprompt() is called, it first tucks the default away where it can be safely recalled later. If this is the first time the function is invoked, it tucks away a null string, which is fine:

```
strcpy( temp, defres);
```

Next, the function adds a line feed to the beginning of the message string, making it easier to read on the screen, and if the default is other than a null string, it adds the default string to the message between angle brackets.

Next, the function tests the value of the default string. If the default is currently a null string, the program calls ads_initget() with a bitcode of 1, disallowing null input from the operator. This forces the operator to enter one of the function's valid keywords. If the default is a string, the program calls ads_initget() with a bitcode of 0, allowing the user to press ↵ without supplying data.

The function then calls ads_getkword(). As it calls this function, it also adds a colon to the end of the prompt string. The operator response is governed by the previous call to ads_initget(). The response is copied to the variable holding the default response.

Lastly, the function tests the value of the default response. If it is a null string (""), the user pressed ↵. The function then copies the value it tucked away back into the default response variable.

Creating an ADS Function from Scratch—FPROMPT.C

If the user entered a response other than the null string, this response is already stored in the default response variable, and no further processing is necessary.

If the function concludes normally, it sends the response string to AutoLISP, and returns RTNORM. Otherwise, it will return another value stored in the val variable, which can be tested and processed as required.

For example, the function is written so that if the user enters Ctrl-C while the function is active, the function returns a message indicating that the user canceled the program, and returns a nil value to AutoLISP. In this case, the val variable will be bound to the value RTCAN.

To use this function, consider what happens with the following code fragment:

```
char defres[6]="No";
char key[]="Yes No Maybe";
char message[]="Yes, No, or Maybe";
fprompt( key , message , defres);
```

AutoCAD would prompt

```
Yes, No, or Maybe <No>:
```

and wait for one of the acceptable answers. If the user entered M (Maybe), for example, the next time the same function was invoked, AutoCAD would display

```
Yes, No, or Maybe <Maybe>:
```

If defres is first initialized to an empty string with the line

```
char defres[6]="";
```

AutoCAD would prompt

```
Yes, No, or Maybe:
```

Whatever response the user gave could be used as the default variable next time.

This function can be used in any program that prompts for character strings from the operator. In the example, literal strings have been supplied as arguments to the function.

Executing Functions in ADS

Having looked in detail at the inner workings of the fprompt() function, you can now examine how ADS goes about the business of linking the function to AutoCAD. The process for doing this is always the same, and is handled in the background, without intervention from the operator:

1. Every ADS application begins with a call to the ads_init() function, which initializes the interface between AutoCAD and the ADS application.

2. After initializing the interface, the ADS application calls ads_link(), which establishes the necessary communication link in memory between AutoCAD and ADS.

3. The first time the function calls ads_link(), AutoCAD returns an integer indicating that it expects the ADS application to call the ads_defun() function, which defines each external function in the application. Ads_defun() will be called for each function you intend to define. In the example, you must write one call to ads_defun() to define the fprompt() function.

Thereafter, subsequent calls to ads_link() will return other integer codes indicating that AutoCAD is expecting a call to other functions in the application. The specific function is controlled by the instructions received from outside the ADS application. These instructions may come from the operator entering commands at the keyboard, a screen or tablet menu, or other command sequence, such as a function call within an AutoLISP application.

The integer codes that control the sequence of steps in an ADS application are not written literally in the source code. Instead, they are represented by various *manifest constants*, such as RQXLOAD, or RQSUBR. You should use these standard constants whenever possible. This allows the same source code to be compiled for a variety of platforms or different versions of ADS, with minimal or no recoding. It is not necessary that you know what actual values are represented by these constants, but if you are curious, you can find their definitions in the library file ADSCODES.h.

For example, the first code sent by AutoCAD after receiving a call from ads_link() is RQXLOAD. The ADS application, upon receiving this integer, should respond by calling ads_defun() for each external function in the program.

TEMPLATE.C

Thereafter, whenever an external function is invoked, AutoCAD will send an RQSUBR integer to the defining application, to which the application responds by executing the defined function's instructions.

TEMPLATE.C

ADS provides a special file, called TEMPLATE.C, that contains the necessary code for calling ads_link() and ads_defun() in correct sequence, plus some basic error trapping if something should go wrong during the loading and linking process. You can use a copy of this file as the base platform for your custom ADS applications.

TEMPLATE.C handles the process of receiving AutoCAD codes and sending ADS responses within a continuous loop. This loop is the C-standard "Main" function of the ADS application. Your custom functions should be called from within this loop when AutoCAD sends a RQSUBR code.

Listing 9.2 shows how to write the fprompt() function into a modified version of TEMPLATE.C, forming the complete application. Take special notice of the comments in this listing, which describe the workings of the program.

Listing 9.2: Complete source code for FPROMPT.C

```
/* FILE NAME:     FPROMPT.c
   Written by:    Bob Thomas    */

/* Include files:   */

#include  <stdio.h>
#include  <string.h>    /* Must include string.h for fprompt() */
#include  "adslib.h"

/* Establish space for the default response */

static char defres[6]="";

/* function prototypes here: */

static int loadfuncs();
int fprompt( char *keyw , char *message , char *defres);

/* Main routine here. This is from TEMPLATE.C   */
```

```c
void main(argc, argv)

  int argc;
  char *argv[];

{
    int stat;
    short scode = RSRSLT;       /* This is the default result code */
    ads_init(argc, argv);       /* Initialize the interface */

/* Endless loop condition set up here: */

    for ( ;; ) {

/* Each time through the loop, call ads_link().
   If return value is less than zero,
   the link failed for some reason.
   Store integer return from ads_link to stat variable.    */

        if ((stat = ads_link(scode)) < 0) {
            printf("FPROMPT: bad status from ads_link() = %d\n", stat);
            fflush(stdout);
            exit(1);
        }
        scode = RSRSLT;    /* Return default value  */

        /* Check for the value of stat returned by ads_link() */

        switch (stat) {

        case RQXLOAD:


    /* ACAD expects ADS to define its external functions.
       You must define functions for each application.
       this is handled with a call to the loadfuncs() function
       This function is also found in TEMPLATE.C, and is standard
       for handling this task
       If loadfuncs() returns RSRSLT, the external functions were
       loaded normally. Otherwise, loadfuncs() returns RSERR.   */

            scode = loadfuncs() ? RSRSLT : RSERR;
            break;
```

TEMPLATE.C

```
       case RQSUBR:

   /* Functions were defined in a previous pass.  Now AutoCAD
      expect ADS to execute an external function. In this
      case, there is only one function to execute, fprompt.
      So here it is, with appropriate arguments.
      Notice that the initial default response is
      a null string (""). */

          fprompt( "Yes No Maybe" ,
                   "Enter Yes, No, or Maybe" ,
                   defres);
          break;

       default:
          break;

       }    /* End Switch */
   }       /* End for(;;) */
}         /* End MAIN    */

/* LOADFUNCS  --  Define external functions
   Call ads_defun() once for each external program to be loaded.
   This can be handled using a loop - refer to the sample ADS
   programs supplied with AutoCAD for examples of different ways
   you can re-write loadfuncs() to handle multiple functions.
   In this example, only one function is being defined; this
   keeps loadfuncs() simple: */

static int loadfuncs()  {

   if (ads_defun("fprompt", 0) == RTNORM)  {
      return 1;
   } else
      return 0;

}   /* End LOADFUNCS    */


/* FPROMPT  --  Format Prompting for Keywords.     */

int fprompt( keyw , message , defres)  {

/* Set up variables for temporary default storage
   and the formatted prompt string:   */
```

```c
        int val;
        char temp[6];
        char prmt[35];

/* Store current default response: */

        strcpy( temp, defres );

/* Put line feed at the top of the message    */

        strcat( strcpy( prmt , "\n" ) , message );

/* If default isn't null, add default to prompt string,
   and allow null (press Enter) response                */

        if ( strcmp( temp , "" ) != 0 ) {
            strcat( strcat( strcat( prmt , " <" ) , temp ) , ">" );
            ads_initget( 0 , keyw );

/* Otherwise, do not allow null response */

        } else
            ads_initget( 1 , keyw );

/* Prompt operator:
   If response is Ctrl-C, display message and return nil to AutoLISP.
   If response is null, copy default to response.
   If a valid response is other than null, it is stored to
   default automatically   */

        if ( (val=ads_getkword( strcat( prmt , ": " ) , defres )) == RTCAN ) {
            ads_printf("\nFunction cancelled.");
            ads_retvoid();

        } else {

            if ( strcmp( defres , "" ) == 0 ) {
                val=RTNORM;
                strcpy( defres , temp );
            }

            ads_retstr(defres);        /* Send response to AutoLISP */
       }
```

```
    return val;                 /* Function return code */
}   /* eof: FPROMPT.C   157 Lines */
```

Testing the Function

Although fprompt() is a useful function with potential for practical application and inclusion in other programs, by itself it is very limited. However, notice how, because it includes special code to return character strings to AutoLISP, it can be tested on its own. Thus, you can test this function separately and be sure you have solid code before adapting it into other applications.

After successfully compiling FPROMPT.C, load it into AutoCAD with the following command:

`(xload "fprompt")`

AutoCAD responds:

`"fprompt"`

Now invoke the new function as follows:

`(fprompt)`

AutoCAD responds:

`Enter Yes, No, or Maybe:`

Try repeatedly invoking the functions and entering various responses to the prompt. This will give you a good feel for what the function does.

CUTOUT.C

After producing this simple, single function, you will now produce a more complex application that makes better use of the power of ADS. The objective of this application is to cut out a rectangular portion of the drawing and move it elsewhere.

This Release 12 application creates a command called CUTOUT. The CUTOUT command prompts you to draw a rectangle using two opposite corner points, then treats that rectangle as a cutting edge for the TRIM command. It cuts entities that intersect the edge (provided those entities can be cut), creates a block from entities enclosed by the rectangle, and allows you to move or copy the closed entities to a different part of the drawing. If you copy these entities, the originals remain in their previous location and condition. If you move the entities, a space remains where you drew the rectangle.

After the cutout is moved elsewhere, you may scale it, rotate it, explode it, or otherwise manipulate it as you would any block. For the sake of simplicity, these post-processing changes were not included in this example ADS application, although you are free to add them if you like.

There are two reasons why it is useful to write this application in ADS rather than AutoLISP:

1. The speed of ADS makes it faster and more efficient than AutoLISP, especially when dealing with large quantities of drawing information.

2. The program creates a temporary external file on the hard disk. Because the program is written in C, you can use standard C functions to clean up this temporary file after you are finished with it, without resorting to unwieldy and cumbersome devices such as the SHELL command, which is slow and forces a flip-screen on single-screen systems.

CUTOUT.C creates temporary drawing files on disk that begin with the letters CUT, followed by a number, starting with zero. However, there are no safety valves that prevent CUTOUT.C from overwriting an existing drawing file with the same name already on disk. If you have existing drawing files with names that begin with the letters CUT followed by a number, you must rewrite the code in CUTOUT.C to use names that do not conflict. For more of a challenge, try writing a function that will test for an existing drawing file and not writing the selection set to disk until a unique name is found.

Several entities present problems when trimming, especially solids and wide polylines. It is possible to include processing to account for these entities, but for the sake of simplicity and to keep you focused on ADS programming issues instead of complicated processing, a few limitations are imposed in this example version of the application.

1. Blocks and dimensions are exploded before the trimming takes place. If you choose CUTOUT.C's copy option, the original entities are left unexploded,

but the copies are moved as primary entities.

2. Several AutoCAD entities are not normally trimmable. These entities include points, solids, 3D faces, attribute definitions, shapes, traces, viewports, and text. In this example application, text entities that have any portion within the cutting rectangle are moved or copied in their entirety. Other non-trimmable entities are ignored. After studying this example, you may decide to refine and enhance CUTOUT.C to handle these entities.

3. Polylines present special problems. The location of vertices in a polyline, relative to the location of the cutting rectangle, influences how the polyline will be trimmed. The simplest way to ensure accurate polyline trimming is to explode the polyline into line segments before trimming. However, when you explode a wide polyline, it loses its width information. This example sacrifices width information for the sake of accurate trimming. After acquainting yourself with the ADS programming concepts used in CUTOUT.C, you may choose to add more complicated functions to account for wide polylines in your own drawings.

The example is written so that you can isolate and change those parts of the code that you would like to enhance. For example, you could treat other nontrimmable entities the same as text, if you want, or ignore the text entities when trimming.

Alternatively, you could choose to handle nontrimmable entities in more complicated ways. It is possible to trim text entities. To do so, you must first export them into a DXB file, then import the file back again. This converts text into a series of tiny line segments, which are trimmable. For more information about DXB files and text, refer to Chapter 3.

Solids may be "trimmed" by redrawing them. You must analyze their orientation and location relative to the cutting rectangle, and redraw them using new intersection points. In a similar fashion, traces may be converted to solids and processed accordingly. Each segment of a wide polyline may be converted to a solid, and processed as a solid. Functions that perform these processes can be found in Appendix B.

Even given the limitations imposed here, this command can be useful and powerful just as it is written. Try it out in its current form first, then feel free to experiment and modify it to suit your own requirements.

Pseudocode for CUTOUT.C

Having defined CUTOUT.C's objectives, you are ready to develop its pseudocode. As you will see, the application objective, although limited in scope, involves many steps. Here is an example of a form your pseudocode might take:

1. Store certain current AutoCAD drawing environment settings, and make certain suitable changes to the AutoCAD drawing environment:
   A. For debugging: Read the current value of the USERI1 variable.
   B. Set default polyline width to zero.
   C. Set EXPERT variable to 5 (minimal ACAD command prompting).
   D. Set UNDO status on.
   E. Based on the value of the USERI1 variable: Turn off command echo, blips, entity highlighting.
2. Place a mark on the undo audit trail.
3. Prompt the operator to choose whether to Move or Copy the cutout. Save the response as the default for next time. Cancel if the operator presses Ctrl-C.
4. Prompt the operator for the opposite points of a rectangle. Cancel if invalid points are entered, or operator presses Ctrl-C.
5. Define the four corners of the rectangle entered by the operator. No matter in what order the points were entered, store them in order as lower left, lower right, upper right, upper left. Use these points to form the cutting rectangle.
6. Define additional rectangle points offset from the cutting rectangle corner points, interior and exterior to the cutting rectangle points.
7. Draw the cutting rectangle using a closed polyline.
8. Create a selection set using the cutting rectangle as a crossing window.
9. Explode all blocks in the selection set (including nested blocks), plus dimensions and polylines.
10. Exclude all nontrimmable entities from the selection set.
11. Trim entities remaining in the selection set. Use the TRIM command with the cutting rectangle, the "fence" option, and the outside offset points.

Pseudocode for CUTOUT.C

12. Create a selection set of entities remaining inside the rectangle, and the rectangle itself.
13. Exclude nontrimmable entities from the selection set, except text. Save entity names as they are excluded.
14. Pick a block name not found in the current block name table.
15. Write the selection set to a temporary file on disk using the WBLOCK command and the new block name.
16. Invoke UNDO BACK to the mark, restoring the original entities.
17. If the operator selected the "Move" option, repeat steps 7 through 10.
18. If the operator selected the "Move" option, trim entities inside the rectangle, using the interior offset points.
19. Create a selection set of entities remaining inside the rectangle.
20. Remove nontrimmable entities from this selection set that were not written to disk earlier.
21. If the operator selected the "Move" option, erase entities remaining inside the rectangle.
22. Invoke the INSERT command with the drawing name, to read the cutout entities into the drawing as a block.
23. Prompt the user for an insertion point only, and place the entities with a one-to-one scale and a rotation angle of zero.
24. Clean up the disk by erasing the temporary drawing file.
25. Reset the drawing environment to default values.

The complete source code for CUTOUT.C appears in Listing 9.3.

Listing 9.3: Source code for CUTOUT.C

```
/* FILE NAME:     CUTOUT.c
   Written by:    Bob Thomas   */
/* Include files:    */

#include   <stdio.h>
#include   <string.h>
#include   <adslib.h>
```

```
/* Define Constants: */

#define CUT_OFFSET 0.05

/* Macros:     */

#define count( array ) ( sizeof(array) / sizeof( (array)[0] ) )

/* Prototypes: */

static int   loadfunc( void );
static int   cutout( void );

   static void  cut_setup( void );
   static int   undo_setup( int val );
   static int   undo_reset( int val );
   static void  cut_reset( int val );

   static int   fprompt( char *keyw , char *message , char *defres);
   static int   cut_setpts( ads_real offset );

   static int   cut_expset( void );
   static void  cut_adjset( ads_name ss );
   static int   cut_etype( ads_name entity , char *ename );
   static int   cut_drwln( ads_point p1 , ads_point p2 ,
                           ads_point p3 , ads_point p4 );
   static void  cut_okblk( char *pf , char *blkname );
   static int   cut_rcut( void );
   static int   cut_rtrim( ads_name tl  , ads_point p1 , ads_point p2 ,
                           ads_point p3 , ads_point p4 );

/* Externals: */

/*   static char blank[2];     */

struct { char *cmdname; int (*cmdfunc)(); }

 cmdtab[] = {
              /* Command Name , Function Name    */
              { "CUTOUT"      , cutout }

            } ;
```

Pseudocode for CUTOUT.C

```c
static char mc_resp[] = "Copy";

static struct resbuf oldcmd , oldexp , oldblp ,
                     oldund , oldhlt , oldplw;

static ads_point p0   , p0a ,
                 pt1  , pt2  , pt3  , pt4  ,
                 i_pt1 , i_pt2 , i_pt3 , i_pt4 ,
                 o_pt1 , o_pt2 , o_pt3 , o_pt4 ;

static ads_name ssx;

/* * * * * * * * * * * * * * * * * * * * * * * * * * * * * * * * */

/* MAIN */

void main( argc , argv )
  int argc;
  char *argv[];

{
    int stat,cindex;
    short scode = RSRSLT;

    ads_init( argc , argv );

    for ( ;; ) {

        if ( ( stat = ads_link( scode ) ) < 0 ) {
        printf( "CUTOUT: bad status from ads_link() = %d\n" , stat );
            fflush( stdout );
            exit( 1 );
        }

        scode = RSRSLT;

        switch ( stat ) {

        case RQXLOAD:

            scode = loadfunc() ? RSRSLT : RSERR;
            break;

        case RQSUBR:
```

```
            if ( (cindex = ads_getfuncode()) >= 0)
               (*cmdtab[cindex].cmdfunc) ();
            else
               ads_retvoid();
            break;

      default:
            break;
      }
   }
}

/* * * * * * * * * * * * * * * * * * * * * * * * * * * * * * * */

int loadfunc()  {

   char cmdbuf[40];
   int i, val;
   strcpy(cmdbuf, "C:");
   for (i = 0; i < count(cmdtab); i++)    {
    strcpy(cmdbuf + 2, cmdtab[i].cmdname);
    if ( ( val=ads_defun(cmdbuf, i) ) != RTNORM)
        break;
   }
   return val;
}

/* * * * * * * * * * * * * * * * * * * * * * * * * * * * * * * */

int cutout()  {

   int val;
   cut_setup();
   if ( ( val=fprompt( "Move Copy" ,
                       "Move or Copy" ,
                       mc_resp ) ) == RTNORM )   {
      if ( ( val=cut_setpts( CUT_OFFSET ) ) == RTNORM )
         val=cut_rcut();
   }

   switch ( val )    {

   case RTNORM:
```

Pseudocode for CUTOUT.C

```
            break;

    case RTCAN:
        ads_prompt( "\n \nCUTOUT: Cancelled. \n" );
        break;
    default:
        ads_printf( "\nCUTOUT: Internal error. Bad value returned: %d"
                    , val );
        break;
    }
    cut_reset(val);
    ads_retvoid();
    return val;
}
/* * * * * * * * * * * * * * * * * * * * * * * * * * * * * * * * * * */

void cut_setup()   {

    struct resbuf rb, user4;
    ads_getvar( "CMDECHO"  , &oldcmd );
    ads_getvar( "BLIPMODE" , &oldblp );
    ads_getvar( "EXPERT"   , &oldexp );
    ads_getvar( "UNDOCTL"  , &oldund );
    ads_getvar( "HIGHLIGHT", &oldhlt );
    ads_getvar( "PLINEWID" , &oldplw );
    ads_getvar( "USERI4"   , &user4 );
    rb.rbnext     = NULL;
    rb.restype    = RTSHORT;

    if ( user4.resval.rint == 5120 )  {
        rb.resval.rint = 1;
        ads_prompt("\nDEBUG on.");
    } else
        rb.resval.rint = 0;
    ads_setvar( "CMDECHO"  , &rb );
    ads_setvar( "BLIPMODE" , &rb );
    ads_setvar( "HIGHLIGHT", &rb );

    rb.resval.rint = 5;
    ads_setvar( "EXPERT" ,    &rb );
    undo_setup( oldund.resval.rint );

    ads_command(
             RTSTR , "_.UNDO" , RTSTR , "GROUP" ,
             RTSTR , "_.UNDO" , RTSTR , "MARK"  ,
```

```c
                       0 );

    return;

}
/* * * * * * * * * * * * * * * * * * * * * * * * * * * * * * * */


/* FPROMPT   --   Format Prompting for Keywords.     */

int fprompt( keyw , message , defres)  {

    int val;
    char temp[6];
    char prmt[35];

    strcpy( temp, defres);
    strcat( strcpy( prmt , "\n" ) , message );
    if ( strcmp( temp , "" ) != 0 ) {
       strcat( strcat( strcat( prmt , " <" ) , temp ) , ">" );
       ads_initget( 0 , keyw );
    } else
       ads_initget( 1 , keyw );

    if ((val=ads_getkword( strcat(prmt,": ") , defres )) == RTCAN ) {
       ads_printf("\nFunction cancelled.");
       ads_retvoid();
    } else  {
       if ( strcmp( defres , "" ) == 0 )  {
            val=RTNORM;
            strcpy( defres , temp );
       }

       ads_retstr(defres);
    }
  return val;
}

/* * * * * * * * * * * * * * * * * * * * * * * * * * * * * * * */

int cut_setpts( offset )  {

   int val=0;
   ads_initget( 1 , NULL);
```

Pseudocode for CUTOUT.C

```c
    if ((val=ads_getpoint(NULL,"\nFirst corner:",p0))==RTNORM) {

        ads_initget( 1 , NULL);
        if ((val=ads_getcorner(p0,"\nOpposite corner:",p0a))==RTNORM) {

            ( p0[X] < p0a[X] ) ? pt1[X] =  p0[X] : pt1[X] = p0a[X];
            ( p0[Y] < p0a[Y] ) ? pt1[Y] =  p0[Y] : pt1[Y] = p0a[Y];
            ( p0[X] > p0a[X] ) ? pt3[X] =  p0[X] : pt3[X] = p0a[X];
            ( p0[Y] > p0a[Y] ) ? pt3[Y] =  p0[Y] : pt3[Y] = p0a[Y];

            pt2[X] = pt3[X];   pt2[Y] = pt1[Y];
            pt4[X] = pt1[X];   pt4[Y] = pt3[Y];

            i_pt1[X] = pt1[X]+offset;   i_pt1[Y] = pt1[Y]+offset;
            i_pt2[X] = pt2[X]-offset;   i_pt2[Y] = pt2[Y]+offset;
            i_pt3[X] = pt3[X]-offset;   i_pt3[Y] = pt3[Y]-offset;
            i_pt4[X] = pt4[X]+offset;   i_pt4[Y] = pt4[Y]-offset;

            o_pt1[X] = pt1[X]-offset;   o_pt1[Y] = pt1[Y]-offset;
            o_pt2[X] = pt2[X]+offset;   o_pt2[Y] = pt2[Y]-offset;
            o_pt3[X] = pt3[X]+offset;   o_pt3[Y] = pt3[Y]+offset;
            o_pt4[X] = pt4[X]-offset;   o_pt4[Y] = pt4[Y]+offset;
        }
    }
    return val;
}
/* * * * * * * * * * * * * * * * * * * * * * * * * * * * * * * */

int cut_rcut()  {

    int val;
    ads_name  trimln, ss1, ent;
    long      *total;
    long      index=1;
    char      bname[32];

    ads_ssadd( NULL , NULL , ssx );
    ads_ssadd( NULL , NULL , ss1 );
    if ( ( val=cut_expset() ) == RTNORM )   {
        if ( ( val=cut_drwln( pt1 , pt2 , pt3 , pt4 ) ) == RTNORM )
            ads_entlast( trimln );
    }
    if ( ( val == RTNORM ) &&
         ( val=cut_rtrim( trimln , o_pt1 , o_pt2 ,
                          o_pt3 , o_pt4 ) ) == RTNORM ) {
```

```
      ads_ssget( "C" , i_pt1 , i_pt3 , NULL , ss1 );
      ads_ssadd( trimln , ss1 , ss1 );
      cut_adjset( ss1 );

      ads_sslength( ss1 , total );

      if ( index < *total ) {
         cut_okblk( "cut" , bname );
         val=ads_command(
                  RTSTR , "_.WBLOCK" , RTSTR , bname , RTSTR , "" ,
                    RTPOINT , pt1 , RTPICKS , ss1 , RTSTR , "" ,
                  RTSTR , "_.UNDO" , RTSTR , "BACK" ,
                  0 );
         ads_ssfree( ss1 );
      } else  {
          ads_ssfree( ss1 );
          val=RTERROR;
      }
   }

   if ( val == RTNORM )  {
      if ( strcmp( mc_resp , "Move" ) == 0 ) {
         cut_expset();
         if ( ( val=cut_expset() ) == RTNORM )  {
            if ( ( val=cut_drwln( pt1 , pt2 , pt3 , pt4 ) ) == RTNORM )
               ads_entlast( trimln );
         }
         if ( ( val == RTNORM ) &&
              ( val=cut_rtrim( trimln , i_pt1 , i_pt2 ,
                              i_pt3 , i_pt4 ) ) == RTNORM ) {
            ads_entdel( trimln );
            ads_ssadd( NULL , NULL , ss1 );
            ads_ssget( "C" , i_pt1 , i_pt3 , NULL , ss1 );
            cut_adjset( ss1 );
            ads_sslength( ss1 , total );
            for ( index=0; index < *total; index++ ) {
               ads_ssname( ss1 , index , ent );
               ads_entdel( ent );
            }
            ads_ssfree( ss1 );
            ads_sslength( ssx , total );
            for ( index=0; index < *total; index++ ) {
               ads_ssname( ssx , index++ , ent );
               ads_entdel( ent );
            }
```

Pseudocode for CUTOUT.C

```
               ads_ssfree( ssx );
               ads_prompt( "\nInsert cutout:" );
            }
         }
         if ( ( val == RTNORM ) &&
                ( val=ads_command(
                            RTSTR , "_.INSERT" , RTSTR , bname , RTSTR , "\\" ,
                              RTSTR , "" , RTSTR , "" , RTSTR , "" ,
                            0 ) ) == RTNORM )  {

            strcat( bname , ".DWG" );
            if ( remove( bname ) == -1 )
               ads_printf( "\nCould not erase %s" , bname );
            else
               ads_printf( "\nErased %s" , bname );
         }
      } else {
         ads_prompt( "\nNothing to cut." );
         val=ads_command(
                         RTSTR , "_.UNDO" , RTSTR , "BACK" ,
                         0 );
      }
      return val;
}

/* * * * * * * * * * * * * * * * * * * * * * * * * * * * * * * */

int cut_expset()  {

      int         val=RTNORM;
      char        etype[20];
      ads_name    ss0, ent;
      int         redo=RTNORM, first=RTNONE;
      long        *total;
      long        index;

      while ( (redo==RTNORM) && (val==RTNORM)) {
         redo=RTNONE;
         ads_ssget( "C" , pt1 , pt3 , NULL , ss0 );
         ads_sslength( ss0 , total );
         index=0;

         while ( index < *total && val==RTNORM) {
            ads_ssname( ss0 , index++ , ent );
            cut_etype( ent , etype );
```

INTRODUCTION TO ADS
CH. 9

```
        if ( strncmp( etype ,"INSERT"   , 6 )   == 0  ||
             strncmp( etype ,"POLYLINE" , 8 ) == 0  ||
             strncmp( etype ,"DIMENSION", 9 )== 0 ) {
            if ( first!=RTNORM )
                first=ads_prompt( "\nExploding blocks/polylines..." );
            redo=RTNORM;
            val=ads_command(
                            RTSTR , "_.EXPLODE" , RTENAME , ent ,
                            0 );
        }
        if ( val==RTNORM )  {
            if ( strcmp( etype , "3DFACE" )   == 0   ||
                 strcmp( etype , "ATTDEF" )   == 0   ||
                 strcmp( etype , "POINT" )    == 0   ||
                 strcmp( etype , "SHAPE" )    == 0   ||
                 strcmp( etype , "SOLID" )    == 0   ||
                 strcmp( etype , "TRACE" )    == 0   ||
                 strcmp( etype , "VIEWPORT" ) == 0 ) {

                ads_ssadd( ent , ssx , ssx );
                ads_entdel( ent );
            }
        }
    }
    ads_ssfree( ss0 );
  }
  return val;
}
/* * * * * * * * * * * * * * * * * * * * * * * * * * * * * * * * */

int cut_etype( entity , etype )  {

   int val;
   struct resbuf *ebuf, *eb;

   if ( ( ebuf = ads_entget( entity ) ) != NULL )  {
      for ( eb = ebuf; ( eb!=NULL && eb->restype!=0 ); eb=eb->rbnext );

      if ( eb != NULL && eb->restype == 0 )  {
         val=RTNORM;
         strcpy( etype , eb->resval.rstring );
      } else
            val=RTERROR;
   } else
         val=RTERROR;
```

Pseudocode for CUTOUT.C

```
      ads_relrb( ebuf );
      return val;
}
/* * * * * * * * * * * * * * * * * * * * * * * * * * * * * * * */

int cut_drwln( p1 , p2 , p3 , p4 )   {

   int check , i;
   struct resbuf *cutrec;
   ads_real *vertices[] = { p1 , p2 , p3 , p4 };

   if ( (cutrec = ads_buildlist(RTDXF0, "POLYLINE",
                            66, 1,
                            70, 1,
                            NULL ) ) == NULL ) {
      ads_fail("\nError building polyline.");
      return RTERROR;
   }
   check = ads_entmake(cutrec);
   ads_relrb(cutrec);
   if (check != RTNORM)   {
      ads_fail("\nERROR continuing polyline.");
      return RTERROR;
   }
   for ( i = 0 ; i < 4 ; i++) {
      cutrec = ads_buildlist(RTDXF0, "VERTEX",
                            10, vertices[i],
                            NULL );
      if (cutrec == NULL )   {
         ads_printf("\nREC: Error building vertex %d.", (i+1));
         return RTERROR;
      }
      check = ads_entmake(cutrec);
      ads_relrb(cutrec);
      if ( check != RTNORM ) {
         ads_printf("\nREC: Error creating vertex %d.", (i+1));
         return RTERROR;
      }
   }

   cutrec = ads_buildlist(RTDXF0, "SEQEND",
                         NULL );
   if (cutrec == NULL )   {
      ads_printf("\nREC: Error building SEQEND.");
```

```
            return RTERROR;
      }

      check = ads_entmake(cutrec);
      ads_relrb(cutrec);

      if ( check != RTNORM ) {
         ads_printf("\nREC: Error finishing polyline.");
         return RTERROR;
      }
      return check;
}
/* * * * * * * * * * * * * * * * * * * * * * * * * * * * * * * */
int cut_rtrim( tl , p1 , p2 , p3 , p4 ) {
      return (ads_command(
               RTSTR , "_.TRIM" , RTENAME , tl , RTSTR , "" ,
               RTSTR , "F" , RTPOINT , p1 , RTPOINT , p2 , RTSTR , "" ,
               RTSTR , "F" , RTPOINT , p2 , RTPOINT , p3 , RTSTR , "" ,
               RTSTR , "F" , RTPOINT , p3 , RTPOINT , p4 , RTSTR , "" ,
               RTSTR , "F" , RTPOINT , p4 , RTPOINT , p1 , RTSTR , "" ,
               RTSTR , "" ,
               0 ));
}

/* * * * * * * * * * * * * * * * * * * * * * * * * * * * * * * */

void cut_okblk( pf , blkname )  {

      char prefix[32];
      char c_index[32];
      long index=0;
      do {  strcpy(   blkname ,
                      strcat(   strcpy( prefix , pf ) ,
                                ltoa( index++ , c_index , 10 )
                            )
                  );
      } while ( ads_tblsearch( "BLOCK" , blkname , 0 ) );
      return;
}
/* * * * * * * * * * * * * * * * * * * * * * * * * * * * * * * */

void cut_adjset( ss )  {

      ads_name ent;
      long *total;
```

Pseudocode for CUTOUT.C

```
      long index=0;
      char etype[20];
      ads_sslength( ss , total );
      while ( index < *total ) {
         ads_ssname( ss , index , ent );
         cut_etype( ent , etype );
         if ( strcmp( etype , "3DFACE" )   == 0   ||
              strcmp( etype , "ATTDEF" )   == 0   ||
              strcmp( etype , "POINT" )    == 0   ||
              strcmp( etype , "SHAPE" )    == 0   ||
              strcmp( etype , "SOLID" )    == 0   ||
              strcmp( etype , "TRACE" )    == 0   ||
              strcmp( etype , "VIEWPORT" ) == 0 ) {
            ads_ssdel( ent , ss );
            --*total;
         } else
            ++index;
      }
      return;
   }
   /* * * * * * * * * * * * * * * * * * * * * * * * * * * * * * */
   void cut_reset( val ) {

      if ( val != RTNORM )
         ads_command(
                     RTSTR , "_.UNDO" , RTSTR , "END" ,
                     RTSTR , "_.U" ,
                     0 );

      undo_reset( oldund.resval.rint );

      ads_setvar( "CMDECHO"  , &oldcmd );
      ads_setvar( "BLIPMODE" , &oldblp );
      ads_setvar( "HIGHLIGHT", &oldhlt );
      ads_setvar( "PLINEWID" , &oldplw );
      ads_setvar( "EXPERT"   , &oldexp );

      return;

   }
   /* * * * * * * * * * * * * * * * * * * * * * * * * * * * * * */

   int undo_setup( val ) {
```

INTRODUCTION TO ADS
CH. 9

```
    int uval=RTNORM;

    switch ( val ) {
       case 0:
          uval=ads_command(
                   RTSTR , "_.UNDO" , RTSTR , "ALL" ,
                   RTSTR , "_.UNDO" , RTSTR , "AUTO" , RTSTR , "OFF" ,
                   0 );
          break;
       case 3:
          uval=ads_command(
                   RTSTR , "_.UNDO" , RTSTR , "CONTROL" , RTSTR , "ALL" ,
                   RTSTR , "_.UNDO" , RTSTR , "AUTO" , RTSTR , "OFF" ,
                   0 );
          break;
       case 5:
          uval=ads_command(
                   RTSTR , "_.UNDO" , RTSTR , "AUTO" , RTSTR , "OFF" ,
                   0 );
          break;
       default:
          break;

    }
    return uval;
}
/* * * * * * * * * * * * * * * * * * * * * * * * * * * * * * * */

int undo_reset( val ) {

    int uval=RTNORM;

    switch ( val ) {
       case 0:
          uval=ads_command(
                  RTSTR , "_.UNDO" , RTSTR , "CONTROL" , RTSTR , "NONE" ,
                  0 );
          break;

       case 1:
          uval=ads_command(
                   RTSTR , "_.UNDO" , RTSTR , "END" ,
                   0 );
          break;
```

```
        case 3:
            uval=ads_command(
                    RTSTR , "_.UNDO" , RTSTR , "END" ,
                    RTSTR , "_.UNDO" , RTSTR , "CONTROL" , RTSTR , "ONE" ,
                    0 );
            break;

        case 5:
            uval=ads_command(
                    RTSTR , "_.UNDO" , RTSTR , "END" ,
                    RTSTR , "_.UNDO" , RTSTR , "AUTO" , RTSTR , "ON" ,
                    0 );
            break;

        default:
            break;
    }

    return uval;
}
/* * * * * * * * * * * * * * * * * * * * * * * * * * * * * * * * * * * *
 eof - CUTOUT.c    660 lines.    */
```

CUTOUT.C has been structured so that one function, cutout(), calls all the other functions in the program. This function is defined by ads_defun() as an AutoCAD command, by appending "C:" to the function name passed to ads_defun(). This is similar to the AutoLISP technique for naming AutoCAD commands.

Function Tables

Technically, CUTOUT.C needs to define only this single function with ads_defun(). All the other functions are local to this command function, and will be called by it. Nevertheless, for the sake of illustration, this source code uses a more general technique you can apply to applications that define more than one command or function. The technique in CUTOUT.C is based on the "function table" technique used in the ADS sample program GRAVITY.C, and you are urged to compare the two.

The function table is set up externally and consists of a structure, illustrated in the following code fragment:

```
struct { char *cmdname; int (*cmdfunc)(); }
 cmdtab[] =  {
                /* Command Name , Function Name  */
                { "CUTOUT"      , cutout }
            } ;
```

The loadfunc() function in CUTOUT.C is more sophisticated than the one used in FPROMPT.C, in that it can loop through each function stored in this table and call ads_defun() for each:

```
int loadfunc()  {
    char cmdbuf[40];
    int i, val;
    strcpy(cmdbuf, "C:");
    for (i = 0; i < count(cmdtab); i++)    {
        strcpy(cmdbuf + 2, cmdtab[i].cmdname);
        if ( ( val=ads_defun(cmdbuf, i) ) != RTNORM)
            break;
    }
    return val;
}
```

Bear in mind, however, that the function table's structure is rigid. Return values and argument structure must be the same for each function in the table. Do not attempt to mix functions with different return value types and argument requirements in the same table. If you need to define functions with different parameters, create different command tables to accommodate them, or call ads_defun() explicitly for each.

Macros and Constants

The loadfunc() function's generality is based on a macro named count(), which returns the number of elements in an array:

```
#define count(array) ( sizeof( array ) / sizeof( (array)[0] ) )
```

This macro must be defined in each program that uses loadfunc().

CUTOUT.C also defines a single manifest constant, named CUT_OFFSET:

```
#define CUT_OFFSET 0.10
```

This constant stores the distance (currently one-tenth of a drawing unit) between the sides of the cutting rectangle and the fence line used in the trim command. Using a constant makes it easy to change the value throughout the program by editing a single line. As an alternative, you may want to give this option to the user by storing the value in an external variable and adding another call to fprompt().

Functions in CUTOUT.C

The following functions appear in CUTOUT.C. Several of these functions are general-purpose, and can be applied to other programs with little or no modification:

Function Name	Purpose
cut_adjset()	Removes nontrimmable entities from a selection set.
cut_drwln()	Draws a closed polyline between four points.
cut_etype()	Extracts the entity type (e.g., "LINE", "INSERT") from an entity definition table.
cut_expset()	Explodes blocks and dimensions in a selection set.
cut_okblk()	Searches the block definition table and binds a name not currently being used to *blkname.
cut_rcut()	Does the real work of the program. Calls cutout functions, writes entities to disk, optionally erasees entities inside the cutting rectangle, and prompts for insertion of cutoutentities in the drawing.
cut_reset()	Restores the saved environment state of the program.
cut_rtrim()	Trims entities using argument points to trime either inside or outside the cutting rectangle.
cut_setpts()	Prompts the operator for the cutting rectangle corners, and sets up the necessary analysis points.

Function Name	Purpose
cut_setup()	Stores current environment variables and sets up the environment state for the CUTOUT command.
cutout()	Becomes the command C:CUTOUT.
fprompt()	Prompts the operator for a keyword. Taken from FPROMPT.C.
loadfunc()	A standard function, defines external functions in a function table.
undo_setup()	Sets up the required UNDO state for the program.
undo_reset()	Restores the previous UNDO state for the program.

External Variables in CUTOUT.C

CUTOUT.C employs a few variables for the sake of programming simplicity and functionality:

External Variable Name	Purpose
static char mc_resp[]	Holds the default response to the Move/Copy prompt.
static struct resbuf oldcmd, oldexp, oldblp, oldund, oldhlt, oldplw	These structures store the environment settings shared by the cut_setup() and cut_reset() functions.
static ads_point p0, p0a, pt1, pt2, pt3, pt4, i_pt1, i_pt2, i_pt3, i_pt4, o_pt1, o_pt2, o_pt3, o_pt4	These variables hold points shared by the cut_setpts() and cut_rcut() functions.
static ads_name ssx	This is a temporary selection set shared by the cut_rcut() and cut_expset() functions.

Using Ads_ssfree() and Ads_relrb()

Whenever a selection set is no longer needed, CUTOUT.C calls ads_ssfree() to release the selection set's memory space. Similarly, CUTOUT.C calls ads_relrb() to release memory used by result buffers. This is an important habit to acquire, because ADS provides no internal mechanism for clearing memory taken up by selection sets and result buffers. In your own programs, you should always release memory used by selection sets and result buffers that are no longer needed. If you do not explicitly release this memory, you will eventually run out and lock the program, or crash AutoCAD.

You can find examples of ads_ssfree() in the functions cut_rcut() and cut_expset(), and examples of ads_relrb() in the functions cut_etype() and cut_drwln().

Managing Program Behavior

Throughout CUTOUT.C, you will notice several If statements that test the values returned by functions, and cancel further processing if the values are not correct for some reason. This is important, not only for debugging purposes, but to help the program behave well if the operator introduces invalid input, or presses Ctrl-C while processing.

CUTOUT.C is structured so that subsequent functions are not processed when abnormal situations are detected. If not normally terminated, CUTOUT.C invokes the UNDO BACK command and restores the drawing to its state when UNDO MARK was invoked. Thus, for example, if the operator cancels processing while trimming is taking place, the program treats it as a full command cancellation, restoring the drawing to its condition at the time the CUTOUT command was entered.

Handling Points

Points in ADS are simply an array of three real numbers, type-defined as ads_point. CUTOUT.C uses 2D points only, meaning that the third point in the array is simply not used.

INTRODUCTION TO ADS
CH. 9

Point values are stored in arrays. The ADS library predefines a data type called ads_point, which is simply an array of three real numbers. The easiest way to assign points to variables with this data type is to assign the coordinates using code blocks, as in the following example:

```
ads_point origin = { 0.0 , 0.0 , 0.0 };
```

This code fragment stores point 0,0,0 in an array value named origin.

Coordinates may also be bound into point arrays one coordinate at a time:

```
ads_point origin;
origin[X] = 0.0;
origin[Y] = 0.0;
origin[Z] = 0.0;
```

The uppercase letters X, Y, and Z are manifest constants in ADS that represent the element location for the X, Y, and Z coordinates in point arrays. Use them whenever you manipulate points in ADS. This makes point arrays easier to read in ADS source code and helps insure portability.

CUTOUT.C contains an example of point coordinate manipulation. To make things easier for the operator, the program will accept any two corners for defining the cutting rectangle, storing them in variables p0 and p0a. Once it receives those points, it uses them to establish the lower-left corner (pt1) and upper-right corner (pt3) of the rectangle:

```
( p0[X] < p0a[X] ) ? pt1[X] = p0[X] : pt1[X] = p0a[X];
( p0[Y] < p0a[Y] ) ? pt1[Y] = p0[Y] : pt1[Y] = p0a[Y];
( p0[X] > p0a[X] ) ? pt3[X] = p0[X] : pt3[X] = p0a[X];
( p0[Y] > p0a[Y] ) ? pt3[Y] = p0[Y] : pt3[Y] = p0a[Y];
```

The code fragment above finds which of the operator-specified points has the lesser X and Y coordinates, and stores the values in the lower-left variable. It stores the greater X and Y values in the upper-right corner. Once these points are defined consistently, other processing becomes much simpler.

Setting Up and Resetting the AutoCAD Environment

Most, if not all, ADS programs will make temporary changes to AutoCAD's extremely flexible drawing environment. CUTOUT.C uses two functions, cut_setup() and cut_reset(), to manage its changes. You can modify these functions to manage changes in your own ADS programs.

For each environmental change, cut_setup() uses an external variable declared as a result buffer to store current environment settings, as the following code fragments demonstrate:

```
struct resbuf rb, user4;    /* Declare variables */
ads_getvar( "USERI4" , &user4 ); /* Reference while processing */
```

These lines store the current value of the USERI4 system variable. Borrowing on an idea demonstrated in the chapter on AutoLISP, this value may be tested and used to affect other settings:

```
if ( user4.resval.rint == 5120 ) {
   rb.resval.rint = 1;
   ads_prompt("\nDEBUG on.");
} else
   rb.resval.rint = 0;
ads_setvar( "CMDECHO"  , &rb );
ads_setvar( "BLIPMODE" , &rb );
ads_setvar( "HIGHLIGHT" , &rb );
```

This code fragment will turn on command echo, blips, and highlighting if the value in the USERI4 system variable is 5120; otherwise, the program turns off these settings. USER14 and the number 5120 were chosen as a combination of system variable and stored value unlikely to conflict with other third-party programs. If this value conflicts with other programs on your system, you should change it to a value that does not conflict.

Using UNDO

CUTOUT.C makes use of AutoCAD's Undo feature to simplify processing. However, to use Undo successfully, you must first learn the status of the Undo feature, remember it, turn the Undo feature on completely, and restore its previous status when processing is interrupted or is complete.

The following code fragment stores the status of the Undo feature and turns the feature on if necessary:

```
struct resbuf oldund;                    /* Define result buffer */
ads_getvar( "UNDOCTL" , &oldund );       /* Store status */
undo_setup( oldund.resval.rint );        /* Turn UNDO on   */
/* ...Some other processing... */
undo_reset( oldund.resval.rint );        /* Restore previous UNDO */
```

The undo_setup() function, defined in CUTOUT.C, uses the value stored in the UNDOCTL system variable to call the UNDO command with the correct sequence of parameters.

Later, the same value will be used by the undo_reset() function (also defined in CUTOUT.C) to call the UNDO command again and restore the feature to its previous state, whether the CUTOUT command is interrupted or completes normally.

Refer to the source code listing of CUTOUT.C for the complete definition of these functions. Notice that the oldund result buffer is defined externally.

The cut_setup() and cut_reset() make one other use of UNDO: to set an Undo Group marker at the start of processing and an Undo End marker at the conclusion of processing. If the operator chooses to Undo the CUTOUT command, these markers will undo the CUTOUT command in a single pass.

Creating Entities in ADS Programs

Many ADS programs will create drawing entities. This process is simplified by using the library functions ads_buildlist() and ads_entmake(). CUTOUT.C uses these functions to construct the cutting rectangle as a closed polyline. The complete process is contained in the function cut_drwln(), found in the source code listing for CUTOUT.C.

The polyline header, each vertex, and the polyline footer must be created individually by separate calls to ads_buildlist() followed by ads_entmake(). The following code fragment creates the polyline header:

```
    int check;
    struct resbuf *cutrec;
    if ( (cutrec = ads_buildlist(RTDXF0, "POLYLINE",
                                 66, 1,
```

Creating Entities in ADS Programs

```
                            70, 1,
                            NULL ) ) == NULL ) {
   ads_fail("\nError building polyline.");
   return RTERROR;
}
```

Ads_buildlist() returns a result buffer containing the elements required to create an entity. The result buffer can then be passed to an ads_entmake() call, adding it to the drawing database:

```
check = ads_entmake(cutrec);
ads_relrb(cutrec);
if (check != RTNORM)  {
   ads_fail("\nERROR adding polyline.");
   return RTERROR;
}
```

Notice how this sequence includes a call to ads_relrb() immediately after the call to ads_entmake(). This releases the memory occupied by the result buffer, an important step.

Since each vertex of the polyline must be added with a separate call to these functions, this sequence is most efficiently handled within a loop:

```
ads_real *vertices[] = { p1 , p2 , p3 , p4 };
for ( i = 0 ; i < 4 ; i++) {
   cutrec = ads_buildlist(RTDXF0, "VERTEX",
                          10, vertices[i],
                          NULL );
   if (cutrec == NULL )  {
      ads_printf("\nREC: Error building vertex %d.", (i+1));
      return RTERROR;
   }
   check = ads_entmake(cutrec);
   ads_relrb(cutrec);
   if ( check != RTNORM ) {
      ads_printf("\nREC: Error creating vertex %d.", (i+1));
      return RTERROR;
   }
}
```

The loop is made possible by predefining an array, named *vertices[], containing pointers to each ads_point variable. The vertex-creating loop then steps through each element of the vertices[] array, adding them to the drawing database (and releasing the memory each time).

The cut_drwln() function concludes by using the same sequence to add the SEQEND list to the drawing database. When this last list is added, the cutting rectangle appears on the screen.

Refer to the source code for CUTOUT.C to study how these fragments are arranged into a working function.

Working with Entities

Many ADS programs will include functions to analyze entities. Entity information is stored in a special data type called a *result* buffer. Several result buffers, each containing some portion of entity information, can be analyzed in sequence. When result buffers are strung together this way, they are called a *linked list*. Thus, a linked list is simply a series of result buffers.

Each result buffer in a linked list contains an integer code (*restype*) indicating the data type, and a union (*resval*) that can hold whatever data type is indicated by the integer code. In addition, the result buffer contains a pointer (*rbnext*) to the memory location of the next result buffer in the list. The end of the list has been reached when the *rbnext* pointer is NULL.

Following is the ADS library definition of the result buffer structure:

```
struct resbuf  {
   struct resbuf *rbnext;
   short restype;
   union ads_u_val resval;
}
```

The union data type referenced in the result buffer structure is a series of data types that can accommodate various types of entity information:

```
union ads_u_val  {
   ads_real rreal;
   ads_real rpoint[3];
   short rint;
   char *rstring;
   long rlname[2];
   long rlong;
   struct ads_binary rbinary;
}
```

Working with Entities

It is useful to know how result buffers are organized, and how they can be chained together into a linked list. When you understand this concept, you can perform sophisticated entity analysis and make changes to entity data.

The following code fragment demonstrates the basic sequence for storing entity information in ADS:

```
ads_name entity;            /* Declare variables   */
struct resbuf *ebuf;
/* Get an entity (e.g., last in database) */
ads_entlast( entity );
/* Store entity information in result buffer ebuf   */
ebuf = ads_entget( entity );
```

The ads_entget() function takes care of setting up the linked list of entity information, and returns the first result buffer in the list. Once the entity information has been extracted in this manner, you can loop through the linked list until you find any desired data.

Ebuf points to a result buffer that contains the first item of the entity's associated data. This is the entity name, which you should leave alone. Ebuf->rbnext will point to the memory location of the next result buffer containing more of this entity's information.

For example, CUTOUT.C needs to find entity types. The following code fragment is a loop that will look through the linked list beginning with ebuf until it reaches the entity type, which is associated with a type code of zero:

```
int val;
struct resbuf *ebuf, *eb;
for ( eb = ebuf; ( eb!=NULL && eb->restype!=0 ); eb=eb->rbnext );
   if ( eb != NULL && eb->restype == 0 ) {
     val=RTNORM;
     strcpy( etype , eb->resval.rstring );
   } else
     val=RTERROR;
ads_relrb( ebuf );
```

This fragment uses a For statement to initialize a copy of the pointer to the result buffer stored in ebuf. The program loops through each result buffer in the linked list eb, until it finds an eb->restype value of zero. When eb->restype equals zero, eb->resval.rstring equals the entity type, and the program copies the eb->resval.rstring value into the etype[] character array. This condition also breaks out of the loop.

INTRODUCTION TO ADS
CH. 9

If the loop goes through the entire linked list without encountering an eb->restype value of zero, the val variable will equal RTERROR. Subsequent processing can test val to be sure that an entity type was found, before processing the etype array.

Refer to the cut_etype() function in the CUTOUT.C source code listing to study how these techniques are assembled into a working ADS function.

Working with Selection Sets

Many ADS programs will include functions to analyze and modify selection sets. Selection sets can be handled using ADS functions that are similar to selection set functions in AutoLISP.

For example, CUTOUT.C creates a selection set using the cutting rectangle as a crossing window. The code for doing this is as follows:

```
ads_name ss1;
ads_point i_pt1, i_pt3;
ads_ssadd( NULL , NULL , ss1 );
ads_ssget( "C" , i_pt1 , i_pt3 , NULL , ss1 );
```

The above code fragment declares the variable ss1 using the ads_name data type, which is a pair of long integers. The variable ss1 is therefore a pointer to the first element of the array.

The call to ads_ssadd() with NULL arguments creates an empty selection set; that is, one that contains no entities. After explicitly creating the empty selection set and storing a pointer to it in the variable ss1, the code fragment calls ads_ssget() to add entities to the set.

The NULL argument in ads_ssget() indicates that the resulting selection set is not filtered according to any common element among the selected entities; in other words, that all entities are to be included in the selection set ss1.

In the above example, the "C" followed by two point arrays creates a selection set of all entities enclosed in or intersecting a rectangle with opposite corners at points stored in variables i_pt1 and i_pt3.

When you have stored entities in selection sets, you can easily loop through them to process their contents. The following code fragment loops through the set

Working with Selection Sets

declared and created in the previous example, without making any changes:

```
ads_name ent;
long     *total, index;
ads_sslength( ss1 , total );
for ( index=0; index < *total; index++ ) {
      ads_ssname( ss1 , index , ent );
/* ...performs some processing on entity in variable ent...*/
}
ads_ssfree( ss1 );
```

The ads_sslength() function requires both a selection set and a pointer to a long integer that stores the number of entities in the selection set. AutoCAD's ADS documentation stresses that variables storing the number of entities in a selection set should be declared as long integers. If you do not declare these variables as long integer types, and the number of entities stored exceeds 65,535, your application will fail in unpredictable ways.

The loop in the above code fragment simply extracts each entity from the selection set in turn, incrementing the index variable by one each time through the loop, to extract the next available entity in the set. In your own applications, you would move on to various entity-processing steps, depending on the application's objectives, within the loop.

Whenever you are finished using a selection set, release it from memory with a call to ads_ssfree(). If you do not explicitly release memory used by selection sets as soon as possible, your application may eventually run out of memory, causing program crashes and other nasty surprises.

CUTOUT.C contains a function, cut_expset(), that takes a selection set and explodes the block, polyline and dimension entities. The following code fragment illustrates this process:

```
int            val=RTNORM;
char           etype[20];
ads_name       ss0, ent;
long           *total;
long           index;
ads_ssget( "C" , pt1 , pt3 , NULL , ss0 );
ads_sslength( ss0 , total );
index=0;
while ( index < *total && val==RTNORM) {
    ads_ssname( ss0 , index++ , ent );
    cut_etype( ent , etype );
```

```
        if ( strncmp( etype ,"INSERT"   , 6 )   == 0  ||
             strncmp( etype ,"POLYLINE" , 8 ) == 0  ||
             strncmp( etype ,"DIMENSION", 9 )== 0  )
           val=ads_command(
                    RTSTR , "_.EXPLODE" , RTENAME , ent ,
                    0 );
   }
   ads_ssfree( ss0 );
```

You will notice that this fragment includes a call to CUTOUT.C's cut_etype() function, which stores the entity type in the etype string variable.

Refer to the cut_expset() function in CUTOUT.C's source code listing for the full implementation of this process.

Searching the Block Table

Some ADS applications will handle blocks, linetypes, named user coordinate systems, views, or other data found in the drawing symbol table. CUTOUT.C, for example, requires that a selection set be written to disk with the WBLOCK command, the UNDO command invoked to restore the drawing to its previous condition, and the selection set called back again with the INSERT command. In order for this simple expediency to work, the drawing on disk must be given a name that is not found in the drawing's block name table. The following code fragment loops through the symbol table, testing for names until it has a name not present:

```
char pf[]="CUT"
char prefix[32];
char c_index[32];
long index=0;
do {
  strcpy( blkname , strcat( strcpy( prefix , pf ) ,
       ltoa( index++ , c_index , 10 ) ) );

  } while ( ads_tblsearch( "BLOCK" , blkname , 0 ) );
```

The above example illustrates a two-stage process:

1. The program assembles a name, converting an integer value to a string and appending it to the letters "CUT." Thus, the first string created is "CUT0."

2. The program calls the ads_tblsearch() function, searching the block table for a name matching the string.

As long as the string is found in the table, the program tries again, incrementing the integer each time, until ads_tblsearch() returns NULL, exiting the loop.

When ads_tblsearch() is successful, it returns a pointer to the first result buffer in a linked list. Depending on your program's objectives, this value may be acted upon by entity functions that analyze and process linked lists, as explained earlier in this chapter.

The zero argument (called the *symnext* argument) in this example indicates that the call to ads_tblsearch() will have no effect on subsequent calls to the ads_tblnext() function. However, CUTOUT.C never calls ads_tblnext(), so there is no concern in this context. However, using an argument other than zero could conceivably have an unwanted effect on other programs that access the same table.

Here is how the symnext argument works: it is useful in situations where you would like to extract several entities from a long symbol table, without having to loop through the table, looking at each entry individually. For example, imagine that this argument was set to any value other than zero. After locating an entity in the table and processing it in some fashion, you could find the next entity in the table by invoking ads_tblnext(), and depending on the arguments you use in that function, you could continue to locate the following entities by repeated calls to ads_tblnext(). This process saves time by allowing you to start anywhere in the table before looping through the entries.

Moving On

ADS is a rich function library that is likely to become more feature-laden and complex in subsequent releases of AutoCAD. C-language enthusiasts, users with special needs, and professional developers will welcome its additional power and flexibility, but ADS will not supplant AutoLISP. AutoLISP will always have the advantage of easier and faster development, at a small sacrifice in power and speed.

INTRODUCTION TO ADS
CH. 9

By the time you have worked through the functions in CUTOUT.C, you will have a solid basis for creating your own ADS applications. This purpose of this chapter is not to turn you into a C programmer overnight, but to allow you to get a feel for how ADS works, and you will find that the ADS documentation provided with AutoCAD is now much easier to understand. Give yourself plenty of time to experiment, and keep your goals modest as you start out.

As you write in ADS, try to develop functions that, whenever necessary, can be used in applications other than the one you are working on. By doing this, you will find that your applications are not only easier to test and debug, but you will quickly develop a library of reliable, pretested ADS functions that can be used repeatedly in a variety of programs. Although progress may seem slow at first, you will pick up speed as you go along, because you will not have to start from scratch each time you develop a new objective.

APPENDIX A

AutoLISP/ADS
Quick Function Reference

AUTOLISP/ADS QUICK FUNCTION REFERENCE
APP. A

This appendix lists AutoLISP functions as of Release 12, with a summary of each function's syntax and general notes regarding usage. It is intended as a "quick reference" to essential information; more details can be found by consulting the AutoLISP *Programmer's Reference*.

If an ADS function exists that corresponds to the AutoLISP function, its syntax and a summary of argument data types are included under the AutoLISP function listing. For example, if you want to look up the Ads_done_dialog function, look under *Done_dialog*.

ADS function declarations are defined in the ADSLIB.H and ADS.H header files. Functions for dialog boxes are defined in the ADSDLG.H header file.

Unlike AutoLISP function arguments, ADS arguments are never optional. In cases where an ADS argument may not be used (for example, a prompt string in Ads_get functions), pass a NULL pointer in its place.

Unless otherwise noted, ADS functions return an RTNORM code when they succeed, and an error code when they fail. Results of ADS function processing are generally placed in variables supplied as additional arguments to the function; result variables and exceptions are noted. Return values for AutoLISP functions are specified in each function listing.

Symbols Used as Functions

+

Adds numbers.

Syntax

(+ *n1 n2* ...)

Return Value: Sum of all argument numbers.

Arguments must be numbers. This function accepts any number of arguments. If all arguments are integers, an integer is returned. If any argument is a real number, a real number is returned.

Symbols Used as Functions

−

Subtracts numbers.

Syntax

(− *n1 n2* ...)

Return Value: Difference between the first argument and the sum of the remaining arguments.

Arguments must be numbers. This function accepts any number of arguments. If all arguments are integers, an integer is returned. If any argument is a real number, a real number is returned. If you supply a single argument, it is subtracted from zero.

*

Multiplies numbers.

Syntax

(* *n1 n2* ...)

Return Value: Product of all arguments.

Arguments must be numbers. This function accepts any number of arguments. If only one argument is supplied, it is multiplied by 1. If all arguments are integers, an integer is returned. Otherwise, a real number is returned.

/

Divides numbers.

Syntax

(/ *n1 n2* ...)

Return Value: Quotient of the first argument divided by the product of the remaining argument.

Arguments must be numbers. This function accepts any number of arguments. If one argument is supplied, it is divided by 1. If two are supplied, the first is divided by the second. If all arguments are integers, an integer is returned. Otherwise, a real number is returned.

=

Tests for numerical equality.

Syntax

(= *arg1 arg2* ...)

Return Value: T if all arguments evaluate to a numerical equivalent; nil otherwise.

Arguments can be numbers or strings. Strings are compared on the basis of numerical equivalence. This function accepts any number of arguments.

/=

Tests for numerical non-equality.

Syntax

(/= *arg1 arg2* ...)

Return Value: T if any arguments are not numerically equivalent; nil if all arguments are numerically equivalent.

Arguments can be numbers or strings. Strings are compared on the basis of numerical equivalence. This function accepts any number of arguments.

<

Tests for less-than relation between arguments.

Syntax

(< *arg1 arg2* ...)

Return Value: T if each argument is numerically less than the argument to its right.

Arguments can be numbers or strings. Strings are compared on the basis of their numerical value. This function accepts any number of arguments.

Symbols Used as Functions

<=

Tests for less-than or equal-to relation between arguments.

Syntax

(<= *arg1 arg2* ...)

Return Value: T if each argument is numerically less than or equal to the argument to its right.

Arguments can be numbers or strings. Strings are compared on the basis of their numerical value. This function accepts any number of arguments.

>

Tests for greater-than relation between arguments.

Syntax

(> *arg1 arg2* ...)

Return Value: T if each argument is numerically greater than the argument to its right.

Arguments can be numbers or strings. Strings are compared on the basis of their numerical value. This function accepts any number of arguments.

>=

Tests for greater-than or equal-to relation between arguments.

Syntax

(>= *arg1 arg2* ...)

Return Value: T if each argument is numerically greater than or equal to the argument to its right.

Arguments can be numbers or strings. Strings are compared on the basis of their numerical value. This function accepts any number of arguments.

~

Returns the bitwise complement of its argument.

Syntax

(~ n)

Return Value: Bitwise complement of n (not the same as zero minus n). N must be an integer.

1+

Increases a number by one.

Syntax

(1+ n)

Return Value: Argument incremented by one.

N must be a number. If an integer, an integer is returned. Otherwise, a real number is returned.

1−

Decreases a number by one.

Syntax

(1− n)

Return Value: Argument decremented by one.

N must be a number. If an integer, an integer is returned. Otherwise, a real number is returned.

Functions Listed Alphabetically

ABS

Converts a number to its absolute value.

Syntax

(abs *n*)

Return Value: The absolute value of *n*.

N must be a number. If an integer, an integer is returned. Otherwise, a real number is returned.

ACTION_TILE

Assigns functions to dialog box tiles.

Syntax

(action_tile *tile function*)

Return Value: Nil.

The Action_tile function requires two arguments. Both are supplied as character strings; that is, they are enclosed in quotes. Refer to the DDGEAR.LSP routine in Chapter 7 for examples of how arguments are supplied to Action_tile.

The *tile* argument is the name of a dialog box tile. *Function* is the function that is to be called when the user activates the specified tile.

ADS Equivalent

```
int ads_action_tile(hdlg, tile, function)
    ads_hdlg hdlg;
    char *tile;
    CLIENTFUNC function;
```

The *function* argument is a pointer to a function to be called when the user selects the tile named in *tile*. The *hdlg* argument is a dialog box handle of the type stored by the Ads_new_dialog function.

ADD_LIST

Adds an item to a list box or popup list.

Syntax

(add_list *item*)

Return Value: Nil.

The required *item* argument is a character string that will be added to the list box or popup list specified in a previous call to the Start_list function. Start_list must be called before this function will work.

ADS Equivalent

```
int ads_add_list(item)
char *item;
```

Adds *item* to the current list specified by ads_start_list().

ADS

Lists loaded ADS applications.

Syntax

(ads)

Return Value: A list of strings. Each string is the application name of a loaded ADS application.

ADS Equivalent

```
struct resbuf *ads_loaded()
```

Returns a pointer to a linked list of result buffers containing ADS applications. If no ADS applications are loaded, this function returns NULL.

ALERT

Displays a dialog box with a warning message.

Functions Listed Alphabetically

Syntax

(alert `str`)

Return Value: nil.

The *str* argument may be any valid string of characters that will appear in the alert box. The argument is required.

ADS Equivalent

```
int ads_alert(str)
    char *str;
```

If Ads_alert fails, it returns an RTERROR code.

ALLOC

Resets the number of nodes in an AutoLISP memory segment.

Syntax

(alloc `n`)

Return Value: The previous number of nodes per segment (default: 514). Resetting the number of nodes per segment can improve the efficiency of large applications. This function is intended for experienced programmers who wish to reserve memory manually in their applications. For details, consult the AutoLISP *Programmer's Reference*.

AND

Tests a series of expressions for values.

Syntax

(and `exp1 exp2 ...`)

Return Value: T if all arguments evaluate to a non-nil value; otherwise, it returns nil.

Arguments to this function can be any valid AutoLISP expression—for example, another function, or a memory variable. This function is often used to test complex criteria in conditional functions, such as the If or While functions.

ANGLE

Calculates the angle formed by two points, in relation to AutoCAD's default angle zero.

Syntax

(angle *pt1 pt2*)

Return Value: The angle formed by the two points, in radians.

Both arguments are required. They must be lists of numbers that can be interpreted by AutoCAD as 2D or 3D points. The angle increases in a counterclockwise direction from angle zero. AutoCAD assumes that a line formed by the two points is in the current construction plane. If the points do not fall within the current construction plane, they are projected onto that plane.

ADS Equivalent

```
ads_real ads_angle(pt1, pt2)
    ads_point pt1, pt2;
```

Ads_angle returns a real number, indicating the angle value in radians.

ANGTOF

Converts a character string into a number representing an angle.

Syntax

(angtof *str mode*)

The *str* argument must be a character string, which expresses a numeric value. The *mode* argument is an integer indicating the current angle format of the string. Valid *mode* values are:

0 = degrees

1 = degrees/minutes/seconds

2 = grads

3 = radians

4 = surveyor's units

Functions Listed Alphabetically

For example:

```
(angtof "90.0" 0)
```

indicates that the string "90.0" expresses ninety degrees.

The *mode* argument is optional. If it is not supplied, the current setting for the AUNITS system variable is used.

ADS Equivalent

```
int ads_angtof(str, unit, result)
    char *str;
    int unit;
    ads_real *result;
```

The conversion result is placed in the *result* argument.

ANGTOS

Converts a number (representing an angle in radians) to a character string.

Syntax

```
(angtos n mode prec)
```

Return Value: A character string representing the angle.

The *mode* argument is an integer, and it is optional. If supplied, the string is returned formatted in the system of angle units as shown in the Angtof function. If *mode* is supplied, the *prec* argument may also be supplied. *Prec* is an integer indicating the number of decimal places to include in the angle string. If neither of these arguments is supplied, AutoCAD uses the current settings for AUNITS and AUPREC for *mode* and *prec*.

ADS Equivalent

```
int ads_angtos(n, unit, prec, str)
    ads_real n;
    int unit, prec;
    char *str;
```

The result is stored in *str*, which must be initialized with enough length to hold the formatted mode and precision; 15 characters is recommended.

APPEND

Builds one list from any number of lists.

Syntax

(append *list1 list2* ...)

Return Value: A single list.

Append can accept any number of arguments, but each argument must be a valid AutoLISP list.

APPLY

Evaluates a function, applying a list of arguments.

Syntax

(apply *func list*)

Return Value: The value returned by the function argument.

The *func* argument may be either a predefined or user-defined AutoLISP function. The *list* argument must be a list of valid arguments for the specified function. The list must contain all the arguments required by the specified function. Apply is used to invoke functions in cases where an AutoLISP routine has created a list of valid arguments.

ASCII

Converts a character into its numeric ASCII code.

Syntax

(ascii *str*)

Return Value: an integer, representing an ASCII code.

The Ascii function requires a character string argument. The string may be of any length, but only the first character in the string is converted.

ASSOC

Locates sublists in an entity association list.

Syntax

(assoc `key list`)

Return Value: The first sublist found in *list*, in which *key* is the first item.

Both arguments are required. The *key* argument can be any valid expression that might appear as the first element in a sublist. The *list* argument must be a list of sublists, such as an AutoCAD entity association list.

ATAN

Calculates the arctangent.

Syntax

(atan `n1 n2`)

Return Value: The arctangent of its arguments, in radians.

The function requires at least one number. If one number is supplied, Atan returns the arctangent of that number. If a second number is supplied, Atan returns the arctangent of the quotient of the first number divided by the second.

If *n2* is zero, Atan returns 1.570796 (90 degrees in radians) if *n1* is positive, or −1.570796 if *n1* is negative.

ATOF

Converts a character string into a real number.

Syntax

(atof `str`)

Return Value: A real number.

The Atof function requires a single character-string argument that represents a numeric value.

ATOI

Converts a character string into an integer.

Syntax

(atoi *str*)

Return Value: An integer.

The Atoi function requires a single character-string argument that represents a valid integer value. If the string represents a real number, the decimal portion is truncated.

ATOM

Tests to determine whether its argument is anything other than a list.

Syntax

(atom *arg*)

Return Value: T if the argument is not a list; otherwise, it returns nil.

ATOMS-FAMILY

Searches for AutoLISP symbols.

Syntax

(atoms-family *format list*)

Return Value: A list of AutoLISP symbols.

The *format* argument is required, and must be either 1 or 0. If 1, the symbols in the returned list are formatted as strings; if 0, the list simply contains the symbol names. The *list* argument is optional. (It is a list of specific symbol names that the function can search for.) If a symbol in the list is not defined, nil appears in the list returned by Atoms-family.

BOOLE

Compares binary bits in integers.

Syntax

`(boole `*`bfunc int1 int2`*` ...)`

Return Value: An integer representing a binary number composed of logical result bits.

The *bfunc*, *int1*, and *int2* arguments are required. They are all integers. Additional optional integer arguments may be supplied. The binary comparisons between the second through last arguments are made between the bits in the first position of each, then the second position, and so forth. In each case, a *result bit* is created in the same position and set to either zero or one. When all positions have been compared, the result is a binary number. The integer equivalent of this number is returned by the function.

The *bfunc* argument is an integer between 1 and 15 indicating which bit values in the remaining arguments will set each result bit to one. The *bfunc* argument may be one of the following integers, or the sum of any combination:

1 = Set result bit to 1 if compared bits are both 1.
2 = Set result bit to 1 if first bit = 1 and second bit = 0.
4 = Set result bit to 1 if first bit = 0 and second bit = 1.
8 = Set result bit to 1 if first bit = 0 and second bit = 0.

BOUNDP

Tests to determine whether a symbol is bound to a value.

Syntax

`(boundp `*`sym`*`)`

Return Value: T if *sym* is bound to a value; nil otherwise.

CAR

Extracts the first element from a list.

Syntax

`(car `*`list`*`)`

Return Value: The first element in the list.

The Car function requires a list as its argument. If the list is empty (same as nil), the function returns nil. If the first element is a sublist, the sublist is returned.

CADR

Extracts the second element from a list.

Syntax

(cadr *list*)

Return Value: The second element in the list.

The Cadr function requires a list as its argument. If the list is empty (same as nil), or the list contains only one element, the function returns nil. If the second element is a sublist, the sublist is returned.

CADDR

Extracts the third element from a list.

Syntax

(caddr *list*)

Return Value: The third element in the list.

The Caddr function requires a list as its argument. If the list is empty (same as nil), or there is no third element in the list, the function returns nil. If the third element is a sublist, the sublist is returned.

CDR

Extracts a list containing all but the first element of a list.

Syntax

(cdr *list*)

Return Value: A list, minus the first element of the argument list.

Functions Listed Alphabetically

The Cdr function requires a list as its argument. If the list is empty (same as nil), the function returns nil. The Cdr function is a convenient means of extracting code values from sublists in entity association lists.

CHR

Converts an integer into an ASCII character.

Syntax

(chr *int*)

Return Value: An ASCII character.

The *int* argument is required, and should be within the range for ASCII character codes. The function returns the character represented by the integer.

CLIENT_DATA_TILE

Associates data with a tile.

Syntax

(client_data_tile *tile data*)

Return Value: nil.

Both arguments are required. The *tile* argument is a character string indicating the name of a tile as specified in the Dialog Control Language (DCL) file. The *data* argument is supplied in the form of a character string. Action expressions linked to tile names in the Action_tile function may access the associated data expression using the metavariable $data.

ADS Equivalent

```
int ads_client_data_tile(hdlg, tile, data)
    ads_hdlg hdlg;
    char *tile;
    void *data;
```

The *hdlg* argument is a dialog box handle of the type stored by the Ads_new_dialog function.

CLOSE

Closes an open file.

Syntax

(close *file*)

Return Value: nil.

The *file* argument must be a valid file descriptor created using the Open function, and bound to a memory variable. Use the memory variable as the argument to this function when you no longer need to access the contents of the file.

COMMAND

Executes AutoCAD commands.

Syntax

(command *command name & valid parameters* ...)

Return Value: nil.

The command function accepts an AutoCAD command name and valid command parameters as if they were typed at the keyboard. Memory variables bound to valid command parameters may be used. There are several restrictions:

1. The drawing editor must be at the Command prompt and awaiting a command when this function is first invoked.
2. String arguments (for example, block names) must be enclosed in quotes.
3. You cannot use Get-functions within the Command function.
4. You cannot invoke DTEXT or SKETCH commands with this function.
5. The SCRIPT command can be invoked, but AutoCAD cannot return to the AutoLISP routine at the conclusion of the script.

The Command function accepts a predefined AutoLISP symbol named *PAUSE*. When this symbol is encountered as an argument to the Command function, AutoCAD pauses and waits for some user input, then proceeds with the routine.

Functions Listed Alphabetically

A backslash character (\) within a string will also pause the routine. If you must use a backslash in a string argument to the Command function, double it ("\\").

You can suspend the Command function by not specifying all the remaining command parameters. You can pick up where you left off by re-invoking the Command function with the correct remaining parameters. For an example of this, refer to the LX.LSP routine in Appendix B.

ADS Equivalent

```
ads_command(rtype, arg, ...)
    int rtype;
```

Ads_command can accept any number of paired arguments. *Rtype* is an integer indicating the data type of the AutoCAD command parameter that is paired with it and follows it; for example:

RTREAL = Real number

RTSHORT = Short integer

RTLONG = Long integer

RT3DPOINT = 3D point

RTPOINT = 2D Point

RTANG = Angle

RTSTR = Character string

RTENAME = Entity name

RTPICKS = Selection set name

RTNONE = End-of-arguments code

The argument sequence always ends in the RTNONE code. You also may use 0 to signal the end of the argument list.

COND

Reads a series of lists. Evaluates the remaining expressions found in the first list whose first element does not evaluate to nil.

Syntax

(cond *list1 list2* ...)

Return Value: The value returned by the last expression in the evaluated list. If no list is evaluated, the Cond function returns nil.

The Cond function is used for conditional branching. The first element in each *list* argument is read in turn. If the first element evaluates to a value (in other words, not nil), then the remaining elements in that list are evaluated. Cond then skips any remaining arguments.

If desired, you can set up a default list to evaluate when all other lists are skipped. The default list should be the last argument, and begin with the symbol T. This symbol will always evaluate to a non-nil value, and therefore the expressions in a list beginning with this symbol will always be evaluated by the Cond function. A list that begins with T should always be the last argument for Cond, because all lists following such a list will be skipped.

CONS

Adds an expression to a list.

Syntax

(cons *exp list/sym*)

Return Value: The new list.

The Cons function requires two arguments. The first argument can be any valid AutoLISP expression. If the second argument is a list, Cons returns a new list with the first argument added as the new first element. If Cons's second argument is not a list, Cons builds a special list called a *dotted pair*. Dotted pairs are used frequently in association lists. For examples of the Cons function used in this way, refer to the use of the Entmake function as described in Chapter 8.

COS

Calculates the cosine of an angle.

Functions Listed Alphabetically

Syntax

(cos *angle*)

Return Value: The cosine of *angle*.

The Cos function requires a number argument, representing an angle expressed in radians.

CVUNIT

Converts a number or list of numbers from one unit of measurement to another.

Syntax

(cvunit *n/list oldstr newstr*)

Return Value: A number (or list of numbers) converted to the unit of measurement represented by the *newstr* argument.

The Cvunit function requires three arguments: *n/list*, a number or list of numbers, followed by two strings: *oldstr*, indicating the current unit of measurement that the number represents, and *newstr*, the unit of measurement into which the number or list will be converted.

The strings representing valid units of measurement are stored in the ASCII file ACAD.UNT, which may be modified by the user. In most cases, both singular and plural forms may be used interchangeably. The default version of ACAD.UNT includes approximately 150 standard units of measurement, including simple mathematical conversions.

If a unit string cannot be found in ACAD.UNT, or if two incompatible units of measurement are chosen, Cvunit returns nil.

ADS Equivalent

```
int ads_cvunit(n, oldstr, newstr, result)
    ads_real n;
    char *oldstr, *newstr;
    ads_real *result;
```

The converted value is stored in the *result* argument. Ads_cvunit returns RTERROR if it fails.

DEFUN

Defines a new AutoLISP function or AutoCAD command.

Syntax

(defun *name arglist exp1 exp2* ...)

Return Value: The new function or command name.

Defun requires the following arguments, in the following order:

1. The name of the function or command that is being created.

2. A list of arguments required by the function, and any memory variables local to that function.

3. A series of valid AutoLISP expressions to be evaluated when the new function is called.

The first argument must be the name of the function being defined. The second argument, *arglist*, is a list of symbols called the *argument list*. The characters in the argument list represent arguments that are required by the new function (if any), plus any *local variables* used within the function.

The arguments in the list are separated from the local variables using a forward slash character. If the list contains no slash character, all members of the list are assumed to be arguments.

If a variable in a function is not explicitly defined as local, it is assumed to be *global*, meaning that it will retain its current value when the function completes its processing. To define a variable as global, simply leave it out of the argument list.

Both global and local variables are useful in AutoLISP, depending on the context. If you use local variables wisely, you can get one variable name to do the work of several different variables, thereby conserving precious node space. You can be sure that your memory variables are not carrying unneeded or incorrect data throughout your routine, which may produce incorrect results. On the other hand, global variables can be passed freely between functions and commands, always holding the data to which they were last bound.

Creating new AutoCAD commands requires almost the same syntax as creating AutoLISP functions: you begin by using AutoLISP's DEFUN function, but enter C:

Functions Listed Alphabetically

in front of the name of the function name. This informs the AutoLISP interpreter that an AutoCAD command, not an AutoLISP function, is being created.

ADS Equivalent

```
int ads_defun(name, i)
    char *name;
    short i;
```

The *i* argument is an integer used to identify the function in subsequent calls from AutoLISP. Refer to the CUTOUT.C routine in Chapter 9 for an example of how to use the Ads_defun function.

DIMX_TILE

Calculates the width of a tile.

Syntax

(dimx_tile *tile*)

Return Value: An integer indicating the tile's maximum X-coordinate.

The *tile* argument is required. It is a character string indicating the name of the tile as specified in the DCL file.

ADS Equivalent

```
int ads_dimensions_tile(hdlg, tile, x_coord, y_coord)
    ads_hdlg hdlg;
    char *tile;
    short x_coord, y_coord;
```

The *hdlg* argument is a dialog box handle of the type stored by the Ads_new_dialog function. Both the X and Y coordinates are stored in *x_coord* and *y_coord*, respectively.

DIMY_TILE

Calculates the height of a tile.

Syntax

(dimy_tile *tile*)

Return Value: An integer indicating the tile's maximum Y-coordinate.

The *tile* argument is required. It is a character string indicating the name of the tile as specified in the DCL file.

ADS Equivalent

```
int ads_dimensions_tile(hdlg, tile, x_coord, y_coord)
    ads_hdlg hdlg;
    char *tile;
    short x_coord, y_coord;
```

The *hdlg* argument is a dialog box handle of the type stored by the Ads_new_dialog function. Both the X and Y coordinates are stored in *x_coord* and *y_coord*, respectively.

DISTANCE

Calculates the distance between two points.

Syntax

(distance *pt1 pt2*)

Return Value: A real number, which is the distance in drawing units between the two points supplied as its arguments.

Distance requires two point lists as its arguments. The point lists can be 2D (two real numbers) or 3D (three real numbers), or a combination. The distance returned by this function is the distance in 3D space between two 3D points supplied as its argument. However, if one or both of the point arguments is 2D, the distance returned is the distance between the points as projected onto the current construction plane. AutoCAD versions prior to Release 9 require 2D coordinate point information only.

ADS Equivalent

```
ads_real ads_distance(pt1, pt2)
ads_point pt1, pt2;
```

Returns a real number indicating the distance between the point arguments. Points can be 2D or 3D.

DISTOF

Converts a string to a real number.

Syntax

(distof *str mode*)

Return Value: A real number.

The *str* argument must be a character string that expresses a real-number value. The *mode* argument is an integer indicating the current numeric format of the string. Valid *mode* values are:

- 1 = Scientific
- 2 = Decimal
- 3 = Engineering
- 4 = Architectural
- 5 = Fractional

The *mode* argument is optional. If it is not supplied, the current setting for the LUNITS system variable is used.

ADS Equivalent

```
int ads_distof(str, mode, result)
    char *str;
    int mode;
    ads_real *result;
```

The conversion result is stored in *result*.

DONE_DIALOG

Ends dialog box processing.

Syntax

(done_dialog *code*)

Return Value: An integer. If *code* was not supplied and the user picked the OK button, 1 is returned. If *code* was not supplied and the user picked anything else, 0 is returned. If *code* was supplied, its value is returned.

The *code* argument is an integer that is returned by the function. You can use the value of this argument to control the flow of AutoLISP processing when the user exits a dialog box.

ADS Equivalent

```
int ads_done_dialog(hdlg, code)
    ads_hdlg hdlg;
    int code;
```

The *hdlg* argument is the dialog box handle stored by Ads_new_dialog in its *hdlg* argument. The *code* argument is required. It may be any application-defined integer code used to control application processing when exiting the dialog box, or the following standard ADS codes:

- DLGOK = User picked the OK button
- DLGCANCEL = User picked the Cancel button, or otherwise canceled processing via Ctrl-C or the ESC key, where applicable.

Additional ADS Equivalent

```
int ads_done_positioned_dialog(hdlg, code, xpt, ypt)
    ads_hdlg hdlg;
    int code, *xpt, *ypt;
```

This function is the same as Ads_done_dialog(), except that this function also returns the coordinate point location of the dialog box in *xpt* and *ypt*, which can be used when you reopen the same dialog box. It is intended for platforms where the dialog boxes can be relocated on screen. This feature keeps track of their location and allows them to be reopened in the same position.

END_IMAGE

Signals the end of image tile processing.

Syntax

(end_image)

Return Value: Nil.

This function has no arguments. You must call this function to indicate the end of processing that was begun with a call to the Start_image function.

ADS Equivalent

```
int ads_end_image(void)
```

END_LIST

Signals the end of list box or popup list processing.

Syntax

```
(end_list)
```

Return Value: Nil.

This function has no arguments. You must call this function to indicate the end of list processing that was begun with a call to the Start_list function.

ADS Equivalent

```
int ads_end_list(void)
```

ENTDEL

Deletes an entity, or restores a deleted entity, in the database.

Syntax

```
(entdel ent)
```

Return Value: The entity name of the entity being deleted or restored.

The Entdel function requires an AutoCAD entity name, a data type like that returned by the Entlast function. If the specified entity name has already been deleted during the current drawing session, it is restored.

ADS Equivalent

```
int ads_entdel(ent)
    ads_name ent;
```

The system variable ERRNO is set to a new value when this function fails.

ENTGET

Extracts the entity association list.

Syntax

(entget *ent list*)

Return Value: The entity association list.

The Entget function requires an entity name, either stored in a memory variable or returned by a nested function.

The *list* argument is optional. If supplied, it must be a list containing the name(s) of registered application(s) that use extended entity data. These names are formatted as strings. If extended entity data exists for the entity specified by *ent*, the extended data for each application named in the list is also returned as part of the entity's association list. Refer to the Regapp function for more details on registering application names.

ADS Equivalent

```
struct resbuf *ads_entget(ent)
    ads_name ent;
```

Returns definition data from entity *ent* as a linked list of result buffers. Otherwise, it returns NULL. The system variable ERRNO is set to a new value when this function fails.

Additional ADS Equivalent

```
    struct resbuf *ads_entgetx(ent, apps)
ads_name ent;
struct resbuf *apps;
```

Returns definition data from entity *ent* plus any extended entity data associated with registered application names as a linked list of result buffers. The *apps* argument must point to a linked list of registered application names. If the *apps* argument is a NULL pointer, this function is equivalent to Ads_entget. If it cannot find the requested entity, the function returns NULL. The system variable ERRNO is set to a new value when this function fails.

ENTLAST

Extracts the name of the last entity in the database.

Syntax

(entlast)

Return Value: An entity name, if undeleted entities exist.

The Entlast function is used without arguments.

ADS Equivalent

```
int ads_entlast(result)
    ads_name result;
```

This function sets *result* to the name of the last non-deleted entity in the database. If this function fails, it returns an RTERROR code.

ENTMAKE

Adds an entity to the database.

Syntax

(entmake *alist*)

Return Value: The entity association list for the newly created entity.

The Entmake function requires a valid entity association list, composed of all information required to draw the entity in AutoCAD. Refer to Chapter 8 for more information on data required by the Entmake function.

ADS Equivalent

```
int ads_entmake(ent)
    struct resbuf *ent;
```

If the function cannot create the entity, it returns an RTREJ code. When it creates a block, it returns RTKWORD, the name of the block. The system variable ERRNO is set to a new value when this function fails.

ENTMOD

Modifies an existing entity in the database.

Syntax

(entmod *alist*)

Return Value: The modified entity's association list. If AutoLISP is unable to update the entity, Entget returns nil.

The Entget function requires an association list that includes the name of an existing AutoCAD entity. Such a list may have been extracted using the Entget function and modified using the Assoc and Subst functions. When called with a valid argument, Entmod changes the entity to reflect modifications made to the association list. Refer to the WALLS.LSP routine in Chapter 8 for an example of Entmod.

ADS Equivalent

```
int ads_entmod(ent)
     struct resbuf *ent;
```

When Ads_entmod fails to update the database, it returns RTREJ. The system variable ERRNO is set to a new value when this function fails.

ENTNEXT

Extracts an entity name from the database in sequence.

Syntax

(entnext *ent*)

Return Value: An entity name.

The *ent* argument to the entnext function is optional. If entnext is called without arguments, it returns the entity name for the first non-deleted entity in the database. If an entity name is supplied as an argument to the Entnext function, it returns the entity name of the next entity in the database. By binding this name to a variable and repeating Entnext, using the variable, it is possible to loop through the database, extracting each entity in turn.

Functions Listed Alphabetically

ADS Equivalent

```
int ads_entnext(ent, result)
    ads_name ent, result;
```

Ads_entnext stores the name of the next entity to *result*. To retrieve the first entity in the database, set *ent* to NULL. Ads_entnext fails if *ent* is the last entity in the database. The system variable ERRNO is set to a new value when this function fails.

ENTSEL

Pauses processing and prompts for the selection of an entity.

Syntax

(entsel *prompt*)

Return Value: A list containing the selected entity name and the point used to select it.

The *prompt* argument is optional. If supplied, this argument is a character string displayed while AutoLISP pauses and waits for the user to pick an entity. If the argument is not supplied, AutoCAD uses the default "Select object:" prompt.

ADS Equivalent

```
int ads_entsel(str, ent, pt)
    char *str;
    ads_name ent;
    ads_point pt;
```

Ads_entsel stores the name of the selected entity in *ent* and the point used to select it in *pt*. This function returns RTCAN if the user presses Ctrl-C. If Ads_initget has been called before this function, this function can return RTKWORD, depending on the arguments supplied to Ads_initget and the user's response to this function. See the discussion of the Initget function in this appendix for details.

ENTUPD

Updates the display of a complex entity, such as a polyline or block.

Syntax

(entupd *ent*)

Return Value: The header association list of the updated entity.

The Entupd function requires an entity name. The argument can be any entity that is part of a more complex entity. The entire complex entity is updated on the screen. In Release 12, if Entupd is called with the name of a simple entity (such as a line or an arc), it works like Entmod.

ADS Equivalent

```
int ads_entupd(ent)
    ads_name ent;
```

The system variable ERRNO is set to a new value when this function fails.

EQ

Tests whether two symbols are bound to the same data.

Syntax

(eq *sym1 sym2*)

Return Value: T if *sym1* and *sym2* are bound to the same data; nil otherwise.

Both arguments are required. *Sym1* and *sym2* may be any valid AutoLISP expression. This function will return T only if the two expressions are bound to the same data, which is not the same as evaluating to the same result. The function will return nil, for example, if the two symbols are bound to two separate but identical lists, or T if both are bound to the same list.

EQUAL

Tests whether two symbols evaluate to equal values.

Syntax

(equal *sym1 sym2 variance*)

Return Value: T if *sym1* and *sym2* evaluate to the same thing; nil otherwise.

The first two arguments are required. *Sym1* and *sym2* may be any valid AutoLISP expression. This function will return T if the two expressions evaluate to equal values. If *sym1* and *sym2* are two real numbers, you may include a third optional argument, *variance*. This argument is also a real number, representing an amount (usually fairly small) by which the two arguments can differ and still be treated as equal by this function.

ERROR

Executes a series of functions if an AutoLISP error condition occurs.

Syntax

`(defun *ERROR*(msg) exp1 exp2 ...)`

Return Value: *ERROR*

AutoLISP's normal error-handling mechanism will display a trace-back of the code which caused the error, from nesting levels of up to 100 functions deep. In complex routines, this can cause seemingly interminable scrolling of long code sequences in the command-prompt area. When others are using your routines, this can be annoying, especially if the user has only canceled the routine by pressing Control-C.

You can redefine *Error* to accept a series of AutoLISP expressions of any length, restore original system variable values, and perform any other necessary clean-up operations required to recover from an error condition. This will eliminate the trace-back.

EVAL

Evaluates expressions

Syntax

`(eval exp)`

Return Value: The value returned by the evaluated expression.

The Eval function requires a single AutoLISP expression, which is evaluated. Use this function in routines where an expression or symbol must be explicitly evaluated at a given point in processing. For example, use it just before exiting a user-defined function, in order for that function to return a result that would otherwise not be returned.

EXIT

Forces the current routine to abort processing.

Syntax

(exit)

Return Value: The message: "quit/exit abort"

This function is called without arguments. Use it as a last-resort "safety valve" in cases where a routine might create unpredictable results if processing is allowed to continue. An example of this function can be found in the DDGEAR.LSP routine, listed in Chapter 7.

ADS Equivalent

```
void ads_exit(stat)
    int stat;
```

The *stat* argument should equal zero for normal termination of processing; or a non-zero value for abnormal termination. Ads_exit() should always be called when an ADS application is no longer required. This function removes an application's code from memory, freeing system resources.

EXP

Calculates the natural antilog of a number.

Syntax

(exp *n*)

Return Value: The exponent raised to the argument's power.

Exp requires a number, real or integer, as its sole argument. This function is used as a natural antilog solving function for scientific and exponential calculations.

EXPAND

Reserves node space by requesting a number of AutoLISP memory segments.

Functions Listed Alphabetically

Syntax

(expand *n*)

Return Value: The number of segments the function was able to allocate from the heap space. (This may be less than the number requested, depending on available space in the heap.)

The Expand function requires an integer indicating the number of memory segments you are requesting from the heap. By default, each segment is equal to 514 nodes, or 6,148 bytes. (You can change this default with the Alloc function, described earlier). This function is intended for experienced programmers who wish to allocate memory manually, and thus improve the efficiency of complex applications.

EXPT

Computes a base number raised to a given power.

Syntax

(expt *base power*)

Return Value: *Base* raised to *power*.

Expt requires two arguments, both numbers. The first is the *base*, the second is the *power* to which the base will be raised. If both numbers are integers, this function returns an integer. Otherwise, it returns a real number.

FILL_IMAGE

Draws a filled rectangle in the current image tile (as specified by a call to the Start_image function).

Syntax

(fill_image *x1 y1 x2 y2 color*)

Return Value: Nil.

All arguments are required. *X1* and *y1* are integers indicating the coordinates of one of the rectangle's corners in the tile's image area; *x2* and *y2* are integers indicating the coordinates of the rectangle's opposite corner in the image area. The image area's origin point is always the upper-left corner, and is always 0,0. The coordinates of the lower-right corner can be obtained by calling the Dimx_tile and Dimy_tile functions.

Color is any available AutoCAD color code integer in the range 0–255, or one of the following:

−2 = Same as AutoCAD graphics screen background color

−15 = Same as dialog box background color

−16 = Same as dialog box text color

−18 = Same as dialog box line color

ADS Equivalent

```
int ads_fill_image(x1, y1, x2, y2, color)
    short x1, y1, x2, y2, color;
```

The *color* argument is any available AutoCAD color code integer in the range 0–255, or one of the following ADS codes:

BGLCOLOR = Same as AutoCAD graphics screen background color

DBGLCOLOR = Same as dialog box background color

DFGLCOLOR = Same as dialog box text color

LINELCOLOR = Same as dialog box line color

FINDFILE

Locates files on AutoCAD's file search path.

Syntax

(findfile *namestr*)

Return Value: The fully qualified file name (file name including path location) if the file was found; nil otherwise.

Findfile requires a character string representing a valid file name. It can be used to search for files when the exact subdirectory location is not known.

You may indicate a drive and subdirectory names in the argument if you like. If a drive letter or subdirectory name is included in the file name, AutoLISP will not

Functions Listed Alphabetically

look for the file along the search path, but instead will confine its search for the file to the named drive/subdirectory, again returning nil if the file is not found, or the full name of the file if found.

When specifying subdirectories in AutoLISP, use the forward slash character (/) rather than the backslash character (\) to separate subdirectory names. AutoLISP reads the backslash character as a signal for control characters rather than a path separator. If you cannot use the forward slash character as part of your file name string, you may use a double backslash (\\) instead.

ADS Equivalent

```
int ads_findfile(namestr, result)
    char *namestr, *result;
```

Ads_findfile stores the fully qualified file name to *result*.

FIX

Converts a real number to an integer.

Syntax

(fix *n*)

Return Value: An integer, or if an integer is not possible, a real number without the fractional portion.

Fix requires a single number, either real or integer. If an integer is supplied as the argument, it is simply returned. If a real number is supplied as the argument, the decimal portion is removed and the number is returned as an integer. If the real number is out of range for integers, the decimal portion is removed and the number is returned with a decimal value of zero.

FLOAT

Converts an integer to a real (floating-point) whole number.

Syntax

(float *i*)

Return Value: A real number.

Float requires a single number as its only argument. The number may be a real or an integer. If the argument is a real number, it is simply returned by the function. If the argument is an integer, it is returned as a real number with a decimal value of zero.

FOREACH

Steps through a list of symbols and evaluates an expression for each symbol in the list.

Syntax

(foreach *sym list exp1* ...)

Return Value: The result of the last expression evaluated.

Foreach requires three arguments, in the following order:

1. A memory variable name (*sym*)
2. A list of symbols (*list*)
3. An AutoLISP expression; often a function (*exp1* ...)

You may include a series of additional expressions after the first one. The series of expressions does not have to be enclosed in parentheses; in other words, it is not required that the series of expressions be a list.

Foreach is a looping function that will repeatedly execute a series of expressions. The first argument is the name of a memory variable. The memory variable need not be already bound to a value. Foreach will sequentially bind it to value(s) in the list supplied as its second argument. After binding the name to a memory variable, Foreach then evaluates the series of functions. In most cases, the series will make use of the memory variable at some point, although it does not have to. The number of times Foreach evaluates the series of expressions is controlled by the number of symbols in the *list* argument. When Foreach runs out of symbols in the list, it stops evaluating the series of expressions and returns the result of the last expression evaluated.

GC

Forces recovery of free node space.

Syntax

(gc)

Return Value: Nil.

The GC function recovers node space that was bound to a symbol then set to nil. Normally, this occurs automatically during processing and is invisible to the user. However, experienced programmers who intend to allocate memory manually may wish to recover this space at explicit times during a routine's processing. The function is called without arguments.

GCD

Calculates the greatest common denominator of two integers.

Syntax

(gcd *i1 i2*)

Return Value: The greatest common denominator.

Gcd requires two integers as its only valid arguments. Gcd is a common-denominator solving function for a variety of mathematical problem solving.

GETANGLE

Pauses processing and waits for the user to enter an angle value.

Syntax

(getangle *pt pstr*)

Return Value: The angle value, in radians.

Getangle requires no arguments, but two optional arguments are allowed: a point (*pt*), which is a list of two or three real numbers, and a prompt string (*pstr*). Either one or both may be used; if both are used, the point argument must appear first.

Getangle is one of two AutoLISP interactive mechanisms for retrieving angle information. (The other is Getorient, described later in this appendix).

You may enter the angle information directly from the keyboard. If entered from the keyboard, the data is accepted in the current angle units format as defined by the

Units command (see Chapter 6), but the angle data returned by the function is always converted to radians, regardless of the input format.

AutoLISP always expresses angles based on AutoCAD's standard angle orientation: that is, zero radians oriented horizontally and to the right in the current construction plane, and incremented in a counterclockwise direction.

Getangle ignores the currently set default direction of angle zero, but obeys the user-configured direction of angle increment.

If you intend that absolute angle information be returned (for instance, the orientation of a baseline), rather than a relative angle, use the Getorient function instead of Getangle.

Alternatively, Getangle will accept data entered by picking two points on the screen. AutoCAD reads the angle formed by the two points and rotates standard angle zero by that number of degrees in the current angle increment direction, returning the AutoCAD standard angle that it finds. If the optional point argument (*pt*) is present, AutoCAD takes that point as the first point entered. A "rubberband" line will appear, extending from this point to the intersection of the crosshairs, and you may enter the second point.

Getangle's prompt argument (*pstr*) can be any appropriate string of characters, which will be displayed as a prompt to the user in the command-prompt area of the screen. If this argument is omitted, no prompt is displayed.

ADS Equivalent

```
int ads_getangle(pt, pstr, result)
    ads_point pt;
    char *pstr;
    ads_real *result;
```

Ads_getangle stores the angle input, in radians, in *result*. This function returns RTCAN if the user presses Ctrl-C. If Ads_initget has been called before this function, this function can return RTKWORD, depending on the arguments supplied to Ads_initget and the user's response to this function. See the discussion of the Initget function in this appendix for details.

GETCORNER

Pauses for input of a point, and draws a "rubberband" rectangle on the screen as the user moves the pointing device.

Syntax

(getcorner *pt pstr*)

Return Value: The point input by the user.

Getcorner requires a point argument (*pt*), which is the first corner of the rubberband rectangle it draws on the screen. The user supplies the opposite corner, and this point is returned by the function. You may also include an optional prompt string as a second argument to this function.

Getcorner will accept a 3D point as its point argument, but the Z-coordinate will be ignored. The corner points are always assumed to be in the current construction plane.

ADS Equivalent

```
int ads_getcorner(pt, pstr, result)
    ads_point pt, result;
    char *pstr;
```

Ads_getcorner stores the selected point in *result*. This function returns RTCAN if the user presses Ctrl-C. If Ads_initget has been called before this function, this function can return RTKWORD, depending on the arguments supplied to Ads_initget and the user's response to this function. See the discussion of the Initget function in this appendix for details.

GETDIST

Pauses for user input of a real number.

Syntax

(getdist *pt pstr*)

Return Value: A real number.

Getdist requires no arguments, but two optional arguments, an anchor point (*pt*) and a prompt string (*pstr*), may be used. You may use either one or both; if both are used, the anchor point must appear first, followed by the prompt string.

You may enter the numeric information directly from the keyboard. If entered from the keyboard, the data is accepted in the current units format as defined by the Units command, but the data returned by the function is always converted to a real decimal number, representing drawing units.

Alternatively, you may enter the numeric data by picking two points on the screen. AutoCAD measures the distance between the two points and returns that value. If the optional anchor point argument is provided, the AutoLISP interpreter assumes this to be the first point, and extends a rubberband line from this point. The user need only pick the second point.

Getdist's prompt argument can be any appropriate string of characters, which will be displayed in the command-prompt area of the screen. If the *pstr* argument is omitted, no prompt is displayed.

ADS Equivalent

```
int ads_getdist(pt, pstr, result)
    ads_point pt;
    char *pstr;
    ads_real *result;
```

Ads_getdist stores the selected distance in *result*. This function returns RTCAN if the user presses Ctrl-C. If Ads_initget has been called before this function, this function can return RTKWORD, depending on the arguments supplied to Ads_initget and the user's response to this function. See the discussion of the Initget function in this appendix for details.

GETENV

Retrieves operating system environment variables.

Syntax

(getenv *varstr*)

Return Value: The value bound to the operating system variable, as a string. If an environment variable is not found or is not set, the function returns nil.

Getenv requires a string representing the name of a valid operating system environment variable. Getenv is useful in cases where the setting of an environment variable might be used to control AutoLISP's processing. For example, Getenv could be used to retrieve the name of the configuration subdirectory stored in ACADCFG, and thus alert you to the current hardware devices being used.

Notice that the Getenv function cannot change environment variables.

GETFILED

Displays a dialog box of file names, and waits for user input.

Syntax

```
(getfiled label fname fext flag)
```

Return Value: The selected file name, as a string; or nil if no file was selected.

All arguments for the Getfiled function are required:

1. The *label* argument specifies a label for the dialog box. You may supply a null string ("") for this argument, in which case the dialog box will appear without a label.

2. The *fname* argument indicates a default file name, including a default path string. You may exclude a path string from the argument, in which case, the current directory is considered the default. The file name portion of this string appears in the File tile of the dialog box. You may also use a null string for this argument, in which case no defaults are set and the Default button in the dialog box is disabled.

3. The *fext* argument is a default file extension that appears in the Pattern tile of the dialog box. If you supply a null string, the dialog box will include all files on the directory.

4. The *flag* argument is a bit-code integer that can be any sum of the following values:

    1 = Indicates that this call to Getfiled is a request to open a new file.
    2 = Disables the Type It button in the dialog box.

4 = Allows the user to override the default file extension.

8 = Searches for the entered file name on the AutoCAD file search path. Do not use this code if you are requesting that a new file be opened.

ADS Equivalent

```
int ads_getfiled(label, fname, fext, flag, result)
    char *title, *fname, *fext;
    int flag;
    struct resbuf *result;
```

Ads_getfiled stores the fully qualified selected file name in *result*. The string in the *result* argument must point to a memory area large enough to hold the file name. The maximum length is platform-dependent; consult your *Programmer's Reference* for details.

GETINT

Pauses to accept input of an integer.

Syntax

(getint *pstr*)

Return Value: The integer entered by the user.

Getint requires no arguments, but an optional prompt string may be provided. Entry of integers by keyboard input or menu picks are the only allowable input.

ADS Equivalent

```
int ads_getint(pstr, result)
    char *pstr;
    int *result;
```

Ads_getint stores the selected integer in *result*. This function returns RTCAN if the user presses Ctrl-C. If Ads_initget has been called before this function, this function can return RTKWORD, depending on the arguments supplied to Ads_initget and the user's response to this function. See the discussion of the Initget function in this appendix for details.

GETKWORD

Pauses processing and waits for user to enter a character string.

Syntax

(getkword *pstr*)

Return Value: The entered string, or a null string (" ") if the user presses Enter without typing anything.

The Getkword function tests the validity of input based on a list of valid keywords set using the Initget function. (The Initget function is discussed later in this appendix.) If an invalid response is entered, Getkword will repeat until a valid response is received. Getkword requires no arguments, but an optional prompt string argument (indicating which responses are valid) is recommended for the user's sake.

Getkword is an alternative to Getstring, which cannot be used with Initget.

ADS Equivalent

```
int ads_getkword(pstr, result)
    char *pstr, *result;
```

Ads_getkword stores the selected input string in *result*. This function returns RTCAN if the user presses Ctrl-C. If Ads_initget has been called before this function, this function can return RTKWORD, depending on the arguments supplied to Ads_initget and the user's response to this function. See the discussion of the Initget function in this appendix for details.

GETORIENT

Pauses processing and waits for user input of an angle.

Syntax

(getorient *pt pstr*)

Return Value: The angle entered by the user, in radians.

Getorient requires no arguments, but two optional arguments are allowed: an anchor point (*pt*) and a prompt string (*pstr*). If both are used, the anchor point must be the first argument.

AUTOLISP/ADS QUICK FUNCTION REFERENCE
APP. A

Getorient returns angle information relative to both the currently set direction of angle zero and the direction of angle increment. Getorient returns an AutoCAD standard angle (expressed in radians) that is found relative to the current angle zero. It will increment the current angle zero by the entered number of degrees, using the current direction for angle increment as set using the Units command, and return the AutoCAD standard angle that it finds.

AutoLISP always expresses angles based on AutoCAD's standard angle orientation: that is, zero radians oriented horizontally and to the right in the current construction plane, and incremented in a counter-clockwise direction. If you have changed the default direction of angle increment using the Units command, some conversion will be done so that the angle returned by this function is relative to AutoLISP's counterclockwise angle increment.

Getorient is useful when you need to input and store absolute angle information (that is, any angle that is expressed relative to the current angle zero—a baseline, for example). If you intend that relative angle information be returned (for example, the angle between items in a polar array), rather than an absolute angle, use the Getangle function instead of Getorient.

You may enter the angle data by picking two points on the screen. Getorient reads the angle formed by the two points relative to the current setting for angle zero, and then increments angle zero by that number of degrees in the current angle increment direction, returning the AutoCAD standard angle that it finds. If the optional point argument is present, Getorient takes that point as the first point entered. A "rubberband" line will appear, extending from this point to the intersection of the crosshairs, and you may enter the second point.

If you are using Release 10 or later, Getorient will accept 3D point input, but the angle is always measured in the current construction plane; 3D points not in the current construction plane will be projected onto that plane, and the angle measurement then taken.

Getorient's prompt argument (*pstr*) can be any appropriate string of characters, which will be displayed in the command-prompt area of the screen. If this argument is omitted, no prompt is displayed.

ADS Equivalent

```
int ads_getorient(pt, pstr, result)
    ads_point pt;
```

Functions Listed Alphabetically

```
char *pstr;
ads_real *result;
```

Ads_getorient stores the selected angle in *result*. This function returns RTCAN if the user presses Ctrl-C. If Ads_initget has been called before this function, this function can return RTKWORD, depending on the arguments supplied to Ads_initget and the user's response to this function. See the discussion of the Initget function in this appendix for details.

GETPOINT

Pauses for user input of a point.

Syntax

(getpoint *pt pstr*)

Return Value: The point entered by the user, as a list of real numbers.

Getpoint requires no arguments, but two optional arguments, an anchor point (*pt*) and a prompt string (*pstr*), may be used. You may use either one or both; if both are used, the anchor point must appear first, followed by the prompt string.

You may enter the point by picking a point on the screen. If the optional anchor point argument is provided, the AutoLISP interpreter extends a "rubberband" line from this point to the intersection of the crosshairs. The point the user picks is returned by the function.

The coordinate point may be entered from the keyboard in the standard fashion, as numbers separated by commas using the current units format, or the decimal equivalent in drawing units.

Getpoint returns 3D points in AutoCAD Release 10 and later. (If you are using Release 10, Getpoint returns 3D points, unless the FLATLAND system variable is not set to zero.)

Getpoint's prompt argument (*pstr*) can be any appropriate string of characters, which will be displayed in the command-prompt area of the screen. If this argument is omitted, no prompt is displayed.

ADS Equivalent

int ads_getpoint(*pt, pstr, result*)

```
ads_point pt;3
char *pstr;
ads_point result;
```

Ads_getpoint stores the selected point in *result*. This function returns RTCAN if the user presses Ctrl-C. If Ads_initget has been called before this function, this function can return RTKWORD, depending on the arguments supplied to Ads_initget and the user's response to this function. See the discussion of the Initget function in this appendix for details.

GETREAL

Pauses for user input of a real number.

Syntax

(getreal *pstr*)

Return Value: The real number entered by the user. If the user enters an integer, it is converted to a real number.

Getreal requires no arguments, but an optional prompt string may be used. You may enter the numeric information directly from the keyboard or from a menu. Picking points is not allowed using Getreal. If entered from the keyboard, the data is accepted in the current units format as defined by the Units command, but the data returned by the function is always converted to a real decimal number.

Getreal's prompt argument (*pstr*) can be any appropriate string of characters, which will be displayed in the command-prompt area of the screen. If this argument is omitted, no prompt is displayed.

ADS Equivalent

```
int ads_getreal(pstr, result)
    char *pstr;
    ads_real *result;
```

Ads_getreal stores the selected value in *result*. This function returns RTCAN if the user presses Ctrl-C. If Ads_initget has been called before this function, this function can return RTKWORD, depending on the arguments supplied to Ads_initget and the user's response to this function. See the discussion of the Initget function in this appendix for details.

GETSTRING

Pauses for user input of a character string.

Syntax

`(getstring `*`spaceOK pstr`*`)`

Return Value: The string entered by the user, or a null string("") if the user pressed Enter without typing characters.

Getstring requires no arguments, but an argument for allowing spaces in the string (*spaceOK*) and an optional prompt string (*pstr*) may be used. If both are used, the *spaceOK* argument must be the first.

Getstring is one of two AutoLISP interactive mechanisms for retrieving string data. (The other is Getkword, which tests the data for validity before accepting it.) Getstring does not automatically test the validity of the data that is entered by the user, and does not obey the Initget function. Any valid string is accepted and returned.

You may enter the string information directly from the keyboard or from a menu. When the string is displayed, it is shown enclosed in quotation marks.

If a non-string argument is supplied and does not evaluate to nil, Getstring will permit spaces to be included in the entered character string. Otherwise, it treats a press of the space bar the same as a press of the Enter key.

There is a limit of 132 characters that can be accepted into any one string requested by this function. If you need to input longer strings, you can input them as several short strings and piece them together using the Strcat function (see the discussion of Strcat in this appendix for details).

Getstring's prompt argument (*pstr*) can be any appropriate string of characters, which will be displayed in the command-prompt area of the screen. If this argument is omitted, no prompt is displayed.

ADS Equivalent

```
int ads_getstring(spaceOK, pstr, result)
    int spaceOK;
    char *pstr, *result;
```

Ads_getstring stores the selected string in *result*. The *result* string may be initialized with space to hold a maximum of 133 characters. This function returns RTCAN if the user presses Ctrl-C.

GETVAR

Extracts a value stored in an AutoCAD system variable.

Syntax

(getvar *vname*)

Return Value: The value of the specified system variable.

Getvar requires the name of a system variable. It is supplied as a string, enclosed in quotes.

ADS Equivalent

```
int ads_getvar(vname, result)
    char *vname;
    struct resbuf *result;
```

Ads_getvar stores the new system variable value in the previously declared result buffer *result*.

GET_ATTR

Extracts the value of a tile's attribute from its Dialog Control Language (DCL) file.

Syntax

(get_attr *tile attname*)

Return Value: A character string, equal to the original value of the tile attribute as specified in the DCL file.

Both arguments to this function are required. The *tile* argument is a character string specifying the tile name. The *attname* argument is a character string specifying the name of one of the tile's DCL file attributes.

ADS Equivalent

```
int ads_get_attr(hdlg, tile, attname, value, len)
    ads_hdlg hdlg;
    char *tile, *attname, *value;
    int len;
```

The *hdlg* argument is a dialog box handle of the type stored by the Ads_new_dialog function. Ads_get_attr stores the new value in the *value* argument. The application must declare enough space for the value of the *value* argument, and supply its length in the *len* argument.

Additional ADS Equivalent

```
int ads_get_attr_string(thandle, attname, value, len)
    ads_htile thandle;
    char attname, *value;
    int len;
```

This function gets an attribute's DCL file value from within callback functions. It works like the Ads_get_attr function, but it accesses the tile via the callback packet's **ads_htile** field.

GET_TILE

Extracts the current value of a tile.

Syntax

(get_tile *tile*)

Return Value: A character string indicating the tile's current value.

The *tile* argument is required by this function. It is a character string indicating the tile's name as defined in the Dialog Control Language (DCL) file.

ADS Equivalent

```
int ads_get_tile(hdlg, tile, val, len)
    ads_hdlg hdlg;
    char *tile, *val;
    int len;
```

The *hdlg* argument is a dialog box handle of the type stored by the Ads_new_dialog function. Ads_get_tile stores the new value in the *val* argument. The application must declare enough memory space for the value of the *val* argument, and supply its length in the *len* argument.

GRAPHSCR

Forces the display of the graphics screen on single-screen systems.

Syntax

(graphscr)

Return Value: Nil.

Graphscr uses no arguments.

ADS Equivalent

int ads_graphscr()

GRCLEAR

Temporarily clears the current viewport.

Syntax

(grclear)

Return Value: Nil.

Grclear uses no arguments. The contents of the cleared viewport may be restored by invoking the Redraw command or calling the Redraw function without arguments.

ADS Equivalent

int ads_grclear()

GRDRAW

Draws a temporary line in the display screen. This line is not part of AutoCAD's drawing database.

Syntax

(grdraw *pt1 pt2 color hlgt*)

Return Value: Nil.

Grdraw requires three arguments, in the following order:

1. A starting 2D or 3D coordinate point (*pt1*), as a list of either 2 or 3 real numbers.
2. An ending 2D or 3D coordinate point (*pt2*), as a list of real numbers.
3. An integer indicating the color of the line (*color*).

Grdraw may include an optional fourth argument, which is an integer. If the argument is present and does not equal zero, the line will be drawn as a highlighted line, such as lines might appear when they are selected for inclusion in a selection set. This optional argument is useful only on display devices that support highlighting of lines.

The *color* argument may also be specified as –1. This value indicates that the line will be the complementary color of all areas that it crosses, including other visible entities.

The lines drawn by the Grdraw function appear on the screen, but they are not part of AutoCAD's drawing database. They will be removed by any command or function that causes a redraw of the screen or drawing regeneration, and they cannot be included in selection sets, nor can their construction points be found with object snap modes.

ADS Equivalent

```
int ads_grdraw(pt1 pt2 color hlgt)
    ads_point from, to;
    int color, hlgt;
```

GRREAD

Reads data from AutoCAD input devices.

Syntax

(grread *track key type*)

Return Value: A list, containing data that indicates the input device that was read, plus the data that was read from the device.

Grread requires no arguments. However, three optional arguments may be supplied:

- *track* This argument may be any AutoLISP expression that does not return nil, which will cause Grread to return a point list, indicating the current location of the intersection of the crosshairs.

- *key* This argument is a bit-code integer that can be the sum of any of the following values:

    1 = Return the crosshair location if the user moves the pointing device without pressing a key.

    2 = Return a value when the user presses any key.

    4 = Activate the *type* argument in the function.

    8 = Disable Ctrl-Break (same as Ctrl-C) for this function.

    16 = Disable the pulldown menu for this function.

- *type* This argument is an integer that controls the crosshair display while the Grread function is active. It can be one of the following values:

    0 = Display crosshairs normally.

    1 = Disable crosshair display.

    2 = Display the AutoCAD object-selection pickbox.

The list returned by Grread has two members: an integer indicating which input device was read, and a second member indicating the data that was read. These lists are summarized below:

Integer Code	Device Read	Data Read
2	Keyboard	ASCII character code for key
3	Pick Button	Coordinate point list, in current UCS
4	On-Screen Menu	Line number (top line: 0)

Functions Listed Alphabetically

Integer Code	Device Read	Data Read
5	Crosshairs	Coordinate point list, in current UCS
6	Pointing Device Buttons	Button number (Pick button not included; first button after pick: 0)
7	Tablet Menu 1	Menu box number
8	Tablet Menu 2	Menu box number
9	Tablet Menu 3	Menu box number
10	Tablet Menu 4	Menu box number
11	Aux Menu	Button number
12	Pointing Device Buttons	Coordinates associated with button number (when Grread is recalled immediately after Point button number was returned).

Grread reacts differently on different types of displays. For example, suppose you have a standard VGA display. If you use Grread to extract a screen menu box number, and make a second call to Grread as the result of pressing a button on the pointing device, Grread will return the crosshair location without pausing for user input, because the memory buffer from the previous call is not empty. One way to clear the Grread buffer is to nest the function within a loop that forces the buffer clear:

```
(while (= (type (nth 1 (grread))))
    'LIST)
)
```

For an example of this technique, refer to the LISTBLK.LSP routine in Appendix B.

ADS Equivalent

```
int ads_grread(track, type, result)
    int track, *type;
    struct resbuf *result;
```

Ads_grread stores the selected value in *result*, and the device type code in *type*. This function can return an RTCAN code if the user presses Ctrl-C or Ctrl-Break, and the *track* argument does not include bit code 8.

GRTEXT

Displays a text string in either the screen menu, status line, or coordinate display areas.

Syntax

(grtext *box text hlgt*)

Return Value: If successful in displaying the text, the character string supplied as the *text* argument; otherwise, nil.

If you call Grtext without arguments, it restores all screen text areas to their normal state. The *box* argument is an integer indicating the area of the screen where the *text* argument is displayed. Integer codes for available locations are as follows:

-2 = Text will be written in the coordinate display area.

-1 = Text will be written in the status display area.

0 and up = Text will be written on a line in the screen menu area. Menu lines are numbered from top to bottom, beginning with zero for the top line.

The *text* argument is a character string that Grtext attempts to display. If the string is too long for the available space on the screen, it is truncated.

Use the optional *hlgt* argument to display the text in highlighted characters, on those displays that support such characters. If you intend to write highlighted text into lines of the screen menu area, first write the text without highlighting it, then write the text again with the highlight code included in the function. This minimizes the chance of unwanted side effects in some drawing displays. Only one line may be highlighted at a time. If you highlight another line, the previously highlighted text is displayed normally.

Text displayed in these menu areas is invisible to AutoCAD; that is, it will be overwritten if any command updates the normal data display in these areas. In addition, if you use Grtext to overwrite a line in the screen menu area, the command sequence for that line will still be activated if you pick that line. To pick the line without activating the command sequence, use the Grread function, described earlier in this appendix.

Functions Listed Alphabetically

ADS Equivalent

```
int ads_grtext(box, text, hlgt)
    int box, hlgt;
    char *text;
```

GRVECS

Displays a series of vectors on the screen.

Syntax

(grvecs *list trans*)

Return Value: Nil if successful; otherwise, the function generates an AutoLISP error message.

Grvecs requires a list containing the following elements, in the following order:

1. An optional integer color code. AutoCAD color codes range from 0 to 255; not all codes are available on all displays. A color code less than zero draws a highlighted vector.

2. A point list indicating the starting point for the vector.

3. A point list indicating the ending point for the vector.

You may repeat this series within the argument list, in order to draw multiple vectors.

The *trans* argument is optional, and used within 3D applications. This argument is also a list, containing a *transformation matrix*, used to relocate your vectors within a given user coordinate system. A transformation matrix is a list of four point sublists. These lists, taken together, describe entity scaling and rotation, and are used to transform an entity's coordinates from its own 3D coordinate system into the world coordinate system. For more detailed information regarding transformation matrices, consult your *Programmer's Reference*.

ADS Equivalent

```
int ads_grvecs(list, trans)
    struct resbuf list;
    ads_matrix trans;
```

HANDENT

Extracts an entity name based on its handle.

Syntax

(handent *handle*)

Return Value: The entity name.

Handent requires a valid entity handle; therefore, this function should be called only when entity handles are enabled. The handle may belong to an entity that was deleted during the current editing session.

ADS Equivalent

```
int ads_handent(handle, ent)
    char *handle;
    ads_name ent;
```

Ads_handent stores the found entity in *ent*. The system variable ERRNO is set to a new value when this function fails.

IF

Evaluates an AutoLISP expression based on whether or not an initial test expression evaluates to nil.

Syntax

(if *test exp1 exp2*)

Return Value: The value returned by the evaluated expression; otherwise, nil.

If requires at least two arguments, both of which are AutoLISP expressions, and will accept a third optional expression. The first argument (*test*) is the test expression. The second argument (*exp1*) is the "do-if-true" expression, evaluated only if the test expression does not return nil. A third argument (*exp2*), the "do-if-nil" expression, is optional, and evaluated if the test expression returns nil.

The If function can only choose between two functions. However, the Progn function can be used to enclose a series of functions within a single function, and passed as an argument to the If function. Another alternative is to use the Cond function, described earlier in this appendix.

INITGET

Controls the validity of responses to an upcoming "Get" function.

Syntax

(initget *value key*)

Return Value: Nil.

Initget must include at least one of the following arguments (it may include both):

- *value* A control-bit integer indicating what data types are valid input for the next "Get" function.
- *key* A character string containing valid keywords that will be accepted by the "Get" function, in addition to its usual form of input.

The following are valid *value* arguments to the Initget function. You may include the sum of any of the following:

1 = Do not accept press of Enter key or space bar without a value.

2 = Do not allow zero input.

4 = Do not allow negative numbers.

8 = Allow points to be selected outside the drawing limits, and temporarily override limits-checking. (Needed only if limits-checking is currently set.)

16 = Return points as 3D points rather than 2D points (for AutoCAD versions prior to Release 10, or in Release 10 if the FLATLAND system variable is not set to zero.)

32 = Use a highlighted line for rubberband lines (if the display device controls the advanced user interface).

64 = Disallow input of a Z-coordinate in response to Getdist.

128 = Return any keyboard input.

The *key* argument contains optional responses that may be accepted by the "Get" function in addition to its regular form of input. For example:

```
(initget "Last Quit")
(setq angvar (getangle "\nLast/Quit/<angle>: "))
```

In the above example, the Getangle function will accept all valid forms of inputs for angles plus the keywords "Last" or "Quit," storing whatever is returned by Getangle in the memory variable *angvar*. This memory variable can then be tested to perform alternate processing based on its contents.

The individual keywords in a keyword string are separated by spaces. Thus, any number of keywords may be used in a single keyword string.

The use of upper and lowercase in the keyword string is important. When a keyword contains both upper and lowercase letters, as in the above example, the user may enter either the entire word or only that portion of the word that appears in uppercase in the keyword string. In the above example, therefore, the user may enter either L or Last for "Last," or Q or Quit for "Quit."

Upon receiving any valid keyword input, the Get function will always return the whole keyword in the format supplied to the Initget function.

ADS Equivalent

```
int ads_initget(value, key)
    int value;
    char *key;
```

The following are valid *value* arguments to the Ads_initget function. You may include the sum of any of the following:

RSG_NONULL = Do not accept press of Enter key or space bar without a value.

RSG_NOZERO = Do not allow zero input.

RSG_NONEG = Do not allow negative numbers.

RSG_NOLIM = Allow points to be selected outside the drawing limits, and temporarily override limits-checking. (Needed only if limits-checking is currently set.)

RSG_DASH = Use a highlighted line for rubberband lines (if the display device controls the advanced user interface).

RSG_2D = Disallow input of a Z-coordinate in response to Getdist.

RSG_OTHER = Return any keyboard input

INTERS

Calculates an intersection point from two line endpoints.

Syntax

(inters *pt1* *pt2* *pt3* *pt4* *inf*)

Return Value: A point list indicating the intersection point of the line formed by *pt1* and *pt2*, and the line formed by *pt3* and *pt4*. If no intersection point is found, the function returns nil.

Inters requires four arguments. They must be point lists. An optional fifth argument (*inf*) may be supplied. If the fifth argument is present and evaluates to nil, the lines are extended infinitely in order to return the intersection point. Otherwise, Inters returns an intersection point only if the line segments actually intersect.

ADS Equivalent

```
int ads_inters(pt1, pt2, pt3, pt4, inf, result)
    ads_point pt1, pt2, pt3, pt4;
    int inf;
    ads_point result;
```

Ads_inters stores the found intersection point in *result*.

ITOA

Converts an integer to a string.

Syntax

(itoa *i*)

Return Value: The character string.

Itoa requires an integer as its only argument. If a real number is supplied, it will produce an error message.

LAMBDA

Applies a list of arguments to a series of expressions.

Syntax

(lambda *arglist exp1* ...)

Return Value: The result of the last expression evaluated.

Lambda requires two arguments: the first (*arglist*) is a list of symbols to be used as arguments. The second is an expression (often a function) that uses the symbols in the list. You may also use a series of expressions following the symbol list.

Lambda is related to the Defun function, in that it will create a new function by evaluating a series of functions and returning a result. Unlike Defun, Lambda creates no function name, and thus does not store the function it creates in memory. Global and local variables are irrelevant, since the function itself is not stored anywhere. Lambda is useful in situations where it would be nice to define a new function, but the function is only needed once, and storing the new function in memory isn't necessary.

LAST

Extracts the last member of a list.

Syntax

(last *list*)

Return Value: The last member of the argument list. If the argument is nil, Last returns a list containing a nil symbol. If the argument is an empty list, Last returns nil.

Last requires a single list as its only allowable argument. The list may contain other lists.

LENGTH

Counts members of a list.

Syntax

(length *list*)

Return Value: An integer indicating the number of members in the argument list.

Length requires a list as its only allowable argument.

LIST

Creates a list from its arguments.

Syntax

(list *exp1* ...)

Return Value: A list of the function's arguments.

List function requires at least one argument, which may be any valid AutoLISP expression or symbol. List is often used to create coordinate point lists from 2 or 3 real numbers, but it can create any form of list, with the exception of dotted pairs. Use the Cons function, described earlier in this appendix, to create dotted pairs.

LISTP

Tests to determine whether its argument is a list.

Syntax

(listp *exp*)

Return Value: T if *exp* is a list; nil otherwise.

Listp requires one argument, which can be any valid AutoLISP expression or symbol. If the argument is a list, the function returns T.

LOAD

Loads an AutoLISP file into memory and evaluates the expressions in the file.

Syntax

(load *file errmsg*)

Return Value: The result of the last expression evaluated.

The *file* argument is the name of a LISP file, enclosed in quotes. It is required. The *errmsg* argument is optional. It is a character string that will be displayed in the command-prompt area of the screen if the Load function is unsuccessful in loading the file for any reason. If the *errmsg* argument is not supplied, failure of this function will generate an AutoLISP error message.

LOAD_DIALOG

Loads a Dialog Control Language (DCL) file.

Syntax

(load_dialog *file*)

Return Value: An integer, to be used as an argument to New_dialog and Unload_dialog files, if loading was successful; otherwise, it returns a negative integer.

Load_dialog requires a character string argument, the name of a DCL file to load. The DCL file may contain as many dialog box definitions. You should always store the integer returned by this function to a memory variable, so that you may access the file in RAM by means of other dialog-box control functions.

ADS Equivalent

```
int ads_load_dialog(file, id)
    char *file;
    int id;
```

Ads_load_dialog stores the dialog box integer handle in *id*.

LOG

Calculates the natural logarithm of a number.

Syntax

(log *n*)

Return Value: A real number.

Log requires a number as its only allowable argument.

LOGAND

Computes a boolean AND comparison of a series of integers.

Syntax

(logand *i1 i2* ...)

Return Value: An integer representing the binary result of the boolean bitwise AND comparison.

Logand requires at least two integers. Real numbers are not allowed. Refer to the Boole function, described in this appendix, for an explanation of bit-comparisons of integers.

LOGIOR

Computes a boolean OR comparison of a series of integers.

Syntax

(logior *i1 i2* ...)

Return Value: An integer representing the binary result of the boolean bitwise OR comparison.

Logand requires at least two integers. Real numbers are not allowed. Refer to the Boole function, described in this appendix, for an explanation of bit-comparisons of integers.

LSH

Computes a bit-shift of binary bits in an integer.

Syntax

(lsh *i shift*)

Return Value: The integer representing the binary number resulting from the bitwise shift.

Lsh requires two arguments: the first (*i*) is the integer on which the bit-shift is to be performed; the second (*shift*) is the number of bit places that are shifted. If the second argument of Lsh is positive, the bits are shifted to the left. If the second argument is negative, the bits are shifted to the right. If the top bit changes, the sign of the integer changes.

MAPCAR

Applies a function to specified lists of arguments.

Syntax

(mapcar *func list1* ...)

Return Value: A list of results from applying the function to each item in the lists.

Mapcar requires the name of a defined function and at least one list of items to supply as the argument for that function. If the named function requires more than one argument, you must supply a separate list of items for each argument required by the named function. Also, the number of items in each list should be the same, so that Mapcar will apply the function consistently to each argument list.

The functions passed to Mapcar as its first argument may be predefined AutoLISP functions or user-defined functions. You may also create a function on the spot and use it as Mapcar's first argument, without bothering to define it separately using the Defun function: Use the Lambda function to define a one-time custom function and pass it to Mapcar as its first argument. Refer to the Lambda function discussed earlier in this appendix for details.

MAX

Extracts the largest value from a series.

Syntax

(max *n1* ...)

Return Value: The largest value found.

Max requires at least one number. It will accept any number of arguments, but they must all be numbers.

MEM

Displays the current state of AutoLISP memory.

Syntax

(mem)

Functions Listed Alphabetically

Return Value: Nil.

Mem is called without arguments. It is generally used by experienced programmers who need to check the status of memory after manual allocation procedures. For most users, AutoLISP's internal memory-allocation procedures are sufficient.

MEMBER

Locates a member in a list.

Syntax

(member *exp list*)

Return Value: A list beginning with the found expression plus any members of the original list that appear after the found member. If the member is not found, this function returns nil.

Member requires an AutoLISP expression (*exp*), which may or may not be a member of the list supplied as its second argument (*list*).

MENUCMD

Switches between the submenus of the currently active AutoCAD menu.

Syntax

(menucmd *mnustr*)

Return Value: Nil.

Menucmd requires a string that consists of a main section letter, equal sign, and a submenu in the currently active menu. Only one string is allowed. The string argument required by Menucmd mimics the submenu reference syntax in the menu file, except that the leading dollar sign is not used.

ADS Equivalent

```
int ads_menucmd(mnustr)
    char *mnustr;
```

MIN

Extracts the smallest value from a series.

Syntax

(min *n1* ...)

Return Value: The smallest value found.

Min requires at least one number. It will accept any number of arguments, but they must all be numbers.

MINUSP

Tests to determine whether a number is less than zero.

Syntax

(minusp *n*)

Return Value: T if the argument *n* is a number and negative, nil otherwise.

Minusp requires a single number, either real or integer, as its only argument.

MODE_TILE

Controls the display and behavior of dialog box tiles.

Syntax

(mode_tile *tile mode*)

Return Value: Nil.

Mode_tile requires two arguments. The *tile* argument is a character string indicating the name of a dialog box tile. The *mode* argument is an integer, indicating how the tile is to behave. You may use one of the following values:

0 = Activate the tile

1 = Deactivate the tile

2 = Set focus to the tile

Functions Listed Alphabetically

3 = Select edit box

4 = Toggle highlighting

ADS Equivalent

```
int ads_mode_tile(hdlg, tile, mode)
    ads_hdlg hdlg;
    char *tile;
    short mode;
```

The *hdlg* argument is a dialog box handle of the type stored by the Ads_new_dialog function. The *mode* argument may be one of the following ADS codes:

MODE_ENABLE = Activate the tile

MODE_DISABLE = Deactiveate the tile

MODE_SETFOCUS = Set focus to the tile

MODE_SETSEL = Select edit box

MODE_FLIP = Toggle highlighting

NENTSEL

Pauses processing and prompts for the selection of an entity nested within a polyline or block.

Syntax

(nentsel *prompt*)

Return Value: A list containing the selected entity name and the point used to select it.

If Nentsel is used to select an entity other than a polyline or block, it functions like Entsel, described earlier in this appendix. If the selected entity is a polyline, this function returns the selected vertex. If the selected entity is a block, this function returns the selected entity nested within that block.

The *prompt* argument is optional. If supplied, this argument is a character string displayed while AutoLISP pauses and waits for the user to pick an entity. If the argument is not supplied, AutoCAD uses the default "Select object:" prompt.

ADS Equivalent

```
int ads_nentsel(str, ent, pt, xform, ref)
    char *str;
    ads_name ent;
    ads_point pt, xform[4];
    struct resbuf **ref;
```

Ads_nentsel() is used to provide compatibility with ADS applications prior to Release 12. All others should use Ads_nentselp().

NENTSELP

Pauses processing and prompts for the selection of an entity nested within a polyline or block, or uses an optional point argument to select an entity without pausing.

Syntax

(nentselp *prompt pt*)

Return Value: A list containing the selected entity name and the point used to select it.

If Nentselp is used without the optional *pt* argument, it functions like Nentsel, described previously. If the optional *pt* argument is supplied (in the form of a point list), this function selects the first entity it finds at the specified point. If no entity is found, the function returns nil.

The *prompt* argument is also optional. If supplied, this argument is a character string displayed while AutoLISP pauses and waits for the user to pick an entity. If the argument is not supplied, AutoCAD uses the default "Select object:" prompt.

ADS Equivalent

```
ads_nentselp(str, ent, pt, flag, xform, ref)
    char *str;
    ads_name ent;
    ads_point pt,
    short flag;
    ads_matrix xform;
    struct resbuf **ref;
```

Functions Listed Alphabetically

The Ads_nentselp function stores the selected entity in *ent* and the point used to select the entity in *pt*. If the *flag* argument is set to the FALSE code, this function prompts the user to select the entity. If TRUE, AutoCAD uses the value of *pt* to select the entity. If the selected entity is contained in a nested block, the *ref* argument is a linked list of result buffers that contain the names of the selected entity's nested parent block structure.

NEW_DIALOG

Displays a dialog box.

Syntax

(new_dialog dbname id default pt)

Return Value: T if the dialog box is displayed; nil otherwise.

New_dialog requires two arguments: *dbname* (the name of a loaded dialog box—which was assigned in a previously loaded Dialog Control Language DCL file) and *id* (the integer code returned by the Load_dialog function call that loaded the DCL file).

The remaining two arguments are optional: *default* is a character string indicating an AutoLISP expression that should be evaluated as a default action, if the user picks a dialog box tile that does not have an action linked to it via the DCL file instructions. You can indicate no default action by supplying this argument as a null string (""). *Pt* is a point list indicating a 2D point. This point is an anchor point on the display screen where the dialog box may appear. This point can be taken from the point list returned by a previous Done-dialog call, allowing the dialog box to reappear in the same location as previous displays.

ADS Equivalent

```
int ads_new_dialog(dbname, id, callback, hdlg)
        char dbname;
        int id;
        CLIENTFUNC callback;
        ads_hdlg *hdlg;
```

If you do not specify an optional *callback* function, this argument must be a NULLCB code. Ads_new_dialog sets *hdlg* to the dialog box handle if it succeeds, and to NULL if it fails. Subsequent calls to ADS dialog box functions require the *hdlg* value that Ads_new_dialog stores.

Additional ADS Equivalent

```
int ads_new_positioned_dialog(dbname, id, callback, xpt, ypt, hdlg)
    char dbname;
    int id;
    CLIENTFUNC callback;
    int xpt, ypt;
    ads_hdlg *hdlg;
```

This function is the same as Ads_new_dialog(), except that this function also returns the coordinate point location of the dialog box in *xpt* and *ypt*, which can be used when you reopen the same dialog box. It is intended for platforms where the dialog boxes can be relocated on screen. This feature keeps track of their location and allows them to be reopened in the same position. To open the dialog box in the default position, supply *xpt* and *ypt* each as –1.

NOT

Tests to determine whether an expression evaluates to nil.

Syntax

(not *exp*)

Return Value: T if the expression returns nil. Otherwise, returns nil.

The Not function requires an AutoLISP expression as its only argument.

NTH

Extracts a member from a specified position in a list.

Syntax

(nth *pos list*)

Return Value: The found member, or nil if a member was not found.

Nth requires two arguments in the following order:

1. *pos* An integer indicating the position within the list.
2. *list* The list from which the member is to be extracted.

Positions within a list are numbered from left to right starting with zero. If the position number specified by the first argument of Nth is greater than the highest position number in the list, Nth returns nil.

NULL

Tests to determine whether an expression evaluates to nil.

Syntax

(null *exp*)

Return Value: T if the expression returns nil. Otherwise, returns nil.

The Null function requires an AutoLISP expression as its only argument.

NUMBERP

Tests to determine whether an expression is a number.

Syntax

(numberp *exp*)

Return Value: T if the function argument is a number, nil otherwise.

Numberp requires a single AutoLISP expression as its sole allowable argument. Numberp will return T if the expression evaluates to either a real number or an integer.

OPEN

Opens a file on disk for reading data or for storing data written to disk.

Syntax

(open *fname mode*)

Return Value: A file descriptor if a file is successfully opened for either reading or writing; nil otherwise.

Open requires two arguments, in the following order:

1. *fname* A string containing the name of the file to be opened. The *fname* argument can be any valid file name. A drive letter and/or subdirectory names may be included as part of the file name, separated from the file name by forward slashes. A single backslash character (\) is not allowed, as the AutoLISP interpreter will mistake it for a control character; however, if you prefer, you may use two backslash characters to separate subdirectory names from file names.

2. *mode* A single lowercase character indicating how the file is to be used:

   - "**a**" indicates that the file is opened in *append mode*. Any data written to the file will be appended to the end of any data currently found there. If no file with the given name exists, the file is created with no data, and data may be written into it.
   - "**r**" indicates that the file is opened in *read mode*. Data may be read from the file, but no data may be written to it.
   - "**w**" indicates that the file is opened in *write mode*. Data may be written to the file; however, if the file already exists at the time the Open function is called, the previous data contained in the existing file is destroyed.

The file descriptor returned by this function is a special data type and cannot be directly accessed by AutoLISP functions. It takes the form:

`<File #nnnnnnnn>`

where *nnnnnnnn* is a number assigned internally by AutoCAD. In order to make use of the file after it has been opened, the file descriptor must be stored in a memory variable. Subsequent processing can then call the file by means of the memory variable name, not by the file descriptor.

OR

Tests a series of expressions for the first expression in the series that evaluates to a non-nil value.

Syntax

(or *exp1* ...)

Return Value: T if any of its expressions does not return nil. If all return nil, the function returns nil.

A series of any number of valid expressions is allowed.

OSNAP

Applies an object-snap override to a point.

Syntax

(osnap *pt mode*)

Return Value: A point list resulting from the object-snap mode being applied to the *pt* argument.

This function requires two arguments: a point list (*pt*), followed by a character string (*mode*) containing a list of valid object-snap overrides, separated by commas.

The reliability of this function depends on a number of factors: the size of the object-snap aperture, the current 3D view, the presence of other entities nearby and whether more than one construction point falls within range. All these factors should be carefully controlled in order for this function to work reliably.

ADS Equivalent

```
int ads_osnap(pt, mode, result)
    ads_point pt, result;
    char *mode;
```

Ads_osnap stores the found point in *result*.

POLAR

Computes a point relative to a given point.

Syntax

(polar *pt angle dist*)

Return Value: A point list, relative to the *pt* argument, at angle *angle* and distance *dist*.

This function requires three arguments, in the following order:

1. *pt* A point list indicating a starting reference point
2. *angle* A reference angle, expressed in radians
3. *dist* A reference distance from the starting reference point

The *angle* argument is always assumed to be in the current construction plane, with angle zero as the positive X-axis, and increasing in a counter-clockwise direction. The point returned, therefore, is always located in the current construction plane.

ADS Equivalent

```
void ads_polar(pt, angle, dist, result)
    ads_point pt, result;
    ads_real angle, dist;
```

Ads_polar stores the found point in *result*. This function does not return a value.

PRIN1

Prints an AutoLISP expression in the command-prompt area or writes it to a file.

Syntax

(prin1 *exp file*)

Return Value: The expression argument.

Prin1 requires the *exp* argument, which can be any valid AutoLISP expression. An optional *file* argument may be added following the expression. This argument must be a symbol bound to a file descriptor of a disk file that has been opened for writing or appending. Refer to the Open and Close functions for details on opening files.

If the *exp* argument is a string, the string is displayed on the screen and/or written to the file including its surrounding quotation marks. Any control characters in a string will be interpreted literally; that is, they will not be evaluated. For example, "\n" in a string will appear on the screen and be written into a file as a backslash character followed by a lowercase n, not a line feed.

Functions Listed Alphabetically

ADS Equivalent

```
int ads_printf(format, args, ...)
    char *format;
```

This function works like the standard printf() function in C, except this function always prints to the AutoCAD text screen. Character strings passed to Ads_printf cannot exceed 132 characters.

PRINC

Prints an AutoLISP expression in the command-prompt area or writes it to a file.

Syntax

(princ *exp file*)

Return Value: The expression argument.

Princ is like Prin1, except that it evaluates control characters. Princ is often used without arguments as the last function in a series. When princ is used without arguments, it will display a null character in the command-prompt area. This is useful when a series of functions would otherwise display the result of the last function in the command-prompt area.

PRINT

Prints a line feed, an AutoLISP expression, and a space in the command-prompt area or writes it to a file.

Syntax

(print *exp file*)

Return Value: The expression argument.

Print requires an expression, which can be any valid AutoLISP expression. An optional memory variable argument may be added following the expression; this memory variable must be bound to a file descriptor of a disk file that has been opened for writing or appending. Refer to the Open and Close functions for details on opening files.

Any control characters in a string will be interpreted literally; that is, they will not be evaluated. For example, "\n" in a string will appear on the screen and be written into a file as a backslash character followed by a lowercase n, not a line feed.

PROGN

Evaluates a series of expressions.

Syntax

(progn *exp1* ...)

Return Value: The last expression evaluated.

Progn accepts any number of valid AutoLISP expressions that are capable of being evaluated in sequence.

PROMPT

Displays a character string in the command-prompt area.

Syntax

(prompt *pstr*)

Return Value: Nil.

Prompt requires a character string as its only valid argument.

ADS Equivalent

```
int ads_prompt(pstr)
    char *pstr;
```

QUIT

Forces the current routine to abort processing.

Syntax

(quit)

Return Value: The message: "quit/exit abort"

Functions Listed Alphabetically

This function is called without arguments. Use it as a last-resort "safety valve" in cases where a routine might create unpredictable results if processing is allowed to continue.

QUOTE

Processes an expression without evaluating it.

Syntax

(quote *exp*)

Alternate Syntax

'*exp*

Return Value: The expression, unevaluated.

The Quote function requires a single argument, which can be any symbol, value, character string, or list, such as a point list to be evaluated by another function.

The alternate apostrophe syntax cannot be used at the Command prompt.

If you are quoting a list that contains other lists, the inner lists will not be evaluated.

READ

Extracts data from character strings.

Syntax

(read *str*)

Return Value: The first item from a character string, or the first list from a character string containing lists.

Read requires a string as its only allowable argument. The Read function operates on strings the way that the Car function operates on lists; that is, it will return the first item (up to the first space) it finds in the string. If the character string contains lists, the first list is returned.

Character strings returned by Read are not surrounded by quotation marks; if you pass them as arguments to other functions, the AutoLISP interpreter will attempt to evaluate them as symbols.

READ-CHAR

Reads characters from the keyboard buffer or file.

Syntax

(read-char *file*)

Return Value: The integer ASCII code for the character read.

Read-char requires no arguments if characters are to be read from the keyboard buffer. If the character is to be read from a file, a memory variable containing a file descriptor of a file open for reading must be supplied.

If the keyboard buffer is empty, read-char pauses for keyboard input. Input can be terminated by pressing the Enter key or space bar. When input is made, the function returns the first character in the buffer. If the function is repeated, the next character is read, and the process is repeated until all characters have been read.

If characters are read from a file open for reading, the first function call reads the first character, and subsequent calls read the following characters until the entire file has been read. When Read-char reaches the end of the file, it returns nil.

READ-LINE

Reads a string of characters from the keyboard or from a file.

Syntax

(read-line *file*)

Read-line requires no arguments if the string of characters is to be read from the keyboard buffer. If the character string is to be read from a file, a memory variable must be supplied containing a file descriptor for a file open for reading.

If the keyboard buffer is empty, Read-line pauses for keyboard input. Input may be terminated by pressing the Enter key; the space bar is considered part of the input.

Functions Listed Alphabetically

When input is made, the function returns the characters entered. When used in this fashion, Read-line works like Getstring with the T argument supplied; refer to the Getstring function for details.

If characters are read from a file open for reading, the first function call reads the first line of characters in the file, and returns that line. Subsequent calls read the following lines until the entire file has been read. When Read-line reaches the end of the file, it returns nil.

REDRAW

Redraws the display screen, or specified entities.

Syntax

(redraw *ent mode*)

Return Value: Nil.

Redraw requires no arguments; without them it redraws the entire screen. It may be supplied with an entity name, in which case it redraws that particular entity. If an entity name is supplied, this function may also be supplied with an integer indicating a particular *redraw mode:*

    1 = Redraw the entity normally. (Same as no integer argument.)

    2 = Blank out the entity. (Entity is not erased, but simply not displayed until the next redraw.)

    3 = Highlight the entity (if the display device supports highlighting).

    4 = Display the entity normally.

If the integer argument is positive and the entity used as the argument to redraw is a block with attributes, the block and its attributes will be operated on by the Redraw function. If the integer argument is negative, only the block is operated on.

ADS Equivalent

```
int ads_redraw(ent, mode)
    ads_name ent;
    int mode;
```

The system variable ERRNO is set to a new value when this function fails.

REGAPP

Registers a third-party application name with AutoCAD. Allows AutoCAD to extract (via the Entget function) extended entity data associated with the registered application.

Syntax

(regapp *appname*)

Return Value: The name of the application, if not previously registered; nil otherwise.

The *appname* argument is required. It is a character string (in quotes) up to 31 characters long. It follows the same naming conventions as any other AutoLISP symbol name.

ADS Equivalent

```
int ads_regapp(appname)
    char *appname;
```

The system variable ERRNO is set to a new value when this function fails.

REM

Calculates the remainder of the division of two numbers.

Syntax

(rem *n1 n2*)

Return Value: The remainder of dividing *n1* by *n2*.

Rem requires two numbers. They may be integers or real numbers. If a real number is used, a real number is returned. If both numbers are integers, an integer is returned.

REPEAT

Repeats each expression in a series a given number of times.

Syntax

(repeat *n exp1* ...)

Functions Listed Alphabetically

Return Value: the result of the last expression evaluated.

Repeat requires at least two arguments. The first (*n*) is an integer, indicating the number of repetitions to be performed. The second argument (*exp1*) is an AutoLISP expression that will be evaluated the indicated number of times. A series of AutoLISP expressions is also accepted by this function; the series need not be enclosed within parentheses.

If a series of expressions is present, each will be evaluated the indicated number of times before the next in the series is evaluated. If you intend that the entire series be evaluated the indicated number of times, enclose the series in the Progn function.

REVERSE

Reverses a list.

Syntax

(reverse *list*)

Return Value: The list with members in reverse order.

Reverse requires a single list. No other arguments are valid.

RTOS

Converts a real number to a character string.

Syntax

(rtos *n mode prec*)

Return Value: A character string.

Rtos requires a number argument (*n*). If the number is an integer, it is interpreted as a real number. If no other arguments are supplied, the number is converted to a string and returned in the current numeric units format and decimal precision as set using the Units command.

You may supply two optional arguments to Rtos:

> *mode*   An integer in the range from 1 to 5 that determines the numeric format of the string, as follows:
>
>> 1 = Scientific units
>>
>> 2 = Decimal units
>>
>> 3 = Engineering units
>>
>> 4 = Architectural units
>>
>> 5 = Fractional units
>
> *prec*   An integer that determines the number of decimal (or fractional) places of accuracy.

Unless the optional arguments are explicitly used, the units format of the string is determined by the settings of LUNITS and LUPREC.

ADS Equivalent

```
int ads_rtos(n, mode, prec, str)
    ads_real n;
    int mode, prec;
    char *str;
```

Ads_rtos places the converted value in *str*. This variable must point to an area of memory large enough to hold the character string.

SET

Binds the value of a symbol to the value of an expression.

Syntax

(set *symbol exp*)

Return Value: The value of the expression.

Set requires two arguments, a symbol (*symbol*) and an expression (*exp*). Set requires that the symbol evaluate to a value that can itself be used as a symbol name. Otherwise, the *symbol* argument should be nested within a Quote function, to prevent evaluation.

Functions Listed Alphabetically

The *exp* argument can be a number, string, list, entity name, file descriptor, or selection set.

If a Set function is used within a Defun function to bind a value to a symbol that is indicated by Defun to be a local variable, the value bound by the Set function is bound only while the defined function is operating. When the function has completed processing, any previous value bound to the variable is returned to the variable. If the variable did not exist previously, it is rebound to nil.

In all other circumstances, the memory variable bound to a value using Set is considered global; that is, the variable will remain bound to that value until another Set or Setq function explicitly binds a new value (or nil) to that variable. Refer to the Defun function for more details regarding local and global variables.

SETQ

Binds unevaluated symbol names to values.

Syntax

(setq *symbol value* ...)

Return Value: The value returned by the last argument in the function.

Setq requires two arguments, a symbol name (*sym*) and a value (*value*). Additional pairs of arguments may be supplied, alternating symbol names and the values to which they are bound.

Setq assumes that the first argument is a quoted symbol name. Setq is generally less confusing to use than Set. Any AutoLISP expression or symbol may be used to supply the value.

A single Setq function may be used to bind several memory variable names to values, if names and values are alternated as arguments to the function.

If a Setq function is used within a Defun function to bind a value to a symbol indicated by Defun to be a local variable, the value bound by Setq to that variable is bound only while that function is operating. When the function has completed its processing, any previous value bound to that variable is returned to the variable. If the variable did not exist previously, it is rebound to nil.

AUTOLISP/ADS QUICK FUNCTION REFERENCE
APP. A

In all other circumstances, the memory variable bound to a value using Setq is considered global; that is, that variable will remain bound to that value until another Setq or Set function explicitly binds a new value (or nil) to that variable. Refer to the Defun function for more details regarding local and global variables.

SETVAR

Changes the value of system variables.

Syntax

(setvar *sysvar val*)

Return Value: The new system variable value.

Setvar requires the name of an AutoCAD system variable (*sysvar*) and a value (*val*) for that variable. The system variable must not be a read-only variable, and the value for that variable must be a value the system variable can accept.

ADS Equivalent

```
int ads_setvar(sysvar, val)
    char *sysvar;
    struct resbuf *val;
```

The system variable ERRNO is set to a new value when this function fails.

SET_TILE

Resets a tile's value.

Syntax

(set_tile *tile val*)

Return Value: Nil.

Both arguments are required. The *tile* argument is a character string indicating the name of the tile. The *value* argument is a character string indicating the tile's new value.

ADS Equivalent

```
int ads_set_tile(hdlg, tile, val)
    ads_hdlg hdlg;
    char *tile, *val;
```

The *hdlg* argument is a dialog box handle of the type stored by the Ads_new_dialog function.

SIN

Calculates the sine of an angle.

Syntax

(sin *ang*)

Return Value: The sine of *ang*.

Sin requires a single numeric argument (*ang*), which should be an angle expressed in radians. Angles expressed in degrees must be converted to radians before being passed to this function.

SLIDE_IMAGE

Displays an AutoCAD slide in the current image tile (as specified by a call to the Start_image function).

Syntax

(slide_image *x1 y1 x2 y2 name*)

Return Value: Nil.

All arguments are required. *X1* and *y1* are integers indicating the coordinates of the slide's insertion point (the upper-left corner) in the tile's image area; *x2* and *y2* are integers indicating the coordinates of the slide's opposite corner in the image area. The image area's origin point is always the upper-left corner, and is always 0,0. The coordinates of the lower-right corner can be obtained by calling the Dimx_tile and Dimy_tile functions.

The *name* argument is the name of any valid AutoCAD slide file, as might be specified in an icon menu or in response to AutoCAD's Vslide command.

If a valid AutoCAD slide does not appear in the image area after a call to this function, it may be that the slide's vectors are being drawn in the same color as the image tile's background color. Try changing the background color of the image tile in the DCL file, or call the Fill_image function first, to change the background color of the current image tile.

ADS Equivalent

```
int ads_slide_image(x1, y1, x2, y2, name)
    short x1, y1, x2, y2;
    char *name;
```

SQRT

Calculates a square root of a number.

Syntax

(sqrt *n*)

Return Value: The square root of *n*.

Sqrt requires one numeric argument (*n*), either integer or real. A real number is always returned.

SSADD

Adds an entity to a selection set.

Syntax

(ssadd *ent sset*)

Return Value: The updated selection set.

Ssadd can be called without arguments. If so, the function will create a new selection set, but it will contain no members (members can be added later). More often, Ssadd is called with two arguments: an entity name (*ent*) followed by a selection set (*sset*). The function adds the entity name referenced as its first argument to the selection set referenced as the second argument.

If the referenced entity is already a member of the selection set, the function does not add it again; instead, it simply returns the selection set with nothing added.

Functions Listed Alphabetically

ADS Equivalent

```
int ads_ssadd(ent, sset, result)
    ads_name ent, sset, result;
```

Ads_ssadd stores the new (or updated) selection set in *result*. The system variable ERRNO is set to a new value when this function fails.

SSDEL

Deletes an entity from a selection set.

Syntax

(ssdel *ent sset*)

Return Value: The updated selection set.

Ssdel requires two arguments: an entity name (*ent*) followed by a selection set (*sset*). The function deletes the entity name referenced as its first argument from the selection set referenced as the second argument. If the referenced entity name is not found in the selection set, this function returns nil.

ADS Equivalent

```
int ads_ssdel(ent, sset)
    ads_name ent, sset;
```

The system variable ERRNO is set to a new value when this function fails.

SSGET

Pauses processing and allows the user to select a group of one or more entities.

Syntax

(ssget *mode pt1 pt2 plist filter*)

Return Value: Returns a selection set containing the selected entities.

Ssget requires no arguments, but may be supplied with one of the following sets of arguments as described below.

If Ssget is called without arguments, it is interactive. AutoLISP will display AutoCAD's "Select Objects:" prompt, and the user is free to use the normal syntax of window, crossing, add, and remove options at will, in order to build a selection set.

The *filter* argument is a list that includes one or more entity group-code sublists. Only entities that include sublists matching the sublists in the *filter* list will be included in the selection set, regardless of other arguments used.

If Ssget is called with an optional selection *mode* argument, it is no longer interactive and will automatically select entities based on the particular mode used. The mode arguments are as follows:

- **(ssget "C" '(*pt1*) '(*pt1*))** Selects entities crossing a window with opposite corners at point lists *pt1* and *pt2*.
- **(ssget "I")** Selects entities in the PICKFIRST selection set.
- **(ssget "L")** Selects the last entity in the database
- **(ssget "P")** Reselects the previously selected set
- **(ssget "P" '(*filter*))** Selects entities in the previously selected set whose sublists match the sublists in the *filter* list.
- **(ssget "W" '(*pt1*) '(*pt1*))** Selects entities contained within a window with opposite corners at point lists *pt1* and *pt2*.
- **(ssget "X")** Selects all entities in the database.
- **(ssget "X" '(*filter*))** Searches the entire database for entities containing sublists that match the sublists in the *filter* list.
- **(ssget '(*pt1*))** Selects the first entity passing through the point list *pt1*.
- **(ssget "WP" '(*plist*))** Selects entities inside a polygon formed by a series of point lists contained in the list *plist*.
- **(ssget "WP" '(*plist*) '(*filter*))** Selects entities inside a polygon formed by a series of point lists contained in the list *plist*, with sublists matching the sublists contained in the *filter* list.
- **(ssget "CP" '(*plist*))** Selects entities inside or crossing a polygon formed by a series of point lists contained in the list *plist*.
- **(ssget "F" '(*plist*))** Selects entities crossing the boundary fence defined by a series of point lists contained in the list *plist*.

Use the Ssget function with the single point argument only in situations where other entities are not very close by. When using this option, AutoLISP will sometimes select the incorrect entity, if more than one entity is very close to the selection point.

ADS Equivalent

```
int ads_ssget(mode, pt1, pt2, filter, sset)
    char *mode;
    void *pt1;
    ads_point pt2;
    struct resbuf filter;
    ads_name sset;
```

The *pt1* and *pt2* arguments are points used by various *mode* options. If a fence or polygon *mode* is specified, *pt1* may contain a linked list of result buffers that specify multiple points. The resulting selection set is stored in *sset*. This function returns RTCAN if the user presses Ctrl-C. The system variable ERRNO is set to a new value when this function fails.

SSLENGTH

Counts entities in a selection set.

Syntax

(sslength *sset*)

Return Value: A number indicating the total entities in the selection set.

Sslength requires a selection set as its only argument.

ADS Equivalent

```
int ads_sslength(sset, length)
    ads_name sset;
    long length;
```

Ads_sslength stores the number of members of the selection set in *length*.

SSMEMB

Determines if an entity is a member of a selection set.

Syntax

`(ssmemb ent sset)`

Return Value: The referenced entity name, if found in the selection set; nil otherwise.

Ssmemb requires two arguments: an entity name (*ent*) and a selection set (*sset*), in that order.

ADS Equivalent

```
int ads_ssmemb(ent, sset)
    ads_name ent, sset;
```

Ads_ssmemb returns RTNORM when the entity *ent* is found in selection set *sset*; RTERROR otherwise. The system variable ERRNO is set to a new value when this function fails.

SSNAME

Extracts entity names from a selection set.

Syntax

`(ssname sset i)`

Return Value: The extracted entity name. If the index argument (*i*) is out of range for the selection set argument (*sset*), the function returns nil.

Ssname requires two arguments in the following order: a selection set (*sset*), and an integer number (*i*). Entity names in selection sets are numbered with integers, starting with integer zero. The *i* argument is the number of the entity within the selection set.

ADS Equivalent

```
int ads_ssname(sset, i, ent)
    ads_name sset, ent;
    long i;
```

Ads_ssname stores the name of the found entity in *ent*.

START_DIALOG

Activates a displayed dialog box.

Syntax

(start_dialog)

Return Value: The value returned by a call to the Done_dialog function.

This function has no arguments. Call this function after you have made a call to the New_dialog and Action_tile functions, to display the dialog box and assign functions to its tiles. Start_dialog remains active until the user makes a call to the Done_dialog function, usually by pressing the OK button, Cancel button, or ESC key.

ADS Equivalent

```
int ads_start_dialog(hdlg, code)
    ads_hdlg hdlg;
    int *code;
```

Ads_start_dialog stores the value returned by the Ads_done_dialog function in *code*. The *hdlg* argument is the dialog box handle stored by Ads_new_dialog in its *hdlg* argument.

START_IMAGE

Starts slide image processing within a tile.

Syntax

(start_image *tile*)

Return Value: Nil.

The *tile* argument is required. It is a character string indicating the tile's name as specified in the Dialog Control Language (DCL) file. You must call this function before calling other image-processing functions, such as Fill_image, Slide_image, or Vector_image.

ADS Equivalent

```
int ads_start_image(hdlg, tile)
    ads_hdlg hdlg;
    char *tile;
```

The *hdlg* argument is a dialog box handle of the type stored by the Ads_new_dialog function.

START_LIST

Starts processing of a list box or popup list.

Syntax

(start_list *tile action index*)

Return Value: Nil.

Your routines should call this function to initialize processing of list boxes or popup lists in dialog boxes; such as calls to the Add_list function. The *tile* argument is required; it is a character string indicating the list box or popup list's tile name. The *action* argument is an integer indicating that some direct action is to take place inside the routine. Choices are:

    1 = Change the contents of the list.

    2 = Add a new item to the list.

    3 = Delete the old list and create a new one.

If no *action* argument is supplied, the default is 3. The *index* argument is required if *action* is 1, and ignored in all other cases. *Index* is an integer indicating which item on the list is to be changed. (The first item on the list is item number 0.)

ADS Equivalent

```
int ads_start_list(hdlg, tile, action, index)
    ads_hdlg hdlg;
    char *tile;
    short action, index;
```

Functions Listed Alphabetically

The *hdlg* argument is a dialog box handle of the type stored by the Ads_new_dialog function. The *action* argument is an ADS code indicating one of the following:

LIST_CHANGE = Change the contents of the list.

LIST_APPEND = Add a new item to the list.

LIST_NEW = Delete the old list and create a new one.

STRCASE

Converts characters in a string to upper or lowercase.

Syntax

(strcase *str mode*)

Return Value: The converted string.

Strcase requires a character string argument (*str*). The *mode* argument is optional, and may be any AutoLISP expression. If the *mode* argument is present and does not evaluate to nil, all characters in the first argument will be converted to lowercase. If the *mode* argument is omitted or nil, the characters in the string will be converted to uppercase. Numbers and punctuation marks are returned unconverted.

STRCAT

Connects (*concatenates*) two or more strings.

Syntax

(strcat *str1 str2* ...)

Return Value: A single combined string.

Strcat requires a series of strings or functions returning strings. This function will only concatenate character-string data.

STRLEN

Counts characters in a string.

Syntax

(strlen *str*)

Return Value: An integer indicating the length of the string, in characters.

Strlen requires a single character-string argument.

SUBST

Searches a list for a specified member. Replaces every occurrence of that member with a specified replacement item.

Syntax

(subst *new old list*)

Return Value: The modified list. If no members are found to replace, the list is returned unmodified.

Subst requires three arguments. The first argument is the replacement member for a list (*new*). The second argument is a current member of a list (*old*). The third argument is the list to be searched (*list*). Subst is often used to replace members of entity association lists.

SUBSTR

Extracts a portion of a character string.

Syntax

(substr *str start length*)

Return Value: The extracted substring.

Substr requires two arguments: a character string (*str*), and an integer indicating the starting position within that string (*start*). You may supply a third, optional, argument, another integer indicating the length of the substring (*length*).

The first character of a string is number 1. If the *length* argument is not present, the function will return a string beginning with the given position and continuing to the end of the original string. If the *length* argument is present, Subst will return a string of the indicated length, beginning with the specified position.

TABLET

Saves and sets tablet calibrations.

Syntax

(tablet *set pt1 pt2 pt3 dir*)

Return Value: A list, containing an integer and four point lists that specify the designated tablet calibration.

Tablet requires the *set* argument. This argument is an integer, either 1 or 0. If 0, the Tablet function returns a list specifying the current tablet calibration. If 1, Tablet will set a new calibration. You must then supply the remaining arguments to the function. *Pt1*, *pt2*, and *pt3* are point lists that define a tablet transformation matrix. These points are similar to the points you enter using AutoCAD's TABLET command, and are used by AutoCAD to calculate the type of tablet transformation: either orthogonal, affine, or projective. The fourth argument, *dir*, is a point list used to identify a direction vector that lies in the drawing planes that the tablet's surface is intended to lie in.

For more detailed information regarding tablet transformations, consult your *Programmer's Reference*, and the TABLET command in the AutoCAD Reference Manual.

ADS Equivalent

```
int ads_tablet(ptlist, result)
    struct resbuf *ptlist, **result;
```

Ads_tablet sets *result* to the new calibration, provided that you supply *result* as a declared result buffer pointer. The alternative is to supply the *result* argument as NULL, in which case the new calibration values are not stored. The system variable ERRNO is set to a new value when this function fails.

TBLNEXT

Extracts the association list for entries in a symbol table.

Syntax

(tblnext *table restart*)

Return Value: The association list for the table entry, or nil if no further entries are present.

The function requires the *table* argument, which is a character string indicating the table name for the symbol table you wish to read—for example, "BLOCK" or "LAYER". The optional *restart* argument may be any AutoLISP expression. If it evaluates to a non-nil value, the function extracts the first association list in the table. Subsequent calls to the Tblnext function, provided they do not include the *restart* argument (or that argument is nil), will extract the next association list in the table. If the *restart* argument is provided and does not evaluate to nil, the function will return the first entry in the table.

ADS Equivalent

```
struct resbuf ads_tblnext(table, restart)
    char *table;
    int restart;
```

Ads_tblnext returns the symbol table entry as a linked list of result buffers. The system variable ERRNO is set to a new value when this function fails.

TBLSEARCH

Extracts a specified entry in a symbol table.

Syntax

(tblsearch *table entry next*)

Return Value: The association list for the specified entry, if found; nil otherwise.

Tblsearch requires at least two arguments. The first, *table*, is a character string indicating the symbol table to search. The second, *entry*, is a character string indicating the name of the table entry (group code 2 in the entry's association list).

The *next* argument is optional, and may be any valid AutoLISP expression. If it is present and does not evaluate to nil, the entry in the table immediately after the found entry will be the entry returned by a subsequent call to the Tblnext function, described previously.

Functions Listed Alphabetically

ADS Equivalent

```
struct resbuf *ads_tblsearch(table entry next)
    char *table, *entry;
    int next;
```

Ads_tblsearch returns the symbol table entry as a linked list of result buffers. The system variable ERRNO is set to a new value when this function fails.

TERM_DIALOG

Cancels all active dialog boxes.

Syntax

(term_dialog)

Return Value: Nil.

Term_dialog uses no arguments. It cancels all active dialog boxes, including nested ones, as if the user had canceled all of them.

ADS Equivalent

```
int ads_term_dialog(void)
```

Ads_term_dialog always returns an RTNORM code.

TERPRI

Prints a line feed in the command-prompt area.

Syntax

(terpri)

Return Value: Nil.

No arguments are allowed with terpri. It affects only the command-prompt area of the screen.

TEXTBOX

Measures the diagonal coordinates of a box surrounding text entities.

Syntax

`(textbox tlist)`

Return Value: A list containing two point lists. The first point list specifies the offset from the text's insertion point to the lower-left corner of the text's boundary box. The second point list indicates the upper-right corner of the boundary box.

The *tlist* argument is required. It must be an association list for a text entity. If the association list argument does not include sublists indicating text style and orientation parameters, the current default parameters are assumed.

ADS Equivalent

```
int ads_textbox(ent, pt1, pt2)
    struct resbuf *ent;
    ads_point pt1, pt2;
```

The *ent* argument must be a linked list of result buffers for a text entity in the drawing (of a kind normally returned by the Ads_entget function). It stores the box's opposite corner coordinate points in *pt1* and *pt2*. The system variable ERRNO is set to a new value when this function fails.

TEXTPAGE

Displays the text screen on single-screen systems, and clears it.

Syntax

`(textpage)`

Return Value: Nil.

Textpage is called without arguments.

ADS Equivalent

`int ads_textpage()`

TEXTSCR

Displays the text screen on single-screen systems.

Functions Listed Alphabetically

Syntax

(textscr)

Return Value: Nil.

Textscr is called without arguments. Unlike the Textpage function, this function does not clear the text screen.

ADS Equivalent

int ads_textscr()

TRACE

Sets a *trace flag* for named functions.

Syntax

(trace *func1* ...)

Return Value: The last named function in the series.

Trace requires at least one name of a previously defined function. Any number of functions may be used as arguments. Trace is an aid to debugging functions, and can be used in situations where your defined functions are working well enough to avoid causing AutoLISP error messages, but you would like to test whether they are returning the results you want.

Each time the function is called when the trace flag is set, AutoLISP will display in the command-prompt area the message "Entering *function:*", where *function* is the name of a function for which the trace flag has been set. AutoLISP will display this message indented by a number of spaces corresponding to the depth to which the function has been nested. Thus if the traced function is nested within two other functions, AutoLISP will display the message indented two spaces. This is helpful if the function is called several times, or if the function is nested within control functions such as If, in which case it might be bypassed. The indentation helps indicate at what point in the processing the function is performing each time the trace message is displayed.

AutoLISP also displays the arguments that are passed to the function. If the arguments are expressions, the results of the expressions are displayed. When the function has completed processing, the result returned by the function is displayed, and the AutoLISP routine continues normally.

TRANS

Translates a point from one coordinate system to another.

Syntax

`(trans pt current new disp)`

Return Value: a point list indicating the point after translation.

Trans requires three arguments in the following order:

1. A 3D coordinate point list, indicating the point to be translated.
2. An integer code or entity name, indicating the current coordinate system of the point expressed in the first argument.
3. An integer code or entity name indicating the coordinate system of the point to be returned by the function.

In addition, the optional *disp* argument may be used. If this argument is present, the 3D point argument is interpreted as a *displacement*, that is, an amount of increment along each axis, translated from one coordinate system to another.

The allowable integer codes for coordinate systems are as follows:

0 = The World Coordinate System

1 = The Current User Coordinate System

2 = The Display Coordinate System

3 = Paper space (used only to/from Code 2)

The World Coordinate System and Current User Coordinate Systems are those standard coordinate systems that can be set current using the Ucs command. The Display Coordinate System is internally interpolated from the viewing angle. When viewing the display screen, you are always in plan view to this coordinate system. The positive Z-axis is measured from the target point to the viewing angle (TARGET to VIEWDIR) system variables, respectively; the positive X-axis is always horizontal and to the right, perpendicular to the Z-axis, and the Y-axis is always perpendicular to both the Z-axis and the X-axis. Thus, if the current UCS is in plan view, both the current User Coordinate System and the Display Coordinate System would be the same.

In addition, you can reference the coordinate system of an individual entity by supplying that entity's name in place of an integer code. Entities that retain coordinate systems of their own include 2D polylines, arcs, blocks, circles, solids, shapes, traces, and text.

Trans is needed because all coordinate point values returned by AutoLISP are relative to the current user coordinate system. Thus if a point is retrieved and stored to a memory variable while in one user coordinate system and the user coordinate system is subsequently changed, the coordinate point in that variable will now reference a completely different point in 3D space. Trans therefore provides the means for "updating" point variables when moving between different coordinate systems.

In addition, point data for entities that maintain their own entity coordinate systems must be translated to the current User coordinate system to be referenced and modified accurately by AutoLISP.

ADS Equivalent

```
int ads_trans(pt, current, new, disp, result)
    ads_point pt;
    struct resbuf *current, *new;
    int disp;
    ads_point result;
```

Ads_trans stores the transformed point in *result*. The system variable ERRNO is set to a new value when this function fails.

TYPE

Extracts the data type of its argument.

Syntax

(type *data*)

Return Value: The data type, as an uppercase string.

Type accepts a single argument, and tests its data type. Type returns one of the following strings (always in uppercase), depending on the data type of the argument:

Returns	When Entity Type Is:
ENAME	Entity name
EXSUBR	ADS (External) Function
FILE	File Descriptor
INT	Integer
LIST	List (A user-defined function is considered to be a list.)
PICKSET	Selection set
PAGETB	Function paging table (when virtual memory is enabled)
REAL	Real number
STR	String
SUBR	AutoLISP predefined function
SYM	Symbol

Type may also return nil if a null argument (such as an unknown symbol name) is supplied.

UNLOAD_DIALOG

Removes a previously loaded Dialog Control Language (DCL) file from RAM.

Syntax

(unload_dialog *id*)

Return Value: Nil.

Unload_dialog requires an integer argument, which is the integer returned by a previous call to the Load_dialog function.

ADS Equivalent

```
int ads_unload_dialog(id)
    int id;
```

This function always returns an RTNORM code.

UNTRACE

Removes the trace flag from functions.

Syntax

(untrace *func1* ...)

Return Value: The name of the last function in the series.

Untrace requires the names of valid functions. If no trace flag exists, nothing happens, but the function name is returned. If a trace flag is set for any function, it is removed from that function.

VECTOR_IMAGE

Draws a line in the current image tile (as specified by a call to the Start_image function.

Syntax

(vector_image *x1 y1 x2 y2 color*)

Return Value: Nil.

All arguments are required. *X1* and *y1* are integers indicating the coordinates of the line's start point in the tile's image area; *x2* and *y2* are integers indicating the coordinates of the line's end point in the image area. The image area's origin point is always the upper-left corner, and is always 0,0. The coordinates of the lower-right corner can be obtained by calling the Dimx_tile and Dimy_tile functions.

Color is any available AutoCAD color code integer in the range 0–255, or one of the following:

–2 = Same as AutoCAD graphics-screen background color

–15 = Same as dialog box background color

–16 = Same as dialog box text color

–18 = Same as dialog box line color

ADS Equivalent

```
int ads_vector_image(x1, y1, x2, y2, color)
    short x1, y1, x2, y2, color;
```

The *color* argument is any available AutoCAD color code integer in the range 0–255, or one of the following ADS codes:

BGLCOLOR = Same as AutoCAD graphics-screen background color

DBGLCOLOR = Same as dialog box background color

DFGLCOLOR = Same as dialog box text color

LINELCOLOR = Same as dialog box line color

VER

Tests the AutoLISP version number.

Syntax

(ver)

Return Value: A character string indicating the version number.

Ver uses no arguments. Ver is useful when routines may be shared among different versions of AutoLISP, in order to choose between alternate processing based on which version is being used.

VMON

Enables virtual function memory paging, in versions prior to Release 12.

Syntax

(vmon)

Return Value: Nil.

Vmon helps conserve memory space when AutoLISP routines define many functions. Its process is transparent to the user. Place it at the beginning of a long AutoLISP routine or in ACAD.LSP. Once enabled, function paging cannot be disabled. This function has no effect in Release 12.

VPORTS

Extracts viewport identification numbers.

Syntax

(vports)

Return Value: A list of viewport identification numbers and corner coordinates for the current viewport configuration.

Vports uses no arguments. The list returned by Vports is a list of sublists. Each sublist contains the following members, in the following order:

1. The viewport identification number, which is always an integer
2. The lower-left corner of the viewport, expressed as a 2D coordinate point list
3. The upper-right corner of the viewport, also a 2D coordinate point list

The currently active viewport is always the first viewport sublist in the list returned by Vports. The values in the coordinate point list are always in the range of 0.0 to 1.0, representing the minimum and maximum values for both X and Y coordinates.

In Release 11 and later, the Vports function returns the viewport configuration in model space if the system variable TILEMODE is set to 1. If TILEMODE is set to zero, the function returns the viewport configuration in paper space.

In paper space, viewport 1 is the paper space area on display when TILEMODE is first set to zero, and the currently active viewport, if any, is listed first.

ADS Equivalent

```
int ads_vports(result)
    struct resbuf **result;
```

Ads_vports stores a linked list of result buffers containing viewport descriptors of the current configuration in *result*. If Ads_vports fails, it returns an RTERROR code.

WCMATCH

Matches a character string to a series of test strings containing special wildcard characters.

Syntax

(wcmatch *str pattern*)

Return Value: T if a successful match is made; nil otherwise.

Wcmatch requires a character string argument (*str*), called the *test string*, as its first argument, followed by a second string argument (*pattern*). If the two strings match, the function returns T. The second string is a special control pattern composed of one or more groups of wildcard characters. Wildcard characters allow the function to return T even if the match is not exact. Each argument may contain up to 500 characters; if a string is longer than this, the excess characters are ignored. The function will return T when a match is made to the following special wildcard characters:

*	The asterisk will match any substring, including no string, anywhere in the test string.
?	The question mark will match any single alphanumeric character anywhere in the pattern.
@	The "at" symbol will match any single alphabetic letter anywhere in the pattern.
#	The "number" or "pound" symbol will match any single numeric character anywhere in the pattern.
.	The period will match any single non-alphanumeric character, including no character, anywhere in the test string.
`	The back-quote character (not the same as the apostrophe) allows you to read wildcard characters literally, instead of as control characters.

If a tilde (~) is the first character within brackets, Wcmatch will return true if the test string does *not* match any of the control pattern characters within the brackets.

You may specify a consecutive range of single characters within brackets by separating the beginning and end of the range with a hyphen (-). Note that this works only for a range of single characters; characters not separated by the hyphen are treated individually.

The comma (,) allows you to separate groups of wildcard characters in the control pattern, thus allowing you to make a comparison to a series of control patterns. A space in the control pattern will match one or more spaces in the test string.

AutoLISP generally interprets the backslash character (\) as a control character whenever it appears in any string; to represent a literal backslash character anywhere in AutoLISP, use two backslashes (\\). If you want to represent a single literal backslash in a control pattern for Wcmatch, use the back-quote character plus two backslashes (`\\).

Square brackets ([]) have a special function in the control pattern string. Wcmatch will return T if any one of the characters within brackets in the control pattern matches the test string. All characters are interpreted literally within brackets; for example, an asterisk appearing within brackets is not interpreted as a wildcard character, but rather as an asterisk.

There are exceptions to this rule of literal characters between brackets, however: As mentioned above, a hyphen within brackets is considered a control character, signifying a range. However, if the hyphen appears first, as in "[-XYZ]" or last, as in "[XYZ-]", or follows a leading tilde, as in "[~-XYZ]", it will be considered a literal character. A leading tilde following an opening bracket is interpreted as a control character, reversing the bracketed match criterion.

If a pair of empty brackets appears in the control pattern, the opening bracket is considered the control character, but the closing bracket will be interpreted as a literal character. This necessitates adding a second closing bracket to the control pattern. For example:

(wcmatch "X]Z" "X[]1-8]Z")

returns T.

Character tests by Wcmatch are case-sensitive; thus, "abc" will not match "A*". However, all symbol names are converted to uppercase by AutoLISP; therefore, use uppercase control patterns to match them.

The wildcard characters described above may be used in any AutoLISP functions that compare string data.

ADS Equivalent

```
int ads_wcmatch(str, pattern)
    char *str, *pattern;
```

Ads_wcmatch returns RTNORM if the string matches the pattern; RTERROR otherwise.

WHILE

Repeatedly evaluates a series of one or more AutoLISP expressions based on whether an initial test expression evaluates to nil or a non-nil value.

Syntax

(while *test exp1* ...)

Return Value: The value of the last evaluated expression.

The While function requires at least two AutoLISP expressions for arguments, but may include a series of any length. The first argument (*test*) is the test expression. The following expressions will be repeatedly evaluated in sequence as long as the test expression does not return nil.

Any processing series may be used inside a looping function, provided that the processing affects the test expression, causing it to return nil at some point. If the test expression never evaluated to nil, the repeated tasks would continue indefinitely. This situation is referred to as an *endless loop*. If you accidentally write an endless loop, the program may appear to be doing nothing, or the same messages may be displayed on the screen over and over. In such a situation, you must cancel the AutoLISP routine by entering Ctrl-C.

WRITE-CHAR

Writes a single character to either the command-prompt area or to a file.

Syntax

(write-char *n file*)

Return Value: The ASCII character code for the character written.

Write-char requires an ASCII integer code for the character being written. ASCII code 0 (null character) is not allowed. If the character is to be written to a file, a memory variable containing a file descriptor of a file open for either writing or appending must be supplied after the ASCII character code integer.

WRITE-LINE

Writes a character string in the command-prompt area or to a file.

Syntax

(write-line *str file*)

Return Value: The character string.

Write-line requires the character string argument *str*. If the character string is to be written to a file, a memory variable containing a file descriptor for a file open for writing or appending must also be supplied.

Like the Print function, Write-line automatically writes each subsequent line to a new line in the file, but unlike the Print function, it does not add a trailing space.

XDROOM

Calculates the amount of extended entity data space available for a named entity.

Syntax

(xdroom *ent*)

Return Value: An integer indicating the number of bytes of available extended entity space.

The maximum amount of available space is 16,383 bytes. Use this function to test whether sufficient space is available for your application's extended entity data.

ADS Equivalent

```
int ads_xdroom(ent, result)
    ads_name ent;
    long *result;
```

Ads_xdroom stores the result of its calculation to *result*. The system variable ERRNO is set to a new value when this function fails.

XDSIZE

Calculates the amount of space required by an extended entity data list.

Syntax

(xdsize *xdlist*)

Return Value: an integer indicating the number of bytes required by the argument list.

The *xdlist* argument must be a list of extended-entity sublists, as described in the AutoLISP *Programmer's Reference*. The entire list must be enclosed within a set of parentheses; therefore, the argument to this function is a list containing a single list, which in turn contains a series of sublists.

ADS Equivalent

```
int ads_xdsize(xdlist, result)
    struct resbuf *xdlist;
    long *result;
```

Ads_xdsize stores the result of its calculation to *result*.

XLOAD

Loads a compiled program developed using AutoCAD's Advanced Development System (ADS).

Syntax

(xload *appname errmsg*)

Return Value: The application name, as specified in the *appname* argument, if the application is successfully loaded; otherwise, an AutoLISP error is generated. If the *errmsg* argument is supplied, an AutoLISP error is not generated, and the *errmsg* character string is returned.

Xload requires a character string naming a valid ADS application file. The file extension (varies, depending on your system) is not required. The *errmsg* argument is optional.

ADS Equivalent

```
int ads_xload(appname)
    char *appname;
```

The system variable ERRNO is set to a new value when this function fails.

XUNLOAD

Removes an ADS program from memory.

Syntax

(xunload *appname errmsg*)

Return Value: The application name, as specified in the *appname* argument, if the application is successfully unloaded; otherwise, an AutoLISP error is generated. If the *errmsg* argument is supplied, an AutoLISP error is not generated, and the *errmsg* character string is returned.

Xunload requires a character string naming a valid ADS application file that was previously loaded into memory. The file extension (varies, depending on your system) is not required. The *errmsg* argument is optional.

ADS Equivalent

```
int ads_xunload(appname)
    char *appname;
```

The system variable ERRNO is set to a new value when this function fails.

ZEROP

Tests to determine whether a number is zero.

Syntax

(zerop *n*)

Return Value: T if the number is exactly zero; nil otherwise.

Zerop requires a number, either real or integer. If the *n* argument is not a number, Zerop returns nil.

APPENDIX B

Short AutoLISP Routines and Useful Functions for Study

SHORT AUTOLISP ROUTINES AND USEFUL FUNCTIONS FOR STUDY
APP. B

This appendix contains useful AutoLISP routines, presented in Listings B.1 through B.22, that you can use as is, modify to your liking, or use as examples for study.

Two-Character Macros

Almost any user can benefit from developing simple, two-character commands that execute frequently invoked command sequences without requiring the original AutoCAD command and without prompting for the necessary option keywords. Use these as a basis for creating your own AutoLISP macro library. Place the most useful macros in your ACAD.LSP file on the AutoCAD system subdirectory.

EL.LSP

EL.LSP, shown in Listing B.1, quickly erases the last entity drawn. It is useful in situations where the Undo command won't work, either because several entities were drawn within an Undo group, or because a custom command made changes to the environment that you don't wish to be undone as well. It is a good way to delete scratch lines. The Oops or Undo command will restore an entity deleted using EL.LSP.

Listing B.1: EL.LSP—Erase Last Object

```
; EL - for AutoCAD Release 9+
(defun C:EL()
  (entdel (entlast))
  (princ)
)
```

LP.LSP

LP.LSP, shown in Listing B.2, is a variation of a classic routine that has existed in one form or another since AutoLISP introduced entity-access functions. This version is especially efficient and compact. LP.LSP creates a macro named LP, which can be invoked from the Command prompt. The Macro prompts you to select an object on the screen, then sets the current layer to be the same as the selected object.

Two-Character Macros

Listing B.2: LP.LSP—Change Layer by Picking Object

```
; LP - for AutoCAD Release 9+
(defun C:LP( / oldech oldsnp olderr esel )
    (setq oldech (getvar "CMDECHO")    ; store current environment
          oldsnp (getvar "OSMODE")
          olderr *ERROR*
    )
    (defun *ERROR* (msg)               ; define new error handler
       (princ " \n") (princ msg)       ; print message
       (setvar "CMDECHO" oldech)
       (setvar "OSMODE"  oldsnp)
       (setq  *ERROR*   olderr)
       (princ)
    )
    (setvar "CMDECHO" 0)               ; reset environment
    (setvar "OSMODE"  512)

    (while (not (setq esel (entsel))))  ; pick entity

    (command ".LAYER" "s"
             (g:entv 8 (car esel)) "")  ; change layer

    (setvar "CMDECHO" oldech)           ; restore environment
    (setvar "OSMODE"  oldsnp)
    (setq *ERROR* olderr)
    (princ)
)
;----------------------------------------------------------------
;
; G:ENTV - Returns entity association list value

(defun g:entv ( code ename )
    (cdr (assoc code (entget ename)))
)
```

Notice that LP.LSP includes a small global function named G:entv. This function can be used in many routines that require values associated with entity group codes. It returns the value associated with a specified group code in an entity's association list. The syntax for the function is as follows:

(g:entv *code entityname*)

The function requires two arguments: the group code being accessed and an entity name. If the group code does not exist, this function returns nil; otherwise, it returns

SHORT AUTOLISP ROUTINES AND USEFUL FUNCTIONS FOR STUDY
APP. B

the value associated with the specified group code.

LX.LSP

LX.LSP, shown in Listing B.3, prompts for a layer name and makes it current, creating it if it does not exist already. Then it freezes all other layers in the drawing. It is useful when you need to isolate the entities on a single layer. This macro will work on AutoCAD Releases 9 and later. After loading the file, enter the command LX.

Listing B.3: LX.LSP—Freeze All But Specified Layer

```
; LX - for AutoCAD Release 9+
(defun C:LX (/ oldech x )

  (setq oldech (getvar "CMDECHO")
        x (getstring "Layer to set: "))

  (setvar "CMDECHO" 0)

  (if (tblsearch "LAYER" x)
     (command ".layer" "t" x "on" x)
     (command ".layer")
  )
  (command "m" x "f" "*" "")

  (setvar "CMDECHO" oldech)
  (princ)

)
```

LT.LSP

LT.LSP, shown in Listing B.4, simply thaws all the layers in the drawing. It is useful as a global recovery from LX.LSP. While LT.LSP thaws all layers, it does not turn layers on if they were turned off when they were frozen. After loading the file, enter the command LT.

Listing B.4: LT.LSP—Thaw All Layers

```
; LT - for AutoCAD Release 9+
(defun C:LT (/ oldech )
```

Two-Character Macros

```
  (setq oldech (getvar "CMDECHO") )
  (setvar "CMDECHO" 0)
  (command ".layer" "t" "*" "")
  (setvar "CMDECHO" oldech)
  (princ)
)
```

UM.LSP

UM.LSP, shown in Listing B.5, is a Release 12 macro that places a mark on the Undo audit trail. If the Undo feature is turned off, it turns it on. After loading the file, enter the command UM:

Listing B.5: UM.LSP—Quick Undo Mark

```
; UM - for AutoCAD Release 12
(defun C:UM( / oldech x )

   (setq oldech (getvar "CMDECHO")
         x      (getvar "UNDOCTL")
   )
   (setvar "CMDECHO" 0)

   (cond ( (= 0 x )
           (command ".undo" "a" ".undo" "a" "on")
         )
         ( (= 3 x )
           (command ".undo" "c" "a")
         )
   )

   (if (<= x 3)
      (prompt "\nUndo ALL now active.")
   )
   (if (>= x 8)
      (command ".undo" "e")
   )

   (command ".undo" "m")
   (prompt "\nMark set.")
```

```
        (setvar "CMDECHO" oldech)
        (princ)

)
```

UB.LSP

UB.LSP, shown in Listing B.6, is a Release 12 macro that activates the UNDO BACK command. It is designed to work as a companion to UM.LSP. If a mark is encountered on the Undo audit trail, it stops at the mark, and reinserts the mark back in place. If no mark is encountered, UB.LSP undoes everything. This macro is useful when you are trying out various options in a drawing and wish to move back quickly to a particular point in the drawing session. After loading the file, invoke the command UB.

Listing B.6: UB.LSP—Quick Undo Back & Mark Reset

```
; UB - for AutoCAD Release 12
(defun C:UB(/ oldech)

    (setq oldech (getvar "CMDECHO") )
    (setvar "CMDECHO" 0)
    (cond ( (= 0 (getvar "UNDOMARKS"))
            (command ".undo" "e" ".undo" "b" "y")
          )
          ( T (command ".undo" "e" ".undo" "b" ".undo" "m")
              (prompt "\nUNDO complete. Mark reset.")
          )
    )

    (setvar "CMDECHO" oldech)
    (princ)

)
```

Remember that the REDO command will reset any changes made using these macros, in case you find you have undone more than you intended.

ZP.LSP

ZP.LSP, shown in Listing B.7, is a fast way to restore the previous viewing angle. After loading the file, enter the command ZP.

Working with Files

Listing B.7: ZP.LSP—Quick Zoom Previous

```
; ZP - for AutoCAD Release 9+
(defun C:ZP(/ oldech )

   (setq oldech (getvar "CMDECHO") )
   (setvar "CMDECHO" 0)
   (command ".zoom" "p")
   (setvar "CMDECHO" oldech)
   (princ)

)
```

Other zoom variations based on this model are possible. For example,

```
; ZW - for AutoCAD Release 9+
(defun C:ZW(/ oldech )

   (command ".zoom" "w" pause pause)
   (princ)

)
```

executes the Zoom window command. The only changes are to the function name, and substitution of the correct parameters in the Command function on line 4. Using this model, you can make two-key macros from many AutoCAD commands to save time and promote efficiency.

Working with Files

G:fname (shown in Listing B.8) is a function, intended for global use, that provides a fair level of error-trapping when accessing files on disk. It is especially useful when working with routines that create files. G:fname verifies that the file name you enter is a legal DOS name, offers an optional default file name, adds a default file extension to the name if desired, and checks for the existence of a file with the same name on the AutoCAD file search path. If a duplicate file is found, G:fname prompts you to confirm that you want to overwrite the existing file before accepting the file name you enter.

The G:fname function has the syntax:

```
(g:fname default extension)
```

Both arguments are optional, but if not supplied, they must be replaced in the function syntax by nil. Following are examples of valid syntax:

```
(g:fname "TEST" "TXT")
(g:fname nil "TXT")
(g:fname "TEST" nil)
(g:fname nil nil)
```

Using the first example, G:FNAME prompts

```
File name <TEST>:
```

and if the user presses ↵, will return

```
TEST.TXT
```

because the default file extension was used.

Even if a default extension is given in the syntax, the user can override the default by entering a file name that includes an extension. G:fname also accepts drive letters and directories as part of the file name.

If you supply a path as part of the file-name argument in the function, you must use double backslashes to separate the path directories; for example:

```
(g:fname "c:\\acad\\sample.txt" "txt")
```

Do not use forward slashes, since these characters are trapped by the Testfn function, which is described just ahead. However, when the G:fname function pauses and prompts you to input a file name, you can easily include a subdirectory path in your response, using the familiar single backslash syntax.

Listing B.8: G:FNAME.LSP—Get File Name with Error-Trapping

```
; G:FNAME function - Gets, verifies, and prompts to overwrite
; a file name

(defun g:fname( defname ext / yn fnvar fqfn)

   (while (not (setq fnvar
              (testfn (g:getstr "\nFile name: " defname nil))
           )
       )
   )

   (if (and ext
```

Working with Files

```
                            (not (findch "." fnvar))
            )
            (setq fnvar (strcat fnvar "." ext))
        )

        (while (and (setq fqfn (findfile fnvar))
                    (/= yn "Yes")
               )
            (initget 1 "Yes No")
            (cond ( (eq "No"
                         (setq yn
                           (getkword
                            (strcat "\nFile " fqfn
                                        " found. Overwrite (Y/N)? "
                            )
                           )
                         )
                    )
                    (setq fnvar (g:getstr "\nFile name: "
                                              defname nil))
                    (if (and ext
                             (not (findch "." fnvar))
                        )
                        (setq fnvar (strcat fnvar "." ext))
                    )
                  )
            )
        )

        (if (eq "Yes" yn)
            fqfn
            fnvar
        )

)
;----------------------------------------------------------------
; G:GETSTR function: - Formatted Getstring

(defun g:getstr(prmt default spaces / temp)

    (if default                          ; if default exists
        (setq temp (getstring spaces (g:str prmt default)))
        (while (not default)             ; while no default
            (setq default (getstring spaces prmt))
        )
```

```
        )
    (if (and temp (/= temp ""))  ; if temp exists (response given)
        (setq default temp)      ; set new default
        default                   ; otherwise, return current
    )
)
;----------------------------------------------------------------
; FINDCH - Locate character within string

(defun findch( chr chrstr lstr )

    (cond ( (and (= (type chrstr) 'STR)
                 (= (type chr) 'STR)
            )
            (setq lstr (strlen chrstr))
            (while (and (> lstr 0)
                        (/= chr (substr chrstr lstr 1))
                   )
                (setq lstr (1- lstr))
            )
          )
    )

    (if (> lstr 0)
        chrstr
    )

)
;----------------------------------------------------------------
; TESTFN - Test string for illegal DOS characters

(defun testfn( chrstr / xstr index valid)

    (setq xstr (strcat "*+=¦[];?/<>," (chr 34))
          index 1
          valid T
    )

    (while (and valid
                (<= index 13)
           )
        (if (findch (substr xstr index 1) chrstr)
            (setq valid nil)
```

Working with Files

```
              (setq index (1+ index))
            )
        )
        (if valid
            chrstr
            (prompt (strcat "\nIllegal character ("
                             (substr xstr index 1)
                             ") in file name.")
            )
        )
    )
)
```

G:FNAME.LSP uses a number of interesting string-handling functions that can be applied to many other AutoLISP routines that manipulate character strings. For example, G:getstr is a formatted version of AutoLISP's getstring function, similar to the formatted Get functions discussed in Chapter 7. Also, notice that G:getstr requires the G:str function, also listed in Chapter 7. You must load that function before attempting to use G:fname.

The Findch function is a string-handling function that tests if a character exists in a given string. The search for the indicated character is not case-sensitive; in other words, lowercase characters will match uppercase. If the character is found, Findch returns the original string. If the character is not found, Findch returns nil. The syntax for Findch is

```
(findch character string)
```

The G:fname function uses Findch to see if a period is included in the file name entered by the user, indicating that the user has supplied a file extension. In such a case, G:fname will not supply a default extension even if one was used as an argument.

The Testfn argument checks the file name string entered by the user for illegal characters. It also makes use of the Findch function for this purpose. Notice how this function tests the entered string against a key string of illegal characters. Because the quote character (') is also illegal in DOS file names, Testfn uses the Strcat and Chr functions to include the quote character in the key string:

```
(strcat "*+=¦[];?/<>," (chr 34))
```

If you included the quote character literally, you would create a situation in which the string delimiters would be unmatched, so this is one method by which you can include a quote character in an AutoLISP string. Syntax for Testfn is

```
(testfn filename)
```

SHORT AUTOLISP ROUTINES AND USEFUL FUNCTIONS FOR STUDY
APP. B

If the string contains one of the illegal characters, the function informs the user and returns nil. Otherwise, it returns the original file name string.

Exporting AutoCAD Text to an ASCII File

TEXTOUT.LSP, shown in Listing B.9, is an example of how to use the G:fname function. It prompts the user to enter a file name and pick a selection set containing AutoCAD text entities. The text entities in the selection set are exported into the named file. Nontext entities in the selection set are ignored.

If you edit text in the drawing, you may change the order in which it appears in the underlying database. Because of this, TEXTOUT.LSP offers two methods for selecting text: using a crossing window or picking the lines individually. If you select text using the crossing window, the entities appear in the file in the order in which they appear in the underlying database. If you pick the text entities individually, they appear in the file in the order selected.

Listing B.9: TEXTOUT.LSP—Write AutoCAD Text to ASCII File

```
; TEXTOUT - for AutoCAD Release 10+
(defun C:TEXTOUT(/ oldech filstr)

    (setq oldech (getvar "CMDECHO"))
    (setvar "CMDECHO" 0)
    (if (setq filstr (g:fname nil "TXT"))
       (export)
    )
    (setvar "CMDECHO" oldech)
    (princ)

)
;-------------------------------------------------------------
; EXPORT - Export AutoCAD text to file

(defun export( / method ll ur lines xpfile
          total alist blist test )

   (while (and (/= method "C")
               (/= method "P")
```

Exporting AutoCAD Text to an ASCII File

```
            )
            (setq method
                (strcase
                    (substr
                        (getstring (strcat "\nSelect text with "
                                           "<C>rossing Window, or "
                                           "<P>ick text lines (C/P): "
                                   )
                        )
                        1 1
                    )
                )
            )
        )
        (cond ( (= method "C")
                (princ (strcat "\nCrossing window used. "
                               "(Non-text entities ignored.)"
                       )
                )
                (setq ll (getpoint "\nFirst Corner: ")
                      ur (getcorner ll "\nOther Corner: ")
                      lines (ssget "C" ll ur)
                )
              )
              ( T (setq lines (ssget))
              )
        )

        (princ (strcat "\nWriting file "
                       (strcase filstr)
                       " -- One moment...\n"
               )
        )
        (setq xpfile (open filstr "w")
              total (1- (sslength lines))
        )
        (cond ( (= method "C")
                (setq blist nil)
                (while (<= 0 total)
                    (prin1 '-)
                    (setq alist (entget (ssname lines total)))

                    (if (= "TEXT" (cdr (assoc 0 alist)))
                        (setq blist (cons (cdr (assoc 1 alist))
```

```
                                                    blist))
                         )
                         (setq total (1- total))
                 )
                 (setq blist (reverse blist))
                 (while blist
                         (prin1 '-)
                         (write-line (car blist) xpfile)
                         (setq blist (cdr blist))
                 )
         )
         ( T   (setq test -1)
               (while (<= (setq test (1+ test)) total)
                       (prin1 '-)
                       (setq alist (entget (ssname lines test)))

                       (if (= "TEXT" (cdr (assoc 0 alist)))
                           (write-line (cdr (assoc 1 alist))
                                       xpfile)
                       )
               )
         )
     )

     (close xpfile)
     (prompt (strcat "\nFile " (strcase filstr) " written.\n"))
 )
```

View Association Lists

It is often helpful, when developing programs, to see the entire contents of an entity's association list. The C:Entlist function, shown in Listing B.10, creates an AutoCAD command that prompts you to select an entity and displays that entity's association list in the command prompt area.

Listing B.10: ENTLIST.LSP—Get Entity Association List

```
; ENTLIST - for AutoCAD Release 9+
(defun C:ENTLIST()

   (princ (entget (setq g:ent (car (entsel)))))
```

Rudimentary Debugging

```
        (princ "\nNext entity: ")
        (princ (entnext g:ent))
        (princ)
)
```

In addition, the entity name is stored in a global variable named G:ent, which can be accessed by the C:NEXT function, shown in Listing B.11. This function creates an AutoCAD command named NEXT, which will return the association list of the entity stored in G:ent, and when repeated, will step through the AutoCAD database, returning the association list of each following entity in turn, until you reach the end of the database.

Listing B.11: NEXT.LSP—Loop through Association Lists

```
; NEXT - for AutoCAD Release 9+
(defun C:NEXT()

    (cond ( (and (= (type g:ent) 'ENAME)
                (setq g:ent (entnext g:ent))
           )
           (princ (entget g:ent))
           (princ "\nNext entity: ")
           (princ (entnext g:ent))
         )
         ( T
           (princ "\nContents of G:Ent variable: ")
           (princ g:ent)
         )
    )
    (princ)

)
```

Rudimentary Debugging

The function shown in Listing B.12 creates an AutoCAD command named DEBUG. When you invoke the command, AutoCAD toggles a global variable named G:debug between being bound to a value and being bound to nil.

SHORT AUTOLISP ROUTINES AND USEFUL FUNCTIONS FOR STUDY
APP. B

Listing B.12: DEBUG.LSP—Toggle Debug Flag On and Off

```
; DEBUG - for AutoCAD Release 9+
(defun C:DEBUG()

   (if g:debug
      (setq g:debug
           (prompt "\nDEBUG now toggled off.")
      )
      (setq g:debug
           (print "DEBUG now toggled on.")
      )
   )
   (princ)
)
```

You can use the status of this variable to make choices within the routines you are developing. For example, the Pauser function, shown in Listing B.13, will temporarily pause a routine and wait for a keypress if G:debug has a value; otherwise, it has no effect and the routine will run normally. The syntax for the function is

(pauser *symbol*)

You can supply the Pauser function with the names of symbols to evaluate before pausing. This can help you identify the status of critical memory variables during processing. To pause processing without evaluating any symbols, use nil as the function's argument.

The symbols you pass to the Pauser function should be enclosed in a list. For example, use the following syntax to pause processing and evaluate the symbols A and B:

(pauser '(A B))

Notice how the list of symbols is preceded by an apostrophe, which is shorthand for AutoLISP's predefined Quote function. This prevents the list of symbols from being interpreted as a nested function. If you omit the apostrophe, the interpreter will return an error message and processing will abort.

Insert the Pauser function at critical stages of processing to track your routine's processes. When the program is fully tested, use your text editor to remove or "comment out" the Pauser functions, or "turn off" the G:debug variable by placing it on the routine's local variable list. This sets the value of G:debug to nil for that routine, ensuring normal processing.

Listing B.13: PAUSER.LSP—Pause AutoLISP Processing

```
; PAUSER function - for AutoCAD Release 9+
(defun pauser( arg )
   (if (and g:debug (= (type arg) 'LIST) )
      (while arg
          (princ "\nVariable ")
          (princ (car arg))
          (princ ": ")
          (princ (eval (car arg)))
          (getstring "\nProgram paused. Press Enter...")
          (setq arg (cdr arg))
      )
      (getstring "\nProgram paused. Press Enter...")
   )
)
```

You can use the status of the G:debug variable to make choices throughout the routine during its development cycle. For example, consider the following framework for choosing between alternate processes, based on the status of G:debug:

```
(cond ( (not g:debug)         ; G:debug not set
                              ;... put normal processes here
       )
       ( T                    ; G:debug is set
                              ;... put debugging variations here
       )
)
```

Later, when the routine is fully developed and debugged, you can permanently "turn off" the G:debug variable by placing it on the routine's local variable list. Alternatively, if your text editor has text search features, it is easy to move through a fully-debugged routine and eliminate all references to G:debug before distributing it to users. This conserves AutoLISP memory space.

While the expedient demonstrated here is no match for a full-featured AutoLISP debugger, it can help you isolate and identify runtime problems in your code with a minimum of fuss.

Toggle System Variables

FRAD.LSP, shown in Listing B.14, is a routine that creates a new AutoCAD command called FRAD. This command prompts you to enter a new fillet radius, storing the current radius. After you run this program the first time, you can repeat it whenever you wish to toggle between the old and new value, or input a new radius value at any time. Use this routine as a model to create two-value toggles for any system variable that is not read-only. (OSMODE, for example, is a good candidate to toggle between two object-snap values).

Listing B.14: FRAD.LSP—Toggle between Two Fillet Radii

```
; FRAD - for AutoCAD Release 9+
(defun C:FRAD( / olderr currad )
   (setq olderr *ERROR*)
   (defun *ERROR*(msg)                     ; define new error handler
      (princ " \n") (princ msg)
      (setq *ERROR* olderr)
      (princ)
   )
                                           ; display current radius
(princ "\nCurrent fillet radius: ")
(princ (setq currad (getvar "FILLETRAD")))

   (if (not g:strad)                       ; disallow null input
      (initget 1)                          ; the first time through
   )
                                           ; get new radius, offering
                                           ; the old as default
(setvar "FILLETRAD" (g:dist nil "\nNew radius: " g:strad))

   (setq g:strad currad)                   ; save the old radius
   (setq *ERROR* olderr)                   ; restore the error handler
   (princ)
)
```

Notice that, as written, FRAD.LSP requires the global functions G:str and G:dist, discussed in Chapter 7. Load these functions before running FRAD.LSP.

More Fun with Fillets

FR.LSP, shown in Listing B.15, offers another way to reset the fillet radius. FR.LSP creates an AutoCAD command called FR, which prompts you to select a circle or an arc on the screen. If you select some other object (or no object at all), AutoCAD prompts you to draw a circle. Then AutoCAD uses the radius of the circle (or arc) to reset the fillet radius. As written, FR.LSP leaves a newly drawn circle on the screen. If you want the routine to delete it automatically, remove the semicolons from the following lines:

```
;; (if newcir
;;   (entdel (entlast))
;; )
```

Alternatively, you can invoke the EL macro (described earlier in this chapter) after executing this command. However, don't use the Undo command to delete the circle, or you will undo the new fillet radius at the same time.

Listing B.15: FR.LSP—Set Fillet Radius from Circle or Arc

```
; FR - for AutoCAD Release 12
(defun C:FR( / oldech oldsnp olderr xpt esel xent etype newcir)

    (setq oldech (getvar "CMDECHO")   ; store current environment
          oldsnp (getvar "OSMODE")
          olderr *ERROR*
    )
    (defun *ERROR* (msg)              ; define new error handler
       (princ " \n") (princ msg)      ; print message
       (setvar "CMDECHO" oldech)
       (setvar "OSMODE"  oldsnp)
       (setq   *ERROR*   olderr)
       (princ)
    )
    (setvar "CMDECHO" 0)              ; reset environment
    (setvar "OSMODE" 512)

    (initget 1)                                 ; pick point
    (setq xpt (getpoint "\nSelect circle or arc: "))

    (cond ( (setq esel (nentselp xpt))    ; if an entity was
            (setq xent (car esel))        ; selected, store it
          )
```

```
            ( T                                    ; otherwise,
              (command ".CIRCLE" xpt pause)        ; draw a circle
              (setq xent (entlast)                 ; and store it
                    newcir T)
            )
          )
                                                  ; if non-circle or non-arc
                                                  ; was selected, then
          (cond ( (not (or (= "CIRCLE"
                              (setq etype (g:entv 0 xent)))
                           (= "ARC" etype)
                       )
                  )
                  (command ".CIRCLE" xpt pause)   ; draw a circle
                  (setq xent (entlast)            ; and store it
                        newcir T)
                )
          )

          (setvar "FILLETRAD" (g:entv 40 xent))    ; set new radius

          ;; (if newcir                           ; option: remove the ";;" symbols
          ;;    (entdel (entlast))                ; to the left, to delete the new
          ;; )                                    ; circle automatically each time

          (princ "\nNew Fillet radius: ")         ; display result
          (princ (getvar "FILLETRAD"))

          (setvar "CMDECHO" oldech)               ; restore environment
          (setvar "OSMODE" oldsnp)
          (setq *ERROR* olderr)
          (princ)
)
```

Notice that FR.LSP also requires the global function G:entv, which was discussed earlier in this appendix. Be certain that G:entv is loaded before you run this routine.

Copy and Rotate

CR.LSP, shown in Listing B.16, creates an AutoCAD command called CR, which prompts you to select any number of objects, followed by a base point and a second point of displacement (which can be the same as the base point). Then AutoCAD copies the objects and prompts you to rotate the copy around the second point of displacement.

Listing B.16: CR.LSP—Copy and Rotate Objects

```
; CR - for AutoCAD Release 9+
(defun C:CR( / olderr oldech p_last x fset)
    (setq oldech (getvar "CMDECHO")
          olderr *ERROR*
          p_last (entlast)
    )
    (setvar "CMDECHO" 0)

    (defun *ERROR*(msg)
      (princ "\nError: ") (princ msg)
      (command) (command ".UNDO" "E" ".U")
      (ssdrw x)
      (setvar "CMDECHO" oldech)
      (setq *ERROR* olderr)
      (princ)
    )

    (command ".UNDO" "G")

    (princ "\nCOPY ")
    (setq x (ssget))
    (prompt "\nProcessing selection set...\n")
    (dup x)
    (setq fset (newss (entnext p_last) (entlast)))

    (command ".MOVE" x)
    (setvar "CMDECHO" 1)
    (command "" pause pause)
    (setvar "CMDECHO" 0)

    (ssdrw fset)
    (prompt "\nROTATE Angle: ")
    (command ".ROTATE" x "" "@" pause)

    (ssdrw fset)
    (command ".UNDO" "E")
    (setvar "CMDECHO" oldech)
    (setq *ERROR* olderr)
    (princ)
)
```

SHORT AUTOLISP ROUTINES AND USEFUL FUNCTIONS FOR STUDY
APP. B

```
;------------------------------------------------------------------
; SSDRAW - Redraws entities in a selection set.
(defun ssdrw( ss / ent index)
   (cond ( (= (type ss) 'PICKSET)
           (setq index -1)
           (while (setq ent (ssname ss (setq index (1+ index))))
                (redraw ent)
           )
         )
   )
)
;------------------------------------------------------------------
; NEWSS - Creates selection set from starting and ending entities
; in the database

(defun newss(start end / ss)
   (setq ss (ssadd start))
   (while (and (setq start (entnext start)) (not (eq start end)))
          (setq ss (ssadd start ss))
   )
   (if start
      (setq ss (ssadd start ss))
      (eval ss)
   )
)
;------------------------------------------------------------------
; DUP - Copies a selection set in place

(defun dup(ss)
   (command ".COPY" ss "" '(0 0 0) '(0 0 0))
)
```

Rotate 3D Objects on Any Axis

PIVOT.LSP, shown in Listing B.17, creates an AutoCAD command called PIVOT, which prompts you to select objects, followed by a base point and an axis in 3D space. Then AutoCAD prompts you for the degree by which to rotate the selected objects around the axis. PIVOT.LSP requires that the G:dtr function be previously loaded.

Listing B.17: PIVOT.LSP—Rotate Objects along 3D Axis

```
; PIVOT - for AutoCAD Release 10+
(defun C:PIVOT( / oldech oldicon oldgrid ss1 bp ap r_ang)

  (setq oldech (getvar "CMDECHO")
        oldicon (getvar "UCSICON")
        oldgrid (getvar "GRIDMODE")
        olderr *error*
  )
  (setvar "CMDECHO" 0)
  (command ".UCS" "s" "$$temp" ".UCS" "w")
  (setvar "GRIDMODE" 0)
  (setvar "UCSICON" 1)
  (defun *error* (msg)
        (princ "\nError: ")
        (princ msg)
        (command ".UCS" "r" "$$temp" ".UCS" "d" "$$temp")
        (setvar "UCSICON" oldicon)
        (setvar "CMDECHO" oldech)
        (setvar "GRIDMODE" oldgrid)
        (setq *error* olderr)
        (princ)
  )

  (setq ss1 (ssget))
  (initget 16)
  (setq bp (getpoint "\nSelect Rotation Base Point: "))
  (initget 16)
  (setq ap (getpoint bp "\nSelect Rotation Axis: ")
        r_ang (g:rtd (getangle bp "\nSelect Rotation Angle: "))
  )

  (command ".UCS" "3point" bp
           (polar bp (- (angle bp ap) (g:dtr 90)) 1) ap
           ".UCS" "x" "90" ".ROTATE" ss1 "" '(0 0 0) r_ang
           ".UCS" "r" "$$temp" ".UCS" "d" "$$temp"
  )

  (setvar "UCSICON" oldicon)
  (setvar "CMDECHO" oldech)
  (setvar "GRIDMODE" oldgrid)
  (setq *error* olderr)
  (princ)
)
```

UND.LSP

If an object on the screen is covered by another object, the UND.LSP function, shown in Listing B.18, allows you to select objects on the screen that are obscured by other objects with a single point pick. It works in a manner similar to object snap. At any "Select objects:" prompt, enter

(und)

and pick an object on the screen. If there is another object hidden behind it, the hidden object will be selected. If multiple objects are hidden, all the hidden objects are selected. Otherwise, the function displays a message telling you that no hidden object was found.

Listing B.18: UND.LSP—Pick Underneath Objects

```
; UND function - for AutoCAD Release 9+
(defun und(/ x ss1)
   (cond ( (not (setq x (cadr (entsel "UNDERNEATH Pick object: "
           ))))
           (princ "\nNo object found.") (princ)
        )
        ( T
          (setq ss1 (ssdel (ssname (ssget x) 0)
                           (ssget "C" (polar x 3.92699 0.15)
                                      (polar x 0.785398 0.15)
                           )
                    )
          )
          (cond ( (= (sslength ss1) 0)
                  (princ "\nNothing underneath.") (princ)
                )
                ( T (eval ss1) )
          )
        )
   )
)
```

XYREC.LSP

XYREC.LSP, shown in Listing B.19, creates an AutoCAD command called XYREC, which draws a rectangle from two points. It using AutoCAD's rubber-band line display to change the rectangle before you enter the second point; and as you move the crosshairs, it displays the dimensions of the rectangle in the screen's coordinate display area. It is intended for 2D or plan view drawing only.

Listing B.19: XYREC.LSP—Display Rectangle Dimensions

```
; XYREC - for AutoCAD Release 11+
(defun C:XYREC( / oldech oldgrd oldcds olderr sp ep)
   (setq oldech (getvar "CMDECHO")
         oldgrd (getvar "GRIDMODE")
         oldcds (getvar "COORDS")
         olderr *ERROR*
   )
   (defun *error* (msg)
         (princ msg)
         (if sp
            (command ".UCS" "OR" (oldorg)))
         (setvar "CMDECHO" oldech)
         (setvar "GRIDMODE" oldgrd)
         (setvar "COORDS" oldcds)
         (setq *error* olderr)
         (princ)
   )
   (setvar "CMDECHO" 0)
   (setvar "GRIDMODE" 0)
   (setvar "COORDS" 1)
   (initget 1)
   (setq sp (getpoint "\nFirst corner: "))
   (command ".UCS" "OR" sp)
   (initget 1)
   (setq ep (getcorner '(0 0) "\nOpposite corner: "))
   (command ".PLINE" '(0 0) (list (car ep) 0)
                     ep (list 0 (cadr ep)) "c"
            "UCS" "OR" (oldorg)
   )
   (setvar "CMDECHO" oldech)
   (setvar "GRIDMODE" oldgrd)
   (setvar "COORDS" oldcds)
   (setq *error* olderr)
```

```
    (princ)
)
;-----------------------------------------------------------------
; OLDORG - Resets the original origin point for C:XYREC

(defun oldorg()
   (list (- 0 (car sp))
         (- 0 (cadr sp))
         (- 0 (caddr sp))
   )
)
```

Calculate Arc Bulge for Shapes

If you are using AutoCAD to draw symbols that will eventually be incorporated into shapes, BULGE.LSP, shown in Listing B.20, will calculate the bulge factor for selected arcs in the drawing, and display the result in the command prompt area. BULGE.LSP requires that the G:dtr and G:rtd functions be previously loaded.

Listing B.20: BULGE.LSP—Calculate Arc Bulge

```
; BULGE - for AutoCAD Release 11+
(defun C:BULGE( / uarc rtod )
  (while (or ( not (setq uarc
                         (car (nentsel "\nSelect arc: ")))
             )
             (/= "ARC" (g:entv 0 uarc))
         )
  )
  (if (< (g:entv 50 uarc) (g:entv 51 uarc) )
      (setq ang1 (- (g:entv 51 uarc) (g:entv 50 uarc) ) )
      (setq ang1 (+ (g:entv 51 uarc)
                    (- (g:dtr 360) (g:entv 50 uarc) )
                 )
      )
  )
  (setq rtod (g:rtd ang1)               ; Convert to degrees
        bulge (* 127 (/ rtod 180))      ; Convert to bulge
  )
  (princ  (strcat "\nArc degrees are: "  ; Display result
                  (rtos rtod 2 0) "    ")
  )
```

```
    (if(< rtod 180)
       (princ (strcat "Bulge for this arc is: "
                 (rtos bulge 2 0) "\n")
       )
       (princ "Arc too large for bulge. Break it first.\n")  )
    (princ)
)
```

Routines for Blocks

Following are two short routines that manipulate blocks.

LISTBLK.LSP

LISTBLK.LSP, shown in Listing B.21, creates an AutoCAD command called LISTBLK, which extracts the names of blocks in the drawing and displays them in the screen menu area. You may then pick the name of a block to insert just like any other screen menu item.

Listing B.21: LISTBLK.LSP—List and Pick Blocks on Screen

```
; LISTBLK - for AutoCAD Release 9+
(defun C:LISTBLK( / blst olderr)

    (setq olderr *ERROR*)
    (defun *ERROR*(msg)
        (princ "\nError: ") (princ msg)
        (grtext)
        (setq *ERROR* olderr)
        (princ)
    )

    (if (setq blst (cdr (assoc 2 (tblnext "BLOCK" 1) ) ) )
        (blk)
        (princ "\n** NO BLOCKS FOUND **")
    )
    (grtext)
    (princ)
)
;----------------------------------------------------------------
(defun blk( / nb alst x_blk num )
```

SHORT AUTOLISP ROUTINES AND USEFUL FUNCTIONS FOR STUDY
APP. B

```
        (prompt "\nExtracting block names. One moment...")
        (setq blst (list (cdr (assoc 2 (tblnext "BLOCK")))
                        blst
                  )
        )

        (while (setq nb (tblnext "BLOCK"))
               (setq blst (cons (cdr (assoc 2 nb))
                                blst
                          )
               )
        )

        (setq alst blst)
        (princ "\nDisplaying block names...")

        (while (and blst (not x_blk) )
               (setq num 0)
               (while (and blst (/= num 19) )
                      (if (/= num 19)
                          (grtext (1+ num) "          ")
                      )
                      (grtext num (car blst))
                      (setq num (1+ num))
                      (setq blst (cdr blst))
               )
               (if blst
                   (grtext num "--MORE--")
               )
               (cond ( blst
                       (princ "\nPick block name ( or <--MORE--> ):")

                       (while (= (type (setq x_blk (nth 1 (grread))))
                                 'LIST)
                       )
                       (if (/= x_blk num)
                           (setq x_blk (nth x_blk alst))
                           (setq x_blk nil)
                       )
                       (setq alst blst)
                     )
                     ( T
                       (princ "\nPick block name: ")
                       (while (= (type (setq x_blk (nth 1 (grread))))
                                 'LIST)
```

Routines for Blocks

```
                            )
                        (setq x_blk (nth x_blk alst))
                        (setq alst blst)
                    )
                )
                (if x_blk
                    (command ".INSERT" x_blk )
                )
            )
        )
    )
```

GBLOCK.LSP

GBLOCK.LSP, shown in Listing B.22, creates an AutoCAD command called GBLOCK, which prompts for two block names (you may select either block by picking it on the screen), then moves through the drawing, replacing all occurrences of the first block with the second. This is useful in cases where you may want to make wholesale changes to the drawing without redefining an existing block.

Listing B.22: GBLOCK.LSP—Global Block Substitution

```
; GBLOCK - for AutoCAD Release 9+
(defun C:GBLOCK( / oldech olderr oldblk oldnam oldset
                newblk newnam test x)

    (setq oldech (getvar "CMDECHO")
          olderr *error*)

    (defun *error* (msg)
        (princ "\nError: ") (princ msg)
        (setvar "CMDECHO" oldech)
        (setq *error* olderr)
        (princ)
    )
    (while (or (not oldnam) (= oldnam ""))
     (initget "Name")
     (setq oldblk (getpoint "\nSelect block (or <N>ame): "))
     (if (= oldblk "Name")
         (setq oldblk nil
               oldnam (cons 2
                       (strcase (getstring "\nBlock Name: ")))
         )
```

SHORT AUTOLISP ROUTINES AND USEFUL FUNCTIONS FOR STUDY
APP. B

```
      )
      (if oldblk
          (cond ( (ssget oldblk)
                  (setq oldblk (ssname (ssget oldblk) 0))
                  (cond ( (= "INSERT"
                             (cdr (assoc 0 (entget oldblk))))
                          (setq oldnam (assoc 2 (entget oldblk)))
                        )
                        ( T
                          (prompt "\nEntity not a block.")
                          (setq oldnam nil)
                          )
                  )
                )
                ( T
                  (prompt "\nNo entity found.")
                  (setq oldnam nil)
                  )
          )
          (if (or (not (cdr oldnam)) (= (cdr oldnam) ""))
              (setq oldnam nil)
          )
      )
  )
  (setq oldset (ssget "X" (list oldnam)))
  (cond ( (not oldset)
          (princ (strcat "\nNo " (cdr oldnam) " blocks found."))
        )
        ( T
          (setq test (sslength oldset))
          (while (not newnam)
              (initget 1 "Name")
              (setq newblk (getpoint
                              "\nSelect new block (or <N>ame): "))
              (cond ( (= newblk "Name")
                      (setq newblk nil
                            newnam (cons 2 (strcase
                                 (getstring "\nNew Block Name: ")
                                            )
                                    )
                      )
              )
              (cond ( (not (tblsearch "BLOCK"
                                       (cdr newnam)))
                      (if(and (cdr newnam)
```

Routines for Blocks

```
                              (/= (cdr newnam) "")
                            )
                            (princ (strcat "\n"(cdr newnam)
                                          " not found."
                                   )
                            )
                          )
                          (setq newnam nil)
                        )
                      )
                    )
                  )
                  (if (and newblk (or (not newnam) (= newnam "")) )
                      (cond ( (ssget newblk)
                              (setq newblk (ssname (ssget newblk) 0))
                              (cond ( (= "INSERT" (cdr (assoc 0
                                                        (entget newblk))))
                                      (setq newnam (assoc 2
                                                     (entget newblk)))
                                    )
                                    ( T
                                      (prompt "\nEntity not block.")
                                      (setq newnam nil)
                                    )
                              )
                            )
                            ( T (prompt "\nNo new entity found.")
                            )
                      )
                  )
                  (while (> test 0)
                      (setq test (1- test)
                            x (subst newnam oldnam
                                     (entget (ssname oldset test))
                              )
                      )
                      (entmod x)
                  )
              )
            )
          )
          (setvar "CMDECHO" oldech)
          (setq *error* olderr)
          (princ)
    )
```

INDEX

Note: This index shows primary explanations of important topics in **boldface** type. Incidental discussions and less important topics appear in regular type. References to illustations appear in *italic* type.

A

$A key character, 87
Abs function, **325**
ACAD variable, **9–10**
ACAD.CFG file, 11
ACAD.LIN file, 5–6, 20, 22, 24
ACAD.LSP file, **221**
ACAD.MNL file, 82, 94
ACAD.MNU file, 7
    copying, **8**
    examining, **91–96**
    icon menus in, **118–120**
ACAD.MNX file, 7
ACAD.PAT file, **8, 26–27**
ACAD.PGP file, **8, 14–16**
ACAD.UNT file, 339
ACADCFG variable, 11
ACADLX.OVL file, 167
Accum function (WALLS), 246, **260–261**
Action_tile function, **325**
activating dialog boxes, 411
active menus, 83, 120
Add a Plotter Configuration command, 77
Add_list function, **326**
addition, 156, **320**
Addset function (WALLS), 244, **261**
Adobe fonts, 69
ADS. *See* AutoCAD Development System (ADS)
Ads function, **326**
Ads_action_tile function, **325**
Ads_add_list function, **326**
Ads_alert function, **327**
Ads_angle function, **328**
Ads_angtof function, **329**
Ads_angtos function, **329**
Ads_buildlist function, 310–311
Ads_client_data_tile function, **335**
Ads_command function, **337**
Ads_cvunit function, **339**
Ads_defun function, 280–281, 303, **341**
Ads_dimensions_tile function, **341–342**
Ads_distance function, **342**
Ads_distof function, **343**
Ads_done_dialog function, **344**
Ads_done_positioned_dialog function, **344**
Ads_end_image function, **345**
Ads_end_list function, **345**
Ads_entdel function, **345–346**
Ads_entget function, 313, **346**
Ads_entlast function, **347**
Ads_entmake function, 310–311, **347**
Ads_entmod function, **348**
Ads_entnext function, **349**
Ads_entsel function, **349**
Ads_entupd function, **350**
Ads_exit function, **352**
Ads_fill_image function, **354**
Ads_findfile function, **355**
Ads_get_attr function, **369**
Ads_get_attr_string function, **369**
Ads_get_tile function, **369–370**
Ads_getangle function, **358**
Ads_getcorner function, **359**
Ads_getdist function, **360**
Ads_getfiled function, **362**
Ads_getint function, **362**
Ads_getkword function, 278, **363**
Ads_getorient function, **364–365**
Ads_getpoint function, **365–366**
Ads_getreal function, **366**
Ads_getstring function, **367–368**
Ads_getvar function, **368**
Ads_graphscr function, **370**
Ads_grclear function, **370**
Ads_grdraw function, **371**
Ads_grread function, **373**

INDEX

Ads_grtext function, **375**
Ads_grvecs function, **375**
ADS.H header file, 274, 320
Ads_handent function, **376**
Ads_init function, 278, 280
Ads_initget function, 278, **378**
Ads_inters function, **379**
Ads_link function, 280–281
Ads_load_dialog function, **382**
Ads_menucmd function, **385**
Ads_mode_tile function, **387**
Ads_nentsel function, **388**
Ads_nentselp function, **388–389**
Ads_new_dialog function, **389–390**
Ads_new_positioned_dialog function, **390**
Ads_osnap function, **393**
Ads_point function, 328, 342
Ads_polar function, **394**
Ads_printf function, **395**
Ads_real function, 328, 342
Ads_redraw function, **399**
Ads_regapp function, **400**
Ads_relrb function, 307, 311
Ads_rtos function, **402**
Ads_set_tile function, **405**
Ads_setvar function, **404**
Ads_slide_image function, **406**
Ads_ssadd function, 314, **407**
Ads_ssdel function, **407**
Ads_ssfree function, 307, 315
Ads_ssget function, 314, **409**
Ads_sslength function, 315, **409**
Ads_ssmemb function, **410**
Ads_ssname function, **410**
Ads_start_dialog function, **411**
Ads_start_image function, **412**
Ads_start_list function, **412–413**
Ads_tablet function, **415**
Ads_tblnext function, 317, **416**
Ads_tblsearch function, 317, **417**
Ads_term_dialog function, **417**
Ads_textbox function, **418**
Ads_textpage function, **418**
Ads_textscr function, **419**
Ads_trans function, **421**
Ads_unload_dialog function, **423**
Ads_vector_image function, **424**
Ads_vports function, **425**
Ads_wcmatch function, **428**
Ads_xdroom function, **429–430**
Ads_xdsize function, **430**
Ads_xload function, **431**
Ads_xunload function, **431**
ADSCODES.h header file, 274, 280
ADSDLG.H header file, 320
ADSLIB.H header file, 274, 320
Alert function, **326–327**
aligning dialog box buttons, 206
Alloc function, **327**
AND comparisons, 382–383
And function, **327**
Angle function, **328**
angle-steel hatch pattern, **27–32**, 32
angles
    arctangents of, 331
    in AutoLISP, **161**
    for blocks, 142
    for bulge arcs, **67**, *68*, **69**
    calculating, 328
    converting, 328–329
    cosines of, 338–339
    hatch patterns, 27–28, 30
    input of, **357–358**, **363–365**
    for octant arcs, 50, *51–52*
    for offset arcs, 62–63
    for rotating crosshairs, 129–130
    in shape files, 41, *41*, 45–46
    sines of, 405
Angtof function, **328–329**
Angtos function, **329**
antilogs, 352
Aperture command, 138
aperture opening, size of, 138
apostrophes ('), 397, 448
Append function, 235–236, **330**
append mode, opening files in, 392
applications
    listing, 326
    loading and unloading, 430–431
    registering, 400
Apply function, **330**
arcs
    bulge, 43, **65–69**, *66*, **458–459**
    creating, 229
    fillet radii from, 451–452
    octant, **49–52**, *50–52*
    offset, **62–65**
    in shape descriptions, **62–69**

signal elements for, 43
arctangents, calculating, 331
arguments and parameters, 155, 177
    dialog boxes for. *See* dialog boxes
    input of, 179–180, **194–196**, **263**
    lists of, applying
        to expressions, 379–380
        to functions, 330
    functions to, 384
    testing, for lists, 332, 381
ASCII characters. *See* characters; strings
ASCII codes
    converting characters into, 330
    for text characters, 70–71
ASCII files, **4**
    for dialog boxes, 201
    exporting text to, **444–446**
    for menus, 83
ASCII function, **330**
Assoc function, 234–235, **331**
association lists, **224–226**
    for entity creation, 227–23
    locating sublists in, **233–237**, 331
    viewing, **446–447**
    WALLS.LSP for. *See* WALLS.LSP
        routine
asterisks (*)
    in hatch pattern definitions, 27
    in line-type definitions, 24
    in menu sections, 86, 106
    for multiplication, 156, **321**
    in shape descriptions, 44
    for text editor prompts, 16
    as wildcard characters, 426
at signs (@) as wildcard characters, 426
Atan function, **331**
Atof function, **331**
Atoi function, **332**
Atom function, **332**
Atoms-family function, **332**
attributes
    blocks with, inserting, **144–146**, 231
    definitions of, creating, 231
    of tiles, retrieving, 368–369
AutoCAD Development System (ADS), **268**
    block table searching with, **316–317**
    compiling in, 269, **272–274**
    cutout routine in, **285–306**
    drawing environment for, **309**
    entities in
        creating, **310–312**
        information about, **312–314**
    features of, **269–270**
    function tables in, **303–304**
    functions in
        creating, **275–279**
        executing, **280–281**
        testing, **285**
    guidelines for, **270–271**
    input validation in, **307**
    points in, **307–308**
    programs from
        listing, 326
        loading and unloading, **430–431**
    requirements for, **271**
    selection sets with, **307**, **314–316**
    source-code files for, 5
    steps in, **275**
    template file for, **281–284**
    UNDO feature in, **309–310**
AUTOEXEC.BAT file, 9–10, 166
AutoLISP, **152**
    data types in, **161–164**
    efficient code for, **168–169**
    functions in, **154–156**
    loading files for, **165**, 381
    memory management in, **165–169**
    nesting in, **159–160**
    planning in, **153–154**
    radians in, **161**
    readability with, **169–171**
    routines for. *See* routines
    source-code files for, 6
    syntax of, **154–161**
    troubles with, **171–172**
    variables in, **157–160**
    versions of, testing for, 424
AutoLISP interpreter, 155
***AUX menu section label, 84, 87

B

$B key character, 87
backquotes (') as wildcard characters, 426
backslashes (\)
    with Command function, 337
    for menus, **89–90**
    with wildcard characters, 427

INDEX

batch files, **12, 17–18**
binary format files for converting text, 76
binding symbols and variables, 157–158, 333, **402–404**
bit-shifts with integers, 383
bitwise complements, 324
blank lines for tiles, **216**
Block command, 96
block tables, searching, **316–317**
blocks
    with attributes, **144–146**, 231
    in DCL files, 204
    definitions for, 231
    editing around, **146–147**
    inserting, **141–142**, *142–143*, **144–146**, *145*, 231
    listing, **459–461**
    replacing, **461–463**
    selecting entities nested in, 387–389
    vs. shape files, **38**
Boole function, **332–333**
Borland C compiler, 272
bound symbols and variables, 157–158, 333, **402–404**
Boundp function, **333**
BOUNDRY line type, **21–24**, *21*
BOUNDRY2 line type, 25, *25*
brackets ([])
    for dialog box files, 204–205
    for menus, **88–89**
    with wildcard characters, 427
Break command in macros, 139
brick paving pattern effect, 32–34, *33*
bulge arcs, **65–69**, *66*
    for shapes, **458–459**
    signal elements for, 43
BULGE.LSP command, **458–459**
buttons in DCL files, **205–206**
***BUTTONS menu section, 84, 87, 91–92

C

.C files, 5
C programming language, 269
    books for, **272**
    requirements for, **271**
Caddr function, **334**
Cadr function, **334**
Calcp function (GEAR), 188, **196**

calibrating tablets, 415
Cancel buttons, **207**
CANCEL control sequences, 92–93
canceling dialog boxes, 417
CAP shape, **64–65**, *64*
Car function, 233, **333–334**
carets (^) with menus, **90**
case of strings, converting, 413
case-sensitivity
    in AutoLISP functions, 156
    in input control, 378
    with menu section labels, 93
    with string matching, 427
C:ddgear function (DDGEAR), 214–216, **218–220**
Cdr function, **334–335**
C:gear function (GEAR), 189–190, **197–198**
characters. *See also* strings; text-font files
    in AutoLISP functions, 156
    converting, 330, 335
    reading, 398
    wildcard, **426–428**
    writing, **428–429**
Chr function, **335**
circles
    creating, 229
    fillet radii from, 451–452
cleaning
    corners, **135**, *136–137*, **138**
    open-cross intersections, **140–141**, *140*
    open-T intersections, **139–140**
    viewports, 370
clearing
    screen **129**, 418
    viewports 370
Client_data_tile function, **335**
Close function, **336**
Closeup function (WALLS), 252–253, **264**
closing files, 336
colors
    isolating, from sublists, **235–236**
    macros for, **147–148**
    in tiles, 354, 423–424
columns in DCL files, 205
combining
    commands
        display with editing, **134–141**
        drawing with editing, **133–134**
    elements of shape descriptions, **52–56**

Command function, **336–337**
commands. *See also* custom menus; macros
    for editing, combining
        with display, **134–141**
        with drawing, **133–134**
            executing, 336–337
            on tablets, **104–106**
commas (,)
    in shape descriptions, 44
    with wildcard characters, 427
***Comment menu section label, 84
comments
    in AutoLISP, **170**
    in batch files, 18
    menu sections for, 84
comparing
    bits, 332–333
    integers, 382–383
    symbols, 350–351
    symbols for, **322–323**
Compile command, 76
compiled programs, loading, 430–431
compiling
    ADS programs, 269, **272–274**
    font files, 76
    menus, **7**, 82–83
    shapes, 39, **46–47**
complements, bitwise, 324
complex shape descriptions, **47–59**
concatenating strings, 413
Cond function, **337–338**
conditional expressions and functions,
    195–196, 337–338, 376
configurations
    multiple, **10–12**
    for plotting, 76–77
    for tablets, **103**
Configure Plotter command, 77
connecting strings, 413
Cons function, 227, 338
console break, **172**
constants
    in AutoLISP, 159
    manifest constants, 280
Control-Break sequence, 172
Control-C sequence, 92–93, 172
control characters
    with menus, 90
    in printing, 395–396

converting
    angles into strings, 329
    case of strings, 413
    characters into ASCII code, 330
    integers
        into characters, 335
        into real numbers, 355–356
        into strings, 379
    numbers, to absolute value, 325
    polylines, 148
    into integers, 355
    into strings, 401–402
    strings
        into angles, 328–329
        into integers, 332
        into real numbers, 331, 343
    text into lines, **76–78**
    units of measurement, 339
coordinate display, displaying strings on, 374
coordinates and coordinate systems
    in hatch patterns, 28
    macros for changing, **148–149**
    in point arrays, 308
    in shape descriptions, 59
    translating points between, 420–421
Copy command and copying
    with hatch patterns, 33
    in macros, **132**, **134**
    with rotating, 452–454
    standard menus, **82**
COPY macro, 132
CORNER1 macro, **135**, *136*, **138**
CORNER2 macro, **135**, *137*, **138**
corners
    cleaning, **135**, *136–137*, **138**
    input of, 359
Cos function, **338–339**
Count() macro, 304
counting
    array elements, 304
    list members, 380
    selection set entities, 409
    string characters, 413–414
covered objects, selecting, **456**
CR.LSP command, **452–454**
crosshairs
    macros for, **129–130**
    reading from, 373
Ctrl-Break sequence, 172

INDEX

Ctrl-C sequence, 92–93, 172
Current User Coordinate System, translating points to, 420–421
curves, octant arcs for, **49–52**, *50–52*
custom menus, **80**
    creating, **80–83**
    icon menus, **114–121**
    loading, **82–83**
    macros on. *See* macros
    organizing commands on, **96–99**, *100*
    pull-down, **107–114**
    routines on, **220**
    sections for, **84–86**
    subsections for, **86–88, 106–107**
    symbols and punctuation for, **88–91**
    syntax for, **85–91**
    for tablets, **101–106**
customizing, **2–3**
    advantages of, **3**
    DOS environment, **8–9**
    hatch patterns. *See* hatch patterns and hatch-pattern definitions
    line types. *See* line types and line-type definitions
    shapes. *See* shape files and shape descriptions
    source-code files, **4–8**
Cut_adjset function (CUTOUT), 300, 305
Cut_drwln function (CUTOUT), 299–300, 305, 307, 312
Cut_etype function (CUTOUT), 298–299, 305, 307, 314, 316
Cut_expset function (CUTOUT), 297–298, 305, 307, 315–316
Cut_okblk function (CUTOUT), 300, 305
Cut_rcut function (CUTOUT), 295–297, 305, 307
Cut_reset function (CUTOUT), 301, 305, 309–310
Cut_rtrim function (CUTOUT), 300, 305
Cut_setpts function (CUTOUT), 294–295, 305
Cut_setup function (CUTOUT), 293–294, 306, 309–310
Cutout function (CUTOUT), 292–293, 306
CUTOUT.C command, **285–287**
    drawing environment for, **309**
    entity creation in, **310–312**
    external variables in, **306**
    function list for, **305–306**
    function tables in, **303–304**
    input validation in, **307**
    listing of, **289–303**
    macros and constants in, **304–305**
    points in, **307–308**
    pseudocode for, **288–289**
    selection sets with, **307, 314–316**
    UNDO feature in, **309–310**
Cvunit function, **339**
C:walls function (WALLS), 239–242, **262–263**

D

D_pwall function (WALLS), 248–249, **264**
D_wwall function (WALLS), 249–251, **264**
data types
    in AutoLISP, **161–164**
    extracting, 421–422
data validation, 201, **208–220**, 307, **377–378**
DCL (Dialog Control Language) files, **5**, 201
    for gears, **202–207**
    loading, 382
    removing, 422–423
DDGEAR.LSP routine, **208–220**
DEBUG.LSP command, **447–449**
debugging, 153
    functions for, **447–449**
    trace flags for, 419–420, 423
decimal points in real numbers, 162
decompiling shapes, **78**
default responses, **190–192**, 278
Defun function, **177–178, 340–341**
degrees
    in AutoLISP, **161**
    converting radians to, **191**
deleting entities, 345–346, 407, 434
descriptions
    for hatch patterns, 27
    for line types, 22
diagonal movement in shape files, 49
dialog boxes, **200–201**
    activating, 411
    canceling, 417
    data input control with, 201, **208–220**
    designing, **202–207**
    displaying, **219**, 326–327, 389–390
    ending processing of, 343–344
    for listing files, 361–362
    source-code files for, 5

tiles for. *See* tiles for dialog boxes
with warning messages, 326–327
diamond shape, 61–62
digitizing tablets. *See* tablets
Dimx_tile function, **341**
Dimy_tile function, **341–342**
direct entity access, **264–265**
direction of octant arcs, 52
directories
    multiple, **8–9**
    for text editors, **13–14**
display commands, combining, with editing, **134–141**
Display Coordinate System, translating points to, 420–421
displaying
    block names, **459–461**
    dialog boxes, **219**, 326–327, 389–390
    graphics screen, 370
    icon menus, **120–121**
    memory status, 384–385
    prompts, 396
    pull-down menus, **109–110**
    slides in tiles, 405–406
    strings, 374–375
    text screens, 418–419
    tiles, 386–387
    variable values, 158
    vectors, 375
distance between points, 342, 359–360
Distance function, **342**
Distof function, **343**
division, 155, **321–322**, 400
dollar signs ($) for subsection references, 86–87
Done_dialog function, 219, **343–344**
DOOR macros, 144–146
door1 macro, **141–142**, *142–143*
doors
    editing around, **146–147**
    inserting, **141–142**, *142–143*, **144–146**, *145*
DOS environment
    customizing, **8–9**
    memory for, 10
dotted pairs in sublists, 225
double quotation marks (") for strings, 163–164, 166, 172
DR menu subsection, revising, **97–99**, *100*

DR2 menu subsection, revising, **97–99**, *100*
DRAW function (GEAR), 188, **197**
drawing commands, combining, with editing, **133–134**
drawing editor for line types, **22–23**
drawing environment for ADS, **309**
Dtext command, 336
dual orientation in text-font files, **74–75**
Dup function (CR), 454
.DXB files, 77
Dxbin command, 78
dynamic dragging feature, 132

E

EDGE shape, **44–46**, *45–46*
edit boxes in DCL files, **206**
editing
    combining commands for
        with display commands, **134–141**
        with drawing commands, **133–134**
    around inserted blocks, **146–147**
    line types, **23–25**
    macros for, **131–140**
    shape files, **39**, **78**
EDITMENU macro, 130
efficient AutoLISP code, **168–169**
EL.LSP macro, **434**
end-of-screen sequences, 232
End_image function, **344–345**
End_list function, **345**
endless loops, 18
Entdel function, **345–346**
Entget function, 234, **346**
entities
    adding, 347, 406–407
    in ADS, **312–314**
    association lists for. *See* association lists
    creating, **227–232**, **310–312**
    deleting, 345–346, 407, 434
    direct access to, **264–265**
    extended, data space for, 429–430
    extracting, 347–348, 376, 410
    handles for, **226**, 376
    input of, 349, 387–389
    modifying, 348
    names of, **161**, 224, 376, 410
    nested, 387–389

INDEX

redrawing, 399
restoring, 345–346
retrieving, **233–237**
selecting, 345–346, 387–389, **407–409**
testing for, 409–410
updating, 349–350
Entlast function, **347**
ENTLIST.LSP function, **446–447**
Entmake function, **227–232**, 347
Entmod function, 235, **348**
Entnext function, **348–349**
Entsel function, 233, **349**
Entupd function, **349–350**
environment
    for ADS, **309**
    customizing, **8–9**
    memory for, 10
environment variables, retrieving, 360–361
Eq function, **350**
Equal function, 350–351
equal signs (=)
    for comparisons, **323**
    for equality tests, **322**
    for subsection references, 86–87
equality, testing for, **322**, 350–351
ERASE macro, 131
erasing entities, 345–346, 407, 434
Error function, **199–200**, 351
error-trapping
    for files, **439–444**
    in GEAR.LSP, **199–200**
ES shape files, 115, *115*
Eval function, 351
evaluating
    AutoLISP functions, 155
    expressions, 351
        conditional, 376
        in lists, 337–338
        loops for, 428
        series of, 396
        for symbols, 356
exclamation points (!) for variables, 158, 164
.EXE files, **5**
Exit function, **352**
exiting from routines, 352, 396–397
.EXP files, **5**
Exp function, **352**
Expand function, **352–353**
exporting text, **444–446**

expressions
    adding, to lists, 338
    applying lists of arguments to, 379–380
    evaluating, 351
        conditional, 376
        in lists, 337–338
        loops for, 428
        series of, 396
        for symbols, 356
    printing, **394–396**
    quoting, 397
    repeating, 400–401
    testing
        for nil, 390–393
        for numbers, 391
        for values, 327
Expt function, **353**
Extended AutoLISP, **167**
extended entities, data space for, 429–430
extended memory, **167**
extensions, file, 5
EXTLISP.EXE file, 167
extracting
    association lists, 346, 415–416
    block names, **459–461**
    data types, 421–422
    entities, 347–348, 376, 410
    list elements, 333–335, 380, 390–391
    string data, 397–398, 414
    system variables, 368
    table entries, 416
    tile values, 369–370
    viewport identification numbers, 425

F

faces
    creating, 230, **258–261**
    editing function for, 263
    in WALLS.LSP, **254**, *254*
F-CURVE macro, 148
file descriptor data type, 162
file handling in functions, 180
files
    ASCII. *See* ASCII files
    batch, **12**, **17–18**
    closing, 336
    DCL. *See* DCL (Dialog Control
        Language) files

error-trapping for, **439–444**
LISP, 152
listing, 361–362
loading, 4, 165, 381–382
locating, 354–355
opening, 391–392
reading from 398–399
shape. *See* shape files and shape descriptions
slide, **116–118**
source-code, **4–8**
temporary, 286
text-font. *See* text-font files
writing
    characters to, 428–429
    expressions to, 394–396
    strings to, 429
Fill_image function, **353–354**
Fillet command in macros, **135**, *136–137*, **138**
fillets, radii for, **450–452**
filter lists for selection sets, 408
Findch function (G:fname), 443
Findfile function, **354–355**
fit-curves, converting polylines to, 148
Fix function, 355
Float function, **355–356**
floating-point numbers. *See* real numbers
fonts. *See* text-font files
Foreach function, 356
foreign-language menu versions, 90
forward slashes (/)
    for division, 155, **321–322**
    for local variables, 178–179
    in non-equality tests, **322**
    in search paths, 165, 355
Fprompt function (CUTOUT), 294, 306
Fprompt.c function
    creating, **275–279**
    template file for, **281–284**
FR.LSP command, **451–452**
fractions in line types, 21
FRAD.LSP command, **450**
freezing layers, macro for, 436
function tables in ADS, **303–304**
functions, **154–156**. *See also* routines
    applying lists of arguments to, 330, 384
    creating, **177–179**, **275–279**
    defining, **340–341**
    executing, **280–281**

memory for, **168–169**
nesting, **159–160**
paging, 424–425
parameters for. *See* arguments and parameters
sharing, **221**
symbols as, **320–324**
testing, 275, **285**
for tiles, 325
trace flag for, 419–420, 423
unbalanced, **172**
variables for, **177–179**, 340
furniture, inserting, **142**, *143*

G

GBLOCK.LSP command, **461–463**
GC function, **356–357**
Gcd function, **357**
G:dist function (GEAR), 186, **193**
G:dtr function (GEAR), 185, **191**
GEAR.DCL file, **202–207**
GEAR.LSP routine, *184*
    enhancements to, **198–199**
    error trapping in, **199–200**
    global functions in, **190–198**
    input validation for, **208–220**
    listing of, **185–190**
    problem stating for, **181–182**
    pseudocode for, **182–183**
Get_attr function, **368–369**
Get_depth function (DDGEAR), 213
Get_hole function (DDGEAR), 212
Get_notch function (DDGEAR), 212–213, **217**
Get_pc function (DDGEAR), **211–212**
Get_teeth function (DDGEAR), 212
Get_tile function, **369–370**
Get_width function (DDGEAR), 213
Get_x function (DDGEAR), 211
Get_y function (DDGEAR), 211
Getangle function, **357–358**
Getcorner function, **359**
Getdist function, **359–360**
Getenv function, **360–361**
Getfiled function, **361–362**
Getint function, 362
Getkword function, 363
Getll function (WALLS), 246–247, **263**
Getoffset function (WALLS), 251–252, **264**

INDEX

Getorient function, **363–365**
Getp function (GEAR), 185–187, **194–196**
Getpoint function, **365–366**
Getreal function, **366**
Getstring function, **367–368**
Getvar function, 160, **368**
Getwindow function (WALLS), 247–248, **264**
G:fname function, **439–444**
G:getstr function (G:fname), 441–443
G:int function (GEAR), 186, **192–193**
global functions in GEAR.LSP, **190–198**
global memory variables, **167–168, 178–179**, 340
Go function (DDGEAR), 210, **217**, 219
GO HOME macro, 148
G:PT function (GEAR), 185–186, **194**
graphics screen, displaying, 370
Graphscr function, **370**
GRAVITY.C program, 303
Grclear function, **370**
Grdraw function, **370–371**
greater-than signs (>)
    for comparisons, **323**
    in pull-down menu symbols, 113
greatest common denominator of integers, 357
group codes in sublists, 225
groups. *See* selection sets
Grread function, **371–373**
Grtext function, **374–375**
Grvecs function, **375**
G:str function (GEAR), 185, **191–192**

H

Handent function, **376**
handles for entities, **226**, 376
hatch patterns and hatch-pattern
    definitions, **25**
        creating, **31–35**
        macro for, **126–128**
        source-code files for, 8
        structure of, **26–31**
header files for ADS compilation, 274, 280, 320
header lines
    for hatch patterns, 27
    for line types, 24
    for shape files, 40, **44**, 48
    for text-font files, 70
headers for polylines, 232, 310–311

height of tiles, 341–342
Help buttons, **207**
hexadecimal numbers, **40–41**
High C compiler, 5, 272–274
highlighted characters, displaying, 374
hyphens (-)
    for character ranges, 427
    with pull-down menus, 113–114
    for subtraction, 156, **321**

I

$I key character, 87
ICON- macros, 149
***ICON menu section, 84, 87, 93
icon menus
    creating, **114–120**
    displaying, **120–121**
    slides for, **116–118**
icons, macros for, 149
If function, **376**
image tiles. *See* tiles for dialog boxes
indentation
    in AutoLISP, **170–171**
    in tracing, 419
Initget function, **377–378**
initializing variables, **216**
input
    of angles, **357–358, 363–365**
    with Command function, 336–337
    of corners for rectangles, 359
    creating function for, **275–279**
    with debugging, **448–449**
    dialog boxes for. *See* dialog boxes
    of entities, 349, 387–389
    of files, 361–362
    of integers, **192–193**, 362
    with menus, 89–90
    of parameters, 179–180, **194–196, 263**
    of points, **193–194**, 365–366
    of real numbers, 366
    of selection set entities, **407–409**
    of strings, 363, 367–368
    validity of, 201, **208–220, 307, 377–378**
input devices, reading from, **371–373**
Insert command in macros, 141
inserted blocks, editing around, **146–147**
inserting blocks, **141–142**, 142–143, **144–146**, 145, 231

insertion points, **56–59**
inserts, creating, 231–232
INSUL shape, **53–58**, *53–54, 57*
INSUL2 shape, **58–59**, *58*
integers, **162–163**
    bit-shifts of, 383
    checking strings for, **216**
    comparing
        bits in, 332–333
        series of, 382–383
    converting
        into characters, 335
        into real numbers, 355–356
        real numbers into, 355
        into strings, 379
        strings into, 332
    greatest common denominator of, 357
    input of, **192–193**, 362
interpreter, AutoLISP, 155
Inters function, 259, **379**
intersection points, calculating, 379
invisible edges on 3D faces, **258–261**
Itoa function, **379**

J

joining strings, 413

K

key characters
    for dialog box objects, 205–206
    for subsection references, **86–87**
key names for dialog box files, 204
keyboard, reading from, 372, 398–399
keystroke saving, macros for, **126–128**
keywords for menus, 92

L

labels
    in DCL files, 204–205
    for menu sections, **85–86**
Lambda function, **379–380**
largest value in series, extracting, 384
last elements, extracting, 380
    from databases, 347
    from lists, 380
Last function, **380**

LayerOff macro, 125
LayerOn macro, 125
layers, macros for, **124–126**
    freezing, 436
    setting, **434–436**
    thawing, 436–437
Layerset macro, **124–126**
length
    of lines, 41, 45
    of lists, 380
    of strings, 164, 413–414
Length function, **380**
Leroy Techic fonts, 76
less-than signs (<)
    for comparisons, **322–323**
    in pull-down menu symbols, 113
    for slide libraries, 117
letters. *See* text-font files
levels of function nesting, 159
libraries
    of line types, 6
    of slide files, **116–118**
LIGHT shape, **60–61**, *61*, **66–67**, *66*
.LIN files, **5–6**, 20
Line command for hatch patterns, 33
line feeds
    printing, 395–396, 417
    in text-font files, 72
line types and line-type definitions, **20–21**
    drawing editor for, **22–23**
    in hatch patterns, 27
    source-code files for, 5–6
    word processors for, **23–25**
lines
    converting text to, **76–78**
    creating, 229
    for hatch patterns, 28, 30, 33
    length of, 41, 45
    parallel, 28, *28*, 30, **133–134**
    reference, **257–258**, **263**
    in shape descriptions, **59–62**
    signal elements for, 43
    temporary, 370–371
    in tiles, 216, 423–424
Linetype command, 6, 22
linked lists, **312–313**
linking ADS functions, 272–274, **280**
LISP. *See* AutoLISP; routines
LISP files, 152

INDEX

LISPHEAP variable, 166
LISPSTACK variable, 166
list boxes
    adding items to, 326
    ending processing of, 345
    starting processing of, 412
List function, 228, **381**
LISTBLK.LSP command, **459–461**
listing
    blocks, **459–461**
    files, 361–362
    loaded ADS applications, 326
Listp function, **381**
lists, 163. *See also* association lists
    adding expressions to, 338
    of arguments, applying
        to expressions, 379–380
        to functions, 330
        functions to, 384
    building, 330
    counting members of, 380
    creating, 381
    evaluating, 337–338, 356
    extracting elements from, 333–335, 380, 390–391
    locating members of, 385, 414
    popup, 326, 345, 412
    replacing members in, 414
    reversing, 401
    testing arguments for, 332, 381
Load function, 165, 220, **381**
Load_dialog function, 218, **382**
Loadfunc function (CUTOUT), 292, **304**, 306
Loadfuncs function (FPROMPT), 283
loading
    ADS programs, 430–431
    AutoLISP routines, **165**, 381
    custom menus, **82–83**
    files, 4, 165, 381–382
local memory variables, **167–168**, **177–179**, **216**, 340
locating
    files, 354–355
    list members, 385
    sublists, 331
lockups, system, 18
Log function, **382**
Logand function, **382–383**
logarithms, 382

Logior function, **383**
loops
    endless, 18
    with Foreach, 356
    with While, 428
lowercase, converting strings to, 413
LP.LSP macro, **434–436**
Lsh function, **383**
.LSP files, **6**
LT.LSP macro, **436–437**
Ltscale command, 23
LX.LSP macro, **436**

M

macros
    for array elements, 304
    for block operations, **141–149**
    for clearing screen, **129**
    for color, **147–148**
    for combining editing commands
        with display commands, **134–141**
        with drawing commands, **133–134**
    for converting polylines, 148
    for coordinate changing, **148–149**
    for corner cleaning, **135**, *136–137*, **138**
    for crosshairs, **129–130**
    for editing around inserted blocks, **146–147**
    for erasing entities, 434
    for hatch patterns, **126–128**
    for inserting blocks, **141–142**, *142–143*, **144–146**, *145*
    for layers, **124–126**, **434–437**
    menu subsection for, **106–107**
    notes for, 81
    for open-cross cleaning, **140–141**, *140*
    for open-T cleaning, **139–140**, *139*
    for patterns, **126–128**
    for selecting, **131–132**
    for tablets, 106
    for thickness, **147–148**
    two-character, **434–439**
    for Undo marks, 437–438
    for undoing, **128**
    for viewing, 438–439
    for word processing, **130**
    for zooming, **128**, 138, 438–439

major sections in menus, **84–85**
Makeface function (WALLS), 246, **258–259**
Makeline function (WALLS), 246, **257–258**
manifest constants, 280
MANYBLKS macro, 134
MANYLINE macro, 134
Mapcar function, **384**
matching, wildcard characters with, **426–428**
matrices, transformation, 375
Max function, **384**
Mem function, **384–385**
Member function, **385**
memory
    in AutoLISP, **165–169**
    displaying status of, 384–385
    for environment, 10
    for nodes, 166, 327, 352–353, 356–357
    paging, 424–425
    recovering, 356–357
    for selection sets, **307**, 315
    for shape files, 38
    for text editors, 14–15
memory variables
    in AutoLISP, **157–159**
    global, **167–168**, **178–179**, 340
    local, **167–168**, **177–179**, **216**, 340
    memory for, 166, **168–169**
menu areas on tablets, **101–106**, *101–102*, *104*
menu bar, 107, *108*
Menu command, 82, 88
Menucmd function, **385**
menus
    custom. *See* custom menus
    displaying strings on, 374
    reading from, 372–373
    source-code files for, 6–7
    switching between submenus, 385
MetaWare High C compiler, 5, 272–274
Microsoft C compiler, 272
Min function, **386**
minus signs (–)
    for character ranges, 427
    with pull-down menus, 113–114
    for subtraction, 156, **321**
Minusp function, **386**
Mirror command, 103
mnemonics for dialog box objects, 205–206
.MNL files, 6
.MNU files, 6–7, 83
.MNX files, 7, 83
Mode_tile function, **386–387**
Modify function (WALLS), 245, **259–260**
Move command, macro for, **132**
MOVE macro, 132
multiple configurations, **10–12**
multiple directories, **8–9**
multiplication, 156, **321**

N

names
    for blocks, **459–461**
    for custom menus, 83
    for dialog box files, 204
    for entities, **161**, 224, 376, 410
    for functions, 177, 179
    for line types, 6, 20, 22
    for routines, 197
    for shapes, 44
    for slide lists, 117
    in text-font files, 71
    for variables, 157–158
narrow-diamond shape, 61–62
natural antilogs, 352
natural logarithms, 382
negative numbers
    in line types, 21
    testing for, 386
Nentsel function, **387–388**
Nentselp function, **388–389**
nested entities, input of, 387–389
nesting
    in AutoLISP, **159–160**
    pull-down submenus, 114
New_dialog function, **389–390**
Newcolor function, 236
NEWCOLOR macro, 147–148
Newss function (CR), 454
next entity, extracting, 348
[next] statement in menu sections, 95
NEXT.LSP function, **447**
nil value
    resetting variables to, 167
    testing for, 390–393
nodes, memory for, 352–353
    allocating, 166
    recovering, 356–357
    resetting, 327

INDEX

non-equality, testing for, **322**
nonstandard entities in shape descriptions
    arcs, **62–69**
    lines, **59–62**
normal block insertions, creating, 231
Not function, **390**
NOTCH function (GEAR), 189, **197**
notes
    for LISP routines, 154
    for preparing custom menus, 81
Nth function, **390–391**
Null function, **391**
number signs (#) as wildcard characters, 426
Numberp function, **391**
numbers. *See also* integers; real numbers;
    values
    absolute value of, 325
    antilogs of, 352
    logarithms of, 382
    negative, 21, 386
    power function for, 353
    square roots of, 406
    testing, for zero, 431–432
    testing for, 391
    units of measurement for, 339
numerical descriptions in shape files, **44–46**

O

object-snap, 393
octant angles, 50, *51–52*
octant arcs, **49–52**, *50–52*
offset arcs, **62–65**
Offset command in macros, **134**
offsets
    function for, 263
    in hatch patterns, 28, *28–29*
OK buttons, **207**
Ok_int function (DDGEAR), 209, **216**
Ok_real function (DDGEAR), 209, **216**
OL_ERRNO.H header file, 274
OLDORG function (XYREC), 458
1+ function, **324**
1- function, **324**
open-cross intersections, cleaning,
    140–141, *140*
Open function, **391–392**
open-T intersections, cleaning, **139–140**, *139*
opening files, 391–392

operators, 155, **320–324**
OR comparisons, 383
Or function, **392–393**
orientation in text-font files, 72, **74–75**
ORIG-PT macro, 149
origin of UCS, macro for, 149
ORTHOMODE system variable, 160
OS/2 operating system, ADS compilers in, 272
Osnap function, **393**
overwriting files, confirmation for, 439

P

$P key character, 87
paging, memory, 424–425
paper space, translating points to, 420
PARALINE macro, **133–134**
parallel lines
    in hatch patterns, 28, *28*, 30
    macro for, **133–134**
parameters. *See* arguments and parameters
parametric programming model, **179–181**
parentheses ()
    for AutoLISP functions, 155, 159
    errors from, 166, 172
    for lists, 163
    in shape descriptions, 60
paths, 354–355
    ACAD variable for, **9–10**
    with AutoLISP, 165, 355
    for text editors, 13
patterns. *See* hatch patterns and hatch-pattern
    definitions
PAUSER.LSP function, **448–449**
pausing for input
    of angles, **357–358**, **363–365**
    with Command function, 336–337
    of corners for rectangles, 359
    creating function for, **275–279**
    with debugging, **448–449**
    of entities, 349, 387–389
    of files, 361–362
    of integers, 362
    with menus, 89–90
    of points, 365–366
    of real numbers, 366
    of selection set entities, **407–409**
    of strings, 363, 367–368
paving pattern effect, 32–34, *33*

pen
    for lines, 20
    for shapes, **47–49**, 59–60
    signal elements for, **42–43**
periods (.)
    in file names, 5
    in real numbers, 162
    as wildcard characters, 426
.PFB files, 69, 76
Phar Lap 386 linker, 272–273
pi constant, 159
pick buttons, reading from, 372
PIVOT.LSP command, **454–455**
planning routines, **153–154**
Plot Configuration dialog box, 77
plotting configurations, 76–77
plus signs (+)
    for addition, 156, **320**
    for menus, **89–91**
pointing devices, reading from, 373
points
    in ADS, **307–308**
    for corners of rectangles, 359
    creating, 229
    distance between, 342, 359–360
    drawing rectangles from, **457–458**
    input of, **193–194**, 365–366
    intersection of, calculating, 379
    object-snap for, 393
    on reference lines, **263**
    relative, calculating, 393–394
    translating, 420–421
Polar function, **393–394**
polylines
    converting, 148
    headers for, 232, 310–311
    selecting entities nested in, 387–389
    trimming, 286–287
    vertices for, 232, 311
***POP menu section, 84, 87, 92
popup lists
    adding items to, 326
    ending processing of, 345
    starting processing of, 412
portability of functions, 176
PostScript fonts, 69, **75–76**
powers, raising numbers to, 353
[previous] statement in menu sections, 95
Prin1 function, **394–395**

Princ function, **395**
Print function, **395–396**
printing
    expressions, **394–396**
    line feeds, 395–396, 417
problem stating for routines, **181–182**
Progn function, **396**
programming. *See* AutoCAD Development System (ADS); AutoLISP
programs
    listing, 326
    loading and unloading, 430–431
    registering, 400
Prompt function, **396**
prompts and prompt area
    ADS function for, **275–279**
    with default responses, **191–192**
    for input. *See* pausing for input
    line feeds for, 417
    in parametric model, 179–180
    for text editors, **15–16**
    writing
        characters to, 428–429
        expressions to, 394–396
        strings to, 164, 396, 429
pseudocode
    for ADS, 275
    for CUTOUT.C, **288–289**
    for FPROMPT.C, 276
    for GEAR.LSP, **182–183**
    for LISP routines, 153
    for WALLS.LSP, **237–238**
pull-down menus
    creating, **107–114**
    displaying, **109–110**
    key character for, 87
    menu sections for, 84
    structure of, **108–109**
    submenus for, **113–114**
    swapping, **110–113**

Q

question marks (?)
    in menu sections, 96
    as wildcard characters, 426
Quit function, **396–397**
quotation marks (" ')
    for quote function, 397, 448

INDEX

for strings, 163–164, 166, 172
Quote function, **397**, 448

R

radians
    in AutoLISP, **161**
    converting, to degrees, **191**
radii
    for fillets, **450–452**
    for octant arcs, 50, 52
Rdwset function (WALLS), 245, **261–262**
Read function, **397–398**
Read-char function, **398**
Read-line function, **398–399**
read mode, opening files in, 392
readability of AutoLISP files, **169–171**
reading
    characters, 398
    from input devices, **371–373**
    strings, 398–399
real numbers, **162–163**
    checking strings for, **216**
    converting
        into integers, 355
        integers into, 355–356
        into strings, 401–402
        strings into, 331, 343
    input of, 366
rectangles
    corners of, input for, 359
    cutout routine for, **285–306**
    drawing, **457–458**
    in tiles, 353–354
Redo command, 438
Redraw function, **399**
redrawing
    screen, 399
    selection set items, **261–262**
reference lines
    drawing, **257–258**
    points on, **263**
Regapp function, **400**
registering applications, 400
relative points, computing, 393–394
Rem function, **400**
REM statements in batch files, 18
remainder function, 400
REMLISP.EXE file, 167

Repeat function, **400–401**
repeating expressions, 400–401
replacing
    blocks, **461–463**
    list members, 414
response codes for text editors, 16
Restore function (DDGEAR), 214
restoring
    entities, 345–346
    viewing angles, 438–439
result bits in comparisons, 333
result buffers, **311–313**
Reverse function, **401**
reversing lists, 401
Roman fonts, 75
rotating
    crosshairs, **129–130**
    objects, **452–455**
    UCS, 149
routines, **176**
    creating functions for, **177–179**
    on custom menus, **220**
    efficient code for, **168–169**
    error trapping in, **199–200**
    exiting from, 352, 396–397
    for gears, **185–198**
    loading, **165**
    memory management in, **165–168**
    parametric model for, **179–181**
    planning, **153–154**
    problem stating for, **181–182**
    pseudocode for, 153, **182–183**
rows in DCL files, 204–205
Rs_error function (DDGEAR), 209, **216**
Rtos function, **401–402**

S

$S key character, 87
Sans-Serif fonts, 75–76
scaling
    blocks, 142, *143*
    line types, 23
    in shape descriptions, **47–48**, 55
    signal elements for, 42
    in text-font files, 71–72
***SCREEN menu section, 84–87, 93–94
screens
    clearing, **129**, 418

graphics, 370
redrawing, 399
text, 418–419
Script command, 336
S-CURVE macro, 148
search paths, 354–355
    ACAD variable for, **9–10**
    with AutoLISP, 165, 355
    for text editors, 13
searching
    block tables, **316–317**
    for files, 354–355
    for list members, 414
    for symbols, 332
sections
    in dialog boxes. *See* tiles for dialog boxes
    in menus, **84–87**
segments, 166, 352–353
selecting
    aperture opening size for, 138
    covered objects, **456**
    entities, 345–346, 387–389, **407–409**
    macros for, **131–132**
selection sets, 164
    adding to, **261**, 406–407
    with ADS, **307**, **314–316**
    counting entities in, 409
    deleting from, 407
    extracting names from, 410
    memory for, **307**, 315
    redrawing items in, **261–262**
    selecting entities for, 349, **407–409**
    testing for entities in, 409–410
semicolons (;)
    in attribute data, 146
    for AutoLISP comments, **170**
    in DCL files, 204
    in macros, 125
    for menus, **89**
SET command, 9–11
Set function, **402–403**
Set_tile function, **404–405**
Setloc function (DDGEAR), 208–209, **216**
Setq function, 157–158, 168, 233, **403–404**
Setvar function, 160, **404**
Shape command, 7
shape files and shape descriptions, 7–8, 38
    arcs in, **62–69**, **458–459**

combining elements of, **52–56**
complex, **47–59**
creating, **44–47**, 230
editing, **39**, **78**
elements in, **40–43**, **52–56**
insertion points in, **56–59**
lines in, **59–62**
octant arcs in, **49–52**, *50–52*
pens and scaling in, **47–49**, **55**
in text-font files, **71–72**. *See also* text-font files
sharing functions and variables, **169**, **221**
shifting integer bits, 383
.SHP files, **7–8**, 70
.SHX files, 69–70, 76, 78
SHX2SHP program, 78
signal elements in shape files, **42–43**
Sin function, **405**
single quotes ('), 397, 448
size
    of aperture opening, 138
    signal elements for, 42
Sketch command, 336
slashes. *See* backslashes (\); forward slashes (/)
.SLD files, 117
Slide_image function, **405–406**
SLIDELIB.EXE file, 115–118
slides
    displaying, 405–406
    files for, **116–118**
    processing, 411–412
smallest value in series, extracting, 386
snapping
    with points, 393
    with shapes, 57
solids
    creating, 230
    trimming, 286–287
source-code files, **4–8**
spaces
    in AutoLISP functions, 155
    in line types, 21
    in lists, 163
    for menus, **89**
speed of ADS programs, 269, 286
spline-curves from polylines, 148
Sqrt function, **406**
square brackets ([])

INDEX

for dialog box files, 204–205
for menus, **88–89**
for wildcard characters, 427
square roots of numbers, 406
Ssadd function, **406–407**
Ssdel function, **407**
Ssdraw function (CR), 454
Ssget function, **407–409**
Sslength function, **409**
Ssmemb function, **409–410**
Ssname function, **410**
standard angles, 41, *41*, 45–46
standard line lengths, 41
Start_dialog function, 219, **411**
Start_image function, **411–412**
Start_list function, **412–413**
starting angles of octant arcs, 50, *51–52*, 52
status line, displaying strings on, 374
Strcase function, **413**
Strcat function, **413**
strings, **163–164**
    connecting, 413
    converting
        into angles, 328–329
        angles into, 329
        case of, 413
        into integers, 332
        integers into, 379
        into real numbers, 331, 343
        real numbers into, 401–402
    displaying, 374–375
    errors from, 166, 172
    extracting data from, 397–398, 414
    input of, 363, 367–368
    length of, 164, 413–414
    memory for, 168
    for prompts, 164, 396, 429
    reading, 398–399
    validity of, checking, **216**
    wildcard characters in, **426–428**
    writing, 429
Strlen function, **413–414**
Style command, 76
sublists for association lists, **224–225**
    in entity creation, 228
    locating, **233–237**, 331
submenus, **113–114**, 385

subsections in menus, **85–88**, **106–107**
Subst function, 235, **414**
Substr function, **414**
swapping pull-down menus, **110–113**
SWING.BAT file, **17–18**
switching between submenus, 385
symbol tables
    association lists for, 415–416
    extracting entries from, 416
symbols
    in AutoLISP, **164**
    binding values to, 157–158, 333, **402–404**
    comparing, 350–351
    evaluating expressions for, 356
    as functions, **320–324**
    searching for, 332
    source-code files for, 7–8
syntax
    of AutoLISP, **154–161**
    for custom menus, **85–91**
system variables
    in AutoLISP, **160**
    extracting values of, 368
    setting, 404
    toggles for, **450**

T

$T key character, 87
tables
    association lists for, 415–416
    extracting entries from, 416
Tablet cfg command, 103
Tablet function, **415**
***TABLET menu section, 84, 87, **104–106**
tablets
    calibrating, 415
    commands on, **104–106**
    configuring, **103**
    custom menus for, **101–106**, *101–102*, 104
    templates for, **102–103**
Tblnext function, **415–416**
Tblsearch function, **416–417**
TEMPLATE.C file, **281–284**
templates
    for ADS, **281–284**

for tablet menus, **102–103**
temporary files, 286
temporary lines, 370–371
Term_dialog function, **417**
Terpri function, **417**
Testfn function (G:fname), 442–443
testing
    for AutoLISP versions, 424
    for bound symbols, 333
    for equality, **322**, 350–351
    functions, 275, **285**
    for lists, 332, 381
    for negative numbers, 386
    for nil, 390–393
    for numbers, 391
    for selection set entities, 409–410
    for values, 327
    for zeros, 431–432
text
    converting, to lines, 76–78
    exporting, **444–446**
Text command, 76
text editors and word processors, **12–14**
    for ACAD.PGP, **14–16**
    batch files for, **17–18**
    for line types, **23–25**
    macros for, **130**
    for shape files, 39
text entities, creating, 230
text-font files, 8, **69**
    ASCII codes for, 70–71
    designing shapes for, **73**, 73
    editing, **78**
    orientation in, 72, **74–75**
    PostScript fonts, **75–76**
    shape descriptions in, **71–72**
    vs. shape files, **70–71**
text screens, displaying, 418–419
Textbox function, **417–418**
TEXTOUT.LSP program, **444–446**
Textpage function, **418**
Textscr function, **418–419**
thawing layers, macro for, 436–437
THICKEN macro, **147–148**
third-party applications, registering, 400
3D faces, creating, 230, **258–261**
3D objects, rotating, **454–455**
3D polyline headers and vertices, 232
tildes (~)
    for bitwise complements, **324**
    in pull-down menus, 114
    with wildcard characters, 426
tiles for dialog boxes, 201
    assigning functions to, 325
    associating data with, 335
    attributes of, retrieving, 368–369
    behavior of, 386–387
    displaying, 386–387
    ending processing of, 344–345
    filled rectangles in, 353–354
    height of, 341–342
    lines in, **216**, 423–424
    setting values of, 404–405
    slides in, 405–406, 411–412
    starting processing in, 411–412
    values of, retrieving, 369–370
    widgets, **207**
    width of, 341
toggles
    in DCL files, **206**
    for system variables, **450**
trace flags, 419–420, 423
Trace function, **419–420**
traces, creating, 230
Trans function, **420–421**
transformation matrices, 375
translating points, 420–421
Trim command in macros, 140–141
trimming, problems in, **286–287**
two-character macros, **434–439**
2D polyline headers and vertices, 232
Type function, **421–422**

U

UB.LSP macro, **438**
UCS PICK macro, 148
UM.LSP macro, **437–438**
unbalanced functions, **172**
UNCURVE macro, 148
UND.LSP command, **456**
underneath objects, selecting, **456**
underscore characters (_) with menus, **90**
Undo back command, 307, 438

INDEX

Undo feature in ADS, **309–310**
Undo macro, **128**
Undo mark command, 307
Undo marks, 307, 437–438
Undo_reset function (CUTOUT), 302–303, 306
Undo_setup function (CUTOUT), 301–302, 306
Units command for hatch patterns, 33
units of measurement, converting, 339
UNIX operating system, ADS compilers in, 272
Unload_dialog function, **422–423**
unloading ADS programs, 431
Untrace function, **423**
updating entities, 349–350
uppercase, converting strings to, 413
User Coordinate System
    macros for, **148–149**
    translating points to, 420–421

V

validity of input, 201, **208–220**, 307, **377–378**
values
    largest, in series, 384
    smallest, in series, 384
    for symbols and variables, 157–158, 333, **402–404**
    testing expressions for, 327
variables
    in AutoLISP, **157–160**, 340
    binding values to, 157–158, 333, **402–404**
    global, **167–168**, **178–179**, 340
    initializing, **216**
    local, **167–168**, **177–179**, **216**, 340
    memory for, 166, **168–169**
    system, **160**, 368, 404, **450**
    in WALLS.LSP, **254–257**
Vector_image function, **423–424**
vectors, displaying, 375
Ver function, **424**
Verify function (DDGEAR), 210–211, **217**
versions, AutoLISP, 424
vertices, 232, 311
viewing
    association lists, **446–447**
    macro for, 438–439

viewports
    clearing, 370
    identification numbers for, extracting, 425
virtual memory, 166, 424–425
Vmon function, **424–425**
Vports function, **425**
Vslide command, 118

W

WALL macro, 134
Wallpt function (WALLS), 244, **263**
WALLS.LSP routine, **237–238**
    drawing faces in, **254**, *254*
    functions in, **257–264**
    listing of, **239–254**
    output from, *239*
    using, **265–266**
    variable names in, **254–257**
warning messages, dialog boxes for, 326–327
WATCOM C 386 compiler, 272
Wcmatch function, **426–428**
Wdraw function (WALLS), 242–243, **263**
Wedit function (WALLS), 243–244, **263**
While function, **428**
widgets in DCL files, **207**
width
    of dialog box buttons, 205
    of tiles, 341
wildcard characters, **426–428**
word processors and text editors, **12–14**
    for ACAD.PGP, **14–16**
    batch files for, **17–18**
    for line types, **23–25**
    macros for, **130**
    for shape files, 39
WORDPROC macro, 130
World Coordinate System, translating points to, 420–421
wrapped around menu text, 91
Write-char function, **428–429**
Write-line function, **429**
write mode, opening files in, 392
writing
    characters, 428–429

expressions, 394–396
strings, 429

X

XBOX shape description, 47–48, *48*
Xdroom function, **429–430**
Xdsize function, **430**
Xload function, **430–431**
Xunload function, **431**
XYREC.LSP command, **457–458**

Z

Zap command, macro for, 129
Z-coordinates with Entmake, 229
Zerop function, **431–432**
zeros, testing for, 431–432
ZOOMIN macro, 128, 138
zooming, macros for, **128**, 138, 438–439
ZOOMOUT macro, 128, 138
Zortech C++ compiler, 272
ZP.LSP macro, **438–439**

FREE BROCHURE!

Complete this form today, and we'll send you a full-color brochure of Sybex bestsellers.

Please supply the name of the Sybex book purchased.

_____

How would you rate it?

_____ Excellent   _____ Very Good   _____ Average   _____ Poor

Why did you select this particular book?

_____ Recommended to me by a friend
_____ Recommended to me by store personnel
_____ Saw an advertisement in _____
_____ Author's reputation
_____ Saw in Sybex catalog
_____ Required textbook
_____ Sybex reputation
_____ Read book review in _____
_____ In-store display
_____ Other _____

Where did you buy it?

_____ Bookstore
_____ Computer Store or Software Store
_____ Catalog (name: _____)
_____ Direct from Sybex
_____ Other: _____

Did you buy this book with your personal funds?

_____ Yes   _____ No

About how many computer books do you buy each year?

_____ 1-3   _____ 3-5   _____ 5-7   _____ 7-9   _____ 10+

About how many Sybex books do you own?

_____ 1-3   _____ 3-5   _____ 5-7   _____ 7-9   _____ 10+

Please indicate your level of experience with the software covered in this book:

_____ Beginner   _____ Intermediate   _____ Advanced

Which types of software packages do you use regularly?

_____ Accounting	_____ Databases	_____ Networks
_____ Amiga	_____ Desktop Publishing	_____ Operating Systems
_____ Apple/Mac	_____ File Utilities	_____ Spreadsheets
_____ CAD	_____ Money Management	_____ Word Processing
_____ Communications	_____ Languages	_____ Other _____
		(please specify)

Which of the following best describes your job title?

_____ Administrative/Secretarial _____ President/CEO

_____ Director _____ Manager/Supervisor

_____ Engineer/Technician _____ Other _____
(please specify)

Comments on the weaknesses/strengths of this book: _____

_____

_____

_____

_____

Name _____
Street _____
City/State/Zip _____
Phone _____

PLEASE FOLD, SEAL, AND MAIL TO SYBEX

SYBEX INC.
Department M
2021 CHALLENGER DR.
ALAMEDA, CALIFORNIA USA
94501

SEAL

Diskette Order Form

If you would like to use the examples shown in this book but do not want to type them out yourself, you may obtain a copy of them on disk. The disk includes a SHP file for an outline bold text font. Please fill out the order form below and return with a check or money order for $17.50 (plus applicable city and county sales taxes, California residents only), payable to Thomas Enterprises. Disk price includes shipping and handling. Allow 2 weeks for delivery. Mail the completed form to:

Thomas Enterprises
400 College Avenue
Santa Rosa, CA 95401

Name: _____

Company: _____

Address: _____

City: _____

State: _____ Zip Code _____

Specify format (check **one** only): 5.25" ☐ 3.5" ☐

No purchase orders or credit card numbers, please. For foreign orders, please send an international money order in U.S. dollars drawn on a U.S. bank.

Thomas Enterprises, ltd. makes no representation or warranties with respect to the contents of the above referenced software and specifically disclaims any implied warranties of merchantability or fitness for any particular purpose. By the act of ordering, purchaser agrees that in any event the sole liability of Thomas Enterprises, ltd. is limited to replacement of the original diskettes should they prove defective within 30 days of the date of shipment.

SYBEX Inc. is not affiliated with Thomas Enterprises, ltd. and makes no representation or warranties with respect to the contents of the above referenced software.

Pull-Down Menu Control Codes

Note: These special control codes for pull-down menus are available in addition to the standard control codes for AutoCAD's screen menu. However, these codes are not available for all display platforms. Check your documentation to be certain that your platform supports special pull-down menu display controls.

Action	Control Code	Comment
Display Icon in Menu	^icon^	(icon = icon slide name)
Evaluate DIESEL Macro	$(	Macro must precede label
Gray-Out Menu Item	~	Tilde must prefix label
Indicate Submenu	->	Characters prefix label
Indicate Last Submenu Item	<-	Characters prefix label
Mark Item	!c	(c = non-alphanumeric character)
Place Check-Mark in Item	!.	Characters prefix label
Separate Menu Items With a Line	--	No other characters allowed
Specify Accelerator Key in Item	/c	(c = Alphanumeric character must appear in label)
Specify Item Font Style	<C	(C = Bold, Italic, Outline, Shadow, Underline)
Terminate Parent Menu	<-<-	Characters prefix label. Each parent menu requires its own <- code.

DIESEL String Expressions

DIESEL string expressions are special macros that can be used as values for the MODEMACRO system variable, in custom menus, macros introduced by the $M= control characters, or as arguments to the Menucmd function in AutoLISP.

Expression	Return Value	Arguments
$(+, n1, n2, ...)	Sum of all numbers	Up to 9 numbers
$(-, n1, n2, ...)	n1 minus sum of other numbers	Up to 9 numbers
$(*, n1, n2, ...)	Product of all numbers	Up to 9 numbers
$(/, n1, n2, ...)	n1 divided by sum of other numbers	Up to 9 numbers
$(=, n1, n2)	1 if both numbers are equal, otherwise 0	Two numbers
$(!=, n1, n2)	1 if numbers aren't equal, otherwise 0	Two numbers
$(<, n1, n2)	1 if n1 less than n2, otherwise 0	Two numbers
$(<=, n1, n2)	1 if n1 less than or equal to n2, otherwise 0	Two numbers
$(>, n1, n2)	1 if n1 greater than n2, otherwise 0	Two numbers
$(>=, n1, n2)	1 if n1 greater than or equal to n2, otherwise 0	Two numbers